Lecture Notes in Artificial Intelligence 12802

Subseries of Lecture Notes in Computer Science

Series Editors

Randy Goebel
University of Alberta, Edmonton, Canada

Yuzuru Tanaka
Hokkaido University, Sapporo, Japan

Wolfgang Wahlster
DFKI and Saarland University, Saarbrücken, Germany

Founding Editor

Jörg Siekmann
DFKI and Saarland University, Saarbrücken, Germany

More information about this subseries at http://www.springer.com/series/1244

Ariel Rosenfeld · Nimrod Talmon (Eds.)

Multi-Agent Systems

18th European Conference, EUMAS 2021
Virtual Event, June 28–29, 2021
Revised Selected Papers

 Springer

Editors
Ariel Rosenfeld ⓘ
Bar-Ilan University
Ramat Gan, Israel

Nimrod Talmon ⓘ
Ben-Gurion University of the Negev
Be'er Sheva, Israel

ISSN 0302-9743   ISSN 1611-3349   (electronic)
Lecture Notes in Artificial Intelligence
ISBN 978-3-030-82253-8   ISBN 978-3-030-82254-5   (eBook)
https://doi.org/10.1007/978-3-030-82254-5

LNCS Sublibrary: SL7 – Artificial Intelligence

This Springer imprint is published by the registered company Springer Nature Switzerland AG
The registered company address is: Gewerbestrasse 11, 6330 Cham, Switzerland

Preface

This volume constitutes the revised post-conference proceedings of the 18th European Conference on Multi-Agent Systems (EUMAS 2021). The conference was held online during June 28–29, 2021. 16 full papers are presented in this volume, each of which carefully reviewed and selected from a total of 51 submissions.

The papers report on research regarding a wide range of topics in the field of multi-agent systems. EUMAS 2021 followed the tradition of previous editions (Oxford 2003, Barcelona 2004, Brussels 2005, Lisbon 2006, Hammamet 2007, Bath 2008, Agia Napa 2009, Paris 2010, Maastricht 2011, Dublin 2012, Toulouse 2013, Prague 2014, Athens 2015, Valencia 2016, Evry 2017, Bergen 2018, and Thessaloniki (virtually) 2020) in aiming to provide the prime European forum for presenting and discussing agents research as the annual designated event of the European Association of Multi-Agent Systems (EURAMAS).

The peer-review process carried out put great emphasis on ensuring the high quality of accepted contributions. The 50-person EUMAS Program Committee accepted 16 submissions as full papers. This volume is structured in sections mirroring the presentation sessions of the virtual conference event (https://biu-ai.com/EUMAS21/). In addition to the papers included in this volume, the program was highlighted by two great keynote talks, the first one by Catholijn M. Jonker (TU Delft), titled Towards Hybrid Intelligence: A vision on the future of AI and Humankind, and the second one by Ariel Procaccia (Harvard University), titled Democracy and the Pursuit of Randomness.

Based on the reviews, the conference chairs presented two awards for papers that especially stood out: a Best Paper Award was awarded to Barak Steindl and Meirav Zehavi for their paper titled Verification of Multi-Layered Assignment Problems; and a Best Paper Runner Up Award was awarded to Cihan Eran, Onur Keskin, Furkan Canturk and Reyhan Aydogan for their paper titled A Decentralized Token-based Negotiation Approach for Multi-Agent Path Finding. The award recipients were invited to submit an extended version of their papers for fast track publication in the Journal of Autonomous Agents and Multi-Agent Systems (JAAMAS). In addition, selected papers were invited to extend their contribution for a special issue of SN Computer Science.

The editors would like to thank the following:

- all members of the Program Committee, and all additional reviewers, for providing their input regarding the submitted papers;
- all authors for submitting to EUMAS;
- all participants of the virtual conference event;
- the invited speakers for their great talks;
- the editors of JAAMAS for inviting the award recipients to extend their papers and enjoy a fast track publication process.

- the editors of SN Computer Science for supporting a special issue of extended selected papers;
- Davide Grossi, for helping in the background.

July 2021   Ariel Rosenfeld
                                                                  Nimrod Talmon

Organization

Program Chairs

Ariel Rosenfeld   Bar-Ilan University, Israel
Nimrod Talmon   Ben-Gurion University, Israel

Program Committee

Ilan Nehama   Bar-Ilan University, Israel
Dušan Knop   Czech Technical University in Prague, Czech Republic
Georgios Chalkiadakis   Technical University of Crete, Greece
Reyhan Aydogan   Ozyegin University, Turkey, and Delft University of
     Technology, The Netherlands
Stanislaw Szufa   Jagiellonian University, Poland
Charilaos Akasiadis   NCSR 'Demokritos', Greece
Erel Segal-Halevi   Ariel University, Israel
Emiliano Lorini   CNRS and IRIT, France
Piotr Faliszewski   AGH University of Science and Technology, Poland
Reshef Meir   Technion – Israel Institute of Technology, Israel
Reuth Mirsky   University of Texas at Austin, USA
Antonis Bikakis   University College London, UK
Krzysztof Sornat   Massachusetts Institute of Technology, USA
Roie Zivan   Ben Gurion University, Israel
Angelina Vidali   American University of Cyprus, Cyprus
Franziska Klügl   Örebro University, Sweden
Sherief Abdallah   British University in Dubai, UAE
Gianluigi Greco   University of Calabria, Italy
Nicolas Maudet   LIP6, Sorbonne University, France
Dominique Longin   CNRS and IRIT, France
Alessandro Ricci   Alma Mater Studiorum–Universita di Bologna, Italy
Gita Sukthankar   University of Central Florida, USA
Andrea Omicini   Alma Mater Studiorum–Università di Bologna, Italy
Alessandro Farinelli   University of Verona, Italy
Robert Bredereck   Humboldt-Universität zu Berlin, Germany
Simon Parsons   University of Lincoln, UK
Ronald de Haan   University of Amsterdam, The Netherlands
Marija Slavkovik   University of Bergen, Norway
Pallavi Jain   Indian Institute of Technology Jodhpur, India
Alberto Castellini   University of Verona, Italy
Piotr Skowron   University of Warsaw, Poland
Ilias Sakellariou   University of Macedonia, Greece
Emmanouil Rigas   Aristotle University of Thessaloniki, Greece

Till Fluschnik	Technische Universität Berlin, Germany
Frederic Moisan	University of Cambridge, UK
Cristiano Castelfranchi	Institute of Cognitive Sciences and Technologies, Italy
Umberto Grandi	University of Toulouse, France
Fred Amblard	IRIT and Toulouse 1 Capitole University, France
Martin Lackner	TU Wien, Austria
Nir Oren	University of Aberdeen, UK
John-Jules Meyer	Utrecht University, The Netherlands
Ana L. C. Bazzan	Universidade Federal do Rio Grande do Sul, Brazil
Gal Shahaf	Weizmann Institute of Science, Israel
Benoit Gaudou	CNRS, IRIT, and University of Toulouse, France
Athanasios Aris Panagopoulos	California State University, Fresno, USA
Gerhard Weiss	Maastricht University, The Netherlands

External Reviewers

Rutvik Page
Furkan Canturk
Dimitrios Troullinos
Neeldhara Misra
Antonis Bikakis
Avshalom Elmalech
Lucas Alegre
Tomáš Valla
Mehmet Onur Keskin

Georgios Papasotiropoulos
Errikos Streviniotis
Anna Rapberger
Aurelie Beynier
William Macke
Lucas Alegre
Sushmita Gupta
Chen Hajaj
Krzysztof Sornat

Contents

Ascending-Price Mechanism for General Multi-sided Markets

Dvir Gilor[1], Rica Gonen[1]([⊠]), and Erel Segal-Halevi[2]

[1] The Open University of Israel, Raanana, Israel
dvir@gilor.com, gonenr@openu.ac.il
[2] Ariel University, Ariel, Israel

Abstract. We present an ascending-price mechanism for a multi-sided market with a variety of participants, such as manufacturers, logistics agents, insurance providers, and assemblers. Each deal in the market may consist of a combination of agents from separate categories, and different such combinations are simultaneously allowed. This flexibility lets multiple intersecting markets be resolved as a single global market. Our mechanism is obviously-truthful, strongly budget-balanced, individually rational, and attains almost the optimal gain-from-trade when the market is sufficiently large. We evaluate the performance of the suggested mechanism with experiments on real stock market data and synthetically produced data.

Keywords: Multi-sided markets · Truthful auctions · Strong budget balance

1 Introduction

The aim of this paper is to automatically arrange the trade in complex multilateral markets. As an example, consider a market for a certain kind of laptop computer, and assume for simplicity that it is made of only two components, e.g. CPU and RAM. Even in this simplified market, there may be several different categories of traders: 1. Buyers, who are interested in a laptop; 2. Laptop producers, who produce whole laptops; 3. CPU producers; 4. RAM producers; 5. Constructors, who construct a laptop from its parts; 6. Transporters, who take a laptop and bring it to an end consumer. A deal in this market can take one of two forms:

- A buyer buys a laptop from a laptop-producer, and asks a transporter to transport it to his place. This involves traders of categories 1, 2 and 6.
- A buyer buys CPU, RAMs and a construction service, and has the final product transported. This involves traders of categories 1, 3, 4, 5 and 6.

The second author would like to thank the Ministry of Science, Technology and Space 995 Binational Israel-Taiwan grant, number 3-16542.

A. Rosenfeld and N. Talmon (Eds.): EUMAS 2021, LNAI 12802, pp. 1–18, 2021.
https://doi.org/10.1007/978-3-030-82254-5_1

In each category there may be many different traders, with potentially different utilities for participating in a deal. Typically, the value of a buyer is positive and the value of a producer or service-provider is negative. The main questions of interest for automatically arranging the trade is *who* will trade and *how much* they will pay (or receive). The answers to these questions should satisfy several natural requirements (see Sect. 2):

(1) *Individual rationality (IR)*: No agent should lose from participating: the amount paid by a trading agent should be at most as high as the agent's value (if the value is negative then the agent should receive money). A non-trading agent should pay nothing.

(2) *Weak budget balance (WBB)*: The total amount paid by all agents together should be at least 0, so that the market manager does not lose money. A stronger requirement called *strong budget balance (SBB)* is that the total amount be exactly 0, i.e., the market manager does not take away money from the market, which might drive traders away.

(3) High *gain-from-trade (GFT)*: The GFT is the sum of values of all agents actively participating in the trade.[1] For example, suppose a certain buyer values a laptop at 1000, the laptop-producer values it at -700 (the cost of production is 700), the CPU and RAM producers and constructor value their efforts at -200 each, and the transporter values the deal at -50 (the cost of transportation is 50). Then, the GFT from a deal involving categories 1, 2, 6 is $1000 - 700 - 50 = 250$, and the GFT from a deal involving categories 1, 3, 4, 5, 6 is $1000 - 200 - 200 - 200 - 50 = 350$. Maximizing the GFT implies that the latter deal is preferred.

(4) *Truthfulness*: The agents' values are their private information. We assume that the agents act strategically to maximize their utility (assumed to be their value minus the price they pay). Truthfulness means that such a utility-maximizing agent reports his true valuation. A stronger requirement called *obvious truthfulness* [12] is that, for each agent, the lowest utility he may get by acting truthfully is at least as high as the highest utility he may get by acting non-truthfully.[2]

1.1 Previous Work

The study of truthful market mechanisms started with Vickrey [20]. He considered a market with only *one category* of traders (buyers), where the famous *second-price auction* attains all four desirable properties: IR, WBB, maximum GFT and truthfulness.

---

[1] We define the categories that receives payments as negative values so we can sum the deal values to calculate the gain from trade.

[2] In the terminology of Li [12], a mechanism is OT if and only if, for all agents, replying truthfully to all queries is an obviously-dominant strategy. Note that Li [12] defines games with actions and not with queries, so in his model, the notion of truthfulness is irrelevant. He defines a mechanism as *obviously strategy-proof* if and only if it has an equilibrium in obviously-dominant strategies..

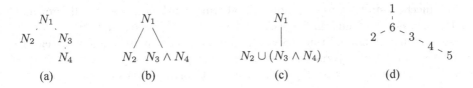

Fig. 1. Examples of trees in a recipe-forest.

When there are *two caterogies* of traders (buyers and sellers), the natural generalization of Vickrey's mechanism is no longer WBB—it may run a deficit. Moreover, Myerson and Satterthwaite [15] proved that *any* mechanism that is IR, truthful and maximizes the GFT must run a deficit. The way out of this impossibility paradox was found by McAfee [13]. In his seminal paper, he presented the first *double auction* (auction for a two-category market) that is IR, WBB, truthful, and *asymptotically* maximizes the GFT. By asymptotically we mean that its GFT is at least $(1 - 1/k)$ of the optimal GFT, where k is the number of deals in the optimal trade. Thus, when k approaches infinity, the GFT approaches the optimum.

McAfee's mechanism has been extended in various ways. Particularly relevant to our setting is the extension by Babaioff and Nisan [1], with *multiple categories* of traders, arranged in a *linear supply chain*. Their model contains a single *producer* category, a single *consumer* category, and several *converter* categories. Each deal must involve a single producer, a single consumer, and a single agent of each converter category. In our laptop example, their model covers either a market with the chain 1,2,6 or a market with the chain 1,3,4,5,6, but not a market where both chains are possible. For this model, they present a mechanism that is IR, WBB, truthful, and attains asymptotically-optimal GFT.

Recently, Gonen and Segal-Halevi [11] considered a multiple-category market in which, like Babaioff and Nisan [1]'s market, all deals must be of the same structure, which they call a "recipe". Their recipes are more general than the linear supply chains of Babaioff and Nisan [1], since they are not restricted to a producer-converters-consumer structure. They present auctions that are IR, SBB, truthful and asymptotically-optimal, but only for a single-recipe market.

Comparison to other supply-chain mechanisms e.g. [9,14] and a survey of more recent works on two-sided markets e.g. [3–7,10,17–19], can be found in the full version of our paper at [8].

1.2   Our Contribution

We study markets with multiple kinds of supply-chains which, following Gonen and Segal-Halevi [11], we call "recipes". In their paper, they have a general single-recipe market. In this paper, we focus on a general multi-recipe market. In such a market, computing the optimal trade—even without strategic considerations—is NP-hard. Moreover, it is NP-hard to compute a trade that attains at least 94/95 of the optimal GFT (see the full version of our paper at [8]). Hence, it is unlikely that a mechanism that runs in polynomial time can be asymptotically-optimal. In this paper, we focus on a special case in which the optimal trade can be computed in polynomial-time (Sect. 3): the case in which the agent categories can be arranged in a *forest* (acyclic graph), and each recipe is a path from a root to a leaf in that forest. Our laptop market corresponds to a forest with the tree in Fig. 1(d).

We present a randomized ascending mechanism for such markets (Sect. 4). Our mechanism is IR, SBB and obviously-truthful. Moreover, all these properties hold *universally*—for every possible outcome of the randomization. The expected GFT of our mechanism is asymptotically-optimal—it approaches the optimum when the optimal number of deals in all recipes approaches infinity (See Sect. 5 for the formal statements). We evaluate the performance of our mechanism on both real and synthetic data (see Sect. 6).

Our mechanism extends [11] in the setting of *binary* recipes, in which each category participates in each recipe either zero or one times. Extending [11] to handle non-binary recipes is beyond the scope of this paper and is the topic of our current research. Some other possible extensions of our mechanism are discussed in the full version of our paper at [8]. In particular, we explain why the limitation to acyclic graphs is economically reasonable.

2 Formal Definitions

2.1 Agents and Categories

A *market* is defined by a set of *agents* grouped into different *categories*. N is the set of agents, G is the set of agent categories, and N_g is the set of agents in category $g \in G$. The categories are pairwise-disjoint, so $N = \sqcup_{g \in G} N_g$.

Each deal in the market requires a certain combination of traders. We call a subset of agents that can accomplish a single deal a *procurement-set* (PS).

A *recipe* is a vector of size $|G|$, denoted by $\mathbf{r} := (r_g)_{g \in G}$, where $r_g \in \mathbb{Z}_+$ for all $g \in G$. It describes the number of agents of each category that should be in each PS: each PS should contain r_1 agents of category 1, r_2 agents of category 2, and so on. The set of recipes available in the market is denoted by R.

In the market of McAfee [13] each deal requires one buyer and one seller, so there is a single recipe and $R = \{(1,1)\}$. In our initial laptop-market example there are two recipes and $R = \{(1,1,0,0,0,1); (1,0,1,1,1,1)\}$. The first one corresponds to deals with a buyer, a producer and a transporter, and the second one corresponds to deals with a buyer, a CPU producer, a RAM producer, a constructor and a transporter. In this paper we assume that recipes are *binary*, i.e., $r_g \in \{0,1\}$ for every recipe $\mathbf{r}$ and every $g \in G$.

Each agent $i \in N$ has a *value* $v_i \in \mathbb{Z}$, which represents the material gain of an agent from participating in the trade. It may be positive, negative or zero. In a two-sided market for a certain good, the value of a buyer is typically positive, while the value of a seller is typically negative and represents the cost of producing the good. However, our model is general and allows the values of different agents in the same category to have different signs. For simplicity, we assume that all the v_i are integer numbers, e.g., all valuations may be given in cents.[3] We also assume that there are publicly known bounds on the possible valuations: for some sufficiently large V, $-V < v_i < V$ for all $i \in N$.

The agents are *quasi-linear in money*: the utility of agent i participating in some PS and paying p_i is $u_i := v_i - p_i$.

2.2   Trades and Gains

The *gain-from-trade* of a procurement-set S, denoted $GFT(S)$, is the sum of values of all agents in S:

$$\text{GFT}(S) := \sum_{i \in S} v_i.$$

In a standard two-sided market, the GFT of a PS with a buyer b and a seller s is $v_b - |v_s|$, since the seller's value is $-|v_s|$.

Given a market $(N, G, \mathbf{r})$, a *trade* is a collection of pairwise-disjoint procurement-sets. I.e, it is a collection of agent subsets, $S_1, \ldots, S_k \subseteq N$, such that for each $j \in [k]$, the composition of agents in S_j corresponds to some recipe $\mathbf{r} \in R$. The total GFT is the sum of the GFT of all procurement-sets participating in the trade:

$$\text{GFT}(S_1, \ldots, S_k) := \sum_{j=1}^{k} \text{GFT}(S_j)$$

A trade is called *optimal* if its GFT is maximum over all trades.

The *value* of agent i given trade $\mathbf{S} = (S_1, \ldots, S_k)$, denoted $v_i(\mathbf{S})$, is either v_i or 0: it is v_i if $i \in S_j$ for some $j \in [k]$, and 0 otherwise.

2.3   Mechanisms

The definitions below cover only the notions used in the present paper. For a more complete treatment of mechanisms and their properties see [16].

A *deterministic direct mechanism* is a function that takes as input a vector $\mathbf{b}$ containing agent bids, and returns as output a trade $\mathbf{S}(\mathbf{b})$ and a price-vector $\mathbf{p}(\mathbf{b})$. The *utility* of each agent i, given a deterministic mechanism and a bid vector $\mathbf{b}$, is $u_i(\mathbf{b}) := v_i(\mathbf{S}(\mathbf{b})) - p_i(\mathbf{b})$.

A deterministic direct mechanism is *truthful* if the utility of every agent i is maximized when the agent bids v_i, for any fixed bids of the other agents. Formally, for every vector $\mathbf{b} = (b_1, \ldots, b_n)$, denote by $\mathbf{b}|_{b_i \leftarrow x}$ the vector $(b_1, \ldots, b_{i-1}, x, b_{i+1}, \ldots, b_n)$. A mechanism is truthful if for every agent i and $\mathbf{b}$:

$$u_i(\mathbf{b}|_{b_i \leftarrow v_i}) \geq u_i(\mathbf{b}).$$

---

[3] This simplifies Algorithm 2.

A deterministic direct mechanism is *individually-rational (IR)* if the utility of every agent i when the agent bids v_i is at least 0, regardless of the bids of the other agents:

$$u_i(\mathbf{b}|_{b_i \leftarrow v_i}) \geq 0.$$

A *randomized direct mechanism* is a lottery over deterministic direct mechanisms. In other words, it is a mechanism in which the functions $\mathbf{S}$ and $\mathbf{p}$ may depend not only on the bids but also on some random variables.

A randomized direct mechanism is called *universally-truthful* if it is a lottery over truthful deterministic direct mechanisms. In a universally-truthful randomized mechanism, the utility of agent i is maximized when the agent bids v_i, regardless of the bids of the other agents, and regardless of the random variable values. Similarly, a randomized direct mechanism is *universally-IR* if it is a lottery over IR deterministic direct mechanisms.

A mechanism is called *obviously truthful* if for every agent i and vectors $\mathbf{b}, \mathbf{b}'$:

$$u_i(\mathbf{b}|_{b_i \leftarrow v_i}) \geq u_i(\mathbf{b}').$$

In other words, the lowest utility the agent can get when reporting truthfully is at least as high as the highest utility the agent can get when reporting untruthfully, where "lowest" and "highest" are w.r.t. all possible reports of the other agents. This is a very strong property that is not satisfied by non-trivial direct mechanisms. However, an analogous property is satisfied by some *sequential mechanisms*.

In a *deterministic sequential mechanism*, at each time, an agent has to choose an *action* from a prespecified set of actions. In order to give meaning to the notion of truthfulness, we assume that the "action" is an answer to a query on the agent's value: at time t, the designer presents a function q_t to some agent i, and the agent is expected to reveal $q_t(v_i)$. Our mechanisms will only use Boolean functions such as "is $v_i > 2$?". Based on the agents' answers so far, the designer may decide to continue asking queries, or to end. When the mechanism ends, the designer examines the vector of answers $\mathbf{a}$, and determines the trade $\mathbf{S}(\mathbf{a})$ and the price-vector $\mathbf{p}(\mathbf{a})$.

Given an answer vector $\mathbf{a}$ and an agent i, denote by $\mathbf{a}|_{a_i \leftarrow x}$ the vector in which the answer of agent i to any function q_t is $q_t(x)$ (and the answers of other agents remain as in $\mathbf{a}$). A deterministic sequential mechanism is called *obviously truthful* if, at any step during the execution, and for any two vectors $\mathbf{a}$ and $\mathbf{a}'$ consistent with the history of answers up to the current step:

$$u_i(\mathbf{a}|_{a_i \leftarrow v_i}) \geq u_i(\mathbf{a}').$$

In other words, the lowest utility the agent can get by answering truthfully, according to v_i, is at least as high as the highest utility he can get by answering untruthfully.

A deterministic direct mechanism is a special case of a deterministic sequential mechanism in which there is only one step of queries and the queries are "what is your value?". If such a mechanism is obviously-truthful, then it is also truthful (set $\mathbf{a} = \mathbf{a}' = \mathbf{b}$ in the definition of obvious-truthfulness).

A *randomized sequential mechanism* is a lottery over deterministic sequential mechanisms; it is called *universally obviously-truthful* if it is a lottery over obviously-truthful deterministic sequential mechanisms.

2.4 Recipe Forests

Recall that a *forest* is an acyclic graph, composed of one or more *trees*; a *rooted forest* is a forest in which, in each tree, one vertex is denoted as its *root*.

Definition 1. *A recipe-set R is called a recipe-forest if there exists a rooted forest T in which the set of nodes is G, and each recipe $\mathbf{r} \in R$ corresponds to a path P from the root of some tree in T to a leaf of that tree (i.e., $r_g = 1$ for each $g \in P$ and $r_g = 0$ for each $g \notin P$).*[4]

We use the same letter g to denote both the category index and the corresponding node in T. As an example, the set $R = \{(1,1,0,0), (1,0,1,1)\}$ is a recipe-forest with a single tree shown in Fig. 1(a). The root category is N_1. The recipe $(1,1,0,0)$ corresponds to a path from N_1 to the leaf N_2. The recipe $(1,0,1,1)$ corresponds to a path from N_1 through N_3 to N_4.[5]

3 Computing Optimal Trade

Table 1. Left: an example market. Right: An optimal trade in that market.

Category	Agents' values
N_1: buyers	**17, 14, 13, 9**, 6, 2
N_2: sellers	**-4, -5**, -8, -10
N_3: A-producers	**-1, -3**, -5
N_4: B-producers	**-1, -4**, -6

Procurement sets
Buyer 17, A-producer −1, B-producer −1
Buyer 14, seller −4
Buyer 13, seller −5
Buyer 9, A-producer −3, B-producer −4

We first present an algorithm for computing an optimal trade assuming all values are known. We illustrate the algorithm on the market in the left of Table 1.

---

[4] In all our examples, the opposite is also true: each path corresponds to a recipe. But it is not necessary to make this assumption explicitly: if some path does not correspond to a recipe in R, then the category corresponding to the leaf of that path can be removed from the market, since it does not participate in any other recipe. This can be repeated until all remaining paths correspond to recipes.

[5] Note that the tree structure is not unique. For example, if R contains a single recipe, then every category can be considered as the root. For our purposes, it is sufficient to fix a single tree and a single root, and consider them as the input to the algorithms (instead of the set R).

The algorithm is based on contracting the recipe-forest down to a single node. Two types of contraction operations are used.

In a **vertical contraction**, a leaf that is a single child is combined with its parent in the following way. Suppose the sets of agent values in the child category are $v_1 \geq v_2 \geq \ldots \geq v_{m_v}$ and the agent values in the parent category are $u_1 \geq u_2 \geq \ldots \geq u_{m_u}$. Replace the parent category by a new category with $m := \min(m_v, m_u)$ values: $u_1 + v_1, u_2 + v_2, \ldots, u_m + v_m$. For example, a vertical contraction on the tree of Fig. 1(a) results in the tree of Fig. 1(b), where $N_3 \wedge N_4$ denotes the elementwise combination of N_3 and N_4. In the Table 1 market, $N_3 \wedge N_4$ contains the value pairs $\{(-1, -1), (-3, -4), (-5, -6)\}$ whose values are $\{-2, -7, -11\}$.

The rationale is that the unique root-leaf path that passes through the parent passes through its child too, and vice-versa. Therefore, any PS that contains an agent of the parent category must contain an agent of the child category, and vice-versa. In economic terms, these two categories are *complements*. Hence, elementwise combination of the two categories leads to a market with identical optimal GFT.

In a **horizontal contraction**, two sibling leaves are combined by taking the union of their categories in the following way. Suppose the sets of agent values in the left sibling category are $v_1, \ldots, v_{m_v}$ and in the right sibling category are $u_1, \ldots, u_{m_u}$. Replace both categories by a new category with $m := m_v + m_u$ values: $v_1, \ldots, v_{m_v}, u_1, \ldots, u_{m_u}$. For example, a horizontal contraction on the tree of Fig. 1(b) results in the tree of Fig. 1(c), where $N_2 \cup (N_3 \wedge N_4)$ denotes the combination of N_2 and $N_3 \wedge N_4$. In the Table 1 market, $N_2 \cup (N_3 \wedge N_4)$ contains the values $\{-4, -5, -8, -10\} \cup \{-2, -7, -11\}$ whose values are $\{-2, -4, -5, -7, -8, -10, -11\}$. If the forest has two or more trees, then all contracted trees (which now contain a single node each) can be further combined to a single node, similarly to a horizontal contraction.

The rationale is that, for every path from the root to one leaf there exists a path from the root to the other leaf, and vice-versa. Therefore, in any PS that contains an agent of one leaf-category, this agent can be replaced with an agent from the other leaf-category. In economic terms, these categories are *substitutes*. Therefore, uniting them leads to a market with the same optimal GFT.

In any tree with two or more vertices, there is a leaf that is either a single child or has a sibling leaf (for example, any leaf farthest from the root). Therefore, any tree admits either a vertical or a horizontal contraction, and it is possible to contract any tree to a single node. For example, a vertical contraction on the tree of Fig. 1(c), in the Table 1 market, yields: $\{17-2, 14-4, 13-5, 9-7, 6-8, 2-10\}$. The optimal trade in this market is the set of all deals with positive values, which in this case contains four deals with values $\{15, 10, 8, 2\}$. This corresponds to an optimal trade with $k = 4$ deals, shown at the right of Table 1.

If the forest has two or more trees, then all contracted trees can be further combined using a horizontal contraction to a single node. The process is shown as **Algorithm 1**.

Algorithm 1. Find the optimal GFT.

Input: A set of categories G, a set of traders N_g for all $g \in G$, and a recipe-forest R based on a rooted forest T. For each agent $i \in \cup_g N_g$, the value v_i is public knowledge.

Output: Optimal trade in the market.

1. If T has a single vertex g:
   Return all agents in N_g with a positive value: $\{i \in N_g | v_i > 0\}$
2. Else, if T has two roots without children g_l and g_s:
   Do a horizontal contraction of g_l into g_s. Go back to step 1.
3. Else, if there is a leaf g_l that is a single child of its parent g_p:
   Do a vertical contraction of g_l into g_p. Go back to step 1.
4. Else, there is a leaf g_l with a sibling leaf g_s:
   Do a horizontal contraction of g_l into g_s. Go back to step 1.

---

4 Ascending Auction Mechanism

4.1 General Description

The ascending-price auction is a randomized sequential mechanism. The general scheme is presented as **Algorithm 2**. For each category g, the auctioneer maintains a price p_g, and a subset $M_g \subseteq N_g$ of all agents that are "in the market" (that is, their value is higher than the current price of their category). At each iteration, the auctioneer chooses a subset of the prices, and increases each price p_g in this subset by 1. After each increase, the auctioneer asks each agent in turn, in a pre-specified order (e.g. by their index), whether their value is still higher than the price. An agent who answers "no" is permanently removed from the market. After each increase, the auctioneer computes the sum of prices of the categories in each recipe, defined as: Prices-sum($\mathbf{r}$) $:= \sum_{g \in G} p_g$. When this sum equals 0, the auction ends and the remaining agents trade in the final prices.

To flesh out this scheme, we need to explain (a) how the prices are initialized, (b) how the set of prices to increase is selected, and (c) how the final trade is determined.

(a) An important challenge in determining the prices is that the sum of prices must be the same for all recipes $\mathbf{r} \in R$, so that the price-sum crosses 0 for all recipes simultaneously, and all deals are simultaneously SBB. For the initial prices, this challenge is handled by the initialization of **Algorithm 2**: the price of each non-leaf category is set to $-V$ (described in Sect. 2), and the price of each leaf category is set to a number which is at most $-V$, computed such that the price-sum in each path from a root to a leaf is the same.

(b) Selecting which prices to increase is handled by **Algorithm 3**. It is a recursive algorithm: if the forest contains only a single category (a root with no children), then of course this category is selected. Otherwise, in each tree, either its root category or its children are selected for increase. The selection is based on the number of agents of each category g who are currently in the market. We denote this number by $m_g := |M_G|$.

We denote the root category of a tree by g_0. The algorithm first compares m_{g_0}

Algorithm 2. Ascending prices mechanism.

Input: A market N, a set of categories G and a recipe-forest R.
Output: Strongly-budget-balanced trade.

1. *Initialization:* Let $M_g := N_g$ for each $g \in G$. Determine initial price-vector **p**:
   For each non-leaf g, set $p_g := -V$;
   For each leaf g, set: $p_g := -V \cdot (\text{MaxDepth} - \text{Depth}(g) + 1)$;
2. Using Algorithm 3, select a set $G^* \subseteq G$ of categories.
3. For each $g^* \in G^*$, ask each agent in $i \in M_{g*}$ whether $v_i > p_{g*}$.
   (a) If an agent $i \in M_{g*}$ answers "no", then remove i from M_{g*} and go back to step 2.
   (b) If all agents in M_{g*} for all $g^* \in G^*$ answer "yes", then for all $g^* \in G^*$, let $p_{g*} := p_{g*} + 1$.
   (c) If after the increase $\sum_{g \in G} p_g \cdot r_g = 0$ for some $\mathbf{r} \in R$, then go on to step 4.
   (d) else go back to step 3.
4. Determine final trade using Algorithm 4.

Algorithm 3. Find a set of prices to increase.

Input: A set of categories G, a set of remaining traders M_g for all $g \in G$,
      and a recipe-forest R based on a forest T.
Output: A subset of G denoting categories whose price should be increased.
0. *Initialization:* For each category $g \in G$, let $m_g := |M_g|$
              = the number of agents of N_g who are in the market.
1. If T contains two or more trees,
   Recursively run Algorithm 3 on each individual tree T'; denote the outcome by $I_{T'}$.
   Return $\bigcup_{T' \in T} I_{T'}$.
2. Let g_0 be the category at the root of the single tree. Let $c_{g_0} := \sum_{g' \in \text{CHILDREN}(g_0)} m_{g'}$.
3. If $m_{g_0} > c_{g_0}$ [or g_0 has no children at all],
   then return the singleton $\{g_0\}$.
4. Else ($c_{g_0} \geq m_{g_0}$), for each child g' of g_0:
   Recursively run Algorithm 3 on the sub-tree rooted at g'; Denote the outcome by $I_{g'}$.
   Return $\bigcup_{g' \in child(g_0)} I_{g'}$.

---

to the sum of the m_g for all children of g_0 (which is denoted by c_{g_0}). If m_{g_0} is larger, then the price selected for increase is the price of g_0; Otherwise (c_{g_0} is larger or equal), the prices to increase are the prices of children categories: for each child category, Algorithm 3 is used recursively to choose a subset of prices to increase, and all returned sets are combined. It is easy to prove by induction that the resulting subset contains exactly one price for each path from a root to a leaf. Therefore, all prices in the subset are increased simultaneously by one unit, and the price-sum in all recipes remains equal.

Consider again the tree of Fig. 1(a), and suppose the numbers of remaining traders in the four categories are $6, 4, 3, 3$. Initially the algorithm compares m_1 to $m_2 + m_3$; since the latter is larger, the algorithm recursively checks the subtrees rooted at $g = 2$ and $g = 3$. In the former there is only one category so it is returned; in the latter, there is one child $g = 4$. Since $m_3 \leq m_4$, the child $g = 4$ is selected. The final set of prices to increase is $\{p_2, p_4\}$. If the counts were $m_1 = 6, m_2 = 3, m_3 = 2, m_4 = 2$ instead, then the set of prices to increase would be $\{p_1\}$. Note that in both cases, a single price is increased in each recipe.

Algorithm 4. Determine a feasible trade.

Input: A set of categories G, a set of remaining traders M_g for all $g \in G$,
 and a recipe-forest R based on a forest T.
Output: A set of PSs with remaining traders, each of which corresponds to a recipe in R.
1. If T has a single vertex g:
  Return M_g — the set of traders remaining in category g.
2. If T has two roots without children g_l and g_s:
  Do a horizontal contraction of g_l into g_s. Go back to step 1.
3. Otherwise, pick an arbitrary leaf category $g_l \in T$.
4. If g_l is a single child of its parent $g_p \in T$:
  Perform a randomized vertical contraction of g_l and g_p. Go back to step 1.
5. Otherwise, g_l has a sibling $g_s \in T$:
  Perform a horizontal contraction of g_l and g_s. Go back to step 1.

The equality of price-sums is preserved by the price-increase. The price-sum increases by 1 at each step, so at some point it reaches 0. At that point, the auction stops.

(c) Once the auction ends, the final trade has to be computed. At this stage, it is possible that in some recipes, the numbers of traders remaining in the market are not balanced. In order to construct an integer number of procurement-sets of each recipe, some agents must be removed from the trade. The traders to remove must be selected at random and not by their value, since selecting traders by value might make the mechanism non-truthful. To this end, we replace the vertical contraction operation with a *randomized vertical contraction*. A leaf that is a single child is combined with its parent in the following way. Denote the leaf and parent category by l and p respectively, and let M_i be the set of traders remaining in category i. Let $n_{min} := \min(|M_l|, |M_p|) =$ the integer number of procurement-sets that can be constructed from the agents in both categories. For each $g \in \{l, p\}$ if $|M_g| > n_{min}$ then choose $|M_g| - n_{min}$ agents uniformly at random and remove them from M_g. Then perform a vertical contraction with the remaining agents.

The horizontal contractions can be performed deterministically, as no traders should be removed. The process of determining the final trade is summarized as **Algorithm 4**.

4.2 Example Run

We illustrate Algorithm 2 using the example in Table 1, where the recipe set is $R = \{(1, 1, 0, 0), (1, 0, 1, 1)\}$ and the recipe-forest contains the single tree shown in Fig. 1(a). The execution is shown in Table 2.

Step 1. The initialization step ensures that (a) the initial sum of prices is the same in each recipe; (b) the price in each category is lower than the lowest possible value of an agent in this category, which we denoted by $-V$. In the example, the initial prices are $-V, -2V, -V, -V$, and the price-sum of each recipe is $-3V$.

Step 2. The categories whose price should be increased are determined using Algorithm 3. In the example, the numbers of remaining traders are $6, 4, 3, 3$. Since $6 < 4 + 3$, the price of the root category (the buyers) is not increased. In the first branch, the seller-price is selected for increase. In the second branch, there is a tie between the A-producer and the B-producer, which is broken in favor of the child. Therefore, the chosen set G^* is $\{2, 4\} = \{\text{seller, B-producer}\}$.

Step 3. The auctioneer increases the prices of each category $g^* \in G^*$ by 1, until one agent of some category $g^* \in G^*$ indicates that his value is not higher than the price, and leaves the trade. The price never skips any agent's integer value, because the initial category price was a big negative integer number $(-V)$ and the increment is done always by 1 so the category price visits every integer from $-V$ to the current category price. In the example, the first agent who answers "no" is B-producer -6. While p_4 has increased to -6, p_2 has increased to $-V - 6$, so the price-sum in all recipes remains the same: $-2V - 6$. After B-producer -6 is removed, we return to step 2 to choose a new set of prices to increase. The algorithm keeps executing steps 2 and 3 as described in Table 2. Finally, while the algorithm increases p_1, before buyer 9 exits the trade, the price-sum in all recipes becomes 0 and the algorithm proceeds to step 4.

Step 4. The final trade is determined by Algorithm 4. In the example, a randomized vertical contraction is first done between the A-producers and B-producers. Since there is one A-producer -1 and one B-producer -1, none of them has to be removed, and the combined category now has a single pair. Next, a horizontal contraction is done between the pair of producers and the remaining two sellers. This results in a combined category of size 3. Finally, a randomized vertical contraction is done between this combined category and the buyers' category. Since there are 4 remaining buyers, but only 3 sets in the child category, one of the buyers is chosen at random and removed from trade. Finally, three deals

Table 2. Execution of Algorithm 2 on market from Table 1

Category counts	G^*	Price-increase stops when	New prices	Price-sum
		[Initialization]	$-V, -2V, -V, -V$	$-3V$
$6, 4, 3, 3$	$2, 4$	B-producer -6 exits	$-V, -V - 6, -V, -6$	$-2V - 6$
$6, 4, 3, 2$	$2, 3$	A-producer -5 exits	$-V, -11, -5, -6$	$-V - 11$
$6, 4, 2, 2$	$2, 4$	seller -10 exits	$-V, -10, -5, -5$	$-V - 10$
$6, 3, 2, 2$	1	buyer 2 exits	$2, -10, -5, -5$	-8
$5, 3, 2, 2$	$2, 4$	B-producer -4 exits	$2, -9, -5, -4$	-7
$5, 3, 2, 1$	$2, 3$	seller -8 exits	$2, -8, -4, -4$	-6
$5, 2, 2, 1$	1	buyer 6 exits	$6, -8, -4, -4$	-2
$4, 2, 2, 1$	$2, 3$	A-producer -3 exits	$6, -7, -3, -4$	-1
$4, 2, 1, 1$	1	price-sum crosses zero	$7, -7, -3, -4$	0

are made: two deals follow the recipe $(1, 1, 0, 0)$ and involve a buyer and a seller, and one deal follows the recipe $(1, 0, 1, 1)$ and involves a buyer, an A-producer and a B-producer.

5   Ascending Auction Properties

Due to space constraints, most proofs can be found in the full version of our paper [8].

A crucial feature of our mechanism is that the price-sum along each path from the same node to a leaf is constant.

Lemma 1. *Throughout Algorithm 2, for any category* $g \in G$, *the price-sum along any path from* g *to a leaf is the same for all paths.*

The economic properties of the auction are summarized in the following theorems.

Theorem 1. *Algorithm 2 is universally strongly-budget-balanced, individually-rational and obviously truthful.*

Proof. Given a fixed priority-ordering on the agents, consider the deterministic variant of the algorithm in which, in step 3 of Algorithm 4, instead of the randomized vertical contraction, the removed agents in each category are selected deterministically by the fixed agent ordering. Algorithm 2 is a lottery on such deterministic mechanisms, where the agent ordering is selected uniformly at random. Therefore, to prove that the randomized mechanism satisfies a property universally, it is sufficient to prove that each such deterministic variant satisfies this property.

Strong budget balance holds since by Lemma 1 (applied to the root category), the price-sum for all recipes remains the same throughout the execution, and the algorithm stops whenever this sum becomes 0. Individual rationality holds since $i \in N_g$ may remain in the market only if $v_i \geq p_g$. To prove obvious-truthfulness, we consider an agent $i \in N_g$ who is asked whether $v_i > p_g$, and check the two possible cases:

- Case 1: $v_i > p_g$. If the agent answers truthfully "yes", then his lowest possible utility is 0 (since the mechanism is IR). If the agent answers untruthfully "no", then his highest possible utility is 0 since he is immediately removed from trade and cannot return.
- Case 2: $v_i \leq p_g$. If the agent answers truthfully "no", then his lowest possible utility is 0 (since he is removed from trade immediately). If the agent answers untruthfully "yes", then his highest possible utility is 0, since the utility is $v_i - p_g$ and the price can only increase.

In both cases, the lowest possible utility of a truthful agent is at least the highest possible utility of a non-truthful agent.

We now show that the ascending auction attains an asymptotically optimal GFT. The analysis assumes that the valuations are *generic*—the sum of valuations in every subset of agents is unique. In particular, the optimal trade is unique. This is a relatively mild assumption, since every instance can be modified to have generic valuations, as explained by Babaioff and Walsh [2].

First, choose a sufficiently large constant $W \geq n + 1$ and replace each value v_i by $2^W \cdot v_i$. This scaling obviously has no effect on the optimal or the actual trade. Then, arbitrarily assign a unique integer index $i \in \{1, \ldots, n\}$ to every agent, and set $v_i' := 2^W \cdot v_i + 2^i$.

Now the sum of valuations in every agent subset is unique, since the n least significant bits in its binary representation are unique. Moreover, for every subset $I \subseteq N$, $\sum_{i \in I} v_i' \approx 2^W \sum_{i \in I} v_i$ plus some "noise" smaller than $2^{n+1} \leq 2^W$.

Therefore, the optimal trade in the new instance corresponds to one of the optimal trades in the original instance, with the GFT multiplied by 2^W. If the constant W is sufficiently large, the "noise" has a negligible effect on the GFT.

Definition 2. *(a) The number of deals in the optimal trade is denoted by k.*
(b) For each recipe $\mathbf{r} \in R$, the number of deals in the optimal trade corresponding to $\mathbf{r}$ is denoted by $k_{\mathbf{r}}$ (so $k = \sum_{\mathbf{r} \in R} k_{\mathbf{r}}$).
(c) The smallest positive number of deals of a single recipe in the optimal trade is denoted by $k_{\min} := \min_{\mathbf{r} \in R, k_{\mathbf{r}} > 0} k_{\mathbf{r}}$.

Theorem 2. *The expected GFT of the ascending-price auction of Sect. 4 is at least $1 - 1/k_{\min}$ of the optimal GFT.*

To prove Theorem 2 we need several definitions. For every category $g \in G$:

(*) $k_g :=$ the number of deals in the optimal trade containing an agent from N_g (equivalently: the number of deals whose recipe-path passes through g). If g is the root category then $k_g = k$. If g is any non-leaf category then

$$k_g = \sum_{g' \text{ is a child of } g} k_{g'}. \tag{1}$$

In the Table 2 market, k_g for categories 1,2,3,4 equals $4, 2, 2, 2$ respectively.

(*) $v_{g,k_g} :=$ the value of the k_g-th highest trader in N_g—the lowest value of a trader that participates in the optimal trade. In the Table 2 market, v_{g,k_g} for categories 1,2,3,4 equals $9, -5, -3, -4$ respectively. Note that, in any path from the root to a leaf, the sum of v_{g,k_g} is positive—otherwise we could remove the PS composed of the agents corresponding to this path, and get a trade with a higher GFT.

(*) $v_{g,k_g+1} :=$ the highest value of a trader that does not participate in the optimal trade (or $-V$ if no such trader exists). In the Table 2 market, v_{g,k_g+1} for categories 1,2,3,4 equals $6, -8, -5, -6$ respectively. Note that, in any path from the root to a leaf, the sum of v_{g,k_g+1} is at most 0—otherwise we could add the corresponding PS and get a trade with a higher GFT.

Recall that, during the auction, $m_g := |M_g|$ = the number of agents of category g currently in the market (whose value is larger than p_g), and

$$c_g := \sum_{g' \text{ is a child of } g} m_{g'}. \tag{2}$$

When the algorithm starts, $m_g \geq k_g$ for all $g \in G$, since all participants of the optimal trade are in the market. Similarly, $c_g \geq k_g$. In contrast to Eq. (1), m_g and c_g need not be equal. By adding dummy agents with value $-V + 1$ to some categories, we can guarantee that, when the algorithm starts, $m_g = c_g$ for all non-leaf categories $g \in G$. For example, in the Table 2 market it is sufficient to add a buyer with value $-V + 1$. This addition does not affect the optimal trade, since no PS in the optimal trade would contain agents with such low values. It does not affect the actual trade either, since the price-sum is negative as long as there are dummy agents in the market. Once $m_g = c_g$, we show that these values remain close to each other throughout the algorithm:

Lemma 2. *For all non-leaf categories $g \in G$,*

$$c_g \leq m_g \leq c_g + 1.$$

Definition 3. *Given a price-vector $\mathbf{p}$, a subset $G' \subseteq G$ is called:*

(a) Cheap—if $p_g \leq v_{g,k_g+1}$ for all $g \in G'$;
(b) Expensive—if $p_g \geq v_{g,k_g}$ for all $g \in G'$.

We apply Definition 3 to paths in trees in the recipe-forest T. Intuitively, in a cheap path, the prices are sufficiently low to allow the participation of agents not from the optimal trade, while in an expensive path, the prices are sufficiently high to allow the participation of agents only from the optimal trade.

Lemmas 3–7 show some cases when Cheap and Expensive paths can and cannot exist in certain forest-trees. These lemmas are then used to prove Lemma 8: *when Algorithm 2 ends, $m_g \in \{k_g, k_g - 1\}$ for all $g \in G$.* With Lemma 8, we prove our main theorem. Lemmas 3–8 and their proofs can be found in the full version of our paper at [8].

Proof (Proof of Theorem 2). By Lemma 8, each recipe $\mathbf{r} \in R$ with $k_{\mathbf{r}} = 0$ does not participate in the trade at all. For each recipe $\mathbf{r} \in R$ with $k_{\mathbf{r}} > 0$, for each category g in $\mathbf{r}$, all k_g optimal traders of g, except maybe the lowest-valued one, participate in the final trade. Therefore, in the random selection of the final traders (Algorithm 4), at least $k_g - 1$ random deals are performed out of the k_g optimal deals. Hence, the approximation ratio of the GFT coming from recipe $\mathbf{r}$ alone is at least $1 - 1/k_{\mathbf{r}}$ of the optimum. Taking the minimum over all recipes yields the ratio claimed in the theorem.

6   Experiments

We evaluated the performance of our ascending auction using simulation experiments.[6] For these preliminary experiments, we used the recipe-forest $\mathbf{R} =$

---

[6] The code used for the experiments and the experiment results are available at https://github.com/dvirg/auctions.

Table 3. Results with stock-market prices and the recipe-forest $\mathbf{R} = \{(1,1, 0,0),(1,0,1,1)\}$.

n	Optimal					Ascending price					
	k	$k_{\min}$	$k_{\max}$	$1-\frac{1}{k_{\min}}$	$OGFT$	k'	$k_{\min}'$	$k_{\max}'$	$\%k'$	GFT	$\%GFT$
2	1.11	1.00	1.00	6.592	106323.0	0.48	0.48	0.48	37.24	60563.5	43.473
4	2.27	1.56	1.83	24.051	231902.7	1.49	1.35	1.38	65.02	194877.0	80.655
6	3.43	1.89	2.65	30.710	348117.4	2.56	1.93	2.22	74.39	322155.4	90.531
10	5.78	2.46	4.31	42.567	594618.4	4.84	2.63	3.89	83.53	578495.9	96.269
16	9.32	3.36	6.79	56.172	953490.8	8.34	3.42	6.37	89.46	943732.1	98.473
26	15.19	5.05	10.91	69.904	1563658.4	14.20	4.88	10.50	93.45	1557792.5	99.401
50	29.34	9.49	20.77	83.685	3010702.2	28.33	9.13	20.37	96.56	3007474.9	99.831
100	58.77	18.86	41.35	91.395	6037200.9	57.74	18.50	40.95	98.25	6035460.2	99.953
500	294.16	90.59	206.05	96.664	30271280.7	293.03	91.92	205.66	99.61	30270801.8	99.997
1000	588.46	176.99	411.96	97.440	60588937.5	587.23	178.03	411.59	99.79	60588643.6	99.999

$\{(1,1,0,0), (1,0,1,1)\}$, which contains a single tree with only binary recipes and two paths ($N_1 \longrightarrow N_2$ and $N_1 \longrightarrow N_3 \longrightarrow N_4$). In the future we plan to do experiments with larger forests and non-binary recipes. For several values of $n \leq 1000$, we constructed a market with n agents of each category g. The agents' values were chosen at random as explained below. For each n, we made 1000 runs and averaged the results. We split the values among the categories uniformly at random, so each category has n values. The results and conclusions can be found in the full version of our paper at [8].

6.1   Agents' Values

We conducted two experiments. In the first experiment, the value of each buyer (root category) was selected uniformly at random from $[1, 1000]$, and the value of each trader from the other three categories was selected uniformly at random from $[-1, -1000]$.

In the second experiment, the values were selected based on real stocks prices on Yahoo's stock market site using 33 stocks. For each stock, we collected the prices from every day from the inception of the stock until September 2020. Every day the stock has 4 values: Open, Close, High and Low. All price values are multiplied by 1000, so they can be represented as integers, to avoid floating-point rounding errors. On each stock, we collected all the price values and used those price values as agents' values at random. For the non-root categories, the values were multiplied by -1. There were more than 1000 values for each category.

6.2   Number of Deals and Gain from Trade

In each run, we calculated k (the number of deals in the optimal trade), $k_{\min}$, $k_{\max}$ (recipe minimum and maximum number of deals in the optimal trade), $1 - \frac{1}{k_{\min}}$ (the theoretical lower bound ratio) and $OGFT$ (the optimal gain-from-trade). We found that the average value of k was approximately $0.6n$. For the ascending-price mechanism, we calculated k' (the actual number of deals done by the mechanism), k_{min}', k_{max}' (the actual recipe minimum and maximum number of deals done by the mechanism) and the GFT (the actual gain-from-trade of deals done by the mechanism). The results are shown in Table 3.

References

1. Babaioff, M., Nisan, N.: Concurrent auctions across the supply chain. J. Artif. Intell. Res. (JAIR) **21**, 595–629 (2004). https://doi.org/10.1613/jair.1316
2. Babaioff, M., Walsh, W.E.: Incentive-compatible, budget-balanced, yet highly efficient auctions for supply chain formation. Decis. Support Syst. **39**(1), 123–149 (2005). https://doi.org/10.1016/j.dss.2004.08.008. ISSN 01679236
3. Blumrosen, L., Mizrahi, Y.: Approximating gains-from-trade in bilateral trading. In: Cai, Y., Vetta, A. (eds.) WINE 2016. LNCS, vol. 10123, pp. 400–413. Springer, Heidelberg (2016). https://doi.org/10.1007/978-3-662-54110-4_28
4. Colini-Baldeschi, R., Goldberg, P.W., de Keijzer, B., Leonardi, S., Roughgarden, T., Turchetta, S.: Approximately efficient two-sided combinatorial auctions. In: Proceedings of the 2017 ACM Conference on Economics and Computation, pp. 591–608. ACM (2017)
5. Feldman, M., Gonen, R.: Removal and threshold pricing: truthful two-sided markets with multi-dimensional participants. In: Deng, X. (ed.) SAGT 2018. LNCS, vol. 11059, pp. 163–175. Springer, Cham (2018). https://doi.org/10.1007/978-3-319-99660-8_15
6. Feldman, M., Frim, G., Gonen, R.: Multi-sided advertising markets: dynamic mechanisms and incremental user compensations. In: Bushnell, L., Poovendran, R., Başar, T. (eds.) GameSec 2018. LNCS, vol. 11199, pp. 227–247. Springer, Cham (2018). https://doi.org/10.1007/978-3-030-01554-1_13
7. Gerstgrasser, M., Goldberg, P.W., de Keijzer, B., Lazos, P., Skopalik, A.: Multi-unit bilateral trade. In: Proceedings of the AAAI 2019, vol. 33, pp. 1973–1980 (2019). arXiv preprint arXiv:1811.05130
8. Gilor, D., Gonen, R., Segal-Halevi, E.: Ascending-price mechanism for general multi-sided markets. In: EUMAS (2021). The full version of the paper is at https://bit.ly/3oY1dZO
9. Gonen, M., Gonen, R., Elan, P.: Generalized trade reduction mechanisms. In: Proceedings of EC 2007, pp. 20–29 (2007)
10. Gonen, R., Egri, O.: COMBIMA: truthful, budget maintaining, dynamic combinatorial market. Auton. Agents Multi Agent Syst. **34**(1), 14 (2020)
11. Gonen, R., Segal-Halevi, E.: Strongly budget balanced auctions for multi-sided markets. In: AAAI, pp. 1998–2005 (2020)
12. Li, S.: Obviously strategy-proof mechanisms. Am. Econ. Rev. **107**(11), 3257–3287 (2017)
13. McAfee, R.P.: A dominant strategy double auction. J. Econ. Theory **56**(2), 434–450 (1992). ISSN 00220531
14. McAfee, R.P.: The gains from trade under fixed price mechanisms. Appl. Econ. Res. Bull. **1**, 1–10 (2008)
15. Myerson, R.B., Satterthwaite, M.A.: Efficient mechanisms for bilateral trading. J. Econ. Theory **29**(2), 265–281 (1983). ISSN 00220531
16. Nisan, N.: Introduction to mechanism design (for computer scientists). In: Nisan, N., Roughgarden, T., Tardos, E., Vazirani, V. (eds.) Algorithmic Game Theory, pp. 209–241. Cambridge University Press (2007). ISBN 978-0521872829

17. Segal-Halevi, E., Hassidim, A., Aumann, Y.: SBBA: a strongly-budget-balanced double-auction mechanism. In: Gairing, M., Savani, R. (eds.) SAGT 2016. LNCS, vol. 9928, pp. 260–272. Springer, Heidelberg (2016). https://doi.org/10.1007/978-3-662-53354-3_21
18. Segal-Halevi, E., Hassidim, A., Aumann, Y.: MUDA: a truthful multi-unit double-auction mechanism. In: Proceedings of AAAI 2018. AAAI Press, February 2018. arXiv preprint arXiv:1712.06848
19. Segal-Halevi, E., Hassidim, A., Aumann, Y.: Double auctions in markets for multiple kinds of goods. In: Proceedings of IJCAI 2018. AAAI Press, July 2018. Previous name: "MIDA: A Multi Item-type Double-Auction Mechanism". arXiv preprint arXiv:1604.06210
20. Vickrey, W.: Counterspeculation, auctions, and competitive sealed tenders. J. Finan. 16(1), 8–37 (1961)

Governing Black-Box Agents
in Competitive Multi-Agent Systems

Michael Pernpeintner[1]([✉])[iD], Christian Bartelt[1][iD],
and Heiner Stuckenschmidt[2][iD]

[1] Institute for Enterprise Systems (InES), University of Mannheim,
Mannheim, Germany
{pernpeintner,bartelt}@es.uni-mannheim.de
[2] University of Mannheim, Mannheim, Germany
heiner@informatik.uni-mannheim.de

Abstract. Competitive Multi-Agent Systems (MAS) are inherently hard to control due to agent autonomy and strategic behavior, which is particularly problematic when there are system-level objectives to be achieved or specific environmental states to be avoided.

Existing solutions for this task mostly assume specific knowledge about agent preferences, utilities and strategies, neglecting the fact that actions are not always directly linked to genuine agent preferences, but can also reflect anticipated competitor behavior, be a concession to a superior adversary or simply be intended to mislead other agents. This assumption both reduces applicability to real-world systems and opens room for manipulation.

We therefore propose a new governance approach for competitive MAS which relies exclusively on publicly observable actions and transitions, and uses the acquired knowledge to purposefully restrict action spaces, thereby achieving the system's objectives while preserving a high level of autonomy for the agents.

Keywords: Multi-agent system · Competition · Stochastic game · Governance · Restriction

1 Introduction

1.1 Motivation

One of the most intriguing and challenging characteristics of an MAS is the fact that its environmental changes depend simultaneously on the actions of all agents, such that a single agent can never simply choose an action and accurately predict the resulting transition. This mutual influence leads to strategic and sometimes even seemingly erratic agent actions—particularly when human agents are involved—, and at the same time decouples *intended* and *observed* system behavior:

© Springer Nature Switzerland AG 2021
A. Rosenfeld and N. Talmon (Eds.): EUMAS 2021, LNAI 12802, pp. 19–36, 2021.
https://doi.org/10.1007/978-3-030-82254-5_2

Example 1. Consider an MAS consisting of two agents X and Y, two states A (initial state) and B, and two actions 0 and 1 for each agent. This results in the joint action set $\{00, 01, 10, 11\}$, where the joint action 10 means that the first player, X, takes action 1, while the second player, Y, takes action 0. The transition function of this MAS is shown in Fig. 1. Imagine now an observer who sees the following sequence of actions and transitions:

$$A \xrightarrow{10} A \xrightarrow{01} A \xrightarrow{00} B$$

If the observer does not know anything about the inner workings of X and Y, it cannot distinguish whether X wanted to stay at state A and changed its action from 1 in the first step to 0 in the second step because it anticipated Y's second action, or X wanted to reach state B, observed the uselessness of its first action and then tried another strategy to reach B (and failed again). This shows that intentions are not immediately linked to observable behavior, and no preference order over the environmental states can be concluded.

Several existing methods, for instance preference elicitation using CP-nets [18], rely on the fact that preferences *can* be observed. However, this requires additional assumptions about the link between actions and preferences.

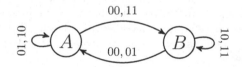

Fig. 1. Transition graph of a simple MAS

In this paper, we are investigating the task of achieving a system objective in the above-mentioned scenario where agents are purely self-interested and pursue their confidential individual goals strategically without an inherent desire for cooperation.

1.2 Governance in Multi-Agent Systems

While full control on the part of an outside authority contradicts the multi-agent property of such a system, some level of control and cooperation can still be achieved by a suitable governance approach. Several ideas have been proposed or adapted over the last decades of MAS research, among them Stochastic Games [36], Deontic Logic [26], Normative Systems [38], and more specifically Normative Multi-Agent Systems [1,5] and Game Theory for MAS [6,21,23]. In all those approaches, there are some "global desirable properties" [35] which are to be fulfilled in addition to the natural, uncontrolled agent behavior. The governance works toward this objective without destroying the multi-agent property of the system.

The simplest way of achieving a system objective would be, of course, to set fixed rules which have to be obeyed by all agents (off-line rule design [38]). While this can be an effective approach, it necessarily suffers from at least one of two drawbacks: Either the agents are so heavily constricted that they lose their autonomy altogether [12], or the system is unable to dynamically cope with unforeseen strategies. Therefore, we propose to make use of the knowledge that can be collected by observing how agents behave in the system, in order to update and refine the governance interventions.

Following the above line of thought, we do not reason in terms of agent preferences or utilities, but rather in terms of actions and transitions. Naturally, there is a conflict between control and autonomy, requiring a relative weighting of the two objectives. We strive here for minimal restriction, subject to a constraint on the expected value of the system objective.

1.3   Overview of the Approach

The overall approach is shown in Fig. 2: A Governance, as formally defined in Sect. 3, observes agent actions and subsequent state transitions in order to predict future agent behavior and to restrict the action spaces from which agents can choose. By looking only at the observable behavior, we avoid the fallacies described in Sect. 1.1 which arise when directly concluding preferences over the environmental states.

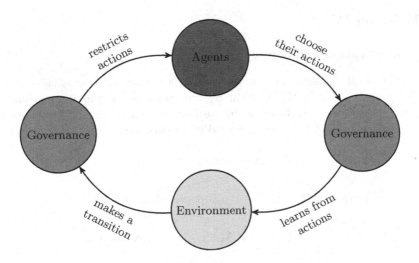

Fig. 2. High-level governance approach

1.4   Contribution

We present a practical approach and corresponding algorithm to immediately turn observations about the history, i.e., the actions and transitions of an MAS, into suitable restrictions of the agents' action spaces, such that the value of a given system objective is optimized (i.e., either minimized or maximized) while agent autonomy is preserved as much as possible.

The theoretical model is intended to be widely applicable to real-world MAS and does therefore not assume any particular structure of agents and environment. The solution method in this paper focuses on Multi-Attribute MAS with binary attributes, but the results carry over quite naturally to attributes with arbitrary finite domains.

Our experimental evaluation indicates that the approach is effective and indeed avoids the above-mentioned problem induced by "observing preferences". However, there are still several open challenges which are listed in the closing section for ongoing and future research.

1.5 Structure

The remainder of this paper is organized as follows: Sect. 2 recaps relevant existing work and places our work within the context of these approaches. Sect. 3 defines the system model and the governing instance. Section 4 describes the logic and implementation of the governance loop, while Sect. 5 provides a quantitative evaluation of two scenarios, demonstrating general feasibility of the approach. Finally, Sect. 6 gives an outlook on open challenges and future work.

2 Existing Work

2.1 Classification and Scope

The fundamental challenge of "guaranteeing the successful coexistence of multiple programs" [38] in a Multi-Agent System obviously requires a measure for "success", as well as an instance which can evaluate and possibly influence the degree of success. MAS research can readily be classified from this perspective:

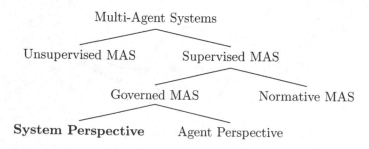

An MAS can either have a supervising entity which interferes with the agents in order to achieve a system objective, or this goal is achieved solely by the interaction of the agents (self-organization and/or emergence [30,42]).

When there is a supervisor, its decisions can be either binding (which we will call a *Governed MAS*) or non-binding (normative). We follow here the reasoning of [4] who state that norms are "a concept of social reality [which does] not physically constrain the relations between individuals. Therefore it is possible to violate them." Note that this terminology is far from being unambiguous; for instance, [32] use the term "Normative Synthesis" for the *enforcement* of equilibria.

There are two perspectives of a Governed MAS: The viewpoint of a participating agent and that of the governing instance. In the latter case, the key points of interest are the level of control–or level of satisfaction of the system objectives–that can be achieved, as well as the necessary interventions.

In the remaining paper, we will focus on Governed MAS from a system perspective only, but the relevant related work (Sect. 2.2) includes also some of the adjacent areas.

2.2   Relevant Related Work

Multi-Agent Learning has been examined from an agent perspective in great detail [16], and there are several approaches which can be partly transferred to the system point of view. In contrast, only few areas, e.g. *Normative Multi-Agent Systems* [5], have been thoroughly examined from an observer's angle.

[16] and [15] identify two main research streams for competitive Multi-Agent Learning: Game theoretic approaches, including auctions and negotiations, and Multi-Agent Reinforcement Learning (MARL) [37]. The latter adds a layer of complexity to classical reinforcement learning [8, 40], since competitive agents all evolve at the same time and therefore disturb the learning process of their opponents (*moving-target problem*) [31]. Both surveys, however, restrict their scope to learning agents, instead of external entities learning *about* agents.

Game theory in this context oftentimes deals with small, well-defined (and mostly contrived) scenarios [3, 14, 39] like two-player games with a fixed payoff matrix, which can be formally examined and sometimes also completely solved in terms of optimal responses and behavioral equilibria. What these solutions lack is widespread applicability to real-world settings where information is incomplete, environments are large and agents do not behave nicely. Therefore, the gap between academic use cases on the one hand, and industrial and societal applications on the other hand is still large.

[38] realized that social laws can be used by designers of Multi-Agent Systems to make agents cooperate without formally controlling them. The authors describe an approach to define such laws off-line and keep them fixed for the entire run-time of the system, and they mention the possibility that their laws are not always obeyed by the agents. From this reasoning, the two notions of *hard norms* and *soft norms* [34, 35] have emerged—the two categories which we call Governed (GMAS) and Normative (NMAS) Multi-Agent Systems, respectively.

[35] argue that "achieving compliance by design can be very hard" due to various reasons, e.g. norm consistency and enforcement complexity. In their view, NMAS are therefore more suitable for open and distributed environments. This lack of hard obligations leads to concepts like sanctions, norm revision, norm

conflict resolution, and others. NMAS have been researched from various perspectives and with a host of theoretical frameworks, among them formal languages and logics [7,13,32], Bayesian networks for the analysis of effectiveness [10], bottom-up norm emergence [30] and on-line norm synthesis [29]. Many of these approaches are also partially applicable to Governed MAS, but require adaptation and generalization. However, the effectiveness of rewards and sanctions fundamentally depends on the agents' susceptibility to this kind of (dis-) incentives, rendering the approach useless when agents simply do not react to sanctions whatsoever.

MARL approaches, naturally built upon the Markov Decision Process (MDP) model, concentrate on two core issues, compared to classical RL: Non-stationarity, by force of unknown and dynamic agents, and scalability, since joint action spaces often grow exponentially in the number of agents. Again, there is vast literature for Multi-Agent learning from the perspective of an agent [40]. [11] specifically look at the balance between individual preferences and shared objectives, but only consider cooperative agents.

Concerning the lack of stationary transition probabilities, multiple methods for model-free learning have been proposed, for example Q-learning [41], DQN [28] and A3C [27]. In contrast, [19] employ a model-based approach for non-stationary environments, assuming a continuous, bounded evolution of both transition and reward.

To fight the scalability issue, [25] apply sequentialization to RL problems with large action spaces at the expense of an increased time horizon. Their technique of binarizing the action space into sequential decisions lends itself particularly well to spaces which are binary themselves, for example all subsets of a fixed set. This, as we will see, is the structure that we face in the MAS Governance problem. Other methods for the reduction of state spaces or action spaces include ϵ-reduction [2,9] as well as exploitation of symmetry [24] and policy structure [22]. [17] apply such techniques to the problem of stochastic shortest paths, while [33] use them for embedding biological state space models into an MDP.

3   Model

Unknown autonomous agents can generally behave in a contradictory manner and thus defy consistent traceability. Probabilistic methods, however, are able to deal with such behavior in a very intuitive way. Therefore, a Stochastic Game [20] was chosen as the underlying model of the black-box MAS observed by the Governance.

The proposed Governance acts by simply allowing and forbidding certain actions for individual agents at run-time. This choice (instead of, for instance, assigning rewards and punishments) is based on two factors: First, the effect of a reward largely depends on an agent's utility function, which we assume to be unknown. Second, Stochastic Games are naturally equipped with a set of *fundamental actions* for each agent, a subset of which (the currently *available actions*) can be chosen at any given time step. This fits nicely into our idea of

Governance which is to transform the set of fundamental actions into a subset of *allowed actions*.

The Governance's knowledge about agent behavior is stored in a data structure similar to a Q-table [41], such that acquisition of new knowledge from observations as well as conclusions about conflicts and optimal action restrictions can be performed as part of an on-line governing cycle.

3.1 Agents and Environment

Consider a discrete-time Stochastic Game (I, S, A, r, δ) with a set $I = \{1, ..., n\}$ of agents, a set S of environmental states, a set $A = \prod_{i \in I} A_i$ of fundamental actions per agent, a confidential reward function $r : S \times A \to \mathbb{R}^n$ and a probabilistic transition function $\delta : S \times A \to \Delta S$, where ΔS denotes the set of all distribution functions $p : S \to [0, 1]$ with $\sum_{s \in S} p(s) = 1$.

At each step t, an agent is given an individual set $A_i^{(t)} \subseteq A_i$ of allowed actions—defined by the Governance—, from which it can choose. The system dynamics of agent i are therefore represented by its confidential stochastic policy $\pi_i : S \times 2^{A_i} \to \Delta A_i$ such that $p_{\pi_i(s, A_i)}(a_i) = 0 \ \forall a_i \notin A_i$. The policies can change dynamically at run-time, reflecting the agents' ability to learn and evolve.

Throughout this paper, variables or functions which are changing over time will be indicated by superscripting the current time step t, as in $\pi_i^{(t)}$.

In this work, we limit our investigation to binary multi-attribute environments, i.e., $S = \mathbb{B}^m$ for some fixed $m \in \mathbb{N}$, where agents can change one attribute per time step (or choose the *neutral action* $\varnothing$), and an attribute is deterministically toggled when at least one agent chooses to change it.

Example 2. Consider a smart home environment consisting of 7 binary variables: $S = T \times O \times W \times B \times H \times L \times A \cong \mathbb{B}^7$, where the variables denote Time (day/night), Occupancy (occupied/empty), Window (open/closed), Blinds (open/closed), Heating (on/off), Lights (on/off) and Alarm (on/off), respectively. The n agents, who each have their individual preferences over the environmental state, can now choose to change at most one of the variables W, B, H, L or A at each step (they cannot, however, influence the Time or the Occupancy of the house).

An exemplary progression of this system could be

$$1100101 \xrightarrow{wa\varnothing} 1110100 \xrightarrow{blb} 1111110$$

$$\xrightarrow{\varnothing\varnothing h} 1111010 \xrightarrow{hlb} 1110100 \xrightarrow{bwl} 1101110,$$

where states are written as binary numbers, and transitions, together with the respective chosen actions, connect subsequent states. There are three agents acting upon the environment with identical action sets $A_i = \{\varnothing, w, b, h, l, a\} \ \forall i$. Time and Occupancy would, of course, be controlled by external forces, but this is omitted here for simplicity.

3.2   Governance

Section 3.1 defines the evolution of an MAS according to the formula

$$s^{(t+1)} = \delta\left(s^{(t)}, \pi(s^{(t)})\right).$$

Since the action policies are at the agents' discretion, it follows immediately that this progression can be influenced via exactly two levers: Either by changing *what agents can do* (altering their action sets) or by changing *what consequences actions have* (altering the transition function).

Our proposed governance model follows a strict separation of concerns: The transition function represents the unalterable evolution of the environment according to the actions taken by all agents, while the restriction of actions is performed by the Governance and therefore artificial. To use an analogy, the transition function accounts for the laws of nature in the system, whereas the Governance plays the role of the legislature.

The Governance $\mathcal{G} = (c_{\mathcal{G}}, \Gamma, \lambda)$ consists of a cost function $c_{\mathcal{G}}$, a restriction function Γ and a learning function λ, which are defined formally in the next sections. We call a MAS together with a Governance a *Governed Multi-Agent System* (GMAS).

Observation and Intervention. The Governance intervenes at each time step t by defining individual *allowed actions* for each agent before the agents choose their respective actions from their restricted action sets:

$$A^{(t)} = \Gamma_{s_{\mathcal{G}}^{(t)}}(s^{(t)}),$$

where $A^{(t)} \sqsubseteq \mathcal{A}$ is a *regular subset* of the fundamental action set $\mathcal{A} = \prod_i \mathcal{A}_i$, i.e., $A^{(t)} = \prod_i A_i^{(t)}$ with $A_i^{(t)} \subseteq \mathcal{A}_i \; \forall i$. The subscript in $\Gamma_{s_{\mathcal{G}}^{(t)}}(s^{(t)})$ hints to the fact that Γ implicitly uses as an input not only the current environmental state $s^{(t)}$, but also the internal state $s_{\mathcal{G}}^{(t)}$ of the Governance, representing the knowledge acquired so far. Since this is always the case, we will henceforth omit the subscript for brevity.

For consistency reasons, each agent i has a *neutral action* $\varnothing_i \in A_i$ which cannot be deleted from the set of allowed actions. Consequently, the joint action $\varnothing$ is always allowed.

As soon as all agents have made their choice of action $a = (a_i)_i \in A^{(t)}$, the Governance can then use the new observation $(s^{(t)}, a^{(t)}, s^{(t+1)})$ to learn about the agents and the effectiveness of Γ. The corresponding learning step is expressed as an update of the Governance's internal state which, in turn, will be used by Γ in the next step, i.e.,

$$s_{\mathcal{G}}^{(t+1)} = \lambda\left(s_{\mathcal{G}}^{(t)}, s^{(t)}, a, s^{(t+1)}\right).$$

As opposed to other authors [4], we do not distinguish between legal and physical power: An agent can, as a matter of fact, only choose from the set of currently allowed actions, which might change from step to step.

System Objective. After defining how the Governance can influence the system behavior, we need to define *why* and *to what purpose* it uses this lever: As mentioned in Sect. 1.1, we assume that there is a certain system objective which is to be fulfilled in addition to the agent-specific goals. Since the Governance has only probabilistic information about the agents' future actions, its objective needs to be compatible with probabilistic reasoning and therefore quantifiable.

Definition 1. *The system objective of an MAS is to minimize a cost function $c_{\mathcal{G}} : \mathcal{S} \to \mathbb{R}$, and to choose a minimal restriction while doing so.*

There are two common types of system objectives: Either minimize (or maximize) a numerical parameter, which can directly be expressed by $c_{\mathcal{G}}$, or distinguish between valid states $\mathcal{S}_+$ and invalid states $\mathcal{S}_- := \mathcal{S} \setminus \mathcal{S}_+$. In the latter case,

$$c_{\mathcal{G}}(s) := \mathbb{1}_{\mathcal{S}_-}(s) \tag{1}$$

describes a system objective which prefers all valid states over all invalid states. Therefore, the Governance will pursue a valid state with minimal restriction of the agents.

In sum, the three components of $\mathcal{G}$ are the functions $c_{\mathcal{G}} : \mathcal{S} \to \mathbb{R}, \Gamma : \mathcal{S} \to 2^{\sqsubseteq \mathcal{A}}$ and $\lambda : \mathcal{S}_{\mathcal{G}} \times \mathcal{S} \times \mathcal{A} \times \mathcal{S} \to \mathcal{S}_{\mathcal{G}}$.

Example 3. As a continuation of Example 2, consider a GMAS where $c_{\mathcal{G}}$ is defined as in Eq. 1 with

$$\mathcal{S}_+ = \left\{ s \in \mathcal{S} : \left(\overline{w}(s) \vee \overline{h}(s)\right) \wedge \left(a(s) \vee o(s)\right) \wedge \left(\overline{l}(s) \vee o(s)\right) \right\},$$

meaning that the system wants to make sure that (a) the window is not open while the heating is turned on, (b) the alarm is on when the house is empty, and (c) the lights are off when there's nobody home.

It is now the task of the Governance to impose minimal restrictions on the agents while keeping $s^{(t)} \in \mathcal{S}_+ \ \forall t \geq 0$.

4 Governance Loop

In this section, we will build and analyze an algorithm to integrate observations into the current knowledge (learning step) and then turn this knowledge into a Pareto-optimal restriction of action sets (restriction step).

Let n be the number of agents, m the number of binary attributes, and q the number of actions for each agent (we assume the same fundamental action set for all agents).

4.1 Observation and Learning Step

Let $\mathcal{S}_{\mathcal{G}} := \mathbb{N}_0^{n \cdot 2^m \cdot q}$, such that the governance state is a simple counter of observed actions per agent per environmental state. Note that the second index of the governance state can naturally be identified with an environmental state s since

$\mathcal{S} \cong \{0, ..., 2^7 - 1\}$. For each observation $(s^{(t)}, a^{(t)})$, the learning function λ increments the respective numbers by one:

$$\lambda(s_{\mathcal{G}}, s^{(t)}, a^{(t)}) = s'_{\mathcal{G}}, \text{ where } s'^{(i,s,j)}_{\mathcal{G}} := \begin{cases} s^{(i,s,j)}_{\mathcal{G}} + 1 & \text{if } a^{(t)}_i = j \wedge s^{(t)} = s \\ s^{(i,s,j)}_{\mathcal{G}} & \text{else} \end{cases}.$$

This gives rise to an (observed) probability distribution

$$P^{(t)}_i(s) := \left(\frac{s^{(i,s,1)}_{\mathcal{G}}}{s^{(i,s)}_{\mathcal{G}}}, ..., \frac{s^{(i,s,q)}_{\mathcal{G}}}{s^{(i,s)}_{\mathcal{G}}} \right) \in \mathbb{P}_q, \text{ where } s^{(i,s)}_{\mathcal{G}} = \sum_{j=1}^{q} s^{(i,s,j)}_{\mathcal{G}}$$

for each agent i and environmental state s, which reflects the knowledge about the agents' past actions up to step t and thus contains the Governance's best guess for the actions at $(t+1)$. It is customary to set $P_i(s) := \left(\frac{1}{q}, ..., \frac{1}{q} \right)$ if $s^{(i,s)}_{\mathcal{G}} = 0$, or to use another initial distribution.

Here, $\mathbb{P}_q := \{x \in \mathbb{R}^q, 0 \le x_i \le 1, \|x\|_1 = 1\}$ denotes the set of probability vectors with q elements. Similarly, let $\mathbb{P}^n_q$ be the set of n-dimensional matrices with size q in each dimension, whose entries lie within $[0, 1]$ and sum up to 1.

Example 4. In the setting of Example 3, the governance state $s_{\mathcal{G}}$ is a three-dimensional matrix of size $3 \times 2^7 \times 6$ (agents × states × actions). Slicing this matrix along its second axis, i.e., at a specific environmental state, gives a (3×6) matrix; at step $t = 5$, the above transition sequence would result in

$$s^{(5)}_{\mathcal{G}}(\Box, 1110100, \Box) = \begin{pmatrix} 0 & 0 & 2 & 0 & 0 & 0 \\ 1 & 0 & 0 & 0 & 1 & 0 \\ 0 & 0 & 1 & 0 & 1 & 0 \end{pmatrix}$$

and consequently

$$P_1(1110100) = \begin{pmatrix} 0 & 0 & 1 & 0 & 0 & 0 \end{pmatrix}$$
$$P_2(1110100) = \begin{pmatrix} \frac{1}{2} & 0 & 0 & 0 & \frac{1}{2} & 0 \end{pmatrix}$$
$$P_3(1110100) = \begin{pmatrix} 0 & 0 & \frac{1}{2} & 0 & \frac{1}{2} & 0 \end{pmatrix}.$$

4.2   Restriction of Action Spaces

We make two independence assumptions regarding the probability of choosing an action: First, the relative probability of choosing an action a_i over another action b_i does not change when a third action is forbidden:

Assumption 1. *Let* $A_i, A'_i \subseteq \mathcal{A}_i$. *Then*

$$\forall a_i, b_i \in A_i \cap A'_i : \frac{P_{A_i}(a_i)}{P_{A_i}(b_i)} = \frac{P_{A'_i}(a_i)}{P_{A'_i}(b_i)} \in \mathbb{R} \cup \{\infty\}.$$

Therefore, we can remove individual actions from $P_i(s)$ and still have a valid distribution (up to normalization) for the remaining actions.

Second, agents exclusively communicate by observing each other's actions, such that their actions are independent from each other at a single time step. Interactions between agents therefore require at least one step between an action and the corresponding reaction.

Assumption 2. *Let $P_i(s)$ be agent i's action probability distribution for state s. Then*

$$P(s) = \prod_i P_i(s) \in \mathbb{P}_q^n$$

is the probability distribution for the joint action of all agents.

This product rule holds for accurate knowledge about the probabilities as well as for the Governance's estimation.

4.3   Algorithm

The Governance loop (see Algorithm 1) works as follows: The n-dimensional matrix $P(s)$ represents a function $P(s) : \mathcal{A} \to \mathbb{R}$ which assigns to each joint action $a \in \mathcal{A}$ the (expected) probability of being chosen. Element-wise multiplication of the matrix with the cost values of the resulting states gives an *expected cost matrix* $C(s) \in \mathbb{R}^{q^n}$ with entries

$$C(s)_a := c_{\mathcal{G}}\left(\delta(s,a)\right) \cdot \prod_i P_i(s)_{a_i} \; \forall a \in \mathcal{A},$$

where an action a is identified with its n-dimensional position in $C(s)$.

Each hyperplane of $C(s)$ along axis i corresponds to an action of agent i. We can therefore see from the expected cost matrix which actions from which agents have the highest expected costs. The matrix $C(s)$ can now be reduced by successively removing maximum-cost hyperplanes (each corresponding to an action by an individual agent) until the sum of all remaining entries drops below a given cost threshold α. Forbidding the removed actions ensures that the expected cost in the next step is less or equal to α, and that no unnecessary restrictions are made. Note that α can be chosen arbitrarily, as long as it is large enough to allow for the neutral action to be chosen. The value of α defines the balance between optimizing restriction and cost.

We will write $C_A := \sum_{a \in A} C_a$ (and in particular $\|C\| := C_{\mathcal{A}}$) for the expected cost of a subset $A \sqsubseteq \mathcal{A}$ of joint actions in an expected cost matrix C. Moreover, we use the component-wise product $X \circ Y := (X_i \cdot Y_i)_i$ for matrices X, Y and the component replacement $(x_{-i}, y_i) := (x_1, x_2, ..., x_{i-1}, y_i, x_{i+1}, ..., x_n)$ for vectors x, y.

Theorem 1. *Let $\alpha > 0$, and assume that $\alpha \geq C_{\delta(s^{(t)}, \varnothing)}$. Then Algorithm 1 produces a restriction $A^{(t)} \sqsubseteq \mathcal{A}$ of actions such that*

$$C_{A^{(t)}} \leq \alpha. \tag{2}$$

This restriction is Pareto minimal, i.e., $\nexists A'^{(t)} \sqsupset A^{(t)}$ with the same property.

Data: Governance cost function $c_{\mathcal{G}}$, fundamental action set $\mathcal{A}$, cost threshold α
Input: Probability distributions $P_i(s^{(t)})$ for the actions of all agents at the
current state $s^{(t)}$
Output: Restricted action set $A^{(t)}$
$P(s^{(t)}) := \prod_i P_i(s^{(t)}) \in \mathbb{P}_q^n$;
$C := P(s^{(t)}) \circ c_{\mathcal{G}} \in \mathbb{R}^{q^n}$;
$A := \mathcal{A}$;
while $\sum_{a \in A} C_a > \alpha$ **do**
$\quad$ $(i, j) := \arg\max_{a_j \in A_i \setminus \{\varnothing\}, i \in [n]} C_{(\square_{-i}, a_j)}$;
$\quad$ $A_i := A_i \setminus \{a_j\}$;
$\quad$ Slice C to remove the corresponding hyperplane;
end
$A^{(t)} := A$;

Algorithm 1: Restricting agent actions

Proof. <u>Termination and threshold</u>: At each step of the **while** loop, an action is removed for one of the agents. Therefore, the loop exits after at most $n \cdot (q - 1)$ passes. Since $\alpha \geq C_{\delta(s^{(t)}, \varnothing)}$, the cost is guaranteed to fall below α at some point, and the loop does not break until this has happened. Therefore, Eq. 2 is satisfied at the end of the algorithm.

<u>Minimality</u>: Let C^* be the cost matrix corresponding to $A^{(t)}$, and assume that $C^* \neq C$. Then C^* was derived from C by successively deleting hyperplanes, i.e. individual actions $a_j \in A_i^{(t)}$. Let such a deleted action be denoted by (i, j). Then the sequence of deletions can be written as

$$C = C_0 \xrightarrow{(i_1, j_1)} C_1 \to \cdots \to C_{x-1} \xrightarrow{(i_x, j_x)} C_x = C^*,$$

where $x > 0$, $\|C_{x-1}\| > \alpha$ and $\|C_x\| \leq \alpha$.

Assume now that there is a restriction $B \sqsupseteq C^*$ with $\|B\| \leq \alpha$. Then $\exists y \leq x$ such that action (i_y, j_y) lies in B. From $\|C_{x-1}\| > \alpha$ we can conclude that $y \neq x$ (otherwise B would be equal to C_{x-1}, which is a contradiction) and therefore $y < x$.

This means that (i_y, j_y) was removed from C before (i_x, j_x), thus $C_{(i_y, j_y)} \geq C_{(i_x, j_x)}$ and consequently

$$\|B\| > \|C_{x-1}\| > \alpha,$$

contradicting the above assumption. $\qquad\square$

If $c_{\mathcal{G}}$ has the structure of Eq. 1 (valid states have cost 0, invalid states have cost 1), then α is precisely an upper bound for the probability of transitioning into an invalid state.

Example 5. Coming back to Example 4 one last time, we see that $s^{(1)} = 1110100$ incurs cost $c_{\mathcal{G}}(s^{(1)}) = 1$ since $s^{(1)} \notin \mathcal{S}_+$. While the Governance probably cannot anticipate and prevent this transition between $t = 0$ and $t = 1$ due to lack of knowledge, it might be able to do so at a later time when enough information has been gathered. For example, at $t = 3$, the Governance could forbid action $h \in \mathcal{A}_1$ such that the joint action hlb cannot happen. If agent 1 now chooses action w instead, $s^{(4)} = \delta(s^{(3)}, wlb) = 1100000 \in \mathcal{S}_+$, and the Governance has therefore successfully prevented an undesirable transition.

4.4 Computational Complexity

The time complexity of Algorithm 1 with regard to the input sizes n, m and q can be derived from the pseudo-code in a straight-forward manner:

- Initialization of P, C, and A: $\mathcal{O}(q^n) + \mathcal{O}(q^n) + \mathcal{O}(qn)$
- **while** loop: $\mathcal{O}(qn)$ passes
  - Checking the break condition: $\mathcal{O}(q^n)$
  - Finding the arg max: $\mathcal{O}(qn \cdot q^n)$
  - Reducing C: $\mathcal{O}(q^n)$
  - Reducing A: $\mathcal{O}(1)$

Altogether, this results in a worst-case time complexity of $\mathcal{O}\left(n^2 \cdot q^{(n+2)}\right)$.

5 Evaluation

To test the validity and efficacy of our approach, we compare unrestricted and restricted evolution of the Smart Home use case from Examples 2, to 5: In the unrestricted case, agents simply act according to their action policies, having the full range of actions at their disposal all the time. The restricted case adds a Governance which employs the governance loop from Sect. 4.

Definition 2. *The degree of restriction imposed by $\mathcal{G}$ at time t is the ratio* $\mathfrak{r}_{\mathcal{G}}^{(t)} := 1 - \frac{|A^{(t)}|}{|\mathcal{A}|} \in [0, 1]$ *of forbidden actions and fundamental actions.*

The average cost over time is shown for unrestricted and restricted simulations, while the degree of restriction only applies to the restricted case.

5.1 Setup

We consider two specific scenarios with different types of action policies: In the deterministic case, each agent i has a fixed mapping of states and actions, i.e., a deterministic action policy $\pi_i : \mathcal{S} \to \mathcal{A}_i$. In the probabilistic case, each agent has a probability distribution for its actions for every state, i.e., an action policy $\pi_i : \mathcal{S} \to \Delta\mathcal{A}_i$.

For each of the two scenarios, we run the simulation with three different numbers of agents $n \in \{2, 3, 5\}$, and with a random initial state. To mitigate the risk of biased results, the data shown in the charts is calculated as the mean of 10 independent runs with identical parameters.

The cost threshold α was chosen such that the cost associated with a uniform probability distribution (i.e., no observation) lies within the allowed margin of error, i.e., $\alpha := \frac{3}{2} \cdot \frac{1}{q^n}$.

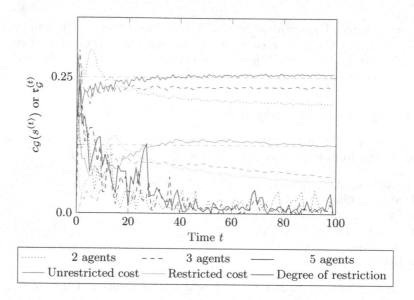

Fig. 3. Evaluation results: deterministic action policies (Color figure online)

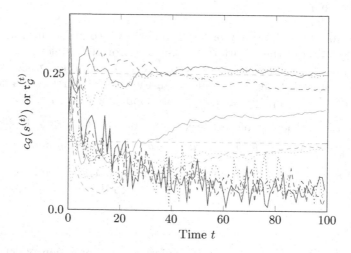

Fig. 4. Evaluation results: probabilistic action policies (Color figure online)

5.2 Results

As can be seen in Figs. 3 and 4, the intervention of the Governance succeeds in reducing the average cost substantially in all cases. If the Governance does not act, the a priori probability of being in a violating state is 25%, which is confirmed by the unrestricted cases (red lines).

Moreover, both the average cost and the degree of restriction decrease over time, which indicates that the Governance indeed learns to predict agent actions and to fine-tune its corrective action. Notably, this learning process is independent from an estimated agent preference order: Indeed, the action policies were created randomly, which means that they most likely do not correspond to a consistent order over the environmental states.

The effect of Governance tends to drop with increasing number of agents. This might be due to the more widespread probability distribution which prevents the Governance from finding clear "dangerous" joint actions. Of course, this suspicion needs to be scrutinized with suitable experiments or supported by theoretical findings before drawing any conclusions.

6   Conclusion

6.1   Summary

In this paper, we have demonstrated that an effective Governance mechanism can be employed for competitive Multi-Agent Systems without further assumptions about agent preferences and utilities. Instead, publicly observable actions and transitions are the only input for the Governance in order to prevent undesirable environmental states by restricting agent action spaces. We have presented, analyzed and tested an algorithm which creates a minimal restriction for a given margin of error and thereby prevents most of the transitions into undesirable environmental states in the test cases.

As opposed to other work which assumes a transparent decision and reasoning process from its agents, or even requires fixed agent preferences, this approach is applicable whenever actions can be observed and restricted by the governing instance.

6.2   Future Work

While the algorithm is functional, it lacks (polynomial) scalability in terms of the number of agents and attributes, and it fully re-evaluates the minimal restriction at every step, thereby reducing continuity of allowed actions over time.

Future work will therefore include a more efficient representation of knowledge (e.g. attribute dependencies and conditional probabilities) as well as environments with continuous attributes or irregular shape, more complex transitions, and the ability to handle open systems (i.e., agents dynamically entering and leaving the MAS). In addition, a more extensive evaluation is necessary to derive significant conclusions about the Governance's asymptotic behavior.

Furthermore, the current approach basically applies two consecutive steps where the value of actions is determined before deriving a suitable restriction policy from this knowledge. In analogy to policy-optimization methods in classical RL, a promising next step is merging these two steps into an immediate policy generation from raw observations.

Note that, by doing so, Assumptions 1 and 2 can be relaxed, resulting in a much more general solution approach.

References

1. Andrighetto, G., Governatori, G., Noriega, P., van der Torre, L.: Normative multi-agent systems (2013). https://doi.org/10.4230/DFU.Vol4.12111.i
2. Asadi, M., Huber, M.: State space reduction for hierarchical reinforcement learning, January 2004
3. Bade, S.: Nash equilibrium in games with incomplete preferences. Econ. Theory **26**(2), 309–332 (2005). www.jstor.org/stable/25055952
4. Balke, T., et al.: Norms in MAS: definitions and related concepts, p. 31, January 2013
5. Boella, G., van der Torre, L., Verhagen, H.: Introduction to normative multiagent systems. Comput. Math. Organ. Theory **12**(2), 71–79 (2006). https://doi.org/10.1007/s10588-006-9537-7
6. Brafman, R.I., Tennenholtz, M.: On partially controlled multi-agent systems. J. Artif. Int. Res. **4**(1), 477–507 (1996)
7. Bulling, N., Dastani, M.: Norm-based mechanism design. Artif. Intell. **239**(C), 97–142 (2016). https://doi.org/10.1016/j.artint.2016.07.001
8. Claus, C., Boutilier, C.: The dynamics of reinforcement learning in cooperative multiagent systems. In: Proceedings of the Fifteenth National/Tenth Conference on Artificial Intelligence/Innovative Applications of Artificial Intelligence, AAAI 1998/IAAI 1998, pp. 746–752. American Association for Artificial Intelligence, Menlo Park (1998). http://dl.acm.org/citation.cfm?id=295240.295800
9. Dean, T., Givan, R., Leach, S.: Model reduction techniques for computing approximately optimal solutions for Markov decision processes. In: Proceedings of the Thirteenth Conference on Uncertainty in Artificial Intelligence, pp. 124–131. UAI 1997, Morgan Kaufmann Publishers Inc., San Francisco (1997)
10. Dell'Anna, D., Dastani, M., Dalpiaz, F.: Runtime revision of norms and sanctions based on agent preferences. In: Proceedings of the 18th International Conference on Autonomous Agents and MultiAgent Systems, AAMAS 2019, pp. 1609–1617. International Foundation for Autonomous Agents and Multiagent Systems, Richland (2019). Event-place: Montreal QC, Canada
11. Durugkar, I., Liebman, E., Stone, P.: Balancing individual preferences and shared objectives in multiagent reinforcement learning, p. 2483, July 2020. https://doi.org/10.24963/ijcai.2020/343
12. Fitoussi, D., Tennenholtz, M.: Choosing social laws for multi-agent systems: minimality and simplicity. Artif. Intell. **119**(1), 61–101 (2000)
13. García-Camino, A., Rodríguez-Aguilar, J., Sierra, C., Vasconcelos, W.: A rule-based approach to norm-oriented programming of electronic institutions. SIGecom Exchanges **5**, 33–40 (2006)
14. Gutierrez, J., Perelli, G., Wooldridge, M.: Imperfect information in reactive modules games. Inf. Comput. **261**, 650–675 (2018)
15. Hernandez-Leal, P., Kartal, B., Taylor, M.E.: A survey and critique of multiagent deep reinforcement learning. Auton. Agent. Multi-Agent Syst. **33**(6), 750–797 (2019). https://doi.org/10.1007/s10458-019-09421-1
16. Hoen, P.J., Tuyls, K., Panait, L., Luke, S., La Poutré, J.A.: An overview of cooperative and competitive multiagent learning. In: Tuyls, K., Hoen, P.J., Verbeeck, K., Sen, S. (eds.) LAMAS 2005. LNCS (LNAI), vol. 3898, pp. 1–46. Springer, Heidelberg (2006). https://doi.org/10.1007/11691839_1
17. Kim, S., Lewis, M.E., White, C.C.: State space reduction for nonstationary stochastic shortest path problems with real-time traffic information. IEEE Trans. Intell. Transp. Syst. **6**(3), 273–284 (2005). https://doi.org/10.1109/TITS.2005.853695

18. Koriche, F., Zanuttini, B.: Learning conditional preference networks. Artif. Intell. **174**(11), 685–703 (2010). https://doi.org/10.1016/j.artint.2010.04.019. http://www.sciencedirect.com/science/article/pii/S000437021000055X

19. Lecarpentier, E., Rachelson, E.: Non-stationary Markov decision processes a worst-case approach using model-based reinforcement learning, April 2019

20. Levy, Y.J., Solan, E.: Stochastic games. In: Meyers, R.A. (ed.) Encyclopedia of Complexity and Systems Science, pp. 1–23. Springer, Heidelberg (2017). https://doi.org/10.1007/978-3-642-27737-5_522-2

21. Littman, M.L.: Markov games as a framework for multi-agent reinforcement learning. In: Proceedings of the eleventh international conference on international conference on machine learning, ICML1994, pp. 157–163. Morgan Kaufmann Publishers Inc., San Francisco (1994)

22. Liu, L., Chattopadhyay, A., Mitra, U.: On solving MDPs with large state space: exploitation of policy structures and spectral properties. IEEE Trans. Commun. **67**(6), 4151–4165 (2019). https://doi.org/10.1109/TCOMM.2019.2899620

23. Liu, T., Wang, J., Zhang, X., Cheng, D.: Game theoretic control of multiagent systems. SIAM J. Control. Optim. **57**, 1691–1709 (2019)

24. Lüdtke, S., Schröder, M., Krüger, F., Bader, S., Kirste, T.: State-space abstractions for probabilistic inference: a systematic review. J. Artif. Int. Res. **63**(1), 789–848 (2018). https://doi.org/10.1613/jair.1.11261

25. Majeed, S.J., Hutter, M.: Exact reduction of huge action spaces in general reinforcement learning (2020)

26. Meyer, J.J.C., Wieringa, R.J. (eds.): Deontic Logic in Computer Science: Normative System Specification. Wiley, USA (1994)

27. Mnih, V., et al.: Asynchronous methods for deep reinforcement learning. In: Proceedings of the 33rd International Conference on International Conference on Machine Learning,ICML2016, vol. 48. pp. 1928–1937. JMLR.org (2016)

28. Mnih, V., et al.: Human-level control through deep reinforcement learning. Nature **518**, 529–33 (2015)

29. Morales, J.: On-line norm synthesis for open multi-agent systems. Ph.D. thesis, Universitat de Barcelona (2016)

30. Morris-Martin, A., De Vos, M., Padget, J.: Norm emergence in multiagent systems: a viewpoint paper. Auton. Agents Multi-Agent Syst. **33**(6), 706–749 (2019). https://doi.org/10.1007/s10458-019-09422-0

31. Nowé, A., Vrancx, P., De Hauwere, Y.M.: Game theory and multi-agent reinforcement learning. In: Wiering, M., van Otterlo, M. (eds.) Reinforcement Learning: State-of-the-Art, pp. 441–470. Springer, Heidelberg (2012). https://doi.org/10.1007/978-3-642-27645-3_14

32. Perelli, G.: Enforcing equilibria in multi-agent systems. In: Proceedings of the 18th International Conference on Autonomous Agents and MultiAgent Systems, AAMAS 2019, pp. 188–196. International Foundation for Autonomous Agents and Multiagent Systems, Richland (2019). Event-place: Montreal QC, Canada

33. Relund Nielsen, L., Jørgensen, E., Højsgaard, S.: Embedding a state space model into a Markov decision process. Ann. Oper. Res. **190**(1), 289–309 (2011). https://doi.org/10.1007/s10479-010-0688-z

34. Rotolo, A.: Norm compliance of rule-based cognitive agents. In: IJCAI International Joint Conference on Artificial Intelligence, pp. 2716–2721, January 2011

35. Rotolo, A., van der Torre, L.: Rules, agents and norms: guidelines for rule-based normative multi-agent systems. In: Bassiliades, N., Governatori, G., Paschke, A. (eds.) RuleML 2011. LNCS, vol. 6826, pp. 52–66. Springer, Heidelberg (2011). https://doi.org/10.1007/978-3-642-22546-8_6

36. Shapley, L.S.: Stochastic games. Proc. Natl. Acad. Sci. U.S.A. **39**(10), 1095–1100 (1953). https://pubmed.ncbi.nlm.nih.gov/16589380
37. Shoham, Y., Powers, R., Grenager, T.: Multi-agent reinforcement learning: a critical survey, June 2003
38. Shoham, Y., Tennenholtz, M.: On social laws for artificial agent societies: off-line design. Artif. Intell. **73**(1), 231–252 (1995). https://doi.org/10.1016/0004-3702(94)00007-N.   http://www.sciencedirect.com/science/article/pii/000437029400007N
39. Stirling, W.C., Felin, T.: Game theory, conditional preferences, and social influence. PLOS One **8**(2), 1–11 (2013). https://doi.org/10.1371/journal.pone.0056751
40. Sutton, R.S., Barto, A.G.: Reinforcement Learning: An Introduction. A Bradford Book, Cambridge (2018)
41. Watkins, C.: Learning from delayed rewards, January 1989
42. Wolf, T.D., Holvoet, T.: Emergence and self-organisation: a statement of similarities and differences (2004)

Path and Action Planning in Non-uniform Environments for Multi-agent Pickup and Delivery Tasks

Tomoki Yamauchi[✉][iD], Yuki Miyashita[iD], and Toshiharu Sugawara[iD]

Computer Science and Communications Engineering, Waseda University,
Tokyo, Japan
{t.yamauchi,y.miyashita,sugawara}@isl.cs.waseda.ac.jp

Abstract. Although the *multi-agent pickup and delivery* (MAPD) problem, wherein multiple agents iteratively carry materials from some storage areas to the respective destinations without colliding, has received considerable attention, conventional MAPD algorithms use simplified, uniform models without considering constraints, by assuming specially designed environments. Thus, such conventional algorithms are not applicable to some realistic applications wherein agents have to move in a more complicated and restricted environment; for example, in a rescue or a construction site, their paths and orientations are strictly restricted owing to the path width, and the sizes of agents and materials they carry. Therefore, we first formulate an N-MAPD problem, which is an extension of the MAPD problem for a non-uniform environment. We then propose an N-MAPD algorithm, the *path and action planning with orientation* (PAPO), to effectively generate collision-free paths meeting the environmental constraints. The PAPO is an algorithm that considers not only the direction of movement but also the orientation of agents as well as the cost and timing of rotations in our N-MAPD formulation by considering the agent and material sizes, node sizes, and path widths. We experimentally evaluated the performance of the PAPO using our simulated environments and demonstrated that it could efficiently generate not optimal but acceptable paths for non-uniform environments.

Keywords: Multi-agent pickup and delivery tasks · Multi-agent path finding · Non-uniform environments

1 Introduction

In recent years, the use of *multi-agent systems* (MAS) for complex and enormous real-world tasks has attracted considerable attention. Examples include robots for automated warehouses [31], autonomous aircraft-towing vehicles in airports [21], ride-sharing services [14], office robots [28] and multiple-drone delivery systems [11]. However, simply increasing the number of agents may result in inefficiencies due to redundancy and resource conflicts between agents such as

© Springer Nature Switzerland AG 2021
A. Rosenfeld and N. Talmon (Eds.): EUMAS 2021, LNAI 12802, pp. 37–54, 2021.
https://doi.org/10.1007/978-3-030-82254-5_3

collisions. Therefore, cooperative and/or coordinated actions that improve the performance and avoid a negative mutual effect are required for actual use. In particular, conflict avoidance is essential in our target application—a pickup and delivery agent system in a restricted environment, where agents are robots that carry heavy and large-size materials.

These problems have often been formulated as a *multi-agent pickup and delivery* (MAPD) problem, wherein several agents are assigned multiple tasks; for each task, an agent has to move to the material storage area, load a specified material, deliver it to the required location, and unload the material there. If we look at the MAPD problem from the planning aspect, it can be considered the repetition of *multi-agent path-finding* (MAPF) wherein leads to multiple agents generating collision-free and optimal or acceptable paths between the start and end; this is because the number of the requested tasks is large in an MAPD problem, and agents have to consequently repeat the MAPF problems one by one as well as avoid possible conflicts. Unfortunately, the MAPF problem is known be NP-hard to obtain the optimal solution [19], and so the MAPD problem is more time-consuming. Nevertheless, we have to efficiently obtain acceptable solutions for the MAPD problems.

There are many studies that focused on the MAPF and MAPD problems [15, 18, 24], and their results are used in real-world applications. However, the applications of these studies assumed that specially designed environments are usually described as grids with uniform aisle widths, ignoring agent and carrying object sizes, and with no constraint regarding the agent's operations such as rotation and moving directions. In contrast, our target application— transportation by forklift-type autonomous agents with a picker in front at a construction site and autonomous arm robots for rescue in a disaster area—is more complicated and has its own constraints. For example, in a construction site, passages/aisles may have various widths. Moreover, agents often have to carry a heavy and large material whose width is wider than the agent's width. Agents may not be able to rotate at certain points owing to obstructions. This suggests that the locations in the environment may have their own constraints and that agents should undertake different paths depending on whether they have materials; owing to these constraints, assuming a simple and uniform environment is not realistic. Furthermore, the widths and topology of the passages easily change because new walls that did not exist the previous day are constructed or new materials are placed on or removed from the passages the next day. This also indicates that the learning method that requires enormous amounts of learning data may not be desirable.

In this study, we first propose another extended MAPD problem formulation, *multi-agent pickup and delivery in non-uniform environment* (N-MAPD) problem, for the above-mentioned complicated situations. For example, in the pickup and delivery problem in a construction site, agents may encounter prohibited activities in certain nodes and paths owing to their widths and area sizes. Similarly, agents have their own sizes (width and size including the materials they carry) to consider; however, in this study, our agents can move in any direction (up, down, left or right) without rotation. In this environment, we must consider additional constraints for movement as well as the constraints for collision avoidance. The simple shortest path without considering the constraints on the sizes of agents, edges, and nodes may not be acceptable because, for example, an edge in the path is so narrow that the agent with a material has to change the orientation to pass but additional rotation may consume considerable time.

Therefore, we propose an N-MAPD algorithm, *path and action planning with orientation* (PAPO), to generate collision-free paths and action sequences in such environments. The PAPO is an algorithm that considers not only the speed and direction of movements but also the orientation of agents and time cost (duration) as well as timing of rotations in our N-MAPD formulation. Furthermore, we have considered a sophisticated process for conflict resolution because agents need to appropriately decide avoidance method such as wait (synchronization), detours, and changes in the order of actions to meet environmental constraints. Subsequently, we experimentally evaluate the performance of PAPO using our simulated environments under various experimental settings by comparing them with the results of the naive centralized method in our environments. We demonstrate that our proposed algorithm could generate not optimal but acceptable paths. We also investigate the effect of agent number on the entire performance. Our formulation can be used in other situations wherein physical constraints such as the multiple-agent disaster-rescue problem need to be considered.

2 Related Work

There are many studies conducted on the MAPF/MAPD problem from different perspectives [7,17,23]. For example, if we focus on the control structure of cooperation between agents, it can be divided into two types: centralized and decentralized. The former includes, for example, the *conflict-based search algorithm* (CBS) [24] for MAPF and its extension [4–6,34], which is a two-stage search comprising *low-level search*, in which each agent determines its own path independently, and *high-level search*, wherein it generates action sequences by removing conflicts between agents. Some decentralized methods guaranteed completeness under certain restrictions [18,22,29,30]. For example, [18] proposed the *token passing* (TP) for MAPD, where agents assign tasks to themselves and generate their paths by using the information in the token, which is a synchronized shared block of memory. However, these studies assume simple environments that ignore constraints such as agent sizes, path widths, duration of movements and speeds of individual agents, thereby limiting the real-world applications.

In contrast, [3,8–10,13,16,20,26,32] modeled agent's rotation, size, and speed differences. For example, [16] proposed the TP-SIPPwRT, an extension of TP by using a novel combinatorial search algorithm called *safe interval path planning with reservation table* (SIPPwRT) to consider the agent direction of movement and rotation. Nevertheless, it is based on a specially designed environment with uniform aisle widths and distances. Therefore, applying it directly to our target environment is almost impossible. There exist studies in the area of trajectory

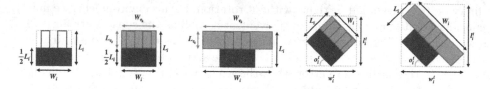

Fig. 1. Definition of agent size (including the materials it carries) and orientation

planning that focuses on kinematic constraints during the planning [1,2,12,27], but our study differs from them in the sense that we aim to more efficiently complete repeated tasks of the MAPD in cluttered and tight environments.

In addition, conventional algorithms may be applied to our N-MAPD problems by adding orientation to the agent's state and considering environmental constraints. As the path planning of conventional algorithms has a two-dimensional search space involving spatial dimension and time dimension, if the orientation dimension involved in various path widths and agent sizes is added to the search space, the search space becomes very large for an N-MAPD problem. Therefore, using naive search to obtain the optimal solution such as conventional algorithms in this three-dimensional search space increases the computational cost. To the best of our knowledge, there have been no studies of path planning on a discrete graph with conflict resolution under the constraint of actions caused by the shape and size of spaces, agents, and the materials carried by them.

3   Problem Formulation and Background

We define the N-MAPD problem, an extension of the conventional MAPD problem, by introducing the width of the paths (edges), sizes of agents and materials, and durations of agent's actions.

3.1   N-MAPD

The N-MAPD problem comprises a set of agents $A = \{1, \ldots, M\}$, a set of tasks $\mathcal{T} = \{\tau_1, \ldots, \tau_N\}$, and an undirected connected graph $G = (V, E)$ embeddable in a two-dimensional Euclidean space described by x- and y-axes. Node $v \in V$ corresponds to a location in the environment and edge $(u, v) \in E$ $(u, v \in V)$ corresponds to the path between locations u and v along which the agents can move. Node v has a width W_v and length L_v. The width and the distance of (u, v) are denoted by W_{uv} and $\text{dist}(u, v)$, respectively, where the distance is defined as the length between the centers of u and v in the Euclidean space. We assume that an agent is a robot for carrying a heavy material such as a forklift robot with a picker in the front. A material is on a rackbase, and the agent can pick up (load) or put down (unload) using its picker with a specific direction at a certain node.

We introduce discrete time $t \in \mathbb{Z}^+$ ($\mathbb{Z}^+$ is the set of positive integers); then, the agent's actions such as the movement toward an adjacent location, rotation, wait action, and loading/unloading of a material require certain durations. Examples of environments are shown in Fig. 2.

Agent $i \in A$ has its size, specified by its width W_i and length L_i. We define the *orientation* $o_i^t \in \mathbb{Z}^+$ and the (moving) *direction* $d_i^t \in \mathbb{Z}^+$ of i at time t, where $0 \leq o_i^t, d_i^t < 360$, in D increments. For example, if $D = 90$, then there are four orientations/directions of $o_i^t, d_i^t = 0, 90, 180, 270$. D can have any number in accordance with the environmental structure but we assume $D = 90$ for the sake of simplicity. We define the north orientation/direction as 0, (so $o_i^t = 0$, $d_i^t = 0$) in G. We also denote the set of possible orientations as $\mathcal{D} = \{0, 90, 180, 270\}$ if $D = 90$. The x-axis length w_i^t and y-axis length l_i^t of i at t are calculated by

$$w_i^t = |L_i \sin o_i^t| + |W_i \cos o_i^t|$$
$$l_i^t = |W_i \sin o_i^t| + |L_i \cos o_i^t|.$$

A material associated with task τ_k has a corresponding size, wherein width and length are W_{τ_k} and L_{τ_k}. When agent i loads it, we assume that the size of i has temporally changed to

$$W_i = \max(W_{\tau_k}, W_i)$$
$$L_i = \max(L_{\tau_k} + \gamma L_i, L_i),$$

where γ ($0 \leq \gamma \leq 1$) is the ratio of the length of agent's body to its fork part. Figure 1 shows examples of the size and orientation of agents with/without materials when $\gamma = 0.5$.

Agents have to move in the environment by considering the constraints of considering the path width and agents' length and width. We refer to the constraints defined in the environment such as the width and size of paths, nodes, and agents as *environmental constraints*.

Agents can perform the following actions—*move, rotate, wait, load* and *unload*. Using the moving distance $l = \text{dist}(u, v)$ between u and v, the rotation angle $\theta \in \mathbb{Z}$ and the waiting time t, we denote the durations of *move, rotate, wait, load* and *unload* as $T_{mo}(l)$, $T_{ro}(\theta)$, $T_{wa}(t)$, T_{ld}, and T_{ul}, respectively. For example, if $l = 1$, then $T_{mo}(1) = 10$ in our experimental setting. Suppose that i is on v at t. In a *move* action, i moves along edge (u, v) to u without changing orientation o_i^t if the edge has enough width. With a *rotate* action, i stays at v and rotates D degrees clockwise (D) or counter-clockwise ($-D$) from o_i^t, i.e., $o_i^{t+T_{ro}(D)} = o_i^t \pm D$, if the node has enough size. Agent i has a unique *parking location* $park_i \in V$ [15], which is its starting location at $t = 0$, and agents return and stay there as long as they have no tasks to perform. Parking locations are expressed by red squares in Fig. 2.

Task τ_j is specified by tuple $\tau_j = (\nu_{\tau_j}^{ld}, \nu_{\tau_j}^{ul}, W_{\tau_j}, L_{\tau_j}, \phi_{\tau_j})$, where $\nu_{\tau_j}^{ld} = (v_{\tau_j}^{ld}, o_{\tau_j}^{ld})$ ($\in V \times \mathcal{D}$) is the location and orientation to load material ϕ_{τ_j}, and $\nu_{\tau_j}^{ul} = (v_{\tau_j}^{ul}, o_{\tau_j}^{ul})$ ($\in V \times \mathcal{D}$) denotes the location and orientation to unload ϕ_{τ_j}, and W_{τ_j} and L_{τ_j} are the width and length of ϕ_{τ_j}, respectively. When an agent loads and unloads material, it needs to be oriented in a specific direction, considering the direction of the picker and the shape of the material. Agents are required to complete all tasks in $\mathcal{T}$ without collision and by not violating any of the environmental constraints. When i completes all tasks in $\mathcal{T}$, it returns to $park_i$ to recharge.

3.2 Well-Formed N-MAPD

While not all MAPD instances are solvable, *well-formed* MAPD instances are always solvable [18]; an MAPD instance is well-formed if and only if (a) the number of tasks is finite, (b) the parking location of each agent is different from all pickup and delivery locations of tasks, and (c) there exists a path between any two start/goal locations that does not traverse the start/goal location of other agents. To reflect the environmental constraint in the N-MAPD, we modify condition (c) to: (c') there exists a feasible path between any two start/goal locations that does not traverse start/goal location of other agents, wherein a feasible path implies that a solution exists in the MAPF instance, considering the environmental constraints. In well-formed (N-)MAPD instances, agents can always return and stay in their parking locations as long as necessary to avoid collisions with other agents; this action reduces the number of agents in an overly crowded environment. The well-formed MAPD instances are a realistic subclass of all MAPD instances because many real-world MAPD instances are well-formed, including those in a construction site, but we need some discussion on condition (c') in N-MAPD. This will be described below.

4 Path and Action Planning with Orientation

We propose PAPO for the N-MAPD problem to generate a collision-free path and subsequently a *plan*, i.e., an action sequence to reach the destination in a non-uniform environment. In this proposed method, agents maintain and use a *synchronized block of information* (SBI) to detect/resolve conflicts. The SBI comprises a *reservation table* (RT) [25] and a *task execution status table* (TEST), which is the set of tuples (τ, v, i), where τ is the currently being executed task by i and v is the load or unload node specified in τ; thus, two tuples are stored to the TEST when one task is assigned an agent. The details of the RT and the TEST are described in the later subsections. The SBI is stored at a centralized memory area and only one agent can access to this area. Although synchronized shared memory often becomes a bottleneck for performance, the robot movements herein are slow compared to the overhead time caused by mutual exclusion; therefore, for a realistic number of agents (e.g., less than 100 agents), we assume that such shared memory exclusion control does not affect agent behaviors. The PAPO algorithm has a two-level structure: *two-stage action planning* (TSAP), wherein the agent first generates numerous shortest paths to the destination and then builds a set of candidate action sequences to follow each of the paths; and *conflict resolution with candidate action sequences* (CRCAS) with which it generates a collision-free (so *approved*) action sequence through which the agent resolves possible conflicts by referring to the previously approved plans of other agents in the SBI.

4.1   Two-Stage Action Planning (TSAP)

In the first stage of the TSAP, agent $i \in A$ generates the first N_K shortest paths (where $N_K \in \mathbb{Z}^+$) from the current location v_s^i to the destination v_d^i, usually the pickup, delivery, or parking location depending on the phase of the task. A path is defined as a sequence of nodes $r = \{v_0(= v_s^i), v_1, \ldots\}$ where any pair of adjacent nodes are edges in E and the distance of r is $\sum_{l=1}^{|r|} \text{dist}(v_{l-1}, v_l)$. There are several algorithms for obtaining the first N_K shortest paths, and we use Yen's algorithm [33] with the Dijkstra method. In this stage, we do not consider the constraints of widths and sizes and use only the topological structure of $G = (V, E)$.

In the second stage, for path $\forall r_k \in \{r_1, \ldots, r_{N_K}\}$ generated in the first stage and for parameter $N_P \in \mathbb{Z}^+$, i builds the first N_P lowest-cost action sequences without using action *wait* to move along path r_k without breaking the environmental constraints, where cost indicates the duration until completing action sequences. We herein elaborate on this stage. First, for path r_k, we generate the weighted state graph $\mathcal{G}_i = (\mathcal{V}_i, \mathcal{E}_i)$ for agent i from G to build the action sequences (subscripts will be abbreviated below) that follow path r_k. Node $\nu = (v, o) \in \mathcal{V}$ ($\subset V \times \mathcal{D}$) corresponds to the location and orientation of i, and an element in $\mathcal{V}$ is called a *state node*. Edge $(\mu, \nu) \in \mathcal{E}$ ($\mu, \nu \in \mathcal{V}$) corresponds to action, *move* or *rotate*, to transmit μ to ν. The weight of edge $\omega(\mu, \nu)$ is defined as the time required for the corresponding action. By denoting the search space as (ν, t_ν), where t_ν is the time at which i will reach state ν, we apply Yen's algorithm with the A^*-search to generate the first N_P lowest-cost action sequences, where the heuristic function h is defined by

$$h(l, \theta) = T_{mo}(l) + T_{ro}(\theta), \tag{1}$$

where l is the distance between the current node and v_d^i, and θ is the difference between the current orientation and the required orientation at v_d^i. Function h is clearly admissible because it does not consider any constraint of the actions and the environment. The required orientation at v_d^i is usually determined by i's task because v_d^i is the location to load or unload material.

In this stage, agent i can prune some state nodes so that i does not violate the environmental constraints by considering its own size with the carrying material and path widths. Suppose that i's state is $\nu = (v, o)$ at t_1 and i schedules a state transition to $\mu = (u, o')$ at time $t_2 = t_1 + \omega(\nu, \mu)$ by (ν, μ). Then, μ will be pruned owing to the violation of constraint between node and agent sizes if $w_i^{t_2} > W_u$ or $l_i^{t_2} > L_u$. Similarly, (ν, μ) is *move* (so $o = o'$ and $(u, v) \in E$) is impossible if $W_{uv} < |l_i^{t_1} \sin d_i^{t_1}| + |w_i^{t_1} \cos d_i^{t_1}|$ depending on orientation o and direction d; therefore, μ after ν is pruned as well. Finally, if (ν, μ) is *rotate* (so $v = u$ but $o \neq o'$), the corresponding action may be impossible; consequently, μ may also

---

Algorithm 1. Conflict Resolution part of PAPO

1: **function** CRCAS(P_i)
2:      // P_i is generated by TSAP(N_K, N_P).
3:      C_{max} ← Maximal duration of the plan in P_i
4:      **while** *true* **do**
5:          **if** $P_i = \varnothing$ **then return** *false*
6:          **end if**
7:          P_i is sorted by duration
8:          p_1 ← the first (shortest duration) plan in P_i
9:          C_1 ← duration of p_1 // Shortest duration in P_i
10:         c_1 ← $(\langle i,j\rangle[t'_s,t'_e],v')$ // The first conflict in p_1 by comparing with the entries in RT.
11:          **if** $c_1 = null$ **then return** p_1
12:          **end if**
13:          C ← all conflicts occurring at v' // so $c_1 \in C$
14:          c_f ← final element $(\langle i,k\rangle,[t_s,t_e],v)$ in C after sorted by occurrence order.
15:          u ← $e_v^k - s_v^i + 1$, $C_1 = C_1 + u$
16:          **if** $C_1 \geq C_{max} + \beta$ **then** // β: tolerance parameter.
17:             P_i ← $P_i \setminus \{p_1\}$ // abandon p_1
18:          **end if**
19:          $wait(u)$ is inserted in p_1 before reaching v with the *modification strategy*.
20:          p_1 in P_i is replaced to the modified p_1 if $p_1 \in P_i$.
21:      **end while**
22: **end function**

---

be pruned owing to the violation of rotation constraint, i.e., as the size of v, W_v and/or L_v is insufficient; this situation can be identified by comparing W_v and L_v with w_i^t and l_i^t between t_1 and t_2, which are maximum, for example, when i's orientation is $45, 135, 225$ or 315 if the agent's shape is square (see Fig. 1).

After the TSAP, the ordered set of at most $N_K \cdot N_P$ action sequences $P_i = \{p_1, \ldots, p_{N_K \cdot N_P}\}$ is generated by sorting them in the ascending order by total duration; clearly, its top element, i.e., the minimum-cost plan is the best candidate but may not be selected owing to conflicts with other agents' plans. This is investigated in the next-stage CRCAS. As the resulting plan p_i is generated to follow the corresponding path r, this relation is denoted by $r = r(p_i)$.

4.2   Conflict Resolution of Candidate Action Sequences (CRCAS)

In the CRCAS, agent i selects the first plan of P_i and tries to find conflicts involved therein and the already approved plans of other agents. This conflict detection is achieved by accessing the SBI. Then, the plan is modified to avoid the conflicts, replaced with the modified one (and P_i is sorted). The basic policy of this modification is that the already approved plans are not requested to be modified. When the first element in P_i is collision-free, it is the output of the CRCAS; thus, the associated reservation data are added to the RT in the SBI and it is approved to be executed. The structure of the RT is explained below.

We define a conflict as the situation wherein multiple agents occupy the same node $v \in V$ simultaneously. If i starts moving at time s_v^i from v to its neighboring node u and i's occupancy intervals for v and u are denoted by $[s_v^i, e_v^i]$ and $[s_u^i, e_u^i]$, respectively, we then set $e_v^i = s_v^i + T_{mo}(l)/2$ and $s_u^i = e_v^i$, where $l = \text{dist}(v, u)$. Similarly, if i starts *rotate*, *wait*, *load* or *unload* at time s_v^i on v, the occupancy intervals of v for the corresponding action can be denoted by $[s_v^i, e_v^i = s_v^i + T_*]$, where T_* is the duration of the action. Furthermore, as agents have physical sizes, we add constant margin $\lambda \geq 0$ to these intervals for safety; therefore, for example, $s_v^i \leftarrow s_v^i - \lambda$, $e_v^i \leftarrow e_v^i + \lambda$. From these calculations, we can generate the *occupancy list* from plan $p_k \in P_i$

$$((v_0, [s_{v_0}, e_{v_0}], i), (v_1, [s_{v_1}, e_{v_1}], i), \ldots, (v_d^i, [s_{v_d^i}, e_{v_d^i}], i)),$$

where $r(p_k) = \{v_0, v_1, \ldots, v_d^i\}$ is the sorted set.

When two intervals of occupations of node v by two agents $i, j \in A$ have an intersection, $[t_s, t_e]$, a conflict occurs and it is represented by a tuple $c = (\langle i, j \rangle, [t_s, t_e], v)$. The occupancy lists of approved plans of other agents is stored into the RT in the SBI. Agent i's plan may have another conflict with the approved plan of another agent k at the same node v; however, the intersection of a conflict appears only between two agents since the plans stored in the SBI have already been approved. Thus, if there exists two conflicts $c_1 = (\langle i, j \rangle, [t_s^1, t_e^1], v)$ and $c_2 = (\langle i, k \rangle, [t_s^2, t_e^2], v)$, then $[t_s^1, t_e^1] \cap [t_s^2, t_e^2] = \varnothing$.

The RT is a collection of lists $(v, [s_v^i, e_v^i], i)$ that is an element in the occupancy list of the approved plan and is not expired yet; thus, when $e_v^i < t_c$ (t_c is the current time), the element is removed from the RT. When the plan p of agent i is approved, i will register all elements in the occupancy list to the RT.

We describe the overall flow of the algorithm of the CRCAS to using the pseudocode in Algorithm 1. We assume that agents can exclusively access the RT in the SBI during function execution. When agent i has generated P_i in the TSAP, for the first element p_1 in P_i, i calculates its occupancy list and then according to the order of visiting nodes, $r(p_1) = \{v_1, v_2, \cdots, \}$, agent i retrieves the lists whose first element is v_l from the RT and tries to detect the conflicts by comparing these lists. If no conflicts are found, p_1 is the result of the CRCAS and will be registered into the RT as the approved plan (line 11). Suppose that c is the first conflict detected at v in the order of visit, where c is represented by $c = (\langle i, j \rangle, [t_s^c, t_e^c], v)$, j is the agent that has the approved plan conflicting with p_1 and $[t_s^c, t_e^c]$ is the intersection of both agents' stay at v. As another conflict with another agent at v is possible, we denote the set of all conflicts at v by C. Subsequently, i sorts C by chronological order and set c_f to the final element of C (line 14). Then, i inserts *wait* action into p_1 using a *plan modification strategy*, which will be explained in the next subsection so that i arrives at v after k departs from v (lines 15 and 19, where e_v^k is the time when k departs from v); therefore, at least the detected conflicts can be avoided. However, if the duration the modified plan is too large to implement the plan by adding the *wait* action, p_1 is abandoned (lines 16 and 17), where β is the *tolerance parameter* to

---

Algorithm 2. Path and Action Planning with Orientation

```
1: function PAPO(i, v_s, v_d) // in agent i
2:     // v_s: current location, v_d: destination.
3:     while true do
4:         P_i ← TSAP(N_K, N_P)
5:         p ← CRCAS(P_i)
6:         if p ≠ false then return p
7:         end if
8:         (N_K, N_P, β) ← RelaxParam(N_K, N_P, β)
9:     end while
10: end function
```

---

retain the selected plan. Subsequently, P_i is sorted by the duration again and i repeats the same process until no conflict occurs in p_1, the first element of P_i.

This process eventually stops. This is because if this process continues forever, the duration for performing the plan increases over $C_{max} + \beta$, and the plan is removed from P_i; then, finally P_i becomes empty. At this point, the function CRCAS returns a false value, i.e., it cannot generate the path from the P_i using the parameters N_K, N_P, and β. In this case, agent i calls the CRCAS again under a relaxed condition, i.e., by providing P_i generated with the increased values of N_K, N_P and/or β.

4.3   Plan Modification Strategy

The plan modification strategy in our context is to decide where action $wait(u)$ is inserted before node v' at which the first conflict is expected in the plan p_i. By denoting $r(p_i) = \{v_0, \dots, v_l(= v'), \dots, v_n(= v_d^i)\}$, the action can be added just before exiting v_k $(0 \le k \le l - 1)$. For example, we can add it to v_{l-1}, but this may cause another conflict. As the added $wait$ is not eliminated, some insertions of $wait$ to avoid another conflict, resulting in longer delay or failure owing to the excessive long wait. Conversely, if it is inserted when i departs from v_0, i can avoid conflicts without failure because when i selected the current task τ by the task selection process (to be described later), its loading and unloading nodes are already stored in the TEST, and no other agents pass through node v_0 by condition (c') in the well-formed N-MAPD. However, this implies that other agents' activities are locked for a while and the entire performance may reduce. The decision on this topic needs further discussion, but we tentatively adopted the strategy in which $wait(u)$ is added at v_k, where $k = \max(0, l - 3)$.

4.4   Flows of Task Selection and PAPO Processes

The task selection process in agent i is performed only when $\mathcal{T} \ne \varnothing$; otherwise, i returns to its parking location $park_i$. Agent i exclusively accesses the current TEST in the SBI during in this process. According to the assumption (c') for the well-formed N-MAPD, i only focuses on task $\tau = (\nu_\tau^{ld}, \nu_\tau^{ul}, W_\tau, L_\tau, \phi_\tau)$ such

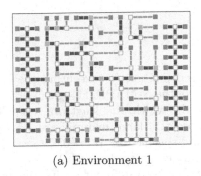

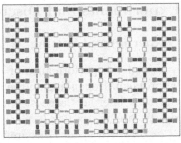

(a) Environment 1   (b) Environment 2

Fig. 2. Experimental environments (red: parking locations, blue: pickup and delivery locations, green-filled: small nodes, hollow green: large nodes, gray: narrow edges, black: wide edges) (Color figure online)

that its loading and unloading nodes, v_τ^{ld} and v_τ^{ul}, do not appear in the TEST of the current SBI. Then, i chooses task τ^* whose value of the heuristic function h used in the A^*-search is the smallest. If i cannot find such tasks, i returns to its parking node and stays there for a while; as other agents may complete their tasks after this, i may be able to select a task after i refrains slightly.

After agent i selects task τ_i, it starts the PAPO process to generate a collision-free action sequence. We show the pseudocode of the PAPO process in Algorithm 2, where v_s is the current node and v_d is v_τ^{ld}, v_τ^{ul}, or $park_i$, depending on the task progress. First, if i can successfully generate plan p via the TSAP and CRCAS processes, i acts in accordance with p, and then $(\tau, v_d, i) \in \mathcal{T} \times V \times A$ is removed from the TEST. Otherwise, i calls the *relaxation function* **RelaxParam** by which the threshold values of parameters N_K, N_P, and β are modified to relax the plan generation condition and performs the planning process again. If i has already relaxed the parameters a few times, this function gives up performing τ_i (so it is returned to $\mathcal{T}$) and set $v_d = park_i$ to return to the parking location; this situation may occur when compared to the size of the current environment, the number of agents is too large to move around in that environment.

We can consider a number of strategies to define the initial values of N_K, N_P, and β and how to increase these values. The small values of N_K, N_P, and β are likely to generate effective plans, but are also likely to fail to generate a plan altogether. Therefore, these initial values appear better in setting small values and increasing them if the agents cannot build a collision-free plan. However, we must consider that frequent changes in parameter values also reduce the planning efficiency. If the parameters continue to increase, i can obtain the collision-free plan (i.e., completeness is guaranteed); owing to the executions of the approved plans progress in other agents, the occupancy list in the RT expires over time, and the constraints are gradually removed.

5 Experiments and Discussion

5.1 Experimental Setting

We evaluated the performance of our proposed method for executing the N-MAPD problem. Depending on the task $\tau \in \mathcal{T}$ of the N-MAPD, an agent carries material that is either large or small, where the width and length of a small material ϕ_τ are $W_\tau = 0.5, L_\tau = 0.25$ and those of a large material are $W_\tau = 1.0, L_{\tau_k} = 0.25$. All agent sizes are identical and specified by $W_i = 0.5, L_i = 0.5$ and $\gamma = 0.5$. The numbers of large and small materials are both $N/2$.

Subsequently, we conducted the experiments in two different environments. The first environment (Env. 1) is a maze-like environment assuming a construction site wherein there are several obstacles such as workspace for other tasks, walls and columns; consequently, it has several environmental constraints such as widths of paths and sizes of nodes (Fig. 2a). Nodes are set at intersections and at ends of edges where the agents load/unload materials. We assume that agents can rotate/wait only at nodes. There are two types of nodes: small nodes v whose width and length are $W_v = 1.0, L_v = 1.0$ and is shown as green-filled squares in Fig. 2, and large nodes v with $W_v = 1.5, L_v = 1.5$ shown as hollow green squares. Thus, agents with large materials cannot rotate at small nodes. Similarly, there are two types of edges; the width of narrow edge (u, v) is $W_{uv} = 0.5$, which are shown by gray edges, and that of wide edge is $W_{uv} = 1.0$, which is shown by black bold edges. Breaks in an edge represent its length; one block indicates a length of 1. Thus, agents with large materials may need to rotate before passing through narrow edges.

The second one (Env. 2) is identical to Env. 1, but we added more nodes on the edges; these nodes usually connect the narrow and wide edges and agents with large materials may have to rotate at this node to pass the narrow edge (Fig. 2b). These nodes on edges can reduce the wait action as rotation at an inter-

Table 1. Parameter values used in experiments

Description	Parameter	Value
No. of agents	M	1 to 40
No. of tasks	N	100
Orientation/direction increments	D	90
Duration of *move* per length 1	$T_{mo}(1)$	10
Duration of *rotate*	$T_{ro}(D)$	20
Durations of *load* and *unload*	T_{ld}, T_{ul}	20
Durations of *wait*	$T_{wa}(t)$	t
Safety intervals	λ	5

section may block other agents' movement. The initial locations of agents are randomly assigned from the parking locations. A hundred tasks are generated and added to $\mathcal{T}$ initially whose pickup and delivery locations are also randomly selected from blue squares.

To evaluate our proposed method, we measured the *operational time per task*, i.e., the average time to complete one task (simply called *operational time*) and *total planning time* for all tasks in $\mathcal{T}$ (simply called *planning time*). Operational time is used to evaluate the quality of generated plans, and planning time denotes

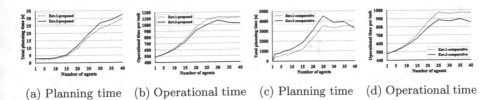

(a) Planning time   (b) Operational time   (c) Planning time   (d) Operational time

Fig. 3. Comparison of Env. 1 and 2

the planning efficiency. Other parameter values in these experiments are listed in Table 1. Our experiments were conducted on a 3.00-GHz Intel 8-Core Xeon E5 with 64-GB RAM. The data shown below are the average values of a hundred trials using different random seeds.

5.2   Exp. 1: Performance Comparison

In the first experiment (Exp. 1), we compared the performance of the proposed method with that of a naive centralized method in Envs. 1 and 2. This comparative method is a centralized planner generating the optimal (shortest) collision-free action sequences, in turn, by assuming that the nodes already reserved by others' plans are temporal obstacles during certain intervals of time. The generated sequence comprises {$move, rotate, wait, load, unload$}, so a state is expressed by $\nu = (v, o, t)$, a tuple of the node, orientation of the agent, and time at which the agent will reach orientation o at node v. All durations are set to be the same as the proposed method. This algorithm can generate optimal plan by assuming that the plans that are already being executed will not be revised. The parameters for the proposed method are set to $N_K = 3$, $N_P = 3$, and $\beta = 100$ and the relaxation function **RelaxParam** increases the parameter values by $N_K \leftarrow N_K + 1$, $N_P \leftarrow N_P$ and $\beta \leftarrow \beta * 2.0$ each time it is called.

We plotted the planning time and operational time in Envs. 1 and 2 in Figs. 3. The data of the comparative method were the average of ten runs because it took an extremely long time to complete all the tasks. Figures 3a and 3c indicate that the planning time for all tasks using our proposed planning method was considerably less than that using the comparative method in both environments, although Figs. 3b and 3d indicate that the operational time when using the proposed method was approx. 10% more than that when using the comparative method. As the comparative method uses naive search to obtain the optimal solution, the quality of the generated sequence of action may be high, but the planning time is extremely long to use in actual environment. We can also improve the operational time by changing the parameters; this is described in the next section.

If we compare the results between Env. 1 and 2 (Figs. 3a and 3b), the operational time of the proposed method in Env. 2 was smaller than that of in Env. 1, but the planning time was the opposite. This is caused by nodes added on some edges. As actions $rotate$ and $wait$ stay at current nodes, they are likely to prevent

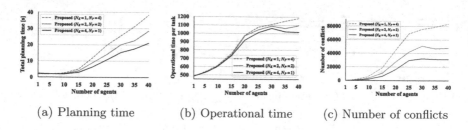

(a) Planning time   (b) Operational time   (c) Number of conflicts

Fig. 4. Combinations of initial values of N_K and N_P

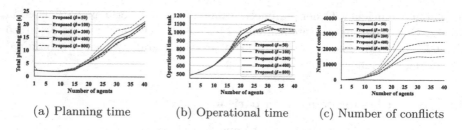

(a) Planning time   (b) Operational time   (c) Number of conflicts

Fig. 5. Initial value of β

other agents' actions if the nodes are intersectional. However, by adding nodes where agents can rotate and wait, agents can reduce such obstructive conditions. In fact, in the proposed method when $M = 25$, the number of detected conflicts in Env. 1 was 82135.07, and that in Env. 2 was 64743.1. This would have made agent movement smoother and likely led to improved operational time approx. 82 (8%), although its planning time in Env. 2 is slightly larger by approx. 2 s (11%) when $M = 25$. Note that $T_{mo}(1) = 10$, so this improvement 82 of the operational time implies the additional running length of 8.2 blocks.

Figures 3c and 3d show that in the comparative method, the operational time became smaller by approx. 90 (9%) in Env. 2 than that in Env. 1, but the planning time in Env. 2 increased by approx. 971 s (27%) when $M = 25$. A considerable increase in planning time also occurred when the number of agents was small, e.g., $M = 2$ and 3. This implies that the increase in the number of nodes considerably affected planning efficiency. In contrast, the proposed method can improve the operational time with a small increase in planning time (Fig. 3a). This discussion suggests that our proposed method is robust enough to increase the number of nodes.

5.3   Exp. 2: Characteristics of the PAPO

In the second experiment (Exp. 2), we examined the impact of the initial values of three parameters, N_K, N_P, and β, on the performance of our proposed method to investigate the characteristics of PAPO. First, we experimented with different combinations of the (initial) values of (N_K, N_P) as (1, 4), (2, 2), and (4, 1) in

Env. 2, so $N_K \times N_p$ is identical. Note that $\beta = 100$ was fixed, and the relaxation function **RelaxParam** was the same as Exp. 1.

We plotted the planning time, operational time, and number of detected conflicts in Fig. 4. These results indicate that $(4, 1)$ was the best combination of values of (N_K, N_P) in Env. 2. This indicates that N_K appears to have a greater impact on performance than N_P. If the agent has no material or a small-sized material, there are no constraints even in Env. 2. Only conflicts between its plans and other agents' plans are of concern and subject to checking. Thus, the more paths that are generated, the more conflicts are prevented from occurring. Clearly, if N_P is fixed, a larger N_K leads to lower operational time.

Even if N_K is large, different paths to the destination may not be generated. Probably, setting large N_K is meaningful as specially designed environments such as automated warehouses have many paths to the destination. However, such parameter setting is not appropriate. In our experiments, we set $N_K = 4$, which was not so large and could generate N_K different paths; thus, a larger N_K could contribute to reducing operational time by avoiding conflict occurrence. Meanwhile, a large N_P can generate various action sequences along each path generated in the first stage of the TSAP by simply changing the timing of rotation without taking long detours or waiting time. Therefore, obtaining collision-free shorter action sequence by setting a larger N_P is possible; of course, this depends on the number of detours and the number of nodes where agents can rotate/wait.

Furthermore, we conducted the same experiments by setting the values of β to 50, 100, 200, 400, and 800. We fixed $N_K = 4, N_P = 1$ and the relaxation function **RelaxParam** was the same as that in Exp. 1. From Fig. 5, as the value of β increases, the planning time and the number of conflicts decrease. A large value of β will reduce the frequency of calling the relaxation function **RelaxParam** because the agent tries to add many *wait* actions to the given set of candidate action sequences to resolve conflicts. As the wait is inserted before the node where the conflict is detected, the agent is likely to wait at the node added on some edges in Env. 2 before the intersection where the conflict is likely to occur, or the start node, i.e., pickup or delivery location. As mentioned in Exp. 1, waiting on nodes on the edge is less likely to prevent other agents actions. Therefore, agents could reduce the number of conflicts, the planning time was also consequently reduced. However, the operational time tends to increase owing to the many uses of the synchronization strategy. Therefore, we can weigh the operational time to improve the quality of generated plans, or the planning time for the planning efficiency by changing the value of β.

6   Conclusion

This paper presented a planning method called *path and action planning with orientation* (PAPO) that is able to generate collision-free plans for MAPD in non-uniform environment (N-MAPD) problems. The N-MAPD problem models a more complex, non-uniform environment where agent actions and orientations are strictly restricted owing to sizes of nodes (locations), agents, and material, as well as path widths. We evaluated the proposed method by comparing it with a naive comparative method. Our experiments demonstrated that the proposed method could generate not optimal but acceptable paths with reasonable lengths for actual applications and that it is sufficiently robust to the increase in the number of nodes. In addition, we analyzed the characteristics of the proposed method and observed that by changing the initial values of the parameters, it can be determined whether to assign weight to the quality of the generated plan or to the efficiency of the planning.

To improve the transportation efficiency even more, we will relax the condition (c') of well-formed N-MAPD. As agents cannot traverse the start/goal locations of other agents owing to condition (c'), the maximum number of agents that can simultaneously perform tasks in an environment depends on the number of nodes where the task is generated.

Acknowledgement. This work was partly supported by JSPS KAKENHI Grant Numbers 17KT0044 and 20H04245.

References

1. Alonso-Mora, J., Beardsley, P., Siegwart, R.: Cooperative collision avoidance for nonholonomic robots. IEEE Trans. Rob. **34**(2), 404–420 (2018). https://doi.org/10.1109/TRO.2018.2793890
2. Bareiss, D., van den Berg, J.: Generalized reciprocal collision avoidance. Int. J. Robot. Res. **34**(12), 1501–1514 (2015). https://doi.org/10.1177/0278364915576234
3. Barták, R., Švancara, J., Škopková, V., Nohejl, D., Krasičenko, I.: Multi-agent path finding on real robots. AI Commun. **32**(3), 175–189 (2019). https://doi.org/10.3233/AIC-190621
4. Bellusci, M., Basilico, N., Amigoni, F.: Multi-agent path finding in configurable environments. In: Proceedings of the 19th International Conference on Autonomous Agents and MultiAgent Systems, pp. 159–167 (2020)
5. Boyarski, E., et al.: ICBS: improved conflict-based search algorithm for multi-agent pathfinding. In: Twenty-Fourth International Joint Conference on Artificial Intelligence (2015)
6. Boyrasky, E., Felner, A., Sharon, G., Stern, R.: Don't split, try to work it out: bypassing conflicts in multi-agent pathfinding. In: Twenty-Fifth International Conference on Automated Planning and Scheduling (2015)
7. Felner, A., et al.: Search-based optimal solvers for the multi-agent pathfinding problem: summary and challenges. In: Tenth Annual Symposium on Combinatorial Search (2017)
8. Ho, F., Salta, A., Geraldes, R., Goncalves, A., Cavazza, M., Prendinger, H.: Multi-agent path finding for UAV traffic management. In: Proceedings of the 18th International Conference on Autonomous Agents and MultiAgent Systems, pp. 131–139. International Foundation for Autonomous Agents and Multiagent Systems (2019)
9. Hönig, W., et al.: Multi-agent path finding with kinematic constraints. In: Twenty-Sixth International Conference on Automated Planning and Scheduling (2016)

10. Kou, N.M., et al.: Multi-agent path planning with non-constant velocity motion. In: Proceedings of the 18th International Conference on Autonomous Agents and MultiAgent Systems, pp. 2069–2071. International Foundation for Autonomous Agents and Multiagent Systems (2019)

11. Krakowczyk, D., Wolff, J., Ciobanu, A., Meyer, D.J., Hrabia, C.-E.: Developing a distributed drone delivery system with a hybrid behavior planning system. In: Trollmann, F., Turhan, A.-Y. (eds.) KI 2018. LNCS (LNAI), vol. 11117, pp. 107–114. Springer, Cham (2018). https://doi.org/10.1007/978-3-030-00111-7_10

12. Li, J., Ran, M., Xie, L.: Efficient trajectory planning for multiple non-holonomic mobile robots via prioritized trajectory optimization. IEEE Robot. Autom. Lett. 6(2), 405–412 (2021). https://doi.org/10.1109/LRA.2020.3044834

13. Li, J., Surynek, P., Felner, A., Ma, H., Kumar, T.K.S., Koenig, S.: Multi-agent path finding for large agents. In: Proceedings of the AAAI Conference on Artificial Intelligence, vol. 33, no. 01, pp. 7627–7634 (2019). https://doi.org/10.1609/aaai.v33i01.33017627

14. Li, M., et al.: Efficient ridesharing order dispatching with mean field multi-agent reinforcement learning. In: The World Wide Web Conference, pp. 983–994. ACM (2019). https://doi.org/10.1145/3308558.3313433

15. Liu, M., Ma, H., Li, J., Koenig, S.: Task and path planning for multi-agent pickup and delivery. In: Proceedings of the 18th International Conference on Autonomous Agents and MultiAgent Systems, pp. 1152–1160. International Foundation for Autonomous Agents and Multiagent Systems (2019)

16. Ma, H., Hönig, W., Kumar, T.S., Ayanian, N., Koenig, S.: Lifelong path planning with kinematic constraints for multi-agent pickup and delivery. In: Proceedings of the AAAI Conference on Artificial Intelligence, vol. 33, pp. 7651–7658 (2019). https://doi.org/10.1609/aaai.v33i01.33017651

17. Ma, H., et al.: Overview: generalizations of multi-agent path finding to real-world scenarios. arXiv preprint arXiv:1702.05515 (2017)

18. Ma, H., Li, J., Kumar, T., Koenig, S.: Lifelong multi-agent path finding for online pickup and delivery tasks. In: Proceedings of the 16th Conference on Autonomous Agents and MultiAgent Systems, pp. 837–845. International Foundation for Autonomous Agents and Multiagent Systems (2017)

19. Ma, H., Tovey, C., Sharon, G., Kumar, T.S., Koenig, S.: Multi-agent path finding with payload transfers and the package-exchange robot-routing problem. In: Thirtieth AAAI Conference on Artificial Intelligence (2016)

20. Machida, M.: Polynomial-time multi-agent pathfinding with heterogeneous and self-interested agents. In: Proceedings of the 18th International Conference on Autonomous Agents and MultiAgent Systems, pp. 2105–2107. International Foundation for Autonomous Agents and Multiagent Systems (2019)

21. Morris, R., et al.: Planning, scheduling and monitoring for airport surface operations. In: Workshops at the Thirtieth AAAI Conference on Artificial Intelligence (2016)

22. Okumura, K., Machida, M., Défago, X., Tamura, Y.: Priority inheritance with backtracking for iterative multi-agent path finding. In: Proceedings of the Twenty-Eighth International Joint Conference on Artificial Intelligence, IJCAI 2019, pp. 535–542. International Joint Conferences on Artificial Intelligence Organization, July 2019. https://doi.org/10.24963/ijcai.2019/76

23. Salzman, O., Stern, R.: Research challenges and opportunities in multi-agent path finding and multi-agent pickup and delivery problems. In: Proceedings of the 19th International Conference on Autonomous Agents and MultiAgent Systems, pp. 1711–1715 (2020)

24. Sharon, G., Stern, R., Felner, A., Sturtevant, N.R.: Conflict-based search for optimal multi-agent pathfinding. Artif. Intell. **219**, 40–66 (2015). https://doi.org/10.1016/j.artint.2014.11.006
25. Silver, D.: Cooperative pathfinding. In: Proceedings of the First AAAI Conference on Artificial Intelligence and Interactive Digital Entertainment, AIIDE 2005, pp. 117–122. AAAI Press (2005)
26. Surynek, P.: On satisfisfiability modulo theories in continuous multi-agent path finding: compilation-based and search-based approaches compared. In: Proceedings of the 12th International Conference on Agents and Artificial Intelligence, ICAART, vol. 2, pp. 182–193. INSTICC, SciTePress (2020). https://doi.org/10.5220/0008980101820193
27. Tang, S., Kumar, V.: Safe and complete trajectory generation for robot teams with higher-order dynamics. In: 2016 IEEE/RSJ International Conference on Intelligent Robots and Systems (IROS), pp. 1894–1901 (2016). https://doi.org/10.1109/IROS.2016.7759300
28. Veloso, M., Biswas, J., Coltin, B., Rosenthal, S.: CoBots: robust symbiotic autonomous mobile service robots. In: Proceedings of the 24th International Conference on Artificial Intelligence, IJCAI 2015, pp. 4423–4429. AAAI Press (2015)
29. Wang, H., Rubenstein, M.: Walk, stop, count, and swap: decentralized multi-agent path finding with theoretical guarantees. IEEE Robot. Autom. Lett. **5**(2), 1119–1126 (2020). https://doi.org/10.1109/LRA.2020.2967317
30. Wang, K.H.C., Botea, A.: MAPP: a scalable multi-agent path planning algorithm with tractability and completeness guarantees. J. Artif. Intell. Res. **42**, 55–90 (2011)
31. Wurman, P.R., D'Andrea, R., Mountz, M.: Coordinating hundreds of cooperative, autonomous vehicles in warehouses. AI Mag. **29**(1), 9 (2008). https://doi.org/10.1609/aimag.v29i1.2082
32. Yakovlev, K., Andreychuk, A., Rybecký, T., Kulich, M.: On the application of safe-interval path planning to a variant of the pickup and delivery problem. In: Proceedings of the 17th International Conference on Informatics in Control, Automation and Robotics, ICINCO, vol. 1, pp. 521–528. INSTICC, SciTePress (2020). https://doi.org/10.5220/0009888905210528
33. Yen, J.Y.: Finding the k shortest loopless paths in a network. Manag. Sci. **17**(11), 712–716 (1971). https://doi.org/10.1287/mnsc.17.11.712
34. Zhang, H., Li, J., Surynek, P., Koenig, S., Kumar, T.S.: Multi-agent path finding with mutex propagation. In: Proceedings of the International Conference on Automated Planning and Scheduling, vol. 30, pp. 323–332 (2020)

Revealed Preference Argumentation and Applications in Consumer Behaviour Analyses

Nguyen Duy Hung[1(✉)] and Van-Nam Huynh[2]

[1] Sirindhorn International Institute of Technology, Pathumthani, Thailand
hung@siit.tu.ac.th
[2] Japan Advanced Institute of Science and Technology, Nomi, Japan
huynh@jaist.ac.jp

Abstract. Consumer preference studies in economics rest heavily on the behavioural interpretation of preference especially in the form of *Revealed Preference Theory* (RPT). Viewing purchasing decisions as a species of human reasoning, in this paper we are interested in generalising behaviourism to preference-based argumentation where existing frameworks are universally governed by the opposing mentalistic interpretation of preference. Concretely we re-construct and unify two main approaches to RPT then develop a so-called *Revealed Preference Argumentation* (RPA) framework which identifies preference as observed reasoning behaviour of an agent. We show that RPA subsumes RPT, by showing that key RPT-based consumer analyses can be translated to and solved as RPA computational tasks. It is argued that RPA may pave the way for future applications of argumentation to behavioural economics.

1 Introduction

There are two opposing views of preference [9]. Mentalism is the view that preference captures real phenomena of people's mental states that shape people's behaviours (thus obtainable by communications provided people speak their minds), while behaviourism is the view that preference is merely a mathematical construct used to describe regularities of human behaviours. Behaviourism is very influential in economics, especially in the form of *Revealed Preference Theory* (aka consumer theory) pioneered by Nobel economic laureate P. Samuelson back in 1938–1948 [26, 27]. Intuitively if a collection of goods b could have been bought by a consumer A within her budget but A in fact was observed to buy another collection of goods a, it is to be presumed by revealed preference theorists that A has revealed a preference for a over b [28]. This intuition provides the basis for approaching such problems as rationality checks, i.e. checking whether a consumer is "kind of" rational given what she bought, or extrapolating her market behaviour to predict what she will buy under new budgets or market conditions. For example, if the above consumer A also bought b while could

© Springer Nature Switzerland AG 2021
A. Rosenfeld and N. Talmon (Eds.): EUMAS 2021, LNAI 12802, pp. 55–71, 2021.
https://doi.org/10.1007/978-3-030-82254-5_4

afford c, and bought c while could afford a (as depicted by the table below), then she would not be viewed as *regular* rational - a kind of rationality that demands transitive preference[1]. For an illustration of behaviour extrapolation, consider another consumer B described by the second table: predictably if B can afford any of five products $a - e$, B shall select either a or e because she ignored c, d when she could afford b; and ignored b when she could afford a, e.

<table>
<tr><td colspan="2" align="center">1. Consumer A</td></tr>
<tr><td>Budgets</td><td>Bought products</td></tr>
<tr><td align="center">a, b</td><td align="center">a</td></tr>
<tr><td align="center">b, c</td><td align="center">b</td></tr>
<tr><td align="center">a, c</td><td align="center">c</td></tr>
</table>

<table>
<tr><td colspan="2" align="center">2. Consumer B</td></tr>
<tr><td>Budgets</td><td>Bought products</td></tr>
<tr><td align="center">a, b, e</td><td align="center">a, e</td></tr>
<tr><td align="center">b, c</td><td align="center">b</td></tr>
<tr><td align="center">b, d</td><td align="center">b</td></tr>
</table>

As purchasing decision is just a species of human reasoning, we might wonder how RPT and behaviourism can be generalized with respect to various forms of reasoning developed in general AI where mentalism dictates for now, as the general objective here is to help agents to state their preferences and compute decisions that maximize their stated preferences. In this paper we are interested in generalizing RPT and behaviourism to AI reasoning using argumentation - a form of reasoning inspired by how people reach conclusions via exchange of arguments in daily life. To the best of our knowledge this problem remains unexplored in the literature of argumentation where much of its recent development rests on the Abstract Argumentation (AA) framework of Dung [10] which is defined simply as a pair (Arg, Att) with a set Arg of arguments and a binary attack relation Att between arguments. Notably existing preference-based argumentation frameworks [1,3,5,6,14] have been defined as triples of the form (Arg, Att, P) where binary relation $P \subseteq Arg \times Arg$ represents the preference over the arguments of otherwise standard AA framework (Arg, Att). One can say that this model of preference-based argumentation is an extension of standard AA with the mentalistic interpretation of preference since relation P must be stated by the reasoning agent (presumably via some form of dialogues), and hence it will be called *Stated Preference Argumentation* (SPA) from now on. The rest of this paper is structured as follows. Section 2 recalls the preliminaries of AA and SPA. Section 3 recalls two main approaches to RPT: the rationalization approach makes sense of an observed consumer behaviour through weak-preference relations "rationalizing" it, while the motivation approach does so through strict-preference relations "motivating" the behaviour[2]. The three subsequent sections present our contributions. First we re-construct and unify the two main approaches to RPT using argumentation terms (Sect. 4). We then develop a so-called *Revealed Preference Argumentation* (RPA) framework (Sect. 5) and show that key RPT-based consumer analyses such as different rationality checks of a consumer behaviour and various kinds of behaviour extrapolations defined in RPT can be translated into RPA computational tasks (Sect. 6). Due to the lack of space, we skip the proofs of theorems and lemmas.

---

[1] Intransitive preference, though seems odd, is not uncommon, see e.g. [25].

[2] Intuitively, a weak preference of x over y is to mean "x is at least as good as y" while a strict one means "x is strictly better than y".

2   Argumentation Frameworks

An **Abstract Argumentation** framework AAF is a pair (Arg, Att) of a set Arg of arguments and an attack relation $Att \subseteq Arg \times Arg$. $S \subseteq Arg$ attacks $A \in Arg$ iff $(B, A) \in Att$ for some $B \in S$. $A \in Arg$ is acceptable wrt to S iff S attacks every argument attacking A. Many "acceptability" semantics for AA have been defined by strengthening this notion of acceptability. In this paper we need just one of them called the *admissibility semantics* according to which an argument A is *(admissibly) acceptable* in AAF, denoted $AAF \vdash_{ad} A$, if it is acceptable wrt an *admissible extension*. An admissible extension is a conflict-free set S of arguments such that each member of S is acceptable wrt to S.

An **AA framework with sub-arguments** is basically a standard AA framework (Arg, Att) equipped with a reflexive, anti-symmetric and transitive relation $Sub \subseteq Arg \times Arg$ representing the sub-argument relationships between arguments. Further Att contains two (not necessarily disjoint) subsets: Att_{pd} consisting of so-called *preference-dependent* attacks (elements of $Att \setminus Att_{pd}$ are called preference-independent attacks), and Att_d consisting of so-called *direct* attacks (elements of $Att \setminus Att_d$ are called *indirect* attacks), where A attacks B iff A *directly* attacks some sub-argument B' of B (i.e. $\forall(A, B) \in Att : \exists(B', B) \in Sub$ s.t. $(A, B') \in Att_d$). As an indirect attack (A, B) is seen as the accumulation of possibly many direct attacks (A, B') where B' is a sub-argument of B, it is assumed that if (A, B) is preference-dependent, then so is (A, B'). Note that a standard AA framework (Arg, Att) can be viewed as an AA framework with sub-arguments (Arg, Att, Sub) where $Sub = \{(A, A) \mid A \in Arg\}$ and $Att_d = Att$. On the other hand without preference information the semantics of (Arg, Att, Sub) is that of the standard AA framework (Arg, Att), and hence in this paper we shall blur distinction between two kinds of frameworks.

A **Stated Preference Argumentation** (SPA[3]) framework $SPAF$ is a pair $SPAF = (AAF, P)$ consisting of an AA framework (possibly with sub-arguments) $AAF = (Arg, Att, Sub)$ and a binary relation $P \subseteq Arg \times Arg$ representing the stated preference between arguments[4]. The semantics of $SPAF$ is defined by reducing $SPAF$ to standard AA as follows [14]. We say that $(A, B) \in Att_{pd}$ is *effective* if A directly attacks some sub-argument B' of B (i.e. $(B', B) \in Sub \wedge (A, B') \in Att_d$) such that B' is not strictly preferred to A (i.e. $(B', A) \notin P \vee (A, B') \in P$); *ineffective* if not effective. The **AA reduction** of $SPAF$ is the AA framework AAR obtained from AAF by removing ineffective preference-dependent attacks, i.e. $AAR = (Arg, Att \setminus \{(A, B) \in Att_{pd} \mid (A, B) \text{ is ineffective}\})$. Define $SPAF \vdash_{as} X$ iff $AAR \vdash_{as} X$ (again, in this paper we focus on $as = ad$ - the **ad**missibility semantics).

Note that the above semantics of SPA is different from the original one by Amgoud and Cayrol [3] whereby an attack (A, B) is ineffective if $(B, A) \in P \wedge (A, B) \notin P$. We do not use Amgoud and Cayrol's semantics as it has gone out of fashion now. Concretely recent accounts of structured argumen-

---

[3] aka preference-based argumentation in [1,3,5,6,14].

[4] We do not impose any constraints on P except that it is a binary relation over Arg.

tation with preferences [11,12,23,24] all demand that preference-independent attacks succeed irrespective of preferences. More seriously as shown in [23,24], disregarding a preference-dependent attack, say (A, B), simply on the ground that $(B, A) \in P \wedge (A, B) \notin P$ as in [3] may lead to violation of the rationality postulates of sub-argument closure [2,23][5] and consistency [8][6]. To avoid these problems, the authors of [11,12,23,24] universally prescribe that a preference-dependent attack (A, B) is disregarded only if for every sub-argument B' of B that A attacks directly, B' is strictly preferred to A. The above semantics of SPA [14] simply follows this finer application of preference in order to capture [11,12,23,24] correctly (readers are referred to [14] more details). Note that SPA is by no means the most general model of extended AA, for example it can be seen as an instance of bipolar argumentation [1] which allows different kinds of supports between arguments including sub-argument relation. Instead of stating preference by a binary preference relation as in [1,3,6], one may consider the case in which arguments are associated values as in [5,15], or arguments express preferences between other arguments as in [4,7,13,22]. Still we can say that all these extended models of AA are governed by the mentalistic interpretation of preference since preference information in these models must be stated by the reasoning agent and hence means to reflect her mental state. In this paper we use SPA for simplicity but feel compelled to replace Amgoud and Cayrol's semantics by that of [14] for the above presented reason.

3   Revealed Preference Theory

Any approaches to RPT dutifully take the same input - a choice representing observed market behaviour of a consumer. In this section we recall the motivation approach and the rationalization approach [18,26,27].

Definition 1. *1. A **budget space** is a pair $(X, \mathcal{B})$ where X is a universe of all possible options and $\mathcal{B} \subseteq 2^X \setminus \{\emptyset\}$ is a set of **budgets** (aka menus).*
*2. A **choice function** (or choice, for short) c over a budget space $(X, \mathcal{B})$ is a function mapping each budget $B \in \mathcal{B}$ to a subset $c(B)$ of B.*

Intuitively $c(B)$ is the set of options chosen (by a consumer) from all affordable options in $B \subseteq X$. For convenience for $R \subseteq X \times X$, let $greatest_R(B)$ denote $\{x \in B \mid \forall y \in B : (x \, R \, y)\}$ - the set of R-greatest elements of B; and $maximal_R(B) \triangleq \{x \in B \mid \forall y \in B : (\neg y \, R \, x)\}$ - the set of R-maximal elements of B. Further $\delta(R)$ denotes the strict core (aka asymmetric core) of R, i.e. $x \, \delta(R) \, y \Leftrightarrow x \, R \, y \wedge \neg(y \, R \, x)$; while $\omega(R)$ denotes the weak relation derived from R as follows: $x \, \omega(R) \, y \Leftrightarrow \neg(y R x)$.

In RPT, preference is simply a binary relation over X. In the motivation approach, such a relation makes sense of a choice by "motivating" it, while in the rationalization approach it does so by "rationalizing" it in the following technical sense.

---

[5] A complete extension contains all sub-arguments of its arguments.
[6] The set of conclusions of arguments in a complete extension is consistent.

Definition 2. *Let c be a choice function over a budget space $(X, \mathcal{B})$ and $R \subseteq X \times X$ be a preference relation.*

1. *We say that R **motivates** (resp. **rationalizes**) c if for any $B \in \mathcal{B}$, $c(B) = maximal_R(B)$ (resp. $c(B) = greatest_R(B)$).*
2. *A choice c is said to be a **motivatable** (resp. **rationalizable**) choice if it can be motivated (resp. rationalized) by some preference relation R.*

Example 1 (rationalizable vs non-rationalizable). Customer A's behaviour in Introduction is described by a choice function $c_A = \{\{a, b\} \mapsto \{a\}, \{b, c\} \mapsto \{b\}, \{a, c\} \mapsto \{c\}\}$. It is clear that $R = \{(a, b), (b, c), (c, a)\} \cup \{(x, x) \mid x \in X = \{a, b, c\}\}$ rationalizes c_A. Hence c_A is a rationalizable choice. Similarly, choice $c_B = \{\{a, b, e\} \mapsto \{a, e\}, \{b, c\} \mapsto \{b\}, \{b, d\} \mapsto \{b\}\}$, which represents consumer B's behaviour, is motivatable since it is motivated by $R = \{(a, b), (e, b), (b, c), (b, d)\}$. Now consider another choice $c = \{B_1 \mapsto \{a\}, B_2 \mapsto \{b\}\}$ where $B_1 = X$ and $B_2 = \{a, b\}$. Assume a relation R rationalizing c. From $c(B_1) = \{a\}$ it is clear that $a \, R \, a$ and $a \, R \, b$. That is $a \in greatest_R(B_2)$ and hence $a \in c(B_2)$ but this is not the case. Hence c is not rationalizable.

Note that a preference relation that makes sense of a choice according to one approach does not necessarily do so according to the other approach, simply because it may motivate a choice but does not rationalize it or vice versa. However rationalizability and motivatability are equivalent properties of a choice.

Lemma 1 *(Theorem 3 of [18]). A choice is rationalizable iff it is motivatable.*

In other words, rationalizable choices and motivatable choices characterize "the same kind" of consumer behaviour. From this equivalence and other equivalences presented below, one can say that two approaches to RPT deliver the same results though they postulate contradictory assumptions about preference. To pin down these assumptions, consider a preference relation R: if R is reflexive then $maximal_R(B) = \emptyset$; and if R is irreflexive then $greasted_R(B) = \emptyset$. Hence if R is to motivate (resp. rationalize) a decisive choice[7], it is presumably irreflexive (resp. reflexive). It is clear that these assumptions have nothing to do with the nature of preference being captured. Rather they are superfluously brought in by the mathematical tools $greatest_R(.)$ and $maximal_R(.)$ the approaches deploy. Lemma 2 below, which is given in [18, 21], says that stating these assumptions explicitly will not change the kind of consumer behaviour being described.

Lemma 2. 1. *(rationalizability $\Leftrightarrow$ reflexive rationalizability) A choice is rationalizable iff it can be rationalized by a reflexive preference relation (for short, reflexive rationalizable).*
2. *(motivatability $\Leftrightarrow$ irreflexive motivatability) A choice is motivatable iff it is irreflexive motivatable.*

---

[7] A choice c is decisive if $c(B) \neq \emptyset$ for any menu $B \in \mathcal{B}$.

Note that many choices that are rationalizable (or equivalently reflexive rationalizable/motivatable/irreflexive motivatable) according to the above technical sense are not really "rational" in common sense. For example, the choice c_1 in Example 1 is rationalizable but clearly a rational consumer is not expected to select c in menu $\{a, c\}$ given that she ignored c when b was available (in menu $\{b, c\}$), and ignored b when a was available (in menu $\{a, b\}$). Proponents of RPT do not see this as a problem, since for them rationalizability (and its equivalences: reflexive rationalizability, motivatability, etc.) aims to be the least stringent in a spectrum of rationality criteria that RPT provides. More stringent criteria can be obtained by assigning extra properties to the preference relation that rationalizes or motivates such a behaviour. Notably, the criteria called regular rationalizability/motivatability defined below require that the rationalizing/motivating preference relation is transitive. In addition they elevate the reflexivity (resp. irreflexivity) assumption to slightly stronger assumption called weak (resp. strict) preference.

Definition 3. *1. A **strict preference relation** $\succ$ is an asymmetric (hence irreflexive) relation over X. A **weak preference relation** $\succeq$ is a reflexive and total relation over X.*
*2. A **regular-weak (regular-strict)** preference relation is a weak preference (resp. strict preference) relation that is **transitive**. A **regular** preference relation is a regular-weak or regular-strict preference relation.*
*3. A choice c is said to be **regular rationalizable** (resp. **regular motivatable**) if it can be rationalized (resp. motivated) by a regular-weak preference relation (resp. a regular-strict preference relation).*

Example 2. Choice c_B is also: 1) regular rationalizable because it is rationalized by $R = \{(a, b), (e, b), (b, c), (b, d), (a, c), (a, d), (e, c), (e, b), (a, e), (e, a), (c, d), (d, c)\} \cup \{(x, x) \mid x \in X\}$, which is regular-weak; and 2) regular motivatable because it is motivated by the asymmetric core $\delta(R)$ of the above relation R, i.e. $\delta(R) = \{(a, b), (e, b), (b, c), (b, d), (a, c), (a, d), (e, c), (e, b)\}$, which is regular-strict.

It is obvious that a regular rationalizable (resp. regular motivatable) choice is also a rationalizable (resp. motivatable) choice but the reverse does not hold.

Example 3. The rationalizable choice c_A is not regular rationalizable because for any relation R, if R rationalizes c_A then $R \supseteq \{a\,R\,b, b\,R\,c, c\,R\,a\}$. Hence if R is regular-weak, then $R = X \times X$, and hence $c_A(B) = B$ for any budget B - but this is not the case. Note that we can obtain a regular rationalizable choice from c_A by selecting c from menu $\{a, c\}$ instead of c. Clearly this new choice is rationalized by $R = \{a\,R\,b, b\,R\,c, a\,R\,c, a\,R\,a, b\,R\,b, c\,R\,c\}$, a regular-weak preference relation.

Regular rationalizability and regular motivatability are equivalent properties of a choice. That is, regular rationalizable choices characterize the same kind of consumer behaviour as regular motivatable choices do.

Lemma 3 *(regular rationalizability $\Leftrightarrow$ regular motivatability). Let c be a choice.*

1. If c is rationalized by a regular-weak preference relation $\succeq$, then c is motivated by $\delta(\succeq)$, which is a regular-strict preference relation (see Lemma 4).
2. If c is motivated by a regular-strict preference relation $\succ$, then c is rationalized $\omega(\succ)$, which is a regular-weak preference relation (see Lemma 4).

Lemma 4. *1. If $\succ$ is a regular-strict preference relation then $\omega(\succ)$ is a regular-weak preference relation. If $\succeq$ is a regular-weak preference relation then $\delta(\succeq)$ is a regular-strict preference relation.*
2. For any regular-strict preference relation $\succ$, it holds that $\succ = \delta(\omega(\succ))$; and for any regular-weak preference relation $\succeq$, it holds that $\succeq = \omega(\delta(\succeq))$.

The following box summarizes and also lists more equivalences and implications between rationality criteria for choices in RPT (see e.g. [18,21]). These criteria are the focal point of the re-construction of RPT in Sect. 4.

---

motivatability $\Leftrightarrow$ irreflexive motivatability $\Leftrightarrow$ rationalizability $\Leftrightarrow$ reflexive rationalizability $\Leftarrow \not\Rightarrow$ total rationalizability $\Leftrightarrow$ total and reflexive rationalizability $\Leftrightarrow$ asymmetric motivatability $\Leftarrow \not\Rightarrow$ regular motivatability $\Leftrightarrow$ regular rationalizability

---

4   RPT in Argumentation

The previous section shows that a rationality criterion of RPT characterizes a certain kind of observed consumer behaviours: the kind characterized by rationalizability is the same as the kind characterized by motivability; the kind characterized by regular rationalizability is also the kind characterized by regular motivability, and so on. Since purchasing decision is just a species of reasoning, one might expect some correspondence between rationality criteria of RPT and argumentation semantics. To the best of our knowledge this correspondence has never been explored so far, and hence in this section we want to fill this gap. In particular we re-construct the elements of RPT in argumentation terms using especially the admissibility semantics of argumentation. To establish the "correctness" of this re-construction we show that it unifies two approaches to RPT presented in Sect. 3. Let us start by viewing each budget not merely as a collection of objects, but a collection of arguments and counter-arguments for choosing those objects, i.e. an argumentation framework.

Definition 4. *We say that an AA framework (possibly with sub-arguments) $AAF = (Arg, Att, Sub)$ represents a budget $B \subseteq X$ if for each option $x \in X$,*

1. *Arg contains an argument for choosing x, denoted arg_x, and*
2. *if $x \in B$ then $AAF \vdash_{ad} arg_x$, otherwise $AAF \not\vdash_{ad} arg_x$.*

Note that Arg may contain arguments other than those for selecting options. For example, the figure below depicts two AAFs representing $B = \{x, y\}$ where the right contains na_z which stands for "z is not available thus not selectable".

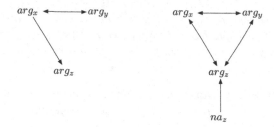

Notation 1. *For convenience wrt a universe of options X, let Arg_X denote the set of arguments $\{arg_x \mid x \in X\}$ and Att_X denote $\{(arg_x, arg_y) \mid x, y \in X, x \neq y\}$. Moreover for a preference relation $R \subseteq X \times X$, $\mathcal{P}_R$ denotes the corresponding argument preference relation, i.e. $(arg_x, arg_y) \in \mathcal{P}_R$ iff $x\,R\,y$.*

The rationale of Definition 4 is as follows. The definition does not spell out a specific argumentation framework but a common "interface" of argumentation frameworks that represent the same budget B. This interface models a minimal introspection into the mind of an agent who is modelled as choosing between the options of B. Concretely, it postulates that for each object $x \in X$, the agent has an argument for choosing x (Property 1 of Definition 4), however does not demand the causes (reasons) behind to be spelled out: arg_x is an abstract argument without internal structure. It is however important that the argument "refers" unambiguously to the option x (this is mechanically done by the subscript x in the notation arg_x). This reference is to prevent such a situation that the agent is observed as choosing x but the agent itself does not believe it did so. Obviously in a situation of this kind, one should not draw any inference regarding the agent's preference[8]. Now that arg_x exists in the agent's mind, the agent should determine whether the argument is acceptable or not when she decides whether to choose option x. Recall that if $AAF \nvdash_{ad} arg_x$ (arg_x is not admissibly acceptable) then arg_x is also not acceptable under any other argumentation semantics, and hence the agent should exclude x from consideration. Clearly this is the case of each and every option $x \in X \setminus B$, as these options are not available. For an available option $x \in B$, $AAF \vdash_{ad} arg_x$ (Property 2) says that the agent probably selects x. Since the agent does not necessarily select x, arg_x must not be required to be acceptable under a more skeptical semantics. Now let's introduce a simple implementation of this interface, called the *canonical representation*, denoted $AAF_B = (Arg_B, Att_B)$. It is clear that Property 1 implies $Arg_B \supseteq Arg_X$. Since arg_x and arg_y for $x \neq y$ attack each other, $Att_B \supseteq Att_X$.

---

[8] For an illustration let's borrow an example from [30]. An economist and her friend visit a sushi restaurant for the first time. The economist has read about wasabi and knows what it looks like. Her friend mistakes it for avocado and devours a whole spoonful. That is, the friend was observed to choose wasabi but did not have an argument for choosing it. If the economist models her friend's choice options as "eating a spoonful of wasabi" and "not doing that", then as a revealed preference theorist, she will conclude that her friend prefers "eating a spoonful of wasabi" to "not doing that", which is obviously wrong.

Definition 5. *The* ***canonical (AA) representation*** *of budget* $B \subseteq X$ *is* $AAF_B \triangleq (Arg_B, Att_B)$ *where* $Arg_B = Arg_X \cup \{na_x \mid x \in X \setminus B\}$, $Att_B = Att_X \cup \{(na_x, arg_x) \mid x \in X \setminus B\}$ *where*

1. na_x *stands for "x cannot be selected as it is* ***not*** *available", and*
2. *each argument in* Arg_B *is a sub-argument of itself only, and all attacks in* Att_B *are direct: attacks of the form* (arg_x, arg_y) *are preference-dependent while* (na_x, arg_x) *is preference-independent.*

Apparently without further information AAF_B is the obvious representation of B, and hence it is assumed in our re-construction of RPT.

Now recall that in the motivation approach (resp. rationalization approach) to RPT, an agent chooses an option x from budget B only if x is a maximal (resp. greatest) element of B wrt a preference relation R ascribed to the agent. It is worth noting that two conditions are contradictory: $x \in maximal_R(B)$ implies that $(x, x) \notin R$ while $x \in greatest_R(B)$ implies that $(x, x) \in R$. The following theorem asserts that when either of two conditions holds, arg_x would be an admissibly acceptable argument wrt the SPA framework obtained from AAF_B and the argument preference relation $\mathcal{P}_R$.

Theorem 1 *(greatest $\vee$ maximal $\Rightarrow$ admissible). Let* $R \subseteq X \times X$ *be a preference relation over options. For any option* x *and budget* B, *if* $x \in greatest_R(B)$ *or* $x \in maximal_R(B)$, *then SPA framework* $(AAF_B, \mathcal{P}_R) \vdash_{ad} arg_x$ *(where* $\mathcal{P}_R$ *is the argument preference relation corresponding to* R*).*

It is important to note that in general the reverse of Theorem 1's assertion may not hold since it may be that $(AAF_B, \mathcal{P}_R) \vdash_{ad} arg_x$ but $x \notin greatest_R(B) \cup maximal_R(B)$ as demonstrated by the example below.

Example 4. Consider $B = \{a, b\}$ and $R = \{(a, b), (b, a)\}$. Clearly $\delta(\mathcal{P}_R) = \emptyset$ and hence the AA reduction of $(AAF_B, \mathcal{P}_R)$ coincides with AAF_B. So $(AAF_B, \mathcal{P}_R) \vdash_{ad} arg_x$ for $x \in \{a, b\}$ but $greatest_R(B) = maximal_R(B) = \emptyset$.

However if the underlying weak-preference/strict-preference assumptions of the two presented approaches to RPT are brought up explicitly, the admissibility of arg_x is equivalent to the disjunction $x \in greatest_R(B) \vee x \in maximal_R(B)$.

Theorem 2. *Let* $B \subseteq X$ *be a budget over a universe of options* X *and* $R \subseteq X \times X$ *be a weak-preference or strict-preference relation. For any option* $x \in B$, $x \in greatest_R(B) \cup maximal_R(B)$ *if and only if* $(AAF_B, \mathcal{P}_R) \vdash_{ad} arg_x$.

The above two theorems say that $(AAF_B, \mathcal{P}_R) \vdash_{ad} arg_x$ is "the right" unification of two conditions $x \in greatest_R(B)$ and $x \in maximal_R(B)$. Note that while the two conditions are not intelligible without their underlying assumptions (i.e. weak preference or strict preference), the admissibility of arg_x is always intelligible. Now the next step of our RPT re-construction is to "lift" this scheme of unification from the level of individual options wrt a fixed budget, to the level of choice functions wrt a budget space. The following definition introduces the notion of *justification* which, as will be shown by Lemma 6, unifies the notions of rationalization and motivation. Note that technically the notion of justification is defined in terms of the admissibility semantics.

Definition 6. *Let c be a choice over a budget space $(X, \mathcal{B})$ and $R \subseteq X \times X$ be a preference relation. We say that R **justifies** c if for every budget $B \in \mathcal{B}$,*

1. *for every $x \in c(B)$, SPA framework $(AAF_B, \mathcal{P}_R) \vdash_{ad} arg_x$*
2. *for every $x \in X \setminus c(B)$, SPA framework $(AAF_B, \mathcal{P}_R) \nvdash_{ad} arg_x$.*

*A choice is **justifiable** if it can be justified by some preference relation.*

Justifiability aims to be the least stringent rationality criterion for a consumer behaviour c based on argumentation semantics. As in RPT, more stringent criteria are defined by assigning extra properties to the preference relations of c.

Definition 7. *A choice c is said to be*

1. ***transitive justifiable*** *if it can be justified by a transitive preference relation.*
2. ***regular** (resp. **regular-strict/regular-weak**) **justifiable** if it can be justified by some regular (resp. regular-strict/regular-weak) preference relation[9].*

Of course in the first case we shall say that c is **transitive-justified** by R and R is a **transitive justification** of c. And in the second case: c is **regular-justified** by R and R is a **regular justification** of c, etc.

Lemma 5 below says that in fact transitive justifiability defined in the first case is equivalent to all three kinds of regular justifiability defined in the second case. In other words, the notion of regularity in our RPT re-construction does not need to commit to either weak preference or strict preference as does the notion of regularity in the two current approaches to RPT.

Lemma 5 *(transitive justifiability ⇔ regular justifiability ⇔ regular-weak justifiability ⇔ regular-strict justifiability). A choice is transitive justifiable iff it is regular justifiable iff it is regular-weak justifiable iff it is regular-strict justifiable.*

Lemma 6 below says that the notion of *justification* unifies the notions of rationalization and motivation.

Lemma 6. *Let c be a choice over budget space $(X, \mathcal{B})$ and $R \subseteq X \times X$ be a preference relation.*

1. *If R is a weak-preference relation, then R justifies c iff R rationalizes c.*
2. *If R is a strict-preference relation, then R justifies c iff R motivates c.*

---

[9] Recall that a regular preference relation is either a regular-weak preference relation or regular-strict preference relation (Definition 3).

Note that in general a preference relation R justifying a choice c may not motivate nor rationalize c. For instance, $R = \{a\,R\,b, b\,R\,a\}$ justifies a choice $c = \{\{a, b\} \mapsto \{a, b\}\}$ but R does not rationalize nor motivate c as $maximal_R(\{a, b\}) = greatest_R(\{a, b\}) = \emptyset$. On the other hand, a preference relation may motivate or rationalize a choice but does not justify it. For example $R = \{a\,R\,b, b\,R\,a\}$ rationalizes $c' = \{\{a, b\} \mapsto \emptyset\}$ but does not justify c'.

Now let's establish the correspondence between justifiability-based rationality criteria for evaluating choices defined in Definition 6 and Definition 7 and different rationality criteria proposed in RPT.

Theorem 3 *(justifiability $\Leftrightarrow$ strict-preference motivatability $\Leftrightarrow$ weak-preference rationalizability). A choice is justifiable iff it can be motivated by a strict-preference relation iff it can be rationalized by a weak-preference relation.*

Theorem 4 *(regular justifiability $\Leftrightarrow$ regular motivatability $\Leftrightarrow$ regular rationalizability). Let c be a choice over budget space $(X, \mathcal{B})$.*

1. *If c is motivated (resp. rationalized) by a regular-strict (resp. regular-weak) preference relation $R \subseteq X \times X$, then c is justified by R.*
2. *If c is justified by a regular preference relation $R \subseteq X \times X$, then c is motivated by $\delta(R)$ and rationalized by $\omega(R)$.*

5   Revealed Preference Argumentation (RPA) Framework

Given that RPT is a particular form of behaviourism that focuses on consumer's preference, one might ask how behaviourism in general works on any agent's preference. To answer this question for argumentative agents, we define a Revealed Preference Argumentation framework as follows.

Definition 8. *A **Revealed Preference Argumentation** (RPA) framework is a pair $RPAF = (Abs, Cbs)$ where*

1. *Abs, which is referred to as the **argument base** of RPAF, is an AA framework (possibly with sub-arguments), and*
2. *Cbs, which is referred to as the **choice base** of RPAF, is a set $\{(A_i = v_i \mid AAF_i)\}_1^m$ of triples $(A_i = v_i \mid AAF_i)$ (referred to as observations) where AAF_i is an AA framework, A_i is an argument in AAF_i and $v_i \in \{\mathbf{acc}, \mathbf{rej}\}$.*

We restrict ourselves to a class of *well-formed* RPA frameworks defined below.

Definition 9. *1. We say that an AA framework (Arg_i, Att_i) is a **preference-invariant extension** of another AA framework (Arg, Att) if and only if $Arg_i \supseteq Arg$, $Att_i \supseteq Att$ such that Att coincides with the projection of Att_i on Arg and $Att_i \setminus Att$ are all preference-independent attacks.*
2. *A RPA framework $RPAF = (Abs, Cbs)$ is said to be **well-formed** if for each observation $(A_i = v_i \mid AAF_i) \in Cbs$, AAF_i is a preference-invariant extension of the argument base Abs.*

Intuitively the argument base Abs of a well-formed RPA framework $RPAF = (Abs, Cbs)$ is supposed to represent the stable knowledge of a reasoning agent whose preference is not yet known but remains unchanged during the period of observations. The choice base Cbs is supposed to represent the agent's observed reasoning behaviour, where an observation $(A_i = v_i \mid AAF_i)$ says that the agent is observed to have accepted or rejected an argument A_i in a condition (experiment) that results in the agent's total knowledge base AAF_i. That is AAF_i extends Abs with additional arguments and attacks that are specific to the condition or the experiment the agent is going through. Moreover these additional attacks are assumed to be preference-independent. For example, of our special interest in the next section is the well-formed RPA framework $RPTinRPA_c$ representing a given choice function c defined as follows.

Definition 10. *For a choice c over a budget space $(X, \mathcal{B})$, $RPTinRPA_c$ denotes the well-formed RPA framework $(Abs_X, Cbs_{\mathcal{B}})$ where*

1. *$Abs_X = (Arg_X, Att_X)$ with $Arg_X = \{arg_x \mid x \in X\}$, $Att_X = \{(arg_x, arg_y) \mid x \neq y \in X\}$, and*
2. *$Cbs_{\mathcal{B}} = \{(arg_x = \mathbf{acc} \mid AAF_B) \mid x \in c(B), B \in \mathcal{B}\} \cup \{(arg_x = \mathbf{rej} \mid AAF_B) \mid x \in B \setminus c(B), B \in \mathcal{B}\}$ where AAF_B is the canonical AA representation of budget B (Definition 5).*

Intuitively an acceptance observation $(arg_x = \mathbf{acc} \mid AAF_B) \in Cbs_{\mathcal{B}}$ (resp. rejection observation $(arg_x = \mathbf{rej} \mid AAF_B) \in Cbs_{\mathcal{B}}$) represents that the option x was chosen (resp. was not chosen) from budget B. For illustration, let's revisit the choice describing the consumer A's behaviour $c_A = \{B_1 = \{a, b\} \mapsto \{a\}, B_2 = \{b, c\} \mapsto \{b\}, B_3 = \{a, c\} \mapsto \{c\}\}$. The choice base of $RPTinRPA_{c_A}$ representing c should contain observations $(arg_a = \mathbf{acc} \mid AAF_{B_1})$ and $(arg_b = \mathbf{rej} \mid AAF_{B_1})$ (where AAF_{B_1} is obtained from AAF_X by adding an attack (na_c, arg_c)) representing that option a was chosen from $B_1 = \{a, b\}$, but not option b.

Now come three definitions that lie at the heart of behaviourism in argumentation. Definition 11 links observed reasoning behaviour (in the form of a choice base) with revealed preference over arguments. That is, one may say that this definition is the counter-part of Definition 2 which links observed market behaviour (in the form of a choice function) with revealed preference over different products.

Definition 11. *Let $RPAF = (Abs, Cbs)$ be a RPA framework. A binary relation P over the set of arguments in Abs is said to be a **revealed preference relation** of $RPAF$ iff for each observation $(A_i = v_i \mid AAF_i) \in Cbs$,*

1. *if $v_i = \mathbf{acc}$, then SPA framework $(AAF_i, P) \vdash_{ad} A_i$,*
2. *otherwise (i.e. $v_i = \mathbf{rej}$), $(AAF_i, P) \nvdash_{ad} A_i$.*

*We say that $RPAF$ is a **preferentially satisfiable** (for short, **p-satisfiable**) RPA framework if it has at least one revealed preference relation.*

Example 5. $RPTinRPA_{c_A}$ (which represents the choice c_A) is p-satisfiable since it has a revealed preference relation $P_1 = \{(arg_a, arg_b), (arg_b, arg_c), (arg_c, arg_a)\}$. $RPTinRPA_{c_B}$ (which represents c_B) is p-satisfiable since it has a revealed preference relation $P_2 = \{(arg_a, arg_b), (arg_e, arg_b), (arg_b, arg_c), (arg_b, arg_d)\}$.

P-satisfiability aims to be the least stringent criterion for a RPA framework to be preferentially satisfiable. More stringent criteria are obtained by associating extra properties to the revealed argumentation preference relations of the concerned RPA framework as follows.

Definition 12. *A RPA framework is said to be*

1. **transitive p-satisfiable** *if it has at least one revealed preference relation that is transitive.*
2. **regular-weak p-satisfiable** *if it has at least one revealed preference relation that is regular-weak (i.e. total, reflexive and transitive).*
3. **regular-strict p-satisfiable** *if it has at least one revealed preference relation that is regular-strict (i.e. asymmetric and transitive).*
4. **regular p-satisfiable** *if it has at least one revealed preference relation that is regular, where an argument preference relation is regular just in case it is regular-weak or regular-strict.*

Obviously if a RPA framework is transitive p-satisfiable then it is also p-satisfiable but the reverse does not hold as exemplified by the following example.

Example 6. Continue Example 5, $RPTinRPA_{c_A}$ is transitive p-satisfiable. To see this assume on the contrary that it has a transitive revealed preference relation P_1'. It is easy to see that $\{(arg_a, arg_b), (arg_b, arg_c), (arg_c, arg_a)\} \subseteq \delta(P_1')$. Since $\delta(P_1')$ is transitive, $(arg_a, arg_c) \in \delta(P_1')$, which contradicts with $(arg_c, arg_a) \in \delta(P_1')$.

Lemma 7. *Let RPAF be a RPA framework. RPAF is transitive p-satisfiable iff RPAF is regular p-satisfiable iff RPAF is regular-weak p-satisfiable iff RPAF is regular-strict p-satisfiable.*

Definition 13 extrapolates observed reasoning behaviour to new conditions.

Definition 13. *Wrt a RPA framework $RPAF = (\mathcal{A}bs, \mathcal{C}bs)$, a **potential extrapolation** e is a triple of the same form $(A = v \mid AAF)$ as an observation of RPAF, and is said to be:*

1. *a **credulous extrapolation** of RPAF, written $RPAF \vdash_{cr} e$, iff there exists some revealed preference relation P of RPAF such that $(AAF, P) \vdash_{ad} A$ if $v = $ **acc**; otherwise $(AAF, P) \nvdash_{ad} A$.*
2. *a **skeptical extrapolation** of RPAF, written $RPAF \vdash_{sk} e$, iff the above condition holds for any revealed preference relation of RPAF.*
3. *a **regular extrapolation** of RPAF, written $RPAF \vdash_{reg} e$, iff the above condition holds for any regular revealed preference relation of RPAF.*

6   RPA as a Complete Computational Framework for RPT-based Consumer Behaviour Analyses

In this section, we show that, given an observed consumer's behaviour in the form of a choice function c, the key RPT-based analyses described below can be translated to and solved as computational tasks wrt the RPA framework $RPTinRPA_c$ that represents c (defined in Definition 10).

- *Rationality check*: Does c satisfy a certain rationality criterion of RPT (e.g. regular rationalizable)?
- *Preference recovery*: Compute the set of all preference relations of a certain class (e.g. regular preference relations) motivating or rationalizing c.
- *Extrapolation*: Given an option x belonging to a new budget B, checking whether for some (resp. any) recovered preference relation R, $x \in maximal_R(B)$ or $x \in greatest_R(B)$, i.e. if the agent is given budget B, whether she would probably (resp. surely) choose option x?

Obviously three analyses are strongly related. For a given choice function c, one first performs a *rationality check*. Passing such a check means that c has a non-empty set of motivating/rationalizing preference relations of the class corresponding to the check. Only then one starts a *preference recovery* to compute this non-empty "answer" set. Having computed this answer set, one can start an extrapolation, asking whether for a given option $x \in B$ where B is a new budget, for some (resp. any) recovered preference relation R in the answer set, $x \in maximal_R(B)$ or $x \in greatest_R(B)$? Note that the computational task here is called an extrapolation because conceptually it extends the given choice function c from its original budget space $(X, \mathcal{B})$ to $(X, \mathcal{B} \cup \{B\})$ by adding a new mapping $B \mapsto maximal_R(B)$ or $B \mapsto greatest_R(B)$. Clearly checking if $x \in maximal_R(B)$ (or $x \in greatest_R(B)$) for some (resp. any) recovered preference relation R is conceptually equivalent to checking if option x belongs to the set-union (resp. set intersection) of $maximal_R(B)$ (or $greatest_R(B)$) where R ranges over the set of all recovered preference relations.

Now let's see how these RPT-based analyses can be translated into computational tasks wrt $RPTinRPA_c$. Theorem 5 says that to check if a choice c is total and reflexive rationalizable, one can check whether $RPTinRPA_c$ is p-satisfiable.

Theorem 5. *Let c be a choice and $RPTinRPA_c$ be the RPA framework representing to c. Then c is total and reflexive rationalizable (or equivalently, asymmetric motivatable) if and only if $RPTinRPA_c$ is p-satisfiable.*

Theorem 6 says that to check whether a choice c is regular rationalizable, one can check whether $RPTinRPA_c$ is regular p-satisfiable.

Theorem 6. *Let c be a choice for a budget space $(X, \mathcal{B})$ and $RPTinRPA_c$ be the RPA framework representing c.*

1. *If c is rationalized (resp. motivated) by a regular-weak (resp. regular-strict) preference relation $R \subseteq X \times X$, then $\mathcal{P}_R \triangleq \{(arg_x, arg_y) \mid x \, R \, y\}$ is a transitive revealed preference relation of $RPTinRPA_c$.*

2. If $RPTinRPA_c$ has a revealed preference relation P that is transitive, then c is motivated by a regular-strict preference relation $\mathcal{R}_{\delta(P)}$ and rationalized by a regular-weak preference relation $\mathcal{R}_{\omega(\delta(P))}$.[10]

It is worth noting that Theorem 6 also offers a method for recovering all regular preference relations motivating/rationalizing a choice c: first find all regular revealed preference-between-arguments relations of $RPTinRPA_c$, and then map each of these relations to a regular-strict (resp. regular-weak) preference relation motivating (resp. rationalizing) c by using functions $\mathcal{R}_{\delta(.)}$ and $\mathcal{R}_{\omega(\delta(.))}$, respectively. Finally, Theorem 7 below says that checking regular extrapolations in RPT can be seen as an instance of checking regular extrapolations in RPA.

Theorem 7. *For any option $x \in B$, $RPTinRPA_c \vdash_{reg} (arg_x = \textbf{acc} \mid AAF_B)$ iff $x \in maximal_R(B)$ for any regular-strict preference relation R that motivates c iff $x \in greatest_R(B)$ for any regular-weak preference relation R rationalizing c.*

7   Conclusions

As early as the beginning of twentieth century, neoclassical economists hypothesize that consumption choices are made so as to maximize utility. Given this hypothesis, it follows that each choice tells us something about the consumer. In other words, choices reveal preferences, and thereby provide information about an underlying utility function [29]. *Revealed Preference Theory* is formulated along this line, but further cuts the ties with human mental states by interpreting preference as merely a mathematical construct used to make sense of observed behaviours, rather than a real mental phenomenon. Hence in RPT, preference elicitation is not an investigation into the agent's mental state (presumably by listening what the agent says), but an analysis of the agent's actions (*It is not what she says but it is what she does that tells what she prefers*). As purchasing decision is just a species of human reasoning, we might wonder how RPT and behaviourism can be generalized with respect to various forms of reasoning developed in AI where mentalism dictates for now. In this paper we answer this question by developing a so-called *Revealed Preference Argumentation* (RPA) framework. We show that RPA lends itself to a complete computational framework for RPT-based consumer behaviour analyses. Given that RPT is one of the most seminal consumer theories till today, we believe that RPA paves the way for future applications of argumentation to behavioural economics - an area unexplored so far to the best of our knowledge. This paper, however, can be viewed as a continuation of our recent work on revealed preference [14], which shares the same general interest with [16,17,19,20] in reversing the standard reasoning flow of SPA to learn about the preference of a SPA framework from a set of accepted arguments or propositions. It is interesting to see how [16,17,19,20] can be extended for consumer's revealed preference.

---

[10] Recall that for an argument preference relation Q, $\mathcal{R}_Q \triangleq \{(x,y) \mid (arg_x, arg_y) \in Q\}$ denotes the corresponding preference relation over options.

Acknowledgment. Nguyen Duy Hung is supported by Center of Excellence in Intelligent Informatics, Speech and Language Technology and Service Innovation (CILS), and Intelligent Informatics and Service Innovation (IISI) Research Center of Sirindhorn International Institute of Technology; Van-Nam Huynh is supported by the US Office of Naval Research Global (ONRG, Grant No. N62909-19-1-2031).

References

1. Amgoud, L., Cayrol, C., Lagasquie-Schiex, M.C., Livet, P.: On bipolarity in argumentation frameworks. Int. J. Intell. Syst. **23**(10), 1062–1093 (2008)
2. Amgoud, L.: Postulates for logic-based argumentation systems. Int. J. Approximate Reason. **55**(9), 2028–2048 (2014). Weighted Logics for Artificial Intelligence
3. Amgoud, L., Cayrol, C.: A reasoning model based on the production of acceptable arguments. Ann. Math. AI **34**(1–3), 197–215 (2002)
4. Baroni, P., Cerutti, F., Giacomin, M., Guida, G.: Encompassing attacks to attacks in abstract argumentation frameworks. In: Sossai, C., Chemello, G. (eds.) ECSQARU 2009. LNCS (LNAI), vol. 5590, pp. 83–94. Springer, Heidelberg (2009). https://doi.org/10.1007/978-3-642-02906-6_9
5. Bench-Capon, T.: Persuasion in practical argument using value-based argumentation frameworks. J. Log. Comput. **13**(3), 429–448 (2003)
6. Bench-Capon, T., Atkinson, K.: Abstract argumentation and values. In: Simari, G., Rahwan, I. (eds.) Argumentation in Artificial Intelligence, pp. 45–64. Springer, Boston (2009). https://doi.org/10.1007/978-0-387-98197-0_3
7. Brewka, G., Woltran, S.: Abstract dialectical frameworks. In: Proceedings of KR 2010, pp. 102–111. AAAI Press (2010)
8. Caminada, M., Amgoud, L.: On the evaluation of argumentation formalisms. Artif. Intell. **171**(5–6), 286–310 (2007)
9. Dietrich, F., List, C.: Mentalism versus behaviourism in economics: a philosophy-of-science perspective. Econ. Philos. **32**(2), 249–281 (2016)
10. Dung, P.M.: On the acceptability of arguments and its fundamental role in non-monotonic reasoning, logic programming and n-person games. Artif. Intell. **77**(2), 321–357 (1995)
11. Dung, P.M.: An axiomatic analysis of structured argumentation with priorities. Artif. Intell. **231**, 107–150 (2016)
12. Dung, P.M., Thang, P.M.: Fundamental properties of attack relations in structured argumentation with priorities. Artif. Intell. **255**, 1–42 (2018)
13. Hanh, D.D., Dung, P.M., Hung, N.D., Thang, P.M.: Inductive defense for sceptical semantics of extended argumentation. J. Logic Comput. **21**(1), 307–349 (2010)
14. Hung, N.D., Huynh, V.-N.: Revealed preference in argumentation: algorithms and applications. Int. J. Approximate Reason. **131**, 214–251 (2021)
15. Kaci, S., van der Torre, L.: Preference-based argumentation: arguments supporting multiple values. Int. J. Approximate Reason. **48**(3), 730–751 (2008). Special Section on Choquet Integration in honor of Gustave Choquet (1915–2006) and Special Section on Nonmonotonic and Uncertain Reasoning
16. Kido, H., Liao, B.: A Bayesian approach to direct and inverse abstract argumentation problems. arXiv e-prints, page arXiv:1909.04319, September 2019
17. Kido, H., Okamoto, K.: A Bayesian approach to argument-based reasoning for attack estimation. In: Proceedings of the Twenty-Sixth International Joint Conference on Artificial Intelligence, IJCAI 2017, pp. 249–255 (2017)

18. Kim, T., Richter, M.K.: Nontransitive-nontotal consumer theory. J. Econ. Theory **38**(2), 324–363 (1986)
19. Mahesar, Q., Oren, N., Vasconcelos, W.W.: Computing preferences in abstract argumentation. In: Miller, T., Oren, N., Sakurai, Y., Noda, I., Savarimuthu, B.T.R., Cao Son, T. (eds.) PRIMA 2018. LNCS (LNAI), vol. 11224, pp. 387–402. Springer, Cham (2018). https://doi.org/10.1007/978-3-030-03098-8_24
20. Mahesar, Q., Oren, N., Vasconcelos, W.W.: Preference elicitation in assumption-based argumentation. In: Uchiya, T., Bai, Q., Maestre, I.M. (eds.) PRIMA 2020. LNCS, vol. 12568, pp. 199–214. Springer, Cham (2021). https://doi.org/10.1007/978-3-030-69322-0_13
21. Richter, M.K.: Preferences, utility, and demand, Chapter 2. In: Rational Choice. Harcourt Brace, Jovanovich (1971)
22. Modgil, S.: Reasoning about preferences in argumentation frameworks. Artif. Intell. **173**(9–10), 901–934 (2009)
23. Modgil, S., Prakken, H.: A general account of argumentation with preferences. Artif. Intell. **195**, 361–397 (2013)
24. Modgil, S., Prakken, H.: The aspic+ framework for structured argumentation: a tutorial. Argument Comput. **5**(1), 31–62 (2014)
25. Panda, S.C.: Rational choice with intransitive preferences. Stud. Microecon. **6**(1–2), 66–83 (2018)
26. Samuelson, P.A.: A note on the pure theory of consumer's behaviour. Economica **5**(17), 61–71 (1938)
27. Samuelson, P.A.: Consumption theory in terms of revealed preference. Economica **15**(60), 243–253 (1948)
28. Sen, A.: Behaviour and the concept of preference. Economica **40**(159), 241–259 (1973)
29. Smeulders, B., Crama, Y., Spieksma, F.C.R.: Revealed preference theory: an algorithmic outlook. Eur. J. Oper. Res. **272**(3), 803–815 (2019)
30. Thoma, J.: In defence of revealed preference theory. Econ. Philos. 1–25 (2020). https://doi.org/10.1017/S0266267120000073

Coordinating Multi-party Vehicle Routing with Location Congestion via Iterative Best Response

Waldy Joe(iD) and Hoong Chuin Lau$^{(\boxtimes)}$(iD)

School of Computing and Information Systems, Singapore Management University,
Singapore, Singapore
waldy.joe.2018@phdcs.smu.edu.sg, hclau@smu.edu.sg

Abstract. This work is motivated by a real-world problem of coordinating B2B pickup-delivery operations to shopping malls involving multiple non-collaborative Logistics Service Providers (LSPs) in a congested city where space is scarce. This problem can be categorized as a Vehicle Routing Problem with Pickup and Delivery, Time Windows and Location Congestion with multiple LSPs (or ML-VRPLC in short), and we propose a scalable, decentralized, coordinated planning approach via iterative best response. We formulate the problem as a strategic game where each LSP is a self-interested agent but is willing to participate in a coordinated planning as long as there are sufficient incentives. Through an iterative best response procedure, agents adjust their schedules until no further improvement can be obtained to the resulting joint schedule. We seek to find the best joint schedule which maximizes the minimum gain achieved by any one LSP, as LSPs are interested in how much benefit they can gain rather than achieving a system optimality. We compare our approach to a centralized planning approach and our experiment results show that our approach is more scalable and is able to achieve on average 10% more gain within an operationally realistic time limit.

Keywords: Vehicle routing problem · Multi-agent systems · Best response planning

1 Introduction

B2B pickup-delivery operations to and from commercial or retail locations involving multiple parties, commonly referred to as Logistics Service Providers (LSPs), more often than not cannot be done in silos. Resource constraints at these locations such as limited parking bays can cause congestion if each LSP adopts an uncoordinated, selfish planning. Thus, some form of coordination is

This research is supported by the National Research Foundation Singapore under its Corp Lab @ University scheme and Fujitsu Limited as part of the A*STAR-Fujitsu-SMU Urban Computing and Engineering Centre of Excellence.

A. Rosenfeld and N. Talmon (Eds.): EUMAS 2021, LNAI 12802, pp. 72–88, 2021.
https://doi.org/10.1007/978-3-030-82254-5_5

needed to deconflict the schedules of these LSPs to minimize congestion thereby maximizing logistics efficiency. This research is motivated by a real-world problem of improving logistics efficiency in shopping malls involving multiple independent LSPs making B2B pickups and deliveries to these locations in small, congested cities where space is scarce.

Collaborative planning for vehicle routing is an active area of research and had been shown to improve efficiency, service level and sustainability [9]. However, collaborative planning assumes that various LSPs are willing to collaborate with each other by forming coalitions, exchanging of information and/or sharing of resources to achieve a common objective. This is different from our problem setting where LSPs are independent entities who can only make decision locally in response to other LSPs' decisions and they do not interact directly with each other to collaborate or make joint decision.

Ideally if we have one single agent who can control the routes and schedules of multiple LSPs with complete information and collaboration amongst the LSPs, we may achieve some form of system optimality. However, an unintended outcome is that some LSPs may suffer more loss than if they adopt their own planning independently. Moreover, such centralized approach is not scalable and not meaningful in solving the real-world problems, since LSPs may not always be willing to collaborate with one another.

To address the above concern, this paper proposes a scalable, decentralized, coordinated planning approach via iterative best response. The underlying problem can be seen as a Vehicle Routing Problem with Pickup and Delivery, Time Windows and Location Congestion with multiple LSPs (or ML-VRPLC in short).

More precisely, we formulate the problem as a strategic game where each LSP is a self-interested agent willing to participate in a coordinated planning (without collaborating directly with other LSPs) as long as there are sufficient incentives. [1] coined the term "loosely-coupled" agent to describe an agent which exhibits such characteristics. Through an iterative best response procedure, multiple agents adjust their schedules until no further improvement can be obtained to the resulting joint schedule. We seek to find the best joint schedule which maximizes the minimum gain achieved by any one LSP, since LSPs are interested in how much benefit they can gain rather than achieving a system optimality. To realize such gains, we propose to use maximum cost deviation from an ideal solution (a solution that assumes no other LSPs exist to compete for the limited resources) as the performance measure. It is clear that the minimum gain is equivalent to the cost deviation of the worst performing LSP from this ideal solution.

This paper makes the following contributions:

- We define a new variant of VRP, ML-VRPLC and formulate the problem as an n-player strategic game.
- We propose a scalable, decentralized, coordinated planning approach based on iterative best response consisting of a metaheuristic as route optimizer with a scheduler based on Constraint Programming (CP) model to solve a large-scale ML-VRPLC.

– We show experimentally that our approach outperforms a centralized approach in solving large-scale problem within a operationally realistic time limit of 1 h.

2   Related Works

VRPLC is essentially a variant of a classical VRP with Pickup and Delivery, and Time Windows (VRPPDTW) but with cumulative resource constraint at each location [13]. Resources can be in the form of parking bays, cargo storage spaces or special equipment such as forklifts. In VRPLC, there are temporal dependencies between routes and schedules that do not exist in classical VRPs. In classical VRPs, arrival times of vehicles are merely used to ensure time window feasibility. In VRPLC, changes to the time schedule of one route may affect the time schedule of another routes in the form of wait time or time window violation. Many existing approaches to VRP do not take into consideration this relationship between routes and schedules.

[13] proposed a branch-and-price-and-check (BPC) approach to solve a single-LSP VRPLC. It is inspired by a branch-and-cut-and-price method for VRP-PDTW [20] and combines it with a constraint programming subproblem to check the VRPPDTW solutions against the resource constraints. However, BPC approach can only find feasible solutions for instances up to 150 pickup-delivery requests and proves optimality for up to 80 requests given a time limit of 2 h. Therefore, this approach is not scalable when applied directly to solve ML-VPRLC since pickup-delivery requests are usually in the region of hundreds per LSP and for our problem setting, solution is expected within a region of 1 h due to operational requirement. In addition, a direct application of BPC to ML-VRPLC assumes a fully centralized, collaborative planning approach which we have concluded earlier that it may not be practical and not meaningful.

ML-VRPLC can be considered as a problem belonging to an intersection between two main, well-studied research areas namely **Multi-Party VRP** and **Multi-Agent Planning** (MAP). Existing approaches to Multi-Party VRP and MAP can broadly be categorized based on the degrees of collaboration and cooperation respectively.

2.1   ML-VRPLC as a Multi-Party VRP

To solve VRPs involving multiple parties similar to ML-VRPLC, many existing works in the literature focus on collaborative planning approaches. [9] coined the term collaborative vehicle routing and it is a big area of research on its own. Collaborative vehicle routing can be classified into centralized and decentralized collaborative planning. The extent of collaboration ranges from forming of alliances or coalitions (for e.g. [6,11]) to sharing of resources such as sharing of vehicles or exchanging of requests through auction (for e.g. [7,23]). We have established earlier that existing works in this area are not directly applicable to our problem due to the non-collaborative nature of the LSPs.

2.2   ML-VRPLC as an MAP Problem

MAP is simply planning in an environment where there exist multiple agents with concurrent actions. Approaches to MAP can be further categorized into cooperative and non-cooperative domains although most MAP problems lie in between the two domains.

Cooperative Domain. Cooperative MAP involves agents that are not self-interested and are working together to form a joint plan for a common goal [22]. [1] introduced MA-STRIPS, a multi-agent planning model on which many cooperative MAP solvers are based on. [19] proposed a two-step approach consisting of centralized planner to produce local plan for each agent followed by solving a distributed constraint satisfaction problem to obtain a global plan. Meanwhile, [2] introduced the concept of planning games and propose two models namely coalition-planning games and auction-planning games. Those two models assume agents collaborate with each other through forming of coalitions or through an auction mechanism; similar to the approaches within the collaborative vehicle routing domain. In general, the approaches in this domain essentially assume cooperative agents working together to achieve a common goal.

Non-cooperative Domain. Planning in the context of multiple self-interested agents where agents do not fully cooperate or collaborate falls into the domain of non-cooperative game theory. MAP problem can be formulated as strategic game where agents interact with one another to increase their individual payoffs.

[15] proposed a sampled fictitious play algorithm as an optimization heuristic to solve large-scale optimization problems. Optimization problem can be formulated as a n-player game where every pure-strategy equilibrium of a game is a local optimum since no player can change its strategy to improve the objective function. Fictitious play is an iterative procedure in which at each step, players compute their best replies based on the assumption that other players' actions follow a probability distribution based on their past decisions [3]. This approach had been applied to various multi-agent optimization problems where resources are shared and limited such as dynamic traffic network routing [10], mobile units situation awareness problem [14], power management in sensor network [4] and multi-agent orienteering problem [5].

Meanwhile, [12] proposed a best-response planning method to scale up existing multi-agent planning algorithms. The authors used existing single-agent planning algorithm to compute best response of each agent to iteratively improve the initial solution derived from an MAP algorithm. It is scalable compared to applying the MAP algorithm directly to an MAP planning problem. However, the authors evaluated their proposed approach only on standard benchmark problems such as those found in the International Planning Competition (IPC) domains. On the other hand, [8] applied a similar best-response planning approach to a real-world power management problem.

2.3   ML-VRPLC as a Non-cooperative MAP Problem

Given that the LSPs in ML-VRPLC are considered as "loosely-coupled" agents, the approach to solve ML-VRPLC will be somewhere in between cooperative and non-cooperative domains of MAP, although it tends to lean more towards the non-cooperative domain since LSPs are still largely independent and self-interested. Our proposed approach includes certain elements that are discussed above such as non-cooperative game theory and best-response planning. Nevertheless, our work differs mainly from other existing works in that we apply techniques from other research fields (MAP and game theory) on a new variant of a well-studied optimization problem (VRP) with a real-world problem scale.

3   Problem Description

Multiple LSPs have to fulfill a list of pickup-delivery requests within a day. They have multiple vehicles which need to go to the pickup locations to load up the goods and deliver them to various commercial or retail locations such as warehouses and shopping malls. The vehicles need to return to their depot by a certain time and every request has a time window requirement. A wait time will be incurred if the vehicle arrives early and time violations if it serves the request late. In addition, every location has limited parking bays for loading and unloading, and a designated lunch hour break where no delivery is allowed. As such, further wait time and time window violations will be incurred if a vehicle arrives in a location where the parking bays are fully occupied or arrives during the designated lunch hour.

The objective of each LSP is to plan for a schedule that minimizes travel time, wait time and time window violations. Given that parking bays at every location are shared among the multiple LSPs, some sort of coordination is needed to deconflict their schedules to minimize congestion.

4   Model Formulation

4.1   ML-VRPLC as a Strategic Game

We formulate ML-VRPLC as an n-player game $\Gamma_{ML-VRPLC}$ with LSPs represented as players $i \in N$ having a finite set of strategies S_i and sharing the same payoff function i.e. $u^1(s) = ... = u^n(s) = u(s)$. $s \in S_1 \times .... \times S_n$ is a finite set since S_i is finite. Table 1 provides the set of notations and the corresponding descriptions used in the model.

Strategy. In this paper, we will use the terms 'strategy', 'solution' and 'schedule' interchangeably since a strategy of a player i.e. an LSP is represented in the form of a schedule. A schedule is a solution of a single-LSP VRPLC which consists of the routes (sequence of locations visited) of every vehicle and the corresponding time intervals (start and end service times) of every requests served by each vehicle. s_i is represented as the following tuple:

Table 1. Set of notations used in $\Gamma_{ML-VRPLC}$.

Notation	Description
N	A set of LSPs, $N \in \{1, 2, ..., n\}$
s_i	A schedule of LSP i, $i \in N, s_i \in S_i$
s	A joint schedule of all LSP, $s = (s_1, s_2, ..., s_n), s \in S$
s_{-i}	A joint schedule of all LSP except LSP i,
	$s_{-i} = (s_1, ..., s_{i-1}, s_{i+1}, ..., s_n)$
(s_i, s_{-i})	A joint schedule where LSP i follows a schedule s_i
	while the rest follows a joint schedule, s_{-i}
$u^i(s)$	Payoff of LSP i when all LSP follows a joint schedule, s
$B_i(s_{-i})$	Best response of LSP i when all other LSPs follow a joint
	schedule, s_{-i}

$$s_i = \langle s_i.routes, s_i.timeIntervals \rangle$$

Potential Function. We define a function, $P(s) = \sum_{i \in N} u^i(s)$ i.e. total weighted sum of travel times, wait times and time violations when all LSP follows a joint schedule s. In this paper, we define the payoff function, $u^i(s)$ as cost incurred (see Eq. (6) for the full definition). $P(s)$ is an *ordinal potential function* for $\Gamma_{ML-VRPLC}$ since for every $i \in N$ and for every $s_{-i} \in S_{-i}$

$$u^i(s_i, s_{-i}) - u^i(s'_i, s_{-i}) > 0 \text{ iff}$$
$$P(s_i, s_{-i}) - P(s'_i, s_{-i}) > 0 \text{ for every } s_i, s'_i \in S_i. \tag{1}$$

Proof.

$$P(s_i, s_{-i}) - P(s'_i, s_{-i}) > 0$$
$$\Rightarrow u^i(s_i, s_{-i}) + \sum_{j \in -i} u^j(s_{-i}) - \left(u^i(s'_i, s_{-i}) + \sum_{j \in -i} u^j(s_{-i}) \right) > 0$$
$$\Rightarrow u^i(s_i, s_{-i}) - u^i(s'_i, s_{-i}) > 0$$

Thus, $\Gamma_{ML-VRPLC}$ is a *finite ordinal potential game* and it possesses a pure-strategy equilibrium and has the Finite Improvement Property (FIP) [17]. Having the FIP means that every path generated by a best response procedure in $\Gamma_{ML-VRPLC}$ converges to an equilibrium. We are able to show conceptually and empirically that our approach converges into an equilibrium in the later sections.

Equilibrium and Local Optimality. $s' = (s'_i, s'_{-i})$ is an equilibrium if

$$u^i(s'_i, s'_{-i}) \leq u^i(s_i, s'_{-i}) \text{ for all } i \in N \text{ where } s_i \in B_i(s_{-i}). \tag{2}$$

An equilibrium of $\Gamma_{ML-VRPLC}$ is a local optimum since no player can improve its payoff/reduce its cost by changing its individual schedule. Conversely, every optimal solution, s^* of $\Gamma_{ML-VRPLC}$ is an equilibrium since $u^i(s^*) \leq u^i(s_i, s^*_{-i})$ for all $i \in N$ where $s_i \in B_i(s^*_{-i})$.

Objective Function. The objective of this problem is to minimize the maximum payoff deviation of any one LSP from an ideal solution.

$$min_{s \in S} f(s) \tag{3}$$

$$f(s) = max_{i \in N} Deviation_{LB}(s, i) \tag{4}$$

$$Deviation_{LB}(s, i) = \frac{u^i(s) - u^i(s^{ideal})}{u^i(s^{ideal})} \times 100\% \tag{5}$$

where s^{ideal} is defined as the joint schedule where all other LSPs do not exist to compete for parking bays. s^{ideal} is a Lower Bound (LB) solution since it is a solution of a relaxed $\Gamma_{ML-VRPLC}$. We are essentially trying to search for solutions where each LSP's payoff is as close as possible to its corresponding LB solution.

We do not define the objective function as $min_{s \in S} \sum_{i \in N} u^i(s)$ because in this game, the players are not concerned about the system optimality (total payoffs of all players) but rather on how much benefit it can obtain by adopting a coordinated planning instead of planning independently.

5   Solution Approach

The key idea of our proposed approach is to improve a chosen joint schedule iteratively by computing the best responses of each player assuming the rest of the players adopt the chosen joint schedule until no improvement can be obtained to the resulting joint schedule or until a given time limit or maximum number of iterations has been reached. Our approach is decentralized in nature because each LSP is an independent agent which can compute its own route and schedule i.e. a central agent does not dictate how each player determine their decisions.

Given that we have established that our problem is a *potential game* and has an FIP, our approach will converge to an equilibrium which has been shown earlier to be equivalent to a local optimal solution. Therefore, our approach seeks to explore multiple local optimal solutions until the terminating conditions are met and returns the best one found so far.

5.1   Iterative Best Response Algorithm

Algorithm 1 describes how the iterative best response algorithm works. At each iteration (lines 3–22), a joint schedule is chosen from a sampling pool of previously obtained improved joint schedules or from the current best joint schedule (line 7). We implement an epsilon greedy sampling policy to allow for exploration

---

Algorithm 1: Iterative Best Response Algorithm to solve ML-VRPLC

Input : Initial joint schedule $s^{initial}$, maximum iteration K, time limit T

Output: Best found joint schedule s^{best}

1   $s^{best} := s^{initial}$, $f_{min} := f(s^{initial})$, $k = 0$

2   Create a sampling pool of joint schedules, $\mathbf{H} = \{s^{initial}\}$

3   **while** $k < K$ and $runTime < T$ and $\mathbf{H} \neq \{\emptyset\}$ **do**

4   **if** $k = 0$ **then**

5 | $s^k := s^{initial}$

6   **else**

7 | With probability ε, $s^k \sim U(\mathbf{H})$ otherwise $s^k := s^{best}$

8   **end**

9   Remove s^k from $\mathbf{H}$

10   Find new joint schedules $\{s^{k,1}, s^{k,2}, ..., s^{k,n}\}$ where
       $s^{k,i} = (s_i^k, s_{-i}^k), u^i(s^{k,i}) < u^i(s^k)$ and $s_i^k \in B_i(s_{-i}^k)$

11   **if** $u^i(s^k) \leq u^i(s^{k,i})$ *for all* $i \in N$ **then**

12 | $k{+}=1$

13 | **continue**

14   **end**

15   **if** $min_{i \in N} f(s^{k,i}) \leq f_{min}$ **then**

16 | $s^{best} := s^{k,i^*}$, $f_{min} := f(s^{k,i^*})$

17 | put $\{s^{k,i}\}_{i \in N \setminus \{i^*\}}$ in $\mathbf{H}$

18   **else**

19 | put $\{s^{k,i}\}_{i \in N}$ in $\mathbf{H}$

20   **end**

21    $k{+}=1$

22 **end**

23 **return** s^{best}

---

of multiple improvements paths (see Fig. 1 for an example of an improvement path) to search for best joint schedule. An improvement step consisting of $n - 1$ best response computations is applied to the chosen joint schedule to obtain new improved joint schedules (line 10). If no further improvement can be made to the sampled joint schedule, we proceed to the next iteration (lines 11–13). We update the current best joint schedule if any of the new joint schedules has a lower $f(s)$ value than f_{min} (lines 15–16). Otherwise, we place the new improved joint schedules into the sampling pool for further improvement steps in the subsequent iterations (lines 17,19). We repeat the process until termination conditions are met. Then, we return the current best joint schedule as the final output.

Initial Solution, Lower Bound and Upper Bound Solutions. The initial joint schedule can be initialized to any random, feasible joint schedule. However, in this paper, we use the uncoordinated joint schedule as the initial solution to be improved by iterative best response algorithm. To compute the initial joint schedule, $s^{initial}$, we first compute the best schedules for each LSP independently assuming no other LSPs exist to compete for the limited resources. This is akin to solving a single-LSP VRPLC. The resulting joint schedule is in fact s^{ideal} and is the LB solution to $\Gamma_{ML-VRPLC}$. Next, a scheduler consisting of a CP model that incorporates the resource capacity constraint at each location is solved for the combined routes of s^{ideal}. This forms an uncoordinated joint schedule, $s^{uncoord}$ which serves as an Upper Bound (UB) solution to $\Gamma_{ML-VRPLC}$ as any coordinated planning approaches should result in solutions that are better than an uncoordinated one. We use the LB and UB solutions in the experiments to evaluate the solution quality of our proposed approach.

Finite Improvement Paths and Convergence. Each improved joint schedule can be represented as a node in a directed tree. A series of nodes with parent-child relationship forms an improvement path as shown in Fig. 1 where $P(s^{k,i}) < P(s^{k-1,i'})$ for all $k \geq 1$ and $i, i' \in N$. Every improvement path is finite since S is a finite set. Every finite improvement path will converge to an equilibrium and every terminal point is a local optimum. However, since the best response is computed heuristically and there is no way to prove optimality, the resulting equilibrium is just an approximate. Nevertheless, we can show empirically in our experiments that our approach will converge to an approximated equilibrium solution after a certain number of iterations.

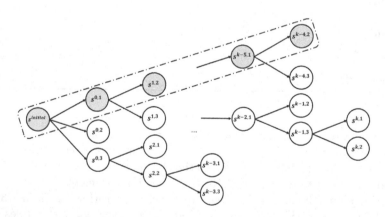

Fig. 1. One example of an improvement path assuming $n = 3$.

In short, our approach explore multiple improvement paths to search for joint schedule that return the best objective value, $f(s)$ with the lowest total payoffs, $P(s)$ as a secondary objective.

5.2   Best Response Computation

At every iteration, best response to a chosen joint schedule, s^k is computed for each LSP (line 10 of Algorithm 1). The best response computation of single LSP is equivalent to solving a single-LSP VRPLC where the resource constraint is determined by the resource utilization of each location by all other LSPs based on s_{-i}^k. Table 2 shows the notations used in this single-LSP VRPLC model.

Table 2. Set of notations used in the single-LSP VRPLC model.

Notation	Description
V	A set of vehicles
R	A set of all requests
M	A set of all locations
R_v	A set of requests served by vehicle v
O_m	A set of requests at location $m \in M$
$C_{m,t}$	Resource capacity at location m at time t
$e_{r,v}$	Lower time window of request r served by vehicle v
$l_{r,v}$	Upper time window of request r served by vehicle v
$prev(r)$	Previous request served prior to request r, $prev(r), r \in R_v$
$d_{x,y}$	Travel time from location of request x to location of request y
$timeInterval_{r,v}$	Time interval when request r in vehicle v is being served, consisting of start and end time
$T_0, coolingRate$	Parameters for acceptance criteria in Simulated Annealing

We propose a heuristic consisting of Adaptive Large Neighbourhood Search (ALNS) as route optimizer and a scheduler based on a CP model to solve this single-LSP VRPLC. Heuristic is proposed as it is more scalable for a real-world problem setting. ALNS is used to search for better routes and the CP model based on the resulting routes is then solved to produce a schedule that meets the resource and time-related constraints. ALNS is chosen because it is probably the most effective metaheuristic for the VRPPDTW [16] and ALNS is widely used to solve large-scale problem [24]. Algorithm 2 details the proposed best response computation consisting of ALNS and CP model.

The ALNS algorithm implemented in this paper is adapted from the vanilla version of ALNS proposed by [21] with differences in the choices of the remove and insert operators and parameters used. However, the key difference in our ALNS implementation lies in line 7 of Algorithm 2. To compute the time intervals and the corresponding payoff of the updated solution, a CP model is solved. The payoff is computed as follow:

$$u^i(s_i) = w_1 \times totalTravelTime(s_i.routes)$$
$$+ minimize \sum_{v \in V} \left\{ w_2 \times \sum_{r \in R_v} waitTime_{r,v} + w_3 \times \sum_{r \in R_v} timeViolation_{r,v} \right\} \quad (6)$$

Algorithm 2: Best Response Computation

Input   : Chosen solution s^k, initial temperature $\overline{T_0}$, *coolingRate*
Output: $B_i(s^k_{-i})$

1 $s^{best}_i := s^k_i, s_i := s^{input}_i, \overline{T} = \overline{T_0}$
2 **while** *termination criteria are not met* **do**
3 $\quad$ $s'_i := s_i$
4 $\quad$ Select removal and insert operators via roulette wheel mechanism
5 $\quad$ Apply the selected removal operator to remove the requests from $s'_i.routes$
6 $\quad$ Apply the selected insert operator to insert the orders into $s'_i.routes$
7 $\quad$ Calculate the cost/payoff, $u^i(s'_i, s^k_{-i})$ and update $s'_i.timeIntervals$
8 $\quad$ **if** $u^i(s'_i, s^k_{-i}) < u^i(s^{best}_i, s^k_{-i})$ **then**
9 $\quad\quad$ $s^{best}_i := s'_i, s_i := s'_i$
10 $\quad$ **else**
11 $\quad\quad$ **if** $u^i(s'_i, s^k_{-i}) < u^i(s_i, s^k_{-i})$ **then**
12 $\quad\quad\quad$ $s_i := s'_i$
13 $\quad\quad$ **else**
14 $\quad\quad\quad$ $s_i := s'_i$ with probability, $\min\{1, e^{(u^i(s_i, s^k_{-i})-u(s'_i, s^k_{-i}))/\overline{T}}\}$
15 $\quad\quad$ **end**
16 $\quad$ **end**
17 $\quad$ Update the weights and scores of the operators accordingly
18 $\quad$ $\overline{T} := \overline{T} * coolingRate$
19 **end**
20 $B_i(s^k_{-i}) := s^{best}_i$
21 **return** $B_i(s^k_{-i})$

---

where

$$w_1, w_2, w_3 \text{are predetermined set of weights,}$$
$$waitTime_{r,v} = min\{0, (start(timeInterval_{r,v})$$
$$- end(timeInterval_{prev(r),v}) - d_{prev(r),r})\},$$
$$timeViolation_{r,v} = min\{0, (end(timeInterval_{r,v}) - l_{r,v})\},$$
$$s_i.timeIntervals = \{timeInterval_{r,v}\}_{r \in R_v, v \in V}$$

The second term of Eq. (6) is the objective function of the CP model with $\{timeInterval_{r,v}\}_{r \in R_v, v \in V}$ as the primary decision variables of the model. The key constraints of the CP model are as follow:

$$CUMULATIVE(\{timeInterval_{r,v} : v \in V, \\ r \in R_v \cap O_m\}, 1, C_{m,t}), \forall m \in M \tag{7}$$

$$noOverlap(\{timeInterval_{r,v} : r \in R_v\}), \forall v \in V \tag{8}$$

$$start(timeInterval_{r,v}) \geq end(timeInterval_{prev(r),v}) \\ + d_{prev(r),r}, \forall r \in R_v, v \in V \tag{9}$$

$$start(timeInterval_{r,v}) \geq e_{r,v}, \forall r \in R_v, v \in V \tag{10}$$

Constraint (7) is used to model the resource capacity constraint at each location at a given time t where $start(timeInterval_{r,v}) \leq t \leq end(timeInterval_{r,v})$ and

$C_{m,t}$ is determined by the resource utilization of all other LSPs based on s^k_{-i}. Constraint (8) ensures that the time intervals of requests within a route do not overlap. Constraints (9) and (10) ensure that the start time of a request must at least be later than the end time of the previous request plus the corresponding travel time and it should not start before its lower time window. Other constraints relating to operational requirements such as no delivery within lunch hours, operating hours of the locations and vehicles are omitted to simplify the discussion as it is fairly straightforward to incorporate these constraints.

Scalability and Flexibility. Our approach is scalable because the best response computations for every LSP can be done in parallel since they are independent of each other. Our approach is also flexible as it also allows any other forms of solution approach to single-LSP VRPLC to be used to compute the best response.

6 Experiments

The objective of the experiment is twofold. Firstly, we would like to empirically verify whether our approach converges to an equilibrium for our problem setting and secondly, to evaluate the solution quality produced by our decentralized approach against a centralized approach with respect to s^{ideal} (LB) and $s^{uncoord}$ (UB). Intuitively, our approach should return solutions with lower payoff/cost than UB solution and within a reasonable deviation from LB solution.

6.1 Experimental Setup

We synthetically generate 30 test instances to simulate a month's worth of pickup-delivery requests for 20 LSPs. These instances are generated based on existing datasets of our trials with several local LSPs. Each test instances consists of 100 requests per LSP and each LSP has 10 vehicles. To simulate congestion at the delivery locations, we narrow down the delivery locations to 15 unique shopping malls with maximum capacity of 4 parking bays per location. Our approach is implemented with K set at 300 with $T = 60$ min.

The solution approach is implemented in Java while CP Optimizer ver. 12.8 is used to solve the CP model. The experiments are run on a server with the following configurations: CentOS 8 with 24 CPU Cores and 32 GB RAM.

Benchmark Algorithm. We chose a centralized, non-collaborative planning approach as a benchmark algorithm. It is centralized since all LSPs are treated as one single LSP and the central agent makes the routing and scheduling decision on behalf of the LSPs. It is non-collaborative as no exchange of requests or sharing of vehicles are allowed i.e. each vehicle can only serve requests from the LSP they belong to. We use a heuristic approach combining ALNS and CP

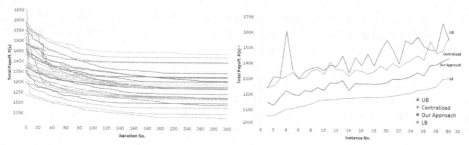

(a) The total payoffs converge for all 30 test instances. Each coloured line represents the result of one test instance.

(b) Our proposed approach outperforms the centralized approach and its solutions are well within the LB and UB solutions.

Fig. 2. Convergence plot and total payoffs across 30 test instances.

model similar to the one used to compute best response to solve this single-LSP VRPLC. The initial solution is constructed via randomized Clarke-Wright Savings Heuristics adapted from [18]. The algorithm is run for 1 h and 2 h for each test instance.

Performance Measures. On top of $f(s)$, we introduce other performance measures to evaluate the two approaches. The other performance measures introduced are as follow:

Maximum Payoff Deviation from an Uncoordinated Solution. $f'(s)$ measures the payoff deviation of the worst performing LSP from the payoff if it follows a schedule based on an uncoordinated planning. A negative deviation value indicates reduction in cost and the lower the value, the higher the improvement gained from the UB solution.

$$f'(s) = max_{i \in N} Deviation_{UB}(s, i) \tag{11}$$

$$Deviation_{UB}(s, i) = \frac{u^i(s) - u^i(s^{uncoor})}{u^i(s^{uncoor})} \times 100\% \tag{12}$$

Average Payoff Deviation from an Ideal Solution. The lower the value, the closer the solution is to the LB solution.

$$g(s) = \frac{1}{n} \times \sum_{i \in N} Deviation_{LB}(s, i) \tag{13}$$

Average Payoff Deviation from an Uncoordinated Solution. Similar to Eq. (11), a negative deviation value indicates reduction in cost.

$$g'(s) = \frac{1}{n} \times \sum_{i \in N} Deviation_{UB}(s, i) \tag{14}$$

6.2 Experimental Results

Convergence. Figure 2a shows that the total payoffs of all players converged after 200 iterations on average for all test instances. This supports our earlier deduction that $\Gamma_{ML-VRPLC}$ possesses an FIP and our proposed algorithm explores multiple improvement path that will converge to an approximated equilibrium. Meanwhile, the average run-time for 200 iterations is around 1 h.

Our Approach vs. Centralized. As shown in Fig. 2b, we intentionally present the results as a line chart and sort the test instances based on increasing total payoff of the ideal solution to better illustrate that our approach returns solutions whose total payoffs are lower than the centralized approach and are well within the UB and LB solutions in all 30 test instances.

Table 3 shows that our approach outperforms the centralized approach on every performance measure even when the run-time for the centralized approach is increased to 2 h. We include results in terms of average and percentiles for a more extensive comparison. In terms of the performance of the worst LSP, our approach is able to ensure that on average, the payoff of the worst performing LSP is still within about 20.7% from the LB solution and at least gain about 2.6% improvement over uncoordinated solution. Meanwhile, even with doubling of the run-time, the centralized approach can only manage to ensure that the payoff of the worst performing LSP is within 31.6% from the LB solution while incurring a 12.9% additional cost as compared to an uncoordinated planning.

On average, across all LSPs, our approach return solutions that are well within 8.3% deviation from the LB solution and improve the payoff of the LSPs by an average of 11.2% from an uncoordinated planning approach. This is contrasted with the centralized approach which can only manage to return solutions that are within 14.4% of LB solution on average and an improvement of about 6.1% from the UB solution even when the run-time is doubled.

We observe that the worst performing LSP in centralized approach consistently returns f' values that are positive (see Table 3) which indicates that the solution for the worst performing LSP is even worse than that of an uncoordinated planning approach. This is because the centralized approach only concerns about the system optimality and not on the performance of each individual LSP. This reiterates our point that a centralized approach may result in some LSPs performing worse than if they are to plan independently.

Experiment Discussion. The experiments show that our proposed decentralized approach outperforms a centralized approach given the available run-time limit of 1 h in all 30 test instances and in all 4 performance measures. Furthermore, we also found that the centralized approach is computationally more expensive and therefore not as scalable as our decentralized approach as it needs longer run-time (>2 h) to return solutions that are at least comparable to our

Table 3. Our approach outperforms the centralized approach on every performance measures across 30 test instances.

Performance measure		Our approach	Centralized (1 h)	Centralized (2 h)
Max payoff	Q1	16.7%	26.3%	24.0%
Deviation from LB	Q2	21.1%	30.7%	27.5%
$f(s)$	Q3	24.0%	36.5%	32.7%
	Avg	**20.7%**	**34.2%**	**31.6%**
Max payoff	Q1	−3.0%	9.9%	6.8%
Deviation from UB	Q2	−1.9%	13.4%	10.1%
$f'(s)$	Q3	−1.1%	16.4%	15.4%
	Avg	**−2.6%**	**12.9%**	**12.9%**
Avg payoff	Q1	5.1%	12.4%	10.3%
Deviation from LB	Q2	8.1%	16.9%	14.2%
$g(s)$	Q3	11.6%	21.5%	18.3%
	Avg	**8.3%**	**16.9%**	**14.4%**
Avg payoff	Q1	−12.4%	−7.1%	−9.5%
Deviation from UB	Q2	−9.1%	1.9%	4.0%
$g'(s)$	Q3	−6.3%	2.9%	0.5%
	Avg	**−11.2%**	**−4.1%**	**−6.1%**

approach. To verify the lack of scalability of the centralized approach, we run another set of experiments with 5 LSPs and find that it indeed performs well with smaller scale problems. Overall, even though there will be LSPs who gain more and others who will gain less, based on our experiments, our approach ensures that there are enough incentives for LSPs to adopt this coordinated planning as compared to them performing their own selfish, independent planning.

7 Conclusion and Future Works

The key idea proposed in this paper is a scalable, decentralized, coordinated planning approach that can be tailored to large-scale optimization problems involving multiple "loosely coupled" entities competing for shared resources. Our proposed iterative best response algorithm decomposes a multi-agent problem into multiple single-agent problems allowing existing single-agent planning algorithms to be applied to a smaller problem.

Even though we assume that the best response algorithms and the payoff functions of each LSP (or agent) are identical, our approach can be extended to problems where each LSP adopts different best response algorithm and payoff function. The best response computation algorithm is akin to a black-box which can be replaced with any solution algorithm to solve single-LSP VRPLC (or single-agent version of the problem). Moreover, even with non-identical payoff functions, the inequality condition in Eq. (1) will still be valid and therefore our approach will still converge to an approximated equilibrium.

One key limitation of our approach is that we assume the environment is static which may not be the case in real-world setting. We assume that every LSP in the system is cooperative in the sense that it participates and adheres to the coordinated planning without any possibility of plan deviation such as dropping out of the system or making changes to their pickup-delivery requests. It is interesting to investigate and enhance our approach to take into consideration uncertainty in the environment and evaluate its robustness in a dynamic environment, as well as to extend it to domains beyond logistics.

Another interesting direction for future work will be to go beyond the empirical study that we did in this paper by further defining and analyzing the theoretical bounds of our approach to n-player game $\Gamma_{ML-VRPLC}$ in terms of the classical notions of Price of Stability (PoS) and Price of Anarchy (PoA).

References

1. Brafman, R.I., Domshlak, C.: From one to many: planning for loosely coupled multi-agent systems. In: Proceedings of the Eighteenth International Conference on International Conference on Automated Planning and Scheduling, pp. 28–35 (2008)
2. Brafman, R.I., Domshlak, C., Engel, Y., Tennenholtz, M.: Planning games. In: IJCAI, pp. 73–78. Citeseer (2009)
3. Brown, G.W.: Iterative solution of games by fictitious play. Activity Anal. Prod. Alloc. **13**(1), 374–376 (1951)
4. Campos-Nañez, E., Garcia, A., Li, C.: A game-theoretic approach to efficient power management in sensor networks. Oper. Res. **56**(3), 552–561 (2008)
5. Chen, C., Cheng, S.F., Lau, H.C.: Multi-agent orienteering problem with time-dependent capacity constraints. Web Intell. Agent Syst. Int. J. **12**(4), 347–358 (2014)
6. Cuervo, D.P., Vanovermeire, C., Sörensen, K.: Determining collaborative profits in coalitions formed by two partners with varying characteristics. Transp. Res. Part C: Emerg. Technol. **70**, 171–184 (2016)
7. Dai, B., Chen, H.: A multi-agent and auction-based framework and approach for carrier collaboration. Logist. Res. **3**(2–3), 101–120 (2011). https://doi.org/10.1007/s12159-011-0046-9
8. De Nijs, F., Spaan, M.T., de Weerdt, M.M.: Best-response planning of thermostatically controlled loads under power constraints. In: Twenty-Ninth AAAI Conference on Artificial Intelligence (2015)
9. Gansterer, M., Hartl, R.F.: Collaborative vehicle routing: a survey. Eur. J. Oper. Res. **268**(1), 1–12 (2018)
10. Garcia, A., Reaume, D., Smith, R.L.: Fictitious play for finding system optimal routings in dynamic traffic networks. Transp. Res. Part B: Methodol. **34**(2), 147–156 (2000)
11. Guajardo, M., Rönnqvist, M., Flisberg, P., Frisk, M.: Collaborative transportation with overlapping coalitions. Eur. J. Oper. Res. **271**(1), 238–249 (2018)
12. Jonsson, A., Rovatsos, M.: Scaling up multiagent planning: a best-response approach. In: Twenty-First International Conference on Automated Planning and Scheduling (2011)

13. Lam, E., Hentenryck, P.V.: A branch-and-price-and-check model for the vehicle routing problem with location congestion. Constraints **21**(3), 394–412 (2016). https://doi.org/10.1007/s10601-016-9241-2
14. Lambert, T.J., Wang, H.: Fictitious play approach to a mobile unit situation awareness problem. Technical report, Univ. Michigan (2003)
15. Lambert Iii, T.J., Epelman, M.A., Smith, R.L.: A fictitious play approach to large-scale optimization. Oper. Res. **53**(3), 477–489 (2005)
16. Li, Y., Chen, H., Prins, C.: Adaptive large neighborhood search for the pickup and delivery problem with time windows, profits, and reserved requests. Eur. J. Oper. Res. **252**(1), 27–38 (2016)
17. Monderer, D., Shapley, L.S.: Potential games. Games Econ. Behav. **14**(1), 124–143 (1996)
18. Nazari, M., Oroojlooy, A., Takáč, M., Snyder, L.V.: Reinforcement learning for solving the vehicle routing problem. In: Proceedings of the 32nd International Conference on Neural Information Processing Systems, pp. 9861–9871 (2018)
19. Nissim, R., Brafman, R.I., Domshlak, C.: A general, fully distributed multi-agent planning algorithm. In: Proceedings of the 9th International Conference on Autonomous Agents and Multiagent Systems, vol. 1, pp. 1323–1330 (2010)
20. Ropke, S., Cordeau, J.F.: Branch and cut and price for the pickup and delivery problem with time windows. Transp. Sci. **43**(3), 267–286 (2009)
21. Ropke, S., Pisinger, D.: An adaptive large neighborhood search heuristic for the pickup and delivery problem with time windows. Transp. Sci. **40**(4), 455–472 (2006)
22. Torreño, A., Onaindia, E., Komenda, A., Štolba, M.: Cooperative multi-agent planning: a survey. ACM Comput. Surv. (CSUR) **50**(6), 1–32 (2017)
23. Wang, X., Kopfer, H.: Collaborative transportation planning of less-than-truckload freight. OR Spectr. **36**(2), 357–380 (2013). https://doi.org/10.1007/s00291-013-0331-x
24. Wang, Y., Lei, L., Zhang, D., Lee, L.H.: Towards delivery-as-a-service: effective neighborhood search strategies for integrated delivery optimization of e-commerce and static O2O parcels. Transp. Res. Part B: Methodol. **139**, 38–63 (2020)

Explaining Ridesharing: Selection of Explanations for Increasing User Satisfaction

David Zar$^{(\boxtimes)}$, Noam Hazon, and Amos Azaria

Computer Science Department, Ariel University, Ariel, Israel
{david.zar,noamh,amos.azaria}@ariel.ac.il

Abstract. Transportation services play a crucial part in the development of modern smart cities. In particular, on-demand ridesharing services, which group together passengers with similar itineraries, are already operating in several metropolitan areas. These services can be of significant social and environmental benefit, by reducing travel costs, road congestion and CO_2 emissions.

Unfortunately, despite their advantages, not many people opt to use these ridesharing services. We believe that increasing the user satisfaction from the service will cause more people to utilize it, which, in turn, will improve the quality of the service, such as the waiting time, cost, travel time, and service availability. One possible way for increasing user satisfaction is by providing appropriate explanations comparing the alternative modes of transportation, such as a private taxi ride and public transportation. For example, a passenger may be more satisfied from a shared-ride if she is told that a private taxi ride would have cost her 50% more. Therefore, the problem is to develop an agent that provides explanations that will increase the user satisfaction.

We model our environment as a signaling game and show that a rational agent, which follows the perfect Bayesian equilibrium, must reveal all of the information regarding the possible alternatives to the passenger. In addition, we develop a machine learning based agent that, when given a shared-ride along with its possible alternatives, selects the explanations that are most likely to increase user satisfaction. Using feedback from humans we show that our machine learning based agent outperforms the rational agent and an agent that randomly chooses explanations, in terms of user satisfaction.

1 Introduction

More than 55% of the world's population are currently living in urban areas, a proportion that is expected to increase up to 68% by 2050 [36]. Sustainable urbanization is a key to successful future development of our society. A key inherent goal of sustainable urbanization is an efficient usage of transportation resources in order to reduce travel costs, avoid congestion, and reduce greenhouse gas emissions.

© Springer Nature Switzerland AG 2021
A. Rosenfeld and N. Talmon (Eds.): EUMAS 2021, LNAI 12802, pp. 89–107, 2021.
https://doi.org/10.1007/978-3-030-82254-5_6

While traditional services—including buses and taxis—are well established, large potential lies in shared but flexible urban transportation. On-demand ridesharing, where the driver is not a passenger with a specific destination, appears to gain popularity in recent years, and big ride-hailing services such as Uber and Lyft are already offering such services. However, despite the popularity of Uber and Lyft [35], their ridesharing services, which group together multiple passengers (Uber-Pool and Lyft-Line), suffer of low usage [15, 28].

In this paper we propose to increase the user satisfaction from a given shared-ride, in order to encourage her to use the service more often. That is, we attempt to use a form of persuasive technology [22], not in order to convince users to take a shared ride, but to make them feel better with the choice they have already made, and thus improve their attitude towards ride-sharing. It is well-known that one of the most influencing factors for driving people to utilize a specific service is to increase their satisfaction form the service (see for example, [46]). Moreover, if people will be satisfied and use the service more often it will improve the quality of the service, such as the waiting time, cost, travel time, and service availability, which in turn further increase the user satisfaction.

One possible way for increasing user satisfaction is by providing appropriate explanations [13], during the shared ride or immediately after the passenger has completed it. Indeed, in recent years there is a growing body of literature that deals with explaining decisions made by AI systems [24, 27]. In our ridesharing scenario, a typical approach would attempt to explain the entire assignment of all passengers to all vehicles. Clearly, a passenger is not likely to be interested in such an explanation, since she is not interested in the assignment of other passengers to other vehicles. A passenger is likely to only be interested with her own current shared-ride when compared to other alternative modes of transportation, such as a private taxi ride or public transportation.

Comparing the shared-ride to other modes of transportation may provide many different possible explanations. For example, consider a shared-ride that takes 20 min and costs $10. The passenger could have taken a private taxi that would have cost $20. Alternatively, the passenger could have used public transportation, and such a ride would have taken 30 min. A passenger is not likely to be aware of the exact costs and riding times of the other alternatives, but she may have some estimations. The agent, on the other hand, has access to many sources of information, and it can thus provide the exact values as explanations. Clearly, the agent is not allowed to provide false information. The challenge is to design an agent that provides the appropriate explanation in any given scenario.

We first model our environment as a signaling game [47], which models the decision of a rational agent whether to provide the exact price (i.e., the cost or the travel time) of a possible alternative mode of transportation, or not. In this game there are three players: nature, the agent and the passenger. Nature begins by randomly choosing a price from a given distribution; this distribution is known both to the agent and the passenger. The agent observes the price and decides whether to disclose this price to the passenger or not. The passenger then determines her current expectation over the price of the alternative. The goal of the agent is to increase the passenger satisfaction, and thus it would like the passenger to believe that the price of the alternative is higher than the price of the shared-ride as much as possible. We use the standard solution concept of Perfect Bayesian Equilibrium (PBE) [23] and show that a rational agent must reveal all of the information regarding the price of the possible alternative to the passenger.

Interacting with humans and satisfying their expectations is a very complex task. Research into humans' behavior has found that people often deviate from what is thought to be the rational behavior, since they are affected by a variety of (sometimes conflicting) factors: a lack of knowledge of one's own preferences, framing effects, the interplay between emotion and cognition, future discounting, anchoring and many other effects [5,14,33,49]. Therefore, algorithmic approaches that use a pure theoretically analytic objective often perform poorly with real humans [6,37,43]. We thus develop an Automatic eXplainer for Increasing Satisfaction (AXIS) agent, that when given a shared-ride along with its possible alternatives selects the explanations that are most likely to increase user satisfaction.

For example, consider again the setting in which a shared-ride takes 20 min and costs $10. The passenger could have taken a private taxi that would have taken 15 min, but would have cost $20. Alternatively, the passenger could have used public transportation. Such a ride would have taken 30 min, but would have cost only $5. A *human* passenger may be more satisfied from the shared-ride if she is told that a private taxi would have cost her 100% more. Another reasonable explanation is that a public transportation would have taken her 10 min longer. It may be even better to provide both explanations. However, providing an explanation that public transportation would have cost 50% less than the shared-ride is less likely to increase her satisfaction. Indeed, finding the most appropriate explanation depends on the specific parameters of the scenario. For example, if public transportation still costs $5 but the shared ride costs only $6, providing an explanation that public transportation would have cost only $1 less than the shared-ride may now become an appropriate explanation.

For developing the AXIS agent we utilize the following approach. We collect data from human subjects on which explanations they believe are most suitable for different scenarios. AXIS then uses a neural network to generalize this data in order to provide appropriate explanations for any given scenario. Using feedback from humans we show that AXIS outperforms the PBE agent and an agent that randomly chooses explanations. That is, human subjects that were faced with shared-ride scenarios, were more satisfied from the ride given the explanations selected by AXIS, than by the same ride when shown all explanations and when the explanations were randomly selected.

The contributions of this paper are threefold:

- The paper introduces the problem of automatic selection of explanations in the ridesharing domain, for increasing user satisfaction. The set of explanations consists of alternative modes of transportation.

- We model the explanation selection problem as a signaling game and determine the unique set of Perfect Bayesian Equilibria (PBE).
- We develop the AXIS agent, which learns from how people choose appropriate explanations, and show that it outperforms the PBE agent an agent that randomly chooses explanations, in terms of user satisfaction.

2   Related Work

Most work on ridesharing has focused on the assignment of passengers to vehicles. See the comprehensive surveys by Parragh et al. [40, 41], and a recent survey by Psaraftis et al. [44]. In particular, the dial-a-ride problem (DARP) is traditionally distinguished from other problems of ridesharing since transportation cost and user inconvenience must be weighed against each other in order to provide an appropriate solution [18]. Therefore, the DARP typically includes more quality constraints that aim at capturing the user's inconvenience. We refer to a recent survey on DARP by Molenbruch et al. [34], which also makes this distinction. In recent years there is an increasing body of works that concentrate on the passenger's satisfaction during the assignment of passengers to vehicles [30, 32, 45]. Similar to these works we are interested in the satisfaction of the passenger, but instead of developing assignment algorithms (e.g., [10]), we emphasize the importance of explanations of a given assignment.

A domain closely related to ridesharing is car-pooling. In this domain, ordinary drivers, may opt to take an additional passenger on their way to a shared destination. The common setting of car-pooling is within a long-term commitment between people to travel together for a particular purpose, where ridesharing is focused on single, non-recurring trips. Indeed, several works investigated car-pooling that can be established on a short-notice, and they refer to this problem as ridesharing [2]. In this paper we focus on ridesharing since it seems that our explanations regarding the alternative modes of transportation are more suitable for this domain (even though they might be also helpful for car-pooling).

In our work we build an agent that attempts to influence the attitude of the user towards ridesharing. Our agent is thus a form of persuasive technology [38]. Persuasion of humans by computers or technology has raised great interest in the literature. In his book [22], Fogg surveyed many technologies to be successful. One example of such a persuasion technology (pg. 50) is bicycle connected to a TV; as one pedals at a higher rate, the image on the TV becomes clearer, encouraging humans to exercise at higher rates. Another example is the Banana-Rama slot machine, which has characters that celebrate every time the gambler wins. Overall, Fogg describes 40 persuasive strategies. Other social scientists proposed various classes of persuasive strategies: Kellermann and Tim provided over 100 groups [26], and Cialdini proposed six principles of influence [17]. More specifically, Anagnostopoulou et al. [4] survey persuasive technologies for sustainable mobility, some of which consider ridesharing. The methods mentioned by Anagnostopoulou et al. include several persuasive strategies such as self-monitoring, challenges & goal setting, social comparison, gamification, tailoring, suggestions and rewards. Overall, unlike most of the works on persuasive technology, our approach is to selectively provide information regarding alternative options. This information aims at increasing the user satisfaction from her action, in order to change her attitude towards the service.

There are other works in which an agent provides information to a human user (in the context of the roads network) for different purposes. For example, Azaria et al. [6–8] develop agents that provide information or advice to a human user in order to convince her to take a certain route. Bilgic and Mooney [9] present methods for explaining the decisions of a recommendation system to increase the user satisfaction. In their context, user satisfaction is interpreted only as an accurate estimation of the item quality.

Explainable AI (XAI) is another domain related to our work [16,19,24]. In a typical XAI setting, the goal is to explain the output of the AI system to a human. This explanation is important for allowing the human to trust the system, better understand, and to allow transparency of the system's output [1]. Other XAI systems are designed to provide explanations, comprehensible by humans, for legal or ethical reasons [20]. For example, an AI system for the medical domain might be required to explain its choice for recommending the prescription of a specific drug [25]. Despite the fact that our agent is required to provide explanations to a human, our work does not belong to the XAI settings. In our work the explanations do not attempt to explain the output of the system to a passenger but to provide additional information that is likely to increase the user's satisfaction from the system. Therefore, our work can be seen as one of the first instances of x-MASE [29], explainable systems for multi-agent environments.

3 The PBE Agent

We model our setting with the following signaling game. We assume that there is a given random variable X with a prior probability distribution over the possible prices of a given alternative mode of transportation. The possible values of X are bounded within the range $[min, max]^1$.

The game is composed of three players: nature, player 1 (agent) and player 2 (passenger). It is assumed that both players are familiar with the prior distribution over X. Nature randomly chooses a number x according to the distribution over X. The agent observes the number x and her possible action, denoted a_1, is either φ (quiet) or x (say). That is, we assume that the agent may not provide false information. This is a reasonable assumption, since providing false information is usually prohibited by the law, or may harm the agent's reputation. The passenger observes the agent's action and her action, denoted a_2, is any number in the range $[min, max]$. The passenger's action essentially means setting her estimate about the price of the alternative. In our setting the agent would like the passenger to think that the price of the alternative is as high as possible,

---

^{1} Without loss of generality, we assume that $Pr(X = min) > 0$ for a discrete distribution, and $F_X(min + \epsilon) > 0$ for a continuous distribution, for every $\epsilon > 0$.

while the passenger would like to know the real price. Therefore, we set the utility for the agent to a_2 and the utility of the passenger to $-(a_2 - x)^2$. Note that we did not define the utility of the passenger to be simply $-|a_2 - x|$, since we want the utility to highly penalize a large deviation from the true value.

We first note that if the agent plays $a_1 \neq \varphi$ then the passenger knows that a_1 is nature's choice. Thus, a rational passenger would play $a_2 = a_1$. On the other hand, if the agent plays $a_1 = \varphi$ then the passenger would have some belief about the real price, which can be the original distribution of nature, or any other distribution. We show that the passenger's best response is to play the expectation of this belief. Formally,

Lemma 1. *Assume that the agent plays $a_1 = \varphi$, and let Y be a belief over x. That is, Y is a random variable with a distribution over $[min, max]$. Then, $\mathrm{argmax}_{a_2} E[-(a_2 - Y)^2] = E[Y]$.*

Proof. Instead of maximizing $E[-(a_2 - Y)^2]$ we can minimize $E[(a_2 - Y)^2]$. In addition, $E[(a_2 - Y)^2] = E[(a_2)^2] - 2E[a_2 Y] + E[Y^2] = (a_2)^2 - 2a_2 E[Y] + E[Y^2]$. By differentiating we get that

$$\frac{d}{da_2} \left((a_2)^2 - 2a_2 E[Y] + E[Y^2] \right) = 2a_2 - 2E[Y].$$

The derivative is 0 when $a_2 = E[Y]$ and the second derivative is positive; this entails that

$$\underset{a_2}{\mathrm{argmin}} \left((a_2)^2 - 2a_2 E[Y] + E[Y^2] \right) = E[Y]$$

□

Now, informally, if nature chooses a "high" value of x, the agent would like to disclose this value by playing $a_1 = x$. One may think that if nature chooses a "low" value of x, the agent would like to hide this value by playing $a_1 = \varphi$. However, since the user adjusts her belief accordingly, she will play $E[X | a_1 = \varphi]$. Therefore, it would be more beneficial for the agent to reveal also low values that are greater than $E[X | a_1 = \varphi]$, which, in turn, will further reduce the new $E[X | a_1 = \varphi]$. Indeed, Theorem 1 shows that a rational agent should always disclose the true value of x, unless $x = min$. If $x = min$ the agent can play any action, i.e., φ, min or any mixture of φ and min. We begin by applying the definition of PBE to our signaling game.

Definition 1. *A tuple of strategies and a belief, $(\sigma_1, \sigma_2, \mu_2)$, is said to be a perfect Bayesian equilibrium in our setting if the following hold:*

1. *The strategy of player 1 is a best response strategy. That is, given σ_2 and x, deviating from σ_1 does not increase player 1's utility.*
2. *The strategy of player 2 is a best response strategy. That is, given a_1, deviating from σ_2 does not increase player 2's expected utility according to her belief.*
3. *μ_2 is a consistent belief. That is, μ_2 is a distribution over x given a_1, which is consistent with σ_1 (following Bayes rule, where appropriate).*

Theorem 1. *A tuple of strategies and a belief, $(\sigma_1, \sigma_2, \mu_2)$, is a PBE if and only if:*

$$- \sigma_1(x) = \begin{cases} x : & x > min \\ anything : & x = min \end{cases}$$

$$- \sigma_2(a_1) = \begin{cases} a_1 : & a_1 \neq \varphi \\ min : & a_1 = \varphi \end{cases}$$

$- \mu_2(x = a_1 | a_1 \neq \varphi) = 1$ *and* $\mu_2(x = min | a_1 = \varphi) = 1$.

Proof. ($\Leftarrow$) Such a tuple is a PBE: σ_1 is a best response strategy, since the utility of player 1 is x if $a_1 = x$ and min if $a_1 = \varphi$. Thus, playing $a_1 = x$ is a weakly dominating strategy. σ_2 is a best response strategy, since it is the expected value of the belief μ_2, and thus it is a best response according to Lemma 1. Finally, μ_2 is consistent: If $a_1 = \varphi$ and according to σ_1 player 1 plays φ with some probability (greater than 0), then according to Bayes rule $\mu_2(x = min | a_1 = \varphi) = 1$. Otherwise, Bayes rule cannot be applied (and it is thus not required). If $a_1 \neq \varphi$, then by definition $x = a_1$, and thus $\mu_2(x = a_1 | a_1 \neq \varphi) = 1$.

($\Rightarrow$) Let $(\sigma_1, \sigma_2, \mu_2)$ be a PBE. It holds that $\mu_2(x = a_1 | a_1 \neq \varphi) = 1$ by Bayes rule, implying that if $a_1 \neq \varphi$, $\sigma_2(a_1) = a_1$. Therefore, when $a_1 = x$ the utility of player 1 is x.

We now show that $\sigma_2(a_1 = \varphi) = min$. Assume by contradiction that $\sigma_2(a_1 = \varphi) \neq min$ (or $p(\sigma_2(a_1 = \varphi) = min) < 1$), then $E[\sigma_2(\varphi)] = c > min$. We now imply the strategy of player 1. There are three possible cases: if $x > c$, then $a_1 = x$ is a strictly dominating strategy. If $x < c$, then $a_1 = \varphi$ is a strictly dominating strategy. If $x = c$, there is no advantage for either playing φ or x; both options give player 1 a utility of c, and thus she may use any strategy, i.e.:

$$\sigma_1(x) = \begin{cases} x : & x > c \\ \varphi : & x < c \\ anything : & x = c. \end{cases}$$

Given this strategy, we need to apply Bayes rule to derive $\mu_2(x | a_1 = \varphi)$. By σ_1, it is possible that $a_1 = \varphi$ only if $x \leq c$. That is, $\mu_2(x > c | a_1 = \varphi) = 0$ and $\mu_2(x \leq c | a_1 = \varphi) = 1$. Therefore, the expected value of the belief, $c' = E[\mu_2(x | a_1 = \varphi)]$, and according to Lemma 1, $\sigma_2(\varphi) = c'$. However, $c' = E[\mu_2(x | a_1 = \varphi)] \leq E[x | x \leq c]$ which is less than c, since $c > min$. That is, $E[\sigma_2(\varphi)] = c' < c$, which is a contradiction. Therefore, the strategy for player 2 in every PBE is determined. In addition, since $\sigma_2(\varphi) = E[\mu_2(x | a_1 = \varphi)]$ according to Lemma 1, then $\mu_2(x | a_1 = \varphi) = min$, and the belief of player 2 in every PBE is also determined.

We end the proof by showing that for $x > min$, $\sigma_1(x) = x$. Since σ_2 is determined, the utility of player 1 is min if $a_1 = \varphi$ and x if $a_1 = x$. Therefore, when $x > min$, playing $a_1 = x$ is a strictly dominating strategy.   □

The provided analysis can be applied to any alternative mode of transportation and to any type of price (e.g. travel-time or cost). We thus conclude that the PBE agent must provide all of the possible explanations.

4   The AXIS Agent

The analysis in the previous section is theoretical in nature. However, several studies have shown that algorithmic approaches that use a pure theoretically analytic objective often perform poorly with real humans. Indeed, we conjecture that an agent that selects a subset of explanations for a given scenario will perform better than the PBE agent. In this section we introduce our Automatic eXplainer for Increasing Satisfaction (AXIS) agent. The AXIS agent has a set of possible explanations, and the agent needs to choose the most appropriate explanations for each scenario. Note that we do not limit the number of explanations to present for each scenario, and thus AXIS needs also to choose how many explanations to present. AXIS was built in 3 stages.

First, an initial set of possible explanations needs to be defined. We thus consider the following possible classes of factors of an explanation. Each explanation is a combination of one factor from each class:

1. Mode of alternative transportation: a private taxi ride or public transportation.
2. Comparison criterion: time or cost.
3. Visualization of the difference: absolute or relative difference.
4. Anchoring: the shared ride or the alternative mode of transportation perspective.

For example, a possible explanation would consist of a private taxi for class 1, cost for class 2, relative for class 3, and an alternative mode of transportation perspective for class 4. That is, the explanation would be "a private taxi would have cost 50% more than a shared ride". Another possible explanation would consist of public transportation for class 1, time for class 2, absolute for class 3, and a shared ride perspective for class 4. That is, the explanation would be "the shared ride saved 10 min over public transportation". Overall, there are $2^4 = 16$ possible combinations. In addition, we added an explanation regarding the saving of CO_2 emission of the shared ride, so there will be an alternative explanation for the case where the other options are not reasonable. Note that the first two classes determine which information is given to the passenger, while the later two classes determine how the information is presented. We denote each possible combination of choosing form the first two classes as a *information setting*. We denote each possible combination of choosing form the latter two classes as a *presentation setting*.

Presenting all 17 possible explanations with the additional option of "none of the above" requires a lot of effort from the human subjects to choose the most appropriate option for each scenario. Thus, in the second stage we collected data from human subjects regarding the most appropriate explanations, in order to build a limited subset of explanations. Recall that there are 4 possible information settings and 4 possible presentation settings. We selected for each information setting the corresponding presentation setting that was chosen (in total) by the largest number of people. We also selected the second most chosen presentation setting for the information setting that was chosen by the largest number of people. Adding the explanation regarding the CO_2 emissions we ended with 6 possible explanations.

In the final stage we collected again data from people, but we presented only the 6 explanation to choose from. This data was used by AXIS to learn which explanations are appropriate for each scenario. AXIS receives the following 7 features as an input: the cost and time of the shared ride, the differences between the cost and time of the shared ride and the alternatives (i.e., the private ride and the public transportation), and the amount of CO_2 emission saved when compared to a private ride. AXIS uses a neural network with two hidden layers, one with 8 neurons and the other one with 7 neurons, and the logistic activation function (implemented using Scikit-learn [42]). The number of neurons and hidden layers was determined based on the performance of the network. AXIS used 10% of the input as a validation set (used for early stopping) and 40% as the test set. AXIS predicts which explanations were selected by the humans (and which explanations were not selected) for any given scenario.

5 Experimental Design

In this section we describe the design of our experiments. Since AXIS generates explanations for a given assignment of passengers to vehicles, we need to generate assignments as an input to AXIS. To generate the assignments we first need a data-set of ride requests.

To generate the ride requests we use the New York city taxi trip data-set [2], which was also used by other works that evaluate ridesharing algorithms (see for example, [11,31]). We use the data-set from 2016, since it contains the exact GPS locations for every ride.

We note that the data-set contains requests for taxi rides, but it does not contain a data regarding shared-rides. We thus need to generate assignments of passengers to taxis, based on the requests from the data-set. Now, if the assignments are randomly generated, it may be hard to provide reasonable explanations, and thus the evaluation of AXIS in these setting is problematic. We thus concentrate on requests that depart from a single origin but have different destinations, since

---

[2] https://data.cityofnewyork.us/Transportation/2016-Green-Taxi-Trip-Data/hvrh-b6nb.

a brute force algorithm can find the optimal assignment of passengers to taxis in this setting.

We use the following brute force assignment algorithm. The algorithm receives 12 passengers and outputs the assignment of each passenger to vehicle that minimizes the overall travel distance. We assume that every vehicle can hold up-to four passengers. The brute force assignment algorithm recursively considers all options to partition the group of 12 passengers to subsets of up to four passengers. We note that there are $3,305,017$ such possible partitions. The algorithm then solves the Travel Salesman Problem (TSP) in each group, by exhaustive search, to find the cheapest assignment. Solving the TSP problem on 4 destinations (or less) is possible using exhaustive search since there are only $4! = 24$ combinations. The shortest path between each combination is solved using a shortest distance matrix between all locations. In order to compute this matrix we downloaded the graph that represents the area of New York from Open Street Map (using OSMnx [12]), and ran the Floyd-Warshall's algorithm.

We set the origin location to JFK Station, Sutphin Blvd-Archer Av, and the departing time to 11:00am. See Fig. 1 where the green location is the origin, and the blue locations are the destinations.

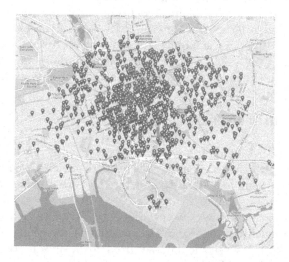

Fig. 1. A map depicting the origin (in green) and destinations (in blue) of all rides considered. (Color figure online)

In order to calculate the duration of the rides we use Google Maps (through Google Maps API). Specifically, the duration of the private taxi ride was obtained using "driving" mode, and the duration of the public transportation was obtained using "transit" mode. The duration of the shared-ride was obtained using "driving" mode with the last passenger's destination as the final destination of the ride and the destinations of the other passengers as way-points. The duration for a specific passenger was determined by using the time required to reach her associated way-point.

In order to calculate the cost of the private ride we use Taxi Fare Finder (through their API)[3]. The cost for public transportation was calculated by the number of buses required (as obtained through Google Maps API), multiplied by $2.5 (the bus fare). The cost for the shared-ride was obtained from Taxi Fare Finder. Since this service does not support a ride with way-points, we obtained the cost of multiple taxi rides, but we included the base price only once. Note that this is the total cost of the shared-ride. The cost for a specific passenger was determined by the proportional sharing pricing function [21], which works as follows. Let c_{p_i} be the cost of a private ride for passenger i, and let $total_s$ be the total cost of the shared ride. In addition, let $f = \frac{total_s}{\sum_i c_{p_i}}$. The cost for each passenger is thus $f \cdot c_{pi}$.

We ran 4 experiments in total. Two experiments were used to compose AXIS (see Sect. 4), and the third and fourth experiments compared the performance of AXIS with that of non-data-driven agents (see below). All experiments used the Mechanical Turk platform, a crowd-sourcing platform that is widely used for running experiments with human subjects [3,39]. Unfortunately, since participation is anonymous and linked to monetary incentives, experiments on a crowd-sourcing platform can attract participants who do not fully engage in the requested tasks [48]. Therefore, the subjects were required to have at least 99% acceptance rate and were required to have previously completed at least 500 Mechanical Turk Tasks (HITs). In addition, we added an attention check question for each experiment, which can be found in the full version of the paper [50].

In the first two experiments, which were designed for AXIS to learn what people believe are good explanations, the subjects were given several scenarios for a shared ride. The subjects were told that they are representatives of a ride sharing service, and that they need to select a set of explanations that they believe will increase the customer's satisfaction. Each scenario consists of a shared-ride with a given duration and cost.

In the third experiment we evaluate the performance of AXIS against the PBE agent. The subjects were given 2 scenarios. Each scenario consists of a shared-ride with a given duration and cost and it also contains either the explanations that are chosen by AXIS or the information that the PBE agent provides: the cost and duration a private ride would take, and the cost and the duration that public transportation would have taken. The subjects were asked to rank their satisfaction from each ride on a scale from 1 to 7.

In the forth experiment we evaluate the performance of AXIS against a random baseline agent. The random explanations were chosen as follows: first, a number between 1 and 4 was uniformly sampled. This number determined how many explanations will be given by the random agent. This range was chosen since over 93% of the subjects selected between 1 and 4 explanations in the second experiment. Recall that there are 4 classes of factors that define an explanation, where the fourth class is the anchoring perspective (see Sect. 4).

---

[3] https://www.taxifarefinder.com/.

The random agent sampled explanations uniformly, but it did not present two explanations that differ only by their anchoring perspective. The subjects were again given 2 scenarios. Each scenario consists of a shared-ride with a given duration and cost and it also contains either the explanations that are chosen by AXIS or the explanations selected by the random agent. The subjects were asked to rank their satisfaction from each ride. The exact wording of the instructions for the experiments can be found in the full version of the paper [50].

953 subjects participated in total, all from the USA. The number of subjects in each experiment and the number of scenarios appear in Table 1. Tables 2 and 3 include additional demographic information on the subjects in each of the experiments. The average age of the subjects was 39.

Table 1. Number of subjects and scenarios in each of the experiments.

	#1	#2	#3	#4	Total
Number of subjects	343	180	156	274	953
Scenarios per subject	2	4	2	2	–
Total scenarios	686	720	312	548	3266

Table 2. Gender distribution for each of the experiments.

	#1	#2	#3	#4	Total
Male	157	66	52	117	392
Female	183	109	104	153	549
Other or refused	3	5	0	4	12

Table 3. Education level for each of the experiments.

	#1	#2	#3	#4	Total
High-school	72	39	38	80	229
Bachelor	183	86	84	131	484
Master	60	29	37	46	172
PhD	15	2	0	10	27
Trade-school	8	4	5	10	27
Refused or did not respond	5	3	0	6	14

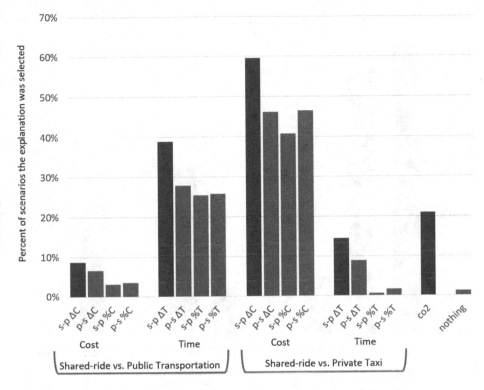

Fig. 2. The percent of scenarios that every explanation was selected in the first experiment. The explanations marked in green were selected for the second experiment. (Color figure online)

6 Results

Recall that the first experiment was designed to select the most appropriate explanations (out of the initial 17 possible explanations). The results of this experiment are depicted in Fig. 2. The x-axis describes the possible explanations according to the 4 classes. Specifically, the factor from the anchoring class is denoted by s-p or p-s; s-p means that the explanation is from the shared-ride perspective, while p-s means that it is from the alternative (private/public) mode of transportation. The factor from the comparison criterion class is denoted by Δ or %; Δ means that the explanation presents an absolute difference while % means that a relative difference is presented. We chose 6 explanations for the next experiment, which are marked in green.

As depicted by Fig. 2, the subjects chose explanations that compare the ride with a private taxi more often than those comparing the ride with public transportation. We believe that this is because from a human perspective a shared-ride resembles a private taxi more than public transportation. Furthermore, when comparing with a private taxi, the subjects preferred to compare the shared-ride with the *cost* of a private taxi, while when comparing to public transportation,

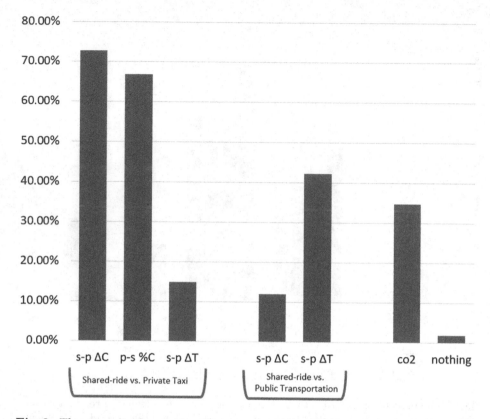

Fig. 3. The percent of scenarios that every explanation was selected in the second experiment. The obtained data-set was used to train AXIS.

the subjects preferred to compare it with the travel time. This is expected, since the travel time by a private taxi is less than the travel time by a shared ride, so comparing the travel time to a private taxi is less likely to increase user satisfaction. We also notice that with absolute difference the subjects preferred the shared ride perspective, while with relative difference the subjects preferred the alternative mode of transportation perspective. We conjecture that this is due to the higher percentages when using the alternative mode prospective. For example, if the shared ride saves 20% of the cost when compared to a private ride, the subjects preferred the explanation that a private ride costs 25% more.

The second experiment was designed to collect data from humans on the most appropriate explanations (out of the 6 chosen explanations) for each scenario. The results are depicted in Fig. 3. This data was used to train AXIS. The accuracy of the neural network on the test-set is 74.9%. That is, the model correctly predicts whether to provide a given explanation in a given scenario in almost 75% of the cases.

The third experiment was designed to evaluate AXIS against the PBE agent; the results are depicted in Fig. 4. AXIS outperforms the PBE agent; the difference is statistically significant ($p < 10^{-5}$), using the student t-test. We note that achieving such a difference is non-trivial since the ride scenarios are identical and only differ by the information that is provided to the user.

The forth experiment was designed to evaluate AXIS against the random baseline agent; the results are depicted in Fig. 4. AXIS outperforms the random agent; the difference is statistically significant ($p < 0.001$), using the student t-test. We note that AXIS and the random agent provided a similar number of explanations on average (2.551 and 2.51, respectively). That is, AXIS performed well not because of the number of explanations it provided, but since it provided appropriate explanations for the given scenarios.

We conclude this section by showing an example of a ride scenario presented to some of the subjects, along with the information provided by the PBE agent, and the explanations selected by the random agent and by AXIS. In this scenario the subject is assumed to travel by a shared ride from JFK Station to 102-3 188th St, Jamaica, NY. The shared ride took 13 min and cost $7.53. The PBE agent provided the following information:

- "A private ride would have cost $13.83 and would have taken 12 min".
- "Public transportation costs $2.5 and would have taken 26 min".

The random agent provided the following explanations:

- "A private taxi would have cost $6.3 more".
- "A ride by public transportation would have saved you only $5.03".

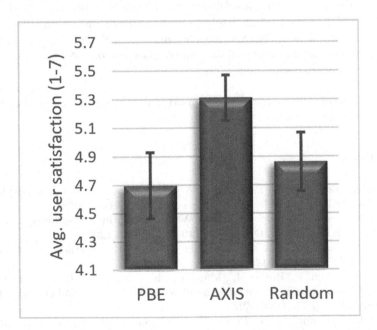

Fig. 4. A comparison between the performance of AXIS, the PBE agent and the random agent. The bars indicate the 95% confidence interval. AXIS significantly outperformed both baseline agents ($p < 0.001$).

Instead, AXIS selected the following explanations:

- "The shared ride had saved you \$6.3 over a private taxi".
- "A private taxi would have cost 83% more".
- "The shared ride saved you 4 min over public transportation".

Clearly, the explanations provided by AXIS seem much more compelling.

7   Conclusions and Future Work

In this paper we took a first step towards the development of agents that provide explanations in a multi-agent system with a goal of increasing user satisfaction. We first modeled the explanation selection problem as a signaling game and determined the unique set of Perfect Bayesian Equilibria (PBE). We then presented AXIS, an agent that, when given a shared-ride along with its possible alternatives, selects the explanations that are most likely to increase user satisfaction. We ran four experiments with humans. The first experiment was used to narrow the set of possible explanations, the second experiment collected data for the neural network to train on, the third experiment was used to evaluate the performance of AXIS against that of the PBE agent, and the fourth experiment was used to evaluate the performance of AXIS against that of an agent that randomly chooses explanations. We showed that AXIS outperforms the other agents in terms of user satisfaction.

In future work we will consider natural language generation methods for generating explanations that are likely to increase user satisfaction. We also plan to extend the set of possible explanations, and to implement user modeling in order to provide explanations that are appropriate not only for a given scenario but also for a given specific user.

Acknowledgment. This research was supported in part by the Ministry of Science, Technology & Space, Israel.

References

1. Adadi, A., Berrada, M.: Peeking inside the black-box: a survey on explainable artificial intelligence (XAI). IEEE Access **6**, 52138–52160 (2018)
2. Agatz, N., Erera, A., Savelsbergh, M., Wang, X.: Optimization for dynamic ride-sharing: a review. Eur. J. Oper. Res. **223**(2), 295–303 (2012)
3. Amir, O., Rand, D.G., et al.: Economic games on the internet: the effect of \$1 stakes. PloS One **7**(2), e31461 (2012)
4. Anagnostopoulou, E., Bothos, E., Magoutas, B., Schrammel, J., Mentzas, G.: Persuasive technologies for sustainable mobility: state of the art and emerging trends. Sustainability **10**(7), 2128 (2018)
5. Ariely, D., Loewenstein, G., Prelec, D.: "Coherent arbitrariness": stable demand curves without stable preferences. Q. J. Econ. **118**(1), 73–106 (2003)

6. Azaria, A., Rabinovich, Z., Goldman, C.V., Kraus, S.: Strategic information disclosure to people with multiple alternatives. ACM Trans. Intell. Syst. Technol. (TIST) **5**(4), 64 (2015)
7. Azaria, A., Rabinovich, Z., Kraus, S., Goldman, C.V., Gal, Y.: Strategic advice provision in repeated human-agent interactions. In: Twenty-Sixth AAAI Conference on Artificial Intelligence (2012)
8. Azaria, A., Rabinovich, Z., Kraus, S., Goldman, C.V., Tsimhoni, O.: Giving advice to people in path selection problems. In: AAMAS, pp. 459–466 (2012)
9. Bilgic, M., Mooney, R.J.: Explaining recommendations: satisfaction vs. promotion. In: Beyond Personalization Workshop, IUI, pp. 13–18 (2005)
10. Bistaffa, F., Farinelli, A., Chalkiadakis, G., Ramchurn, S.D.: A cooperative game-theoretic approach to the social ridesharing problem. Artif. Intell. **246**, 86–117 (2017)
11. Biswas, A., Gopalakrishnan, R., Tulabandhula, T., Mukherjee, K., Metrewar, A., Thangaraj, R.S.: Profit optimization in commercial ridesharing. In: Proceedings of the 16th Conference on Autonomous Agents and MultiAgent Systems, pp. 1481–1483. International Foundation for Autonomous Agents and Multiagent Systems (2017)
12. Boeing, G.: OSMnx: new methods for acquiring, constructing, analyzing, and visualizing complex street networks. Comput. Environ. Urban Syst. **65**, 126–139 (2017)
13. Bradley, G.L., Sparks, B.A.: Dealing with service failures: the use of explanations. J. Trav. Tour. Market. **26**(2), 129–143 (2009)
14. Camerer, C.F.: Behavioral Game Theory. Experiments in Strategic Interaction, chapter 2, pp. 43–118. Princeton University Press (2003)
15. Campbell, H.: Seven reasons why rideshare drivers hate uberpool & lyft line (2017). https://maximumridesharingprofits.com/7-reasons-rideshare-drivers-hate-uberpool-lyft-line/
16. Carvalho, D.V., Pereira, E.M., Cardoso, J.S.: ML interpretability: a survey on methods and metrics. Electronics **8**(8), 832 (2019)
17. Cialdini, R.B.: Harnessing the science of persuasion. Harv. Bus. Rev. **79**(9), 72–81 (2001)
18. Cordeau, J.-F., Laporte, G.: A tabu search heuristic for the static multi-vehicle dial-a-ride problem. Transp. Res. Part B: Methodol. **37**(6), 579–594 (2003)
19. Core, M.G., Lane, H.C., Van Lent, M., Gomboc, D., Solomon, S., Rosenberg, M.: Building explainable artificial intelligence systems. In: Proceedings of the 18th Conference on Innovative Applications of Artificial Intelligence, pp. 1766–1773 (2006)
20. Doran, D., Schulz, S., Besold, T.R.: What does explainable AI really mean? A new conceptualization of perspectives. arXiv preprint arXiv:1710.00794 (2017)
21. Fishburn, P., Pollak, H.: Fixed-route cost allocation. Am. Math. Mon. **90**(6), 366–378 (1983)
22. Fogg, B.J.: Persuasive technology: using computers to change what we think and do. Ubiquity **2002**(December), 2 (2002)
23. Fudenberg, D., Tirole, J.: Perfect Bayesian equilibrium and sequential equilibrium. J. Econ. Theory **53**(2), 236–260 (1991)
24. Gunning, D.: Explainable artificial intelligence (XAI). Defense Advanced Research Projects Agency (DARPA), p. 2 (2017)
25. Holzinger, A., Biemann, C., Pattichis, C.S., Kell, D.B.: What do we need to build explainable AI systems for the medical domain? arXiv preprint arXiv:1712.09923 (2017)
26. Kellermann, K., Cole, T.: Classifying compliance gaining messages: taxonomic disorder and strategic confusion. Commun. Theory **4**(1), 3–60 (1994)

27. Kleinerman, A., Rosenfeld, A., Kraus, S.: Providing explanations for recommendations in reciprocal environments. In: Proceedings of the 12th ACM Conference on Recommender Systems, pp. 22–30 (2018)
28. Koebler, J.: Why everyone hates uberpool? (2016). https://motherboard.vice.com/en_us/article/4xaa5d/why-drivers-and-riders-hate-uberpool-and-lyft-line
29. Kraus, S., et al.: AI for explaining decisions in multi-agent environments. In: The Thirty-Fourth AAAI Conference on Artificial Intelligence, pp. 13534–13538 (2019)
30. Levinger, C., Hazon, N., Azaria, A.: Human satisfaction as the ultimate goal in ridesharing. Future Gener. Comput. Syst. **112**, 176–184 (2020)
31. Lin, J., Sasidharan, S., Ma, S., Wolfson, O.: A model of multimodal ridesharing and its analysis. In: 2016 17th IEEE International Conference on Mobile Data Management (MDM), vol. 1, pp. 164–173. IEEE (2016)
32. Lin, Y., Li, W., Qiu, F., Xu, H.: Research on optimization of vehicle routing problem for ride-sharing taxi. Procedia Soc. Behav. Sci. **43**, 494–502 (2012)
33. Loewenstein, G.: Willpower: a decision-theorist's perspective. Law Philos. **19**, 51–76 (2000)
34. Molenbruch, Y., Braekers, K., Caris, A.: Typology and literature review for dial-a-ride problems. Ann. Oper. Res. **259**, 295–325 (2017). https://doi.org/10.1007/s10479-017-2525-0
35. Molla, R.: Americans seem to like ride-sharing services like Uber and Lyft (2018). https://www.vox.com/2018/6/24/17493338/ride-sharing-services-uber-lyft-how-many-people-use
36. United Nations: 2018 revision of world urbanization prospects (2018)
37. Nay, J.J., Vorobeychik, Y.: Predicting human cooperation. PloS One **11**(5), e0155656 (2016)
38. Oinas-Kukkonen, H., Harjumaa, M.: A systematic framework for designing and evaluating persuasive systems. In: Oinas-Kukkonen, H., Hasle, P., Harjumaa, M., Segerståhl, K., Øhrstrøm, P. (eds.) PERSUASIVE 2008. LNCS, vol. 5033, pp. 164–176. Springer, Heidelberg (2008). https://doi.org/10.1007/978-3-540-68504-3_15
39. Paolacci, G., Chandler, J., Ipeirotis, P.G.: Running experiments on amazon mechanical turk. Judgm. Decis. Mak. **5**(5), 411–419 (2010)
40. Parragh, S.N., Doerner, K.F., Hartl, R.F.: A survey on pickup and delivery problems. Part I: transportation between customers and depot. J. für Betriebswirtschaft **58**(1), 21–51 (2008). https://doi.org/10.1007/s11301-008-0036-4
41. Parragh, S.N., Doerner, K.F., Hartl, R.F.: A survey on pickup and delivery problems. Part II: transportation between pickup and delivery locations. J. für Betriebswirtschaft **58**(1), 81–117 (2008). https://doi.org/10.1007/s11301-008-0036-4
42. Pedregosa, F.: Scikit-learn: machine learning in Python. J. Mach. Learn. Res. **12**, 2825–2830 (2011)
43. Peled, N., Gal, Y.K., Kraus, S.: A study of computational and human strategies in revelation games. In: AAMAS, pp. 345–352 (2011)
44. Psaraftis, H.N., Wen, M., Kontovas, C.A.: Dynamic vehicle routing problems: three decades and counting. Networks **67**(1), 3–31 (2016)
45. Schleibaum, S., Müller, J.P.: Human-centric ridesharing on large scale by explaining AI-generated assignments. In: Proceedings of the 6th EAI International Conference on Smart Objects and Technologies for Social Good, pp. 222–225 (2020)
46. Singh, H.: The importance of customer satisfaction in relation to customer loyalty and retention. Acad. Mark. Sci. **60**(193–225), 46 (2006)
47. Spence, A.M.: Market Signaling: Informational Transfer in Hiring and Related Screening Processes, vol. 143. Harvard Univ Press, Cambridge (1974)

48. Turner, A.M., Kirchhoff, K., Capurro, D.: Using crowdsourcing technology for testing multilingual public health promotion materials. J. Med. Internet Res. **14**(3), e79 (2012)
49. Tversky, A., Kahneman, D.: The framing of decisions and the psychology of choice. Science **211**(4481), 453–458 (1981)
50. Zar, D., Hazon, N., Azaria, A.: Explaining ridesharing: selection of explanations for increasing user satisfaction. arXiv preprint arXiv:2105.12500 (2021)

Large-Scale, Dynamic and Distributed Coalition Formation with Spatial and Temporal Constraints

Luca Capezzuto$^{(\boxtimes)}$ ⓘ, Danesh Tarapore ⓘ, and Sarvapali D. Ramchurn ⓘ

School of Electronics and Computer Science, University of Southampton, Southampton, UK
{luca.capezzuto,d.s.tarapore,sdr1}@soton.ac.uk

Abstract. The *Coalition Formation with Spatial and Temporal constraints Problem* (CFSTP) is a multi-agent task allocation problem in which few agents have to perform many tasks, each with its deadline and workload. To maximize the number of completed tasks, the agents need to cooperate by forming, disbanding and reforming coalitions. The original mathematical programming formulation of the CFSTP is difficult to implement, since it is lengthy and based on the problematic Big-M method. In this paper, we propose a compact and easy-to-implement formulation. Moreover, we design D-CTS, a distributed version of the state-of-the-art CFSTP algorithm. Using public London Fire Brigade records, we create a dataset with 347588 tasks and a test framework that simulates the mobilization of firefighters in dynamic environments. In problems with up to 150 agents and 3000 tasks, compared to DSA-SDP, a state-of-the-art distributed algorithm, D-CTS completes $3.79\% \pm [42.22\%, 1.96\%]$ more tasks, and is one order of magnitude more efficient in terms of communication overhead and time complexity. D-CTS sets the first large-scale, dynamic and distributed CFSTP benchmark.

Keywords: Task allocation · Coalition formation · Distributed constraint optimization problem · Large-scale · Dynamic · Disaster response

1 Introduction

Consider the situation after a disaster, either natural, such as Hurricane Maria in 2017, or man-made, such as the Beirut explosion in 2020. A complex response phase takes place, which includes actions such as extinguishing fires, clearing the streets and evacuating civilians. If the number of first responders is limited, they need to cooperate to act as fast as possible, because any delay can lead to further tragedy and destruction [1]. Cooperation is also necessary when tasks require combined skills. For example, to extract survivors from the rubble of a collapsed building, rescue robots detect life signs with their sensors, firefighters dig and

© Springer Nature Switzerland AG 2021
A. Rosenfeld and N. Talmon (Eds.): EUMAS 2021, LNAI 12802, pp. 108–125, 2021.
https://doi.org/10.1007/978-3-030-82254-5_7

paramedics load the injured into ambulances. In addition, at any moment new fires could break out or other buildings could collapse, therefore first responders must be ready to deploy to other areas.

Disaster response is a fundamental research topic for multi-agent and multi-robot systems [17,29]. Within this field, we are interested in the *Coalition Formation with Spatial and Temporal constraints Problem* (CFSTP) [5,42]. In the CFSTP, tasks (e.g., save victims or put out fires) have to be assigned to agents (e.g., ambulances or fire brigades). The assignment is determined by the spatial distribution of the tasks in the disaster area, the time needed to reach them, the workload they require (e.g., how large a fire is) and their deadlines (e.g., estimated time left before victims perish). In addition to these constraints, the number of agents may be much smaller than the number of tasks, hence the agents need to cooperate with each other by forming, disbanding and reforming coalitions. A *coalition* is a short-lived and flat organization of agents that performs tasks more effectively or quickly than single agents [5]. The objective of the CFSTP is to define which tasks (e.g., sites with the most victims and the strongest fires) to allocate to which coalitions (e.g., the fastest ambulances and fire trucks with the largest water tanks), in order to complete as many tasks as possible.

Despite having similarities with classic problems such as Generalized Assignment Problem [44] and Job-Shop Scheduling [4], the importance of the CFSTP lies in the fact that it was the first generalization of the Team Orienteering Problem [42, Sect. 4.2] to consider coalition formation. For this reason, it has been applied in contexts such as human-agent collectives [43], multi-UAV exploration [2] and law enforcement [30].

There are two main issues in the CFSTP literature. First, its original mathematical programming formulation [42, Sect. 5] is based on 3 sets of binary variables, 1 set of integer variables and 23 types of constraints, 8 of which use the Big-M method. So many variables and constraints make implementation difficult, while the Big-M method introduces a large penalty term that, if not chosen carefully, leads to serious rounding errors and ill conditioning [11]. Second, there is no algorithm that is simultaneously scalable, distributed and able to solve the CFSTP in systems with a *dynamic environment evolution*[1] (i.e., systems in which, at any time, agents can join in or leave, and new tasks can appear) [10]. Below, we discuss this in detail.

The state-of-the-art CFSTP algorithm, *Cluster-based Task Scheduling* (CTS) [5], transforms the CFSTP into a sequence of $1 - 1$ task allocations. In other words, instead of allocating each task to a coalition of agents, it forms coalitions by *clustering* or grouping agents based on the closest and most urgent tasks. CTS is anytime (i.e., it returns a partial solution if interrupted before completion), has a polynomial time complexity and can be used in dynamic environments. Its main limitation is being a centralized algorithm. In real-world domains such as disaster response, this leads to three major issues. First, a centralized solver

---

[1] Also referred to as *open* systems [13]. For brevity, we call them *dynamic environments*.

is a single point of failure that makes the system fragile and not robust to unexpected events, such as malfunctions or communication disturbances between agents far apart [35]. Second, if the agents have limited computational resources and the problem is not small, electing a centralized solver might not be possible, while distributing computations always improves scalability. Third, a centralized approach might not be as effective as a distributed approach, given that the situation can evolve rapidly and there could be significant communication delays [27].

To date, only Ramchurn et al. [41] have proposed a dynamic and distributed solution to the CFSTP. They reduced it to a *Dynamic Distributed Constraint Optimization Problem* (DynDCOP) [10] and solved it with *Fast Max-Sum* (FMS), a variant of the Max-Sum algorithm [9] specialized for task allocation. However, unlike CTS, FMS is not guaranteed to convergence, it is not anytime, and its runtime is exponential in the number of agents. Pujol-Gonzalez et al. [37] proposed another Max-Sum variant called *Binary Max-Sum* (BinaryMS), which, compared to FMS, lowers the runtime to polynomial and achieves the same solution quality. Nonetheless, even BinaryMS is not guaranteed to converge and not anytime. In addition, it requires a preprocessing phase with exponential runtime to transform the problem constraints into binary form, which makes it not suitable for dynamic environments. Against this background, we propose the following contributions:

1. A novel mathematical programming formulation of the CFSTP, based only on binary variables and 5 types of constraints, which do not use the Big-M method.
2. D-CTS, a distributed version of CTS that preserves its properties, namely being anytime, scalable and guaranteed to convergence [5].
3. The first large-scale and dynamic CFSTP test framework, based on real-world data published by the London Fire Brigade [22,23].

The rest of the paper is organized as follows. We begin with a discussion of related work in Sect. 2, then we give our formulation of the CFSTP in Sect. 3 and present D-CTS in Sect. 4. Finally, we evaluate D-CTS with our test framework in Sect. 5 and conclude in Sect. 6.

2   Related Work

The CFSTP is NP-hard [42], while CTS is an *incomplete* or non-exact algorithm with a search-based approach [5]. Since we reduce the CFSTP to a DynDCOP in Sect. 4 and propose a realistic test framework in Sect. 5, we briefly recall incomplete search-based algorithms and realistic test frameworks, for both DCOPs and DynDCOPs. For a more in-depth look, see [10,19].

2.1   Incomplete Search-Based Algorithms

Among the most popular incomplete search-based DCOP algorithms are MGM [24] and DSA [53]. In MGM, each agent iteratively chooses its assignment based on the current neighbor assignments. DSA is an extension of MGM where, to escape from local minima, assignments are chosen stochastically. Both algorithms are efficient, and although they have no quality guarantees on the solutions found, numerous studies have proven their efficacy in many domains. In particular, DSA is a touchstone for novel DCOP algorithms [10]. We use DSA-SDP [54], the state-of-the-art DSA variant, as the baseline in our tests.

Other notable algorithms are k-optimal [34], SBDO [3] and GDBA [33]. The class of k-optimal algorithms decomposes a DCOP into a set of subproblems, each of which involves at most k agents. The solution process continues until no subset of k or fewer agents can improve the global solution. These algorithms are anytime and guaranteed to find a lower bound on the solution quality. However, to eliminate conflicts between partial solutions, each agent may need to communicate with every other agent. Consequently, communication is not local, and both time and space complexity are exponential. Such limitations are also present in the variants proposed in [15,49]. SBDO is a DynDCOP algorithm in which agents exchange arguments about partial solutions. More precisely, each agent tries to send stronger arguments over time to influence its neighbors. Despite being anytime, SBDO has an exponential runtime [10]. GDBA is an extension of the Distributed Breakout Algorithm [51] aimed at solving DCOPs. It is not anytime, but it can be made so by using the Anytime Local Search framework [54]. Moreover, it has polynomial space and time complexity. The results reported in [26,54] suggest that GDBA has similar performance to DSA-SDP.

Dynamic environments pose a challenge to the DCOP research community [19,20,35], to the extent that SBDO and FMS are the only incomplete DynD-COP algorithms proposed to date [10].

2.2 Realistic Test Frameworks

Although the DCOP model can capture numerous real-world problems, researchers usually perform their empirical evaluations on hard random problems or classic combinatorial problems, such as graph coloring and resource allocation [10]. To the best of our knowledge, to date only the following works have conducted tests based on real-world data. Mahesrawan et al. [25] considered resource-constrained multiple-event scheduling problems occurring in office environments. Junges and Bazzan [14] evaluated the performance of complete DCOP algorithms in traffic light synchronization problems. Kim et al. [16] developed heuristics for applying Max-Sum to problems based on the real-time sensor system NetRad. Amador Nelke et al. [30] studied law enforcement problems inspired by police logs. However, none of these test frameworks is as large as ours.

3 Problem Formulation

We formulate the CFSTP as a *Binary Integer Program* (BIP) [50]. After giving our definitions, we detail our decision variables, constraints and objective function. For constraint programming formulations of the CFSTP, see [5,42].

3.1 Definitions

Let $V = \{v_1, \ldots, v_m\}$ be a set of m tasks and $A = \{a_1, \ldots, a_n\}$ be a set of n agents. Let L be the finite set of all possible task and agent locations. Time is denoted by $t \in \mathbb{N}$, starting at $t = 0$, and agents travel or complete tasks with a base time unit of 1. The time units needed by an agent to travel from one location to another are given by the function $\rho : A \times L \times L \rightarrow \mathbb{N}$. Having A in the domain of ρ allows to characterize different agent features (e.g., speed or type). Let l_v be the fixed location of task v, and let $l_a^t \in L$ be the location of agent a at time t, where l_a^0 is its initial location and is known a priori.

Task Demand. Each task v has a *demand* (γ_v, w_v) such that γ_v is the *deadline* of v, or the time until which agents can work on v [32], and $w_v \in \mathbb{R}_{\geq 0}$ is the *workload* of v, or the amount of work required to complete v [5]. We call $t_{max} = \max_{v \in V} \gamma_v$ the *maximum problem time*.

Coalition and Coalition Value. A subset of agents $C \subseteq A$ is called a *coalition*. For each coalition and task there is a *coalition value*, given by the function $u : P(A) \times V \rightarrow \mathbb{R}_{\geq 0}$, where $P(A)$ is the power set of A. The value of $u(C, v)$ is the amount of work that coalition C does on task v in one time unit. In other words, when C performs v, $u(C, v)$ expresses how well the agents in C work together, and the workload w_v decreases by $u(C, v)$ at each time.

3.2 Decision Variables

Similar to [42, Sect. 5], we use the following indicator variables:

$$\forall v \in V, \forall t \leq \gamma_v, \forall C \subseteq A, \ \tau_{v,t,C} \in \{0, 1\} \tag{1}$$

$$\forall v \in V, \ \delta_v \in \{0, 1\} \tag{2}$$

where: $\tau_{v,t,C} = 1$ if coalition C works on task v at time t, and 0 otherwise; $\delta_v = 1$ if task v is completed, and 0 otherwise. Specifying indicator variables for individual agents is not necessary, since they can be inferred from Eq. 1.

3.3 Constraints

There are 3 types of constraints: structural, temporal and spatial.

Structural Constraints. At each time, at most one coalition can work on each task:

$$\forall v \in V, \forall t \leq \gamma_v, \ \sum_{C \subseteq A} \tau_{v,t,C} \leq 1 \tag{3}$$

Temporal Constraints. Tasks can be completed only by their deadlines:

$$\forall v \in V, \ \delta_v \leq 1 \tag{4}$$

$$\forall v \in V, \ \sum_{t \leq \gamma_v} \sum_{C \subseteq A} u(C, v) \cdot \tau_{v, t, C} \geq w_v \cdot \delta_v \tag{5}$$

Spatial Constraints. An agent cannot work on a task before reaching its location. This identifies two cases: when an agent reaches a task from its initial location, and when an agent moves from one task location to another. The first case imposes that, for each task v, time $t \leq \gamma_v$ and coalition C, the variable $\tau_{v, t, C}$ can be positive only if all agents in C can reach location l_v at a time $t' < t$:

$$\forall v \in V, \ \forall C \subseteq A, \ \text{if } \lambda = \max_{a \in C} \rho(a, l_a^0, l_v) \leq \gamma_v \ \text{then} \ \sum_{t \leq \lambda} \tau_{v, t, C} = 0 \tag{6}$$

λ is the maximum time at which an agent $a \in C$ reaches l_v, from its initial location at time $t = 0$. Conditional constraints are usually formulated using auxiliary variables or the Big-M method [50]. However, such approaches further enlarge the mathematical program or can cause numerical issues (Sect. 1). Consequently, in the preprocessing step necessary to create our BIP, we can implement Eq. 6 simply by excluding the variables that must be equal to zero.

The second case requires that if an agent cannot work on two tasks consecutively, then it can work on at most one:

$$\forall v_1, v_2 \in V, \ \forall C_1, C_2 \subseteq A \text{ such that } C_1 \cap C_2 \neq \emptyset,$$
$$\forall t_1 \leq \gamma_{v_1}, \ \forall t_2 \leq \gamma_{v_2} \text{ such that } t_1 + \max_{a \in C_1 \cap C_2} \rho(a, l_{v_1}, l_{v_2}) \geq t_2, \tag{7}$$
$$\tau_{v_1, t_1, C_1} + \tau_{v_2, t_2, C_2} \leq 1$$

Hence, coalition C_2 can work on task v_2 only if all agents in $C_1 \cap C_2$ can reach location l_{v_2} by deadline γ_{v_2}. Eq. 7 also implies that an agent cannot work on multiple tasks at the same time.

There are no synchronization constraints [32]. Thus, when a task v is allocated to a coalition C, each agent $a \in C$ starts working on v as soon as it reaches its location, without waiting for the remaining agents. This means that v is completed by a temporal sequence of subcoalitions of C: $\exists S \subseteq P(C)$ such that $\forall C' \in S, \exists t \leq \gamma_v, \tau_{v, t, C'} = 1$, where $P(C)$ is the power set of C.

3.4 Objective Function

Let τ be a *solution*, that is, a value assignment to all variables, which defines the route and schedule of each agent. The objective is to find a solution that maximizes the number of completed tasks:

$$\arg\max_{\tau} \sum_{v \in V} \delta_v \text{ subject to Equations 1–7} \tag{8}$$

Both creating all decision variables (Sect. 3.2) and finding an optimal solution exhaustively (Eq. 8) may require to list all $\mathcal{L}$-tuples over $P(A)$, where $\mathcal{L} = |V| \cdot t_{max}$. This implies a worst-case time complexity of:

$$O\left(\left(2^{|A|}\right)^{\mathcal{L}}\right) = O\left(2^{|A| \cdot |V| \cdot t_{max}}\right) \tag{9}$$

Theorem 1. *Equation 8 is equivalent to the original mathematical program of the CFSTP [42, Sect. 5].*

Proof sketch. Since we use the original objective function [42, Eq. 9], it suffices to verify that our constraints imply the original ones [42, Eqs. 10–32] as follows. Equations 4 and 5 imply [42, Eqs. 10 and 11]. Equation 3 implies [42, Eqs. 12 and 16]. We do not need [42, Eq. 13] because $t \leq \gamma_v$ for each $\tau_{v,t,C}$ (Eq. 1). Equations 6 and 7, combined with the objective function, imply [42, Eqs. 14, 15, 17–19]. Equation 7 implies [42, Eqs. 20–22]. Equations 5–7 imply [42, Eqs. 25–30]. Equations 3 and 7 imply [42, Eq. 31]. Equation 6 implies [42, Eq. 32].□

Having significantly fewer constraints than the original, our BIP can be used more effectively by exact algorithms based on branch-and-cut or branch-and-price [47, Sect. 3.1.1]. A trivial way to solve the CFSTP would be to implement Eq. 8 with solvers such as CPLEX or GLPK. Although this would guarantee anytime and optimal solutions, it would also take exponential time to both create and solve our BIP (Eq. 9). This limits this practice to offline contexts or very small problems. For example, using CPLEX 20.1 with commodity hardware and the test setup of [42], we can solve problems where $|A| \cdot |V| \leq 50$ in hours. With bigger problems, the runtime increases rapidly to days.

Another major issue with centralized generation of optimal solutions is that, in real-time domains such as disaster response, it can be computationally not feasible (Sect. 1) or economically undesirable, especially when the problem changes frequently [5]. For these reasons, the next section presents a scalable, dynamic and distributed algorithm.

4   A Scalable, Dynamic and Distributed CFSTP Algorithm

We reduce the CFSTP to a DynDCOP, then we show how CTS, the state-of-the-art CFSTP algorithm [5], can solve it. We use the DynDCOP formalism because it has proven largely capable of modeling disaster response problems [10].

4.1   Reduction of the CFSTP to a DynDCOP

Following [10], we formalize a DynDCOP as a sequence $\mathcal{D} = \{\mathcal{D}_t\}_{t \leq t_{max}}$, where each $\mathcal{D}_t = (A^t, X^t, D^t, F^t)$ is a DCOP such that $A^t \subseteq A$ and:

- $X^t = \{x_1^t, \ldots, x_k^t\}$ is a set of $k = |A^t| \leq n$ variables, where x_i^t is the task performed by agent $a_i^t \in A^t$.

- $D^t = \{D_1^t, \ldots, D_k^t\}$ is a set of k variable domains, such that $x_i^t \in D_i^t$. A set $d = \{d_1, \ldots, d_k\}$, where $d_i \in D_i^t$, is called an *assignment*. Each $d_i \in d$ is called the i-th *variable assignment* and is the value assigned to variable x_i^t.
- $F^t = \{f_1^t, \ldots, f_h^t\}$ is a set of $h \leq m$ functions, where f_i^t represents the constraints on task v_i^t. In particular, each $f_i^t : D_{i_1}^t \times \cdots \times D_{i_{h_i}}^t \to \mathbb{R}_{\geq 0}$ assigns a non-negative real cost to each possible assignment to the variables $X_{h_i}^t \subseteq X^t$, where $h_i \leq h$ is the arity of f_i^t.

The objective is to find an assignment that minimizes all costs:

$$\forall t \leq t_{max}, \arg\min_{d \in D^t} \sum_{f_i^t \in F^t} f_i^t(d_{i_1}, \ldots, d_{i_{h_i}}) \tag{10}$$

It is typically assumed that if x_i^t is in the scope of f_j^t, then agent a_i^t knows f_j^t [10, Sect. 4.2]. To reduce the CFSTP to a DynDCOP, we define A^t, D^t and F^t as follows. At time t, let A^t be the set of agents that are not working on nor traveling to a task (i.e., *free* or *idle* agents [5]), and let $V_{allocable}^t$ be the set of tasks that have not yet been completed. The domain of each variable x_i^t is:

$$D_i^t = \left\{ v \in V_{allocable}^t \text{ such that } t + \rho(a_i^t, l_{a_i^t}, l_v) \leq \gamma_v \right\} \cup \{\varnothing\} \tag{11}$$

where $\varnothing$ means that no task is allocated to agent a_i^t. Hence, A^t satisfies the structural constraints, while D_i^t contains the tasks that at time t can be allocated to a_i^t satisfying the spatial constraints (Sect. 3.3). Let $\tau_i \subseteq \tau$ be a *singleton solution*, that is, a solution to task v_i. At time t, let $\tau_i^t \subseteq \tau_i$ be a singleton solution corresponding to $f_i^t(d_{i_1}, \ldots, d_{i_{h_i}})$, defined as follows. Each $\tau_{v_i, t, C} \in \tau_i^t$ is such that C is a subset of the agents that control the variables in the scope of f_i^t, while $\tau_{v_i, t, C} = 1$ if $d_{i_{h_i}} = v_i$, for each h_i-th agent in C, and 0 otherwise. To satisfy the temporal constraints (Sect. 3.3), each i-th function is defined as follows:

$$f_i^t(d_{i_1}, \ldots, d_{i_{h_i}}) = \min_{\tau_i^t, t' \leq \gamma_{v_i}} \sum_{s \leq t', \tau_{v_i, s, C} \in \tau_i^t} u(C, v) \geq w_v \tag{12}$$

with the convention that $f_i^t(d_{i_1}, \ldots, d_{i_{h_i}}) = +\infty$ if v_i cannot be completed by deadline γ_v. Hence, the solution space of $\mathcal{D}$ satisfies all CFSTP constraints, while minimizing all costs implies minimizing the time required to complete each task (Eqs. 10 and 12), which implies maximizing the total number of completed tasks, as required by the objective function of the CFSTP (Eq. 8).

4.2 Distributed CTS

At each time, CTS executes in sequence the following two phases [5]:

1. For each free agent a, associate a with an uncompleted task v such that v is the closest to a and deadline γ_v is minimum.
2. For each uncompleted task v, allocate v to a coalition C such that $|C|$ is minimum and each agent $a \in C$ has been associated with v in Phase 1.

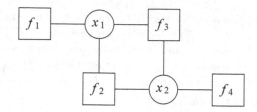

Fig. 1. The factor graph of a DCOP with 2 agents and 4 tasks. In our formulation, a DCOP represents the state of a CFSTP at a certain time, in which circles are variables of free agents, squares are cost functions of uncompleted tasks, and each edge connects an agent to a task it can reach by its deadline.

To represent a DCOP, we use a *factor graph* [18,21], which decomposes the problem into three parts: *variable nodes*, representing the variables; *factor nodes*, representing the constraints; undirected edges between each factor node and the variable nodes in its scope. As an example, Fig. 1 shows the factor graph of the function $F(X) = f_1(x_1) + f_2(x_1, x_2) + f_3(x_1, x_2) + f_4(x_2)$.

In a factor graph G, a solution is found by allowing nodes to exchange messages. Hence, to execute CTS on G, we have to define how the nodes communicate and operate. Below, we present a communication protocol and algorithms for both variable and factor nodes. Based on the well-established formalism of Yokoo et al. [52], the nodes communicate in the following way:

- Node i can message node j only if i knows the address of j. In our context, if x_i^t is in the scope of f_j^t, then x_i^t knows the address of f_j^t, and vice versa.
- Each node i has a message queue Q_i, to which messages are delivered with a finite delay.
- Node i can use the function RECEIVE() to dequeue a message from Q_i, and the function SEND(j, illoc_force, [args]) to send a message to j. Node j will receive a message in the format (sender, illoc_force, [args]), where sender is the identifier of node i, illoc_force is its illocutionary force, and [args] is an optional list of arguments. By *illocutionary force*, we mean either an information or a command [48].

We assume that the node of each function is controlled by an agent in its scope. Algorithm 1 presents the operation of variable node x_i^t. If there is an uncompleted task v_j^t that can be allocated to free agent a_i^t (lines 1–3), then variable node x_i^t communicates to factor node f_j^t the ability of a_i^t to work on v_j^t, also specifying the time at which it can reach and start working on it (lines 4–6). After that, it waits until it gets a reply from f_j^t or a predetermined time interval expires (lines 7–9). If it receives the approval of f_j^t, then v_j^t is allocated to a_i^t (lines 10–11). At line 2, v_j^t is chosen such that it is the closest to a_i^t and $\gamma_{v_j^t}$ is the shortest deadline [5]. Phase 1 is completed after that each x_i^t executes line 6.

Algorithm 1: CTS node of variable x_i^t

---

1   $x_i^t \leftarrow \varnothing$ ▷ initialize to *idle*
2   $d_j \leftarrow$ get task allocable to agent a_i^t at time t ▷ [5, Algorithm 5]
3   **if** $d_j \neq \varnothing$ **then**
4      $s_i \leftarrow$ time at which agent a_i^t can start working on task d_j
5      $f_j^t \leftarrow$ factor node of d_j
6   SEND(f_j^t, assignable, s_i)
7   msg $\leftarrow$ NIL
8   **while** *msg not received from* f_j^t *or not time out* **do**
9   msg $\leftarrow$ RECEIVE()
10   **if** *msg* $= (f_j^t, allocate)$ **then**
11        $x_i^t \leftarrow d_j$

Algorithm 2: CTS node of factor f_j^t

---

1   **while** *not all neighbors sent an* **assignable** *message or not time out* **do**
2   msg $\leftarrow$ RECEIVE()
3   $\Pi_{v_j}^t \leftarrow$ list of all assignable agents sorted by arrival time to v_j
4   $C^* \leftarrow$ minimum coalition in $\Pi_{v_j}^t$ that can complete v_j by γ_v ▷ Equation 12
5   **for** $a_i^t \in C^*$ **do**
6   SEND(x_i^t, allocate)
7   $C_{v_j}^t \leftarrow$ all agents working on v_j at time t
8   **if** $C_{v_j}^t \neq \emptyset$ **then**
9     $w_{v_j} \leftarrow w_{v_j} - u(C_{v_j}^t, v_j)$

Algorithm 2 presents the operation of factor node f_j^t. The loop at lines 1–2 is a synchronization step that allows f_j^t to know which agents in its neighborhood can work on v_j^t. Lines 3–6 enacts Phase 2, while lines 7–9 update workload w_{v_j}.

We call *Distributed CTS* (D-CTS) the union of Algorithms 1 and 2. The size of each message is $O(1)$, since it always contains a node address, a message flag and an integer. At time t, each variable node x_i^t sends at most 1 message (line 6 in Algorithm 1), while each factor node f_j^t sends $O(|A|)$ messages (lines 5–6 in Algorithm 2). Assuming that all tasks can be completed, the total number of messages sent is $O(|A| + |V| \cdot |A|) = O(|V| \cdot |A|)$.

The runtime of Algorithm 1 is $O(|V|)$, because line 2 selects a task in the neighborhood of an agent. The runtime of Algorithm 2 is $O(|A| \log |A|)$, due to the sorting at line 3 [8]. Since both algorithms are executed up to t_{max} times, the overall time complexity of D-CTS is the same as CTS [5, Eqs. 10 and 11]:

$$\Omega\left(t_{max} \cdot (|V| + |A| \log |A|)\right) \text{ and } O\left(t_{max} \cdot |V| \cdot |A| \log |A|\right) \tag{13}$$

where the lower bound represents the case in which the operations of each phase are executed in parallel. The advantages of D-CTS are as follows:

1. It is anytime, since it decomposes a CFSTP into a set of independent sub-problems (Sect. 1). This property is not trivial to guarantee in distributed systems [54], and is missing in main DCOP algorithms (e.g., ADOPT, DPOP, OptAPO and Max-Sum [10, Table 4]).
2. It is self-stabilizing [10, Definition 6], being guaranteed to converge [5, Theorem 1], and given that each agent can only work on a new task after completing the one to which it is currently assigned (Algorithm 1).
3. The phase-based design has two performance benefits. First, the algorithm is not affected by the structure of factor graphs. For instance, in a cyclic graph like the one in Fig. 1, where the same $a > 1$ tasks can be allocated to the same $b > 1$ agents, inference-based DCOP algorithms (e.g., Max-Sum and BinaryMS) in general are not guaranteed to converge, unless they are augmented with specific techniques (e.g., damping [7] or ADVP [55]). Second, the algorithm is robust to *disruptions*, that is, to the addition or removal of nodes from a factor graph [41, Sect. 6.2]. Disruptions are typical of real-world domains [5]. For instance, in disaster response, tasks are removed if some victims have perished, and are added if new fires are discovered. Likewise, new agents are added to reflect the availability of additional workforce, while existing ones are removed when they deplete their resources or are unable to continue due to sustained damages. Unlike D-CTS, the majority of DCOP algorithms (e.g., Max-Sum and DPOP) cannot handle disruptions, unless they are properly modified or extended (e.g., FMS and S-DPOP [10]). Hence, besides being a DynDCOP algorithm, D-CTS can also cope with runtime changes in a DCOP formulation.
4. Unlike most DCOP algorithms (e.g., ADOPT and DPOP), the communication overhead (i.e., the number of messages exchanged) is at most linear, and each agent does not need to maintain an information graph of all other agents.
5. Finally, performance does not depend on any tuning parameters, as is the case with other algorithms (e.g., DSA variants).

5   Empirical Evaluation in Dynamic Environments

We created a dataset[2] with 347588 tasks using open records published by the London Fire Brigade over a period of 11 years. Then, we wrote a test framework in Java[3] and compared D-CTS against DSA-SDP [54], a state-of-the-art incomplete, synchronous and search-based DCOP algorithm.

We adapted DSA-SDP to solve our DynDCOP formulation (Sect. 4.1), which decomposes the CFSTP into a sequence of independent subproblems. Hence, although originally a DCOP algorithm, its performance is not penalized in our test framework. We chose it as our baseline because, similarly to D-CTS, it has a polynomial coordination overhead and is scalable (Sect. 2). We kept the parameters of [54] and ran $|V_{allocable}^t|$ iterations at each time t, since we found that, in our test framework, running more iterations can only marginally improve the

---

[2] https://zenodo.org/record/4728012.
[3] https://zenodo.org/record/4764646.

solution quality, while requiring a significant increase in communication overhead and time complexity. Below, we detail our setup and discuss the results.

5.1 Setup

Let $\mathcal{N}$ and $\mathcal{U}$ denote the normal and uniform distribution, respectively. A test configuration consists of the following parameters:

- Since there are currently 150 identical London fire engines in operation, $|A| = 150$ for each problem. All agents have the same speed, but each may perform differently in different coalitions.
- $|V| = |A| \cdot k$, where $k \in \mathbb{N}^+$ and $k \leq 20$. Thus, problems have up to 3000 tasks.
- Each task v is a fire or a special service, and its demand is defined by a record dated between 1 January 2009 and 31 December 2020. More precisely, γ_v is the attendance time (in seconds) of the firefighters, and since the median attendance time in the whole dataset is about 5 minutes, we set $w_v \sim \mathcal{U}(10, 300)$ to simulate wide ranging workloads.
- For each task-to-agent ratio $|V|/|A|$, the nodes of a problem are chosen in chronological order. That is, the first problem always starts with record 1, and if a problem stops at record q, then the following one will use records $q + 1$ to $q + 1 + |V|$.
- The locations are latitude-longitude points, and the travel time $\rho(a, l_1, l_2)$ is given by the distance between locations l_1 and l_2 divided by the (fixed) speed of agent a.
- In addition to task locations, L contains the locations of the 103 currently active London fire stations. In each problem, each agent starts at a fire station defined by the record of a task.
- To generate coalition values, we start by taking from [38, Sect. 4] the following well-known distributions:
  1. *Normally Distributed Coalition Structures* (NDCS): $u(C, v) \sim \mathcal{N}(|C|, \sqrt[4]{|C|})$.
  2. *Agent-based*: each agent a has a value $p_a \sim \mathcal{U}(0, 10)$ representing its individual performance and a value $p_a^C \sim \mathcal{U}(0, 2 \cdot p_a)$ representing its performance in coalition C. The value of a coalition is the sum of the values of its members: $u(C, v) = \sum_{a \in C} p_a^C$.

  Then, we decrease each $\mu_v = u(C, v)$ by $r \sim \mathcal{U}(\mu_v/10, \mu_v/4)$ with probability $\gamma_v/(t_{max} + 1)$, and by $q \sim \mathcal{U}(\mu_v/10, \mu_v/4)$ with probability $|C|/(|A|+1)$. The perturbation r simulates real-time domains, where the earlier the deadline for a task, the higher the reward [45]. The perturbation q simulates situations where the more agents there are, the greater the likelihood of congestion and thus of reduced performance, as it can happen in large-scale robot swarms [12]. We call the resulting distributions UC_NDCS and UC_Agent-based, where UC means *Urgent and Congested*. NDCS does not to favor solutions containing fewer coalitions [40], while Agent-based tends to do the opposite. By using them, we obtain solution spaces in which higher values are first associated

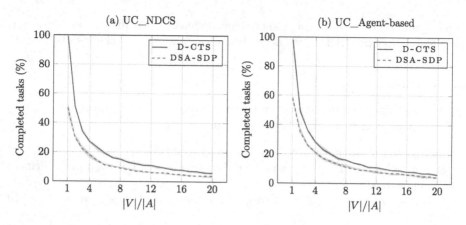

Fig. 2. Performance of DSA-SDP and D-CTS in our test framework. Each subfigure denotes a coalition value distribution, while each point is the median and 95% confidence interval over 100 problems of the percentage of tasks completed. The X-axis is the task-to-agent ratio.

with smaller coalitions and then with larger coalitions. Both distributions are neither superadditive nor subadditive [39]. Hence, it is not possible to define a priori an optimal coalition for each task.

During the solution of each problem, we gradually removed agents to simulate *degradation* scenarios. The removal rate was calculated with a Poisson cumulative distribution function $Pois_{CDF}(\boldsymbol{a}, \lambda)$, where $\boldsymbol{a}$ contains all firefighter arrival times in the dataset, and the rate λ is the average number of incidents per hour and per day. For each test configuration and algorithm, we solved 100 problems and measured the median and 95% confidence interval of: number of messages sent; *network load*, or the total size of messages sent; number of *Non-Concurrent Constraint Checks* (NCCCs) [28]; percentage of tasks completed, and CPU time[4].

5.2   Results

Figure 2 and 3 show our results. D-CTS completes 3.79% ± [42.22%, 1.96%] more tasks than DSA-SDP (Fig. 2). For both algorithms, the performance drops rapidly as the task-to-agent ratio increases. This is due to the Urgent component in the coalition value distributions: the higher the ratio, the higher the median task completion time. Conversely, the Congested component can reduce the percentage of tasks completed more in problems with smaller task-to-agent ratios, where agents can form larger coalitions and thus increase the likelihood of congestion.

---

[4] Based on an Intel Xeon E5-2670 processor (octa-core 2.6 GHz with Hyper-Threading).

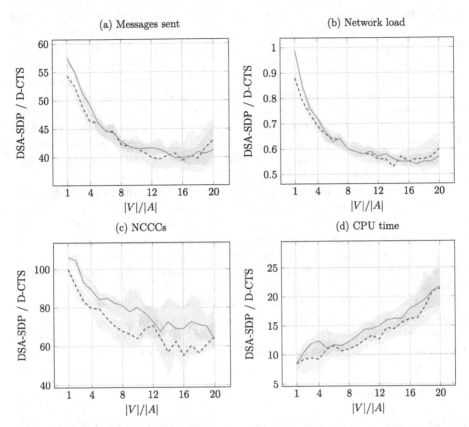

Fig. 3. Ratio of DSA-SDP performance to D-CTS performance. Each subfigure denotes a performance metric m, while each point is the median and 95% confidence interval over 100 problems of m_a/m_b, where m_a (resp. m_b) is the value of DSA-SDP (resp. D-CTS) for m. The X-axis is the task-to-agent ratio.

The network load of DSA-SDP is $0.59 \pm [0.41, 0.02]$ times that of D-CTS (Fig. 3b). This is because a DSA-SDP message contains only a task address, while a D-CTS message also contains a binary flag and an integer (Sect. 4.2). In Java, an address requires 8 bytes, a flag requires 1 byte, and an integer requires 1–4 bytes. Hence, while a DSA-SDP message always requires 8 bytes, a D-CTS message requires 10–13 bytes. This is line with the results obtained. However, the situation would be reversed if we performed 1000 DSA-SDP iterations as suggested in [53], since $median(\{|V_{allocable}^t|\}_{t \leq t_{max}}) \ll 1000$ in our tests.

The remaining metrics put DSA-SDP at a distinct disadvantage (Fig. 3a, c, d). The overload compared to D-CTS is $41.72 \pm [12.45, 0.42]$ times more messages sent, $72.78 \pm [34.79, 27.79]$ times more NCCCs, and $13.82 \pm [4.52, 3.71]$ times more CPU time. This is explained as follows. While the number of messages sent is $O(|V|\cdot|A|)$ in D-CTS (Sect. 4.2), it is $O(|V|\cdot|A|^2)$ in DSA-SDP, since the agents exchange their assignments [54]. In D-CTS, analyzing in sequence the agents that can be assigned to each task (line 4 in Algorithm 2) requires $O(|V|\cdot|A|)$ NCCCs. DSA-SDP does a similar analysis, but for each message exchanged between two agents, which requires $O(|V|^2\cdot|A|^2)$ NCCCs. Finally, the time complexity of DSA-SDP is $O(t_{max}\cdot|V|\cdot|A|^2)$, where $O(|V|\cdot|A|)$ is required by the message exchange phase at each time, and $O(|A|)$ is required by each agent to calculate the assignment costs (Eq. 12). Hence, DSA-SDP is asymptotically slower than D-CTS (Eq. 13). Overall, D-CTS took $525\pm[281,482]$ ms, while DSA-SDP took $6.97\pm[5.84,6.2]$ seconds. In accordance with the above, the ratio of DSA-SDP performance to D-CTS performance tends to increase with regard to CPU time, and to decrease with regard to the other metrics.

In a dynamic environment, desirable features of a distributed algorithm include being robust to disruptions and minimizing communication overhead (Sect. 4.2). The latter feature is particularly important in real-world domains such as disaster response, where agent communication can be costly (i.e., non *free-comm* environment [36]) or there might be operational constraints, such as low bandwidth or limited network topology (e.g., sparse robot swarms searching for shipwrecks on the seabed or monitoring forest fires [46]). In our tests, compared to DSA-SDP, D-CTS achieves a slightly better solution quality (Fig. 2), and is one order of magnitude more efficient in terms of communication overhead and time complexity (Fig. 3). This affirms its effectiveness as a scalable and distributed CFSTP algorithm for dynamic environments.

6   Conclusions

We gave a novel mathematical programming formulation of the CFSTP, which is significantly shorter and easier to implement than the original [42]. By reducing the CFSTP to a DynDCOP, we also designed D-CTS, the first distributed version of the state-of-the-art CFSTP algorithm. Finally, using real-world data provided by the London Fire Brigade and a large-scale test framework, we compared D-CTS against DSA-SDP, a state-of-the-art distributed algorithm. In situations where the number of agents monotonically decreases over time, D-CTS has slightly better median performance, as well as significantly lower communication overhead and time complexity. Future work aims at extending our test framework by:

1. Comparing D-CTS with other state-of-the-art distributed algorithms, such as DALO [15], SBDO [3], GDBA [33], D-Gibbs [31] and FMC_TA [30].
2. Adding more realistic coalition value distributions.
3. Studying *exploration* scenarios [10], that is, designing tests in which tasks are gradually added to the system.

We also want to transfer our work to the MARSC model [6], which, unlike the CFSTP, can capture situations where there are soft deadlines, tasks are not all equally important, and there may be an order of completion.

Finally, given its advantages (Sect. 4.2) and the scarcity of incomplete Dyn-DCOP algorithms (Sect. 2), we want to design a D-CTS extension with provable bounds on solution quality and able to solve general DynDCOPs.

Acknowledgments. We thank Alessandro Farinelli for his suggestions, and the anonymous reviewers for helping us correct and improve the manuscript. This research is sponsored by UKRI and AXA Research Fund. Luca Capezzuto acknowledges the use of the IRIDIS High Performance Computing facility at the University of Southampton.

References

1. Alexander, D.E.: Principles of Emergency Planning and Management. Oxford University Press, Oxford (2002)
2. Baker, C.A.B., Ramchurn, S., Teacy, W.L., Jennings, N.R.: Planning search and rescue missions for UAV teams. In: ECAI, pp. 1777–1782 (2016)
3. Billiau, G., Chang, C.F., Ghose, A.: SBDO: a new robust approach to dynamic distributed constraint optimisation. In: Desai, N., Liu, A., Winikoff, M. (eds.) PRIMA 2010. LNCS (LNAI), vol. 7057, pp. 11–26. Springer, Heidelberg (2012). https://doi.org/10.1007/978-3-642-25920-3_2
4. Brucker, P.: Scheduling Algorithms, 5th edn. Springer, Heidelberg (2007). https://doi.org/10.1007/978-3-540-69516-5
5. Capezzuto, L., Tarapore, D., Ramchurn, S.D.: Anytime and efficient multi-agent coordination for disaster response. SN Comput. Sci. **2**(165) (2021, online)
6. Capezzuto, L., Tarapore, D., Ramchurn, S.D.: Multi-agent routing and scheduling through coalition formation. In: OptLearnMAS-21 (2021)
7. Cohen, L., Zivan, R.: Max-sum revisited: the real power of damping. In: Sukthankar, G., Rodriguez-Aguilar, J.A. (eds.) AAMAS 2017. LNCS (LNAI), vol. 10643, pp. 111–124. Springer, Cham (2017). https://doi.org/10.1007/978-3-319-71679-4_8
8. Cormen, T.H., Leiserson, C.E., Rivest, R.L., Stein, C.: Introduction to Algorithms, 3rd edn. MIT Press, Cambridge (2009)
9. Farinelli, A., Rogers, A., Petcu, A., Jennings, N.R.: Decentralised coordination of low-power embedded devices using the max-sum algorithm. In: AAMAS, vol. 2, pp. 639–646 (2008)
10. Fioretto, F., Pontelli, E., Yeoh, W.: Distributed constraint optimization problems and applications: a survey. JAIR **61**, 623–698 (2018)
11. Griva, I., Nash, S.G., Sofer, A.: Linear and Nonlinear Optimization. Society for Industrial and Applied Mathematics, 2nd edn. (2009)
12. Guerrero, J., Oliver, G., Valero, O.: Multi-robot coalitions formation with deadlines: complexity analysis and solutions. PloS one **12**(1), e0170659 (2017)
13. Hewitt, C.: The Challenge of Open Systems, pp. 383–395. Cambridge University Press, Cambridge (1990)
14. Junges, R., Bazzan, A.L.C.: Evaluating the performance of DCOP algorithms in a real world, dynamic problem. In: AAMAS, vol. 2, pp. 599–606 (2008)
15. Kiekintveld, C., Yin, Z., Kumar, A., Tambe, M.: Asynchronous algorithms for approximate distributed constraint optimization with quality bounds. In: AAMAS, pp. 133–140 (2010)

16. Kim, Y., Krainin, M., Lesser, V.: Effective variants of the max-sum algorithm for radar coordination and scheduling. In: IEEE/WIC/ACM International Conferences on Web Intelligence and Intelligent Agent Technology, vol. 2, pp. 357–364 (2011)

17. Kitano, H., Tadokoro, S.: Robocup rescue: a grand challenge for multiagent and intelligent systems. AI Mag. **22**(1), 39 (2001). https://rescuesim.robocup.org

18. Kschischang, F.R., Frey, B.J., Loeliger, H.A.: Factor graphs and the sum-product algorithm. IEEE Trans. Inf. Theory **47**(2), 498–519 (2001)

19. Leite, A.R., Enembreck, F., Barthes, J.P.A.: Distributed constraint optimization problems: review and perspectives. Expert Syst. Appl. **41**(11), 5139–5157 (2014)

20. Lesser, V., Corkill, D.: Challenges for multi-agent coordination theory based on empirical observations. In: AAMAS, pp. 1157–1160 (2014)

21. Loeliger, H.A.: An introduction to factor graphs. IEEE Sig. Proc. Mag. **21**(1), 28–41 (2004)

22. London Datastore: London Fire Brigade Incident Records (2021). https://data.london.gov.uk/dataset/london-fire-brigade-incident-records

23. London Datastore: London Fire Brigade Mobilisation Records (2021). https://data.london.gov.uk/dataset/london-fire-brigade-mobilisation-records

24. Maheswaran, R.T., Pearce, J.P., Tambe, M.: Distributed algorithms for dcop: A graphical-game-based approach. In: International Conference on Parallel and Distributed Computing Systems, pp. 432–439 (2004)

25. Maheswaran, R.T., Tambe, M., Bowring, E., Pearce, J.P., Varakantham, P.: Taking DCOP to the real world: efficient complete solutions for distributed multi-event scheduling. In: AAMAS, vol. 1, pp. 310–317 (2004)

26. Mahmud, S., Khan, M.M., Jennings, N.R.: On population-based algorithms for distributed constraint optimization problems. arXiv:2009.01625 (2020)

27. Mailler, R., Zheng, H., Ridgway, A.: Dynamic, distributed constraint solving and thermodynamic theory. JAAMAS **32**(1), 188–217 (2018)

28. Meisels, A.: Distributed Search by Constrained Agents. Springer, Heidelberg (2007). https://doi.org/10.1007/978-1-84800-040-7

29. Murphy, R.R.: Disaster Robotics. MIT Press, Cambridge (2014)

30. Nelke, S.A., Okamoto, S., Zivan, R.: Market clearing-based dynamic multi-agent task allocation. ACM Trans. Int. Syst. Tech. **11**(1), 1–25 (2020)

31. Nguyen, D.T., Yeoh, W., Lau, H.C., Zivan, R.: Distributed Gibbs: a linear-space sampling-based DCOP algorithm. JAIR **64**, 705–748 (2019)

32. Nunes, E., Manner, M., Mitiche, H., Gini, M.: A taxonomy for task allocation problems with temporal and ordering constraints. JRAS **90**, 55–70 (2017)

33. Okamoto, S., Zivan, R., Nahon, A., et al.: Distributed breakout: beyond satisfaction. In: IJCAI, pp. 447–453 (2016)

34. Pearce, J.P., Tambe, M.: Quality guarantees on k-optimal solutions for distributed constraint optimization problems. In: IJCAI, pp. 1446–1451 (2007)

35. Petcu, A.: A class of algorithms for distributed constraint optimization. Ph.D. thesis, École polytechnique fédérale de Lausanne (2007)

36. Ponda, S.S., Johnson, L.B., Geramifard, A., How, J.P.: Cooperative mission planning for multi-UAV teams. In: Valavanis, K., Vachtsevanos, G. (eds.) Handbook of Unmanned Aerial Vehicles, pp. 1447–1490. Springer, Dordrecht (2015). https://doi.org/10.1007/978-90-481-9707-1_16

37. Pujol-Gonzalez, M., Cerquides, J., Farinelli, A., Meseguer, P., Rodriguez-Aguilar, J.A.: Efficient inter-team task allocation in robocup rescue. In: AAMAS, pp. 413–421 (2015)

38. Rahwan, T., Michalak, T., Jennings, N.: A hybrid algorithm for coalition structure generation. In: AAAI, vol. 26 (2012)
39. Rahwan, T., Michalak, T.P., Wooldridge, M., Jennings, N.R.: Coalition structure generation: a survey. AI **229**, 139–174 (2015)
40. Rahwan, T., Ramchurn, S.D., Jennings, N.R., Giovannucci, A.: An anytime algorithm for optimal coalition structure generation. JAIR **34**, 521–567 (2009)
41. Ramchurn, S.D., Farinelli, A., Macarthur, K.S., Jennings, N.R.: Decentralized coordination in robocup rescue. Comput. J. **53**(9), 1447–1461 (2010)
42. Ramchurn, S.D., Polukarov, M., Farinelli, A., Truong, C., Jennings, N.R.: Coalition formation with spatial and temporal constraints. In: AAMAS, pp. 1181–1188 (2010)
43. Ramchurn, S.D., et al.: Human-agent collaboration for disaster response. JAAMAS **30**(1), 82–111 (2016)
44. Ross, G.T., Soland, R.M.: A branch and bound algorithm for the generalized assignment problem. Math. Program. **8**(1), 91–103 (1975)
45. Stankovic, J.A., Spuri, M., Ramamritham, K., Buttazzo, G.C.: Deadline Scheduling for Real-time Systems: EDF and Related Algorithms, vol. 460. Springer, Heidelberg (2013). Reprint of the original 1998 edition
46. Tarapore, D., Groß, R., Zauner, K.P.: Sparse robot swarms: moving swarms to real-world applications. Front. Robot. AI **7**, 83 (2020)
47. Vansteenwegen, P., Gunawan, A.: Orienteering Problems: Models and Algorithms for Vehicle Routing Problems with Profits. Springer, Switzerland (2019). https://doi.org/10.1007/978-3-030-29746-6
48. Vieira, R., Moreira, Á.F., Wooldridge, M., Bordini, R.H.: On the formal semantics of speech-act based communication in an agent-oriented programming language. JAIR **29**, 221–267 (2007)
49. Vinyals, M., et al.: Quality guarantees for region optimal DCOP algorithms. In: AAMAS, vol. 1, pp. 133–140 (2011)
50. Wolsey, L.A.: Integer Programming, 2nd edn. Wiley, Hoboken (2020)
51. Yokoo, M., Hirayama, K.: Distributed breakout algorithm for solving distributed constraint satisfaction problems. In: Proceedings of the 2nd International Conference on MAS, pp. 401–408. MIT Press Cambridge (1996)
52. Yokoo, M., Ishida, T., Durfee, E.H., Kuwabara, K.: Distributed constraint satisfaction for formalizing distributed problem solving. In: Proceedings of the 12th International Conference on Distributed Computing System, pp. 614–621. IEEE (1992)
53. Zhang, W., Wang, G., Xing, Z., Wittenburg, L.: Distributed stochastic search and distributed breakout: properties, comparison and applications to constraint optimization problems in sensor networks. AI **161**(1–2), 55–87 (2005)
54. Zivan, R., Okamoto, S., Peled, H.: Explorative anytime local search for distributed constraint optimization. AI **212**, 1–26 (2014)
55. Zivan, R., Parash, T., Cohen, L., Peled, H., Okamoto, S.: Balancing exploration and exploitation in incomplete min/max-sum inference for distributed constraint optimization. JAAMAS **31**(5), 1165–1207 (2017)

Convention Emergence with Congested Resources

Priel Levy[1(✉)] and Nathan Griffiths[2]

[1] Bar-Ilan University, Ramat Gan, Israel
priel.levy@biu.ac.il
[2] University of Warwick, Coventry, UK
nathan.griffiths@warwick.ac.uk

Abstract. Norms and conventions enable coordination in populations of
agents by establishing patterns of behaviour, which can emerge as agents
interact with their environment and each other. Previous research on
norm emergence typically considers pairwise interactions, where agents'
rewards are endogenously determined. In many real-life domains, however, individuals do not interact with one other directly, but with their
environment, and the resources associated with actions are often congested. Thus, agents' rewards are exogenously determined as a function
of others' actions and the environment. In this paper, we propose a framework to represent this setting by: (i) introducing congested actions; and
(ii) adding a central authority, that is able to manipulate agents' rewards.
Agents are heterogeneous in terms of their reward functions, and learn
over time, enabling norms to emerge. We illustrate the framework using
transport modality choice as a simple scenario, and investigate the effect
of representative manipulations on the emergent norms.

Keywords: Norm emergence · Conventions · Congestion games

1 Introduction

Norms and conventions enable populations of agents to interact in complex environments, by establishing patterns of behaviour that are beneficial, and enabling
coordination. Norms are viewed as equilibria, in which the interacting agents
act in some expected way [38], either choosing the same action (in coordination
games) or different actions (in anti-coordination games).[1] Existing norm emergence research often focuses on the population level phenomena that result from
pairwise interactions between individual agents [16,28].

In many real-life scenarios, however, individuals do not interact with one
another through pairwise interactions, but instead select actions (which have
a cost) according to some individual strategy, and receive rewards which are,
at least in part, determined by the action choices of others. Thus, individuals interact with their environment, rather than directly with others. Furthermore, resources are often *congested*, meaning that an individual's valuation of a

---

[1] Note that such equilibria are not necessarily Nash equilibria.

© Springer Nature Switzerland AG 2021
A. Rosenfeld and N. Talmon (Eds.): EUMAS 2021, LNAI 12802, pp. 126–143, 2021.
https://doi.org/10.1007/978-3-030-82254-5_8

resource (and consequently their reward) is not endogenously determined, but rather depends on the number of others using the resource (i.e., it is a function of others' actions) [26]. This congestion effect manifests in many economic and social environments, where individuals 'compete' for some resource, with such congestion games being widely studied from a game theoretic perspective. However, in such environments, while it is often desirable to establish norms to facilitate coordination, the number of individuals who can benefit from choosing a particular action is limited. Examples include transport modality or route choices, bandwidth or compute allocation, and public service consumption.

One important aspect of many economic and social environments, in addition to congested resources and which is not accounted for by traditional congestion games, is that of an authority figure with preferences about the distribution of individuals' action choices, and having some (but not complete) control over the payoffs they receive. While norms often emerge in the absence of an authority, the authority may manipulate the rewards of individuals or groups of individuals in order to 'nudge' the system towards a particular state. Consider, for example, the scenario of commuters choosing a transport modality (e.g., bus, car or walk) and route. Such choices are made individually, but rewards are determined by the current state of the environment and are affected both by others' choices and the city authority. Many individuals choosing the bus may result in overcrowding and low rewards, but few individuals choosing the bus may cause the city authority to increase prices. Moreover, the city authority may have preferences in terms of reducing car use and increasing active travel, and so may impose charges for car use or offer rewards for walking. In London, for example, the city authority facilitates bike loans, encourages employers to offer financial or holiday incentives for employees who do not drive, and imposes charges for private car use.[2]

The way a norm is evaluated depends on the perspective and associated preferences, either that of an individual agent or of the authority. Behaviours and norms that are beneficial from one perspective may not be beneficial from another, a factor not typically considered in congestion games. Individual agents evaluate a norm by considering its impact on their own rewards, which are influenced by others' actions. Alternatively, the authority may evaluate it from a system level, considering whether it is appropriate for the system as a whole, potentially considering factors such as the long-term or indirect effects of a norm [16]. While the authority may aim to maximise social welfare (i.e., the sum of individuals' rewards), it may have its own preferences regarding resource utilisation, namely, which actions are selected and by what proportion of agents.

To illustrate this difference in perspectives, consider the example of transport modality choice and the possible norms of driving and walking. From an individual's perspective, choosing to drive may broadly result in two possible scenarios: either a high individual reward (if relatively few others choose to drive and so traffic is light), or a low individual reward (if many others choose to drive, resulting in congestion). Similarly, from an individual's perspective walking may have a medium reward, regardless of others' transport choices. From the authority's

---

[2] See, for example, http://content.tfl.gov.uk/tfl-active-recovery-toolkit.pdf.

perspective, assuming a preference of decreasing car use and encouraging active travel, the situation is independent of the individual rewards: there is higher value to the authority when fewer individuals choose to drive, and the highest value would be for all individuals to walk and not drive. Other norms may be more complex, for example, individuals may prefer to be on buses with a reasonable number of other passengers (for perceived personal safety), but not so many that they have to sit next to a fellow traveller, while the authority might prefer the bus to be full to capacity (i.e., full utilisation of the resource).

In this paper, we propose a framework that: (i) introduces congested actions into the norm emergence setting; (ii) adds a central authority to such congestion games, such that the authority is able to manipulate (but not fully control) the rewards of agents and groups of agents; and (iii) accounts for the different perspectives of the agents and authority in terms of their preferences. We illustrate the framework using a simplified transport modality choice example, and show the impact of manipulations on the emergent norms in the population.

2   Related Work

Norm emergence has been widely studied in the context of agents who learn (or reproduce) based on the rewards received from their interactions with others. Such interactions typically take the form of an n-player m-action game, in which each agent's reward is a discrete function of others' actions and is determined according to a payoff matrix, which is typically common knowledge. Most literature on norm emergence either models cooperation using the Prisoner's Dilemma [3,17,18] or learning to choose common actions in a coordination game [16,19,28,35,36,39,44]. Such work typically focuses on pairwise interactions where agents select from two possible actions, i.e., $n = 2$ and $m = 2$. In this paper, we consider norm emergence from a more general perspective, in which individual agents select from a wider set of actions ($m \geq 2$) and receive rewards which are only partially determined by other agents' choices (i.e., interactions are not pairwise). While some studies have considered the more general setting of $n \geq 2$ and $m \geq 2$, they have typically focused on cases with small numbers of agents and actions per interaction [1,27] and do not consider congested resources or the inclusion of an authority figure. Other work has considered the impact of large action spaces [31], but only from the perspective of agents learning common actions, rather than the more general setting.

Our setting is similar to the El-Farol Bar Problem (EFBP), a well-known congestion game which shares some characteristics with norm emergence [4,12, 33]. In the EFBP, a group of n agents, representing people, independently decide whether to visit a bar on a certain evening, with the most enjoyable visits being when the bar is not too crowded, i.e., when the number of visitors is less than some (unknown) threshold. Choices are unaffected by previous visits and there is no communication or information on others' choices. Each agent only knows its own choice and the subsequent reward. The EFBP illustrates the key features of our setting, namely that agents compete for a resource (space in the bar), agents are rational (their rewards provide information on attendance, and they use this strategically), and there is limited information (agents do not know others' strategies, but their rewards provide information on other agents' actions). In this paper, we introduce an authority figure that can influence agents' rewards, which can be viewed as adding a bar owner to the EFBP, and considering rewards from both the owner and customer perspectives.

Our setting is also similar to the Multi-Armed Bandit (MAB) problem, where each individual sequentially pulls one of several arms (representing choosing actions), with each pull resulting in a reward from some distribution (which is unknown to the agent and may differ over time) [5,7,15,22]. While we could represent rewards in a MAB setting as being influenced by other agents' action choices through the use of a non-stationary distribution, such a representation is not intuitive. Moreover, it is less clear how an authority that can reward or penalise certain action choices might be introduced into the MAB setting.

Various forms of intervention have been considered to encourage norm emergence. One of the earliest studies was Axelrod's Norms Game [8], in which a population of agents repeatedly make decisions about whether to comply with a desired norm or defect, and whether to punish those who are seen to defect. More informed punishment methods, such as experience based punishment, have been developed for the Norms Game [24,25], but these are peer-based and do not consider an authority figure. Other approaches have considered incentives and sanctions [30,32], or the use of non-learning fixed strategy agents [13,27,36] to influence the emergence of norms, but typically in settings where rewards are a direct function of the choices of those involved in an interaction, and so can be represented as a simple payoff matrix. In this paper, we introduce an authority that is able to influence agents' rewards, by changing the costs of performing actions and the sensitivities of agents to the results. Similar manipulations have been considered in non-stationary MABs, for example adding constant noise [14], using adversarial (arbitrary) rewards [2,6,20,34], varying the expected values of the reward distributions [45], or assuming arms are contextual (i.e., no prior knowledge about the arms exists except for some historical data or some action features) [23,37,42]. To the best of our knowledge, we are the first to consider such a perspective in the context of norm emergence with congested actions, where rewards are partially determined by the actions of others.

3 Modelling Norm Emergence with Congested Actions

We consider a population of n agents, or players, $P = \{p_1, ..., p_n\}$ and a single centralized authority, ψ. Agents are heterogeneous and may be of different types, or belong to different groups, which determine their preferences over actions and influence the rewards they receive. Agents interact with their environment by playing a repeated game in which they select an action, or option, o from a set of $m \geq 2$ alternatives, $O = \{o_1, ..., o_m\}$. At a given time t each agent p simultaneously interacts with the environment by choosing an action $o_{p,t}$ for which it receives a reward (which could be positive or negative). For simplicity, unless it is ambiguous, we assume that t refers to the current time and write o_p for the action selected by p.

Each action is viewed as requiring some resource, and we assume that resources are *congested*, meaning that there is a limit to how many agents can simultaneously use the resource and receive maximal individual reward. Let $\omega_o^* \in (0, 1]$ denote the maximum proportion of agents in the population who can simultaneously select o and receive maximal reward, i.e., ω_o^* represents the *capacity* of the resource associated with action o. Thus, if $\omega_o^* = 1/n$ then only a single agent can receive maximal reward for selecting the action at any time, while if $\omega_o^* = 1$ then all agents would receive the maximal reward if they simultaneously selected the action. We assume that agents are fully rational, self-interested and act independently and simultaneously at any given time, without any knowledge of others choices or strategies.

3.1   Actions and Congested Resources

The reward an agent receives for selecting an action is determined both by its individual preferences, represented by its type, and the value associated with the action, which is a function of the environment and others' action choices. We use the terms *value* and *reward* respectively to distinguish between the benefit resulting from an action in the current setting, independent of an agent's preferences, and the benefit an agent receives taking into account its preferences. Let $v_{o,t}$ denote the *value* that is associated with selecting action o in time step t. Again, unless it is ambiguous in the current context, we assume that t refers to the current time, and so we simply write v_o. For generality, we assume that the value of an action o is determined by some valuation function $\mathcal{V}_o(\omega_o)$ which maps the proportion of agents, ω_o, selecting action o to the value of the action,

$$v_o = \mathcal{V}_o(\omega_o). \tag{1}$$

The proportion of agents, $\omega_o \in [0, 1]$, who select action o in the current time step, is defined as

$$\omega_o = \frac{|\{p | p \in P \wedge o_p = o\}|}{|P|} \tag{2}$$

where o_p is the action selected by p.

Some actions might not be congested, or have sufficient capacity that $\omega_o^* = 1$, and so the value v_o associated with such actions is independent of the proportion of agents selecting that action, so

$$\mathcal{V}_o(\omega_o) = y \tag{3}$$

meaning that the value associated with o has a constant value of y.

For actions associated with congested resources, the capacity of the resource plays an important role in determining the value of such actions. There are two cases: the resource associated with action o is *in-capacity* if $\omega_o \leq \omega_o^*$ or is *over-capacity* if $\omega_o > \omega_o^*$. For such actions, we assume that $\mathcal{V}_o(\omega_o)$ appropriately reflects the valuation function in both situations.

In the simplest case, the valuation function can be modelled in the same manner for the in- and over-capacity cases. For example, we might use a uni-modal Normal function with mean $\mu_o = \omega_o^*$ and variance σ_o^2 (with σ_o being the standard deviation), such that agents receive the maximal value when the resource is at capacity, i.e., $\omega_o = \omega_o^*$,

$$\mathcal{V}_o(\omega_o) = \frac{1}{\sqrt{2\pi\omega_o^*}} e^{\frac{-(\omega_o - \omega_o^*)^2}{2\sigma_o^2}}. \tag{4}$$

In the more general case, the distributions defining the value for the in-capacity and over-capacity cases may be different. For example, if we use a uni-modal Normal distribution for both cases this could be represented using σ_o^2 and $\sigma_o'^2$ to represent the variance for the in- and over-capacity cases respectively (noting that the mean is fixed at the capacity),

$$\mathcal{V}_o(\omega_o) = \begin{cases} \frac{1}{\sqrt{2\pi\omega_o^*}} e^{\frac{-(\omega_o - \omega_o^*)^2}{2\sigma_o^2}}, & \text{if } \omega_o \leq \omega_o^* \\ \frac{1}{\sqrt{2\pi\omega_o^*}} e^{\frac{-(\omega_o - \omega_o^*)^2}{2\sigma_o'^2}}, & \text{otherwise, i.e., } \omega_o > \omega_o^*. \end{cases} \tag{5}$$

We might also model the in- or over-capacity cases using constant values if they do not depend on ω_o.

3.2 Agent Types: Mapping Values to Rewards

Each individual agent's reward from choosing action o is a function of the value, v_o, of the action and the agent's type. We assume that the agents are partitioned into a set G of disjoint *types*, or *groups*, $G = \{g_1, g_2, \ldots, g_l\}$ such that $\forall g_i \in G, g_i \subseteq P, g_1 \cup g_2 \cup \ldots \cup g_l = P$ and $\forall g_i, g_j \in G, g_i \cap g_j = \emptyset$. We use agent types to represent that the cost and relative reward associated with a given action may vary for different agents. For example, in the context of selecting transport modalities in a city, the relative cost of a congestion charge for car use may be low for wealthy individuals compared to those on low incomes, while the relative reward of using a low polluting mode of transport may be higher for individuals who are concerned about environmental issues.

We model such differences by associating each agent type g with a cost, $c_{o,g}$, and *sensitivity*, $s_{o,g}$, for each action o. For simplicity, we assume that the cost and sensitivity of each action for each agent type is predetermined and fixed over time, unless subject to manipulation by the authority. Rewards are defined at the group level, such that any agent in group g will receive reward $r_{o,g}$ for selecting action o, determined by multiplying the value v_o of the action by the corresponding sensitivity and subtracting the corresponding cost,

$$r_{o,g} = s_{o,g} \cdot v_o - c_{o,g} \tag{6}$$

where $s_{o,g}$ represents the sensitivity for action o, and $c_{o,g}$ the cost of action o for group g. Thus, the reward $r_{o,p}$ that an individual agent p receives for selecting action o is determined by p's group g, namely,

$$r_{o,p} = r_{o,g} \ni p \in g. \tag{7}$$

3.3 Authority Preferences and Influence on Rewards

We assume that the system contains an authority that has preferences over the state of the system in terms of the proportions of agents selecting each of the actions, and is able to influence the rewards agents receive by manipulating the sensitivities and costs of agent types. The authority's preferences with respect to a given action o are determined by the overall proportion of agents it desires to choose the action, $\hat{\omega}_o$, along with a utility function $\mathcal{U}_o(\omega_o)$ mapping the proportion of agents who choose the action, ω_o, to the utility from the authority's perspective. We assume that the utility function accounts for the potentially different distributions in the cases where $\omega_o \leq \hat{\omega}_o$ and $\omega_o > \hat{\omega}_o$. We use the term *utility* for the authority's perspective to distinguish from individual agent's rewards and action values. The utility u_o of action o from the authority's perspective is therefore

$$u_o = \mathcal{U}_o(\omega_o). \tag{8}$$

The authority's utility function for a given action can be modelled in a similar manner to the valuation functions in Eqs. 3, 4 and 5, using a constant value ($\hat{y}$), variance ($\hat{\sigma}_o^2$), or pair of variance values ($\hat{\sigma}_o^2$ and $\hat{\sigma}_o'^2$) for the in- and over-capacity cases respectively.

The overall utility u to the authority of the current action choices of the population is simply the aggregation of the utility (from the authority's perspective) of each individual agent's choice,

$$u = \sum_{p \in P} u_{o_p} \tag{9}$$

where u_{o_p} represents the utility to the authority of agent p selecting action o.

While the authority is not able to directly control the action choices of agents, or the values associated with those actions, we assume that it is able to exert influence over the rewards agents receive, which in turn may cause agents to adopt different strategies. There are two methods we consider through which the authority can affect rewards, namely, modifying the cost or the sensitivity associated with an action for a group of agents. Thus, the authority is able to replace the default sensitivity $s_{o,g}$, or cost $c_{o,g}$, of group g for action o with modified values $\tilde{s}_{o,g}$ and $\tilde{c}_{o,g}$ respectively. The reward is then calculated using these updated values in Eq. 6, i.e.,

$$r_{o,g} = \tilde{s}_{o,g} \cdot v_o - \tilde{c}_{o,g}. \tag{10}$$

3.4 Agent Learning

Norms can emerge through social learning [11], such that an individual's estimate of the desirability of each possible action is affected by others' actions in the environment. To illustrate our framework, we assume that agents use Q-learning [41], since this has been shown as effective for norm emergence [1,9,29,36,40,43], although other methods such as HCR [38] or WoLF-PHC [10] can also be used.

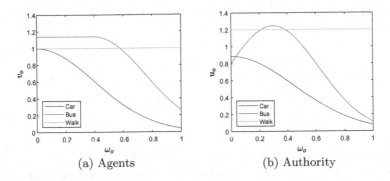

Fig. 1. Value functions of (a) agents and (b) authority.

For each action $o \in O$, each agent maintains a Q-value that estimates the benefit of choosing that action. The Q-values are initially set to zero and are updated based on the rewards received. Whenever agent p selects action o and receives reward $r_{o,p}$, it will update its Q-value for o using

$$Q(o) \leftarrow (1 - \alpha)Q(o) + \alpha\left(r_{o,p} + \gamma \max_{o'} Q(o')\right) \tag{11}$$

where $0 < \alpha \leq 1$ is the learning rate and γ is the discount factor.

We assume that agents use ϵ-greedy action selection ($0 \leq \epsilon \leq 1$), such that an agent selects a random action with probability ϵ, and with probability $1 - \epsilon$ selects the action with the highest Q-value.

4   Experimental Methodology

In this section, we describe our simulation and experimental methodology using transport modality choice as an illustrative example. The environment contains $n = 3,000$ agents who select from actions $O = \{Car, Bus, Walk\}$, i.e., $m = 3$, representing the available transport modalities. In each iteration (i.e., time step) every agent selects an action, receives a reward, and updates its Q-values. We ran the simulation for $10,000$ iterations and averaged our results over 10 runs. We used $\epsilon = 0.05$, $\alpha = 0.1$ and $\gamma = 0.75$ as representative values for the exploration rate, learning rate and discount factor respectively.

We assume that the *Walk* action is not associated with a congested resource, and so for simplicity we define its value as $\mathcal{V}_{Walk}(\omega_{Walk}) = 1$, while both the *Car* and *Bus* actions are assumed to be congested. We define $\mathcal{V}_{Car}(\omega_{Car})$ using a uni-modal Normal function with $\omega^*_{Car} = 0$ and $\sigma^2_{Car} = 0.4$ (see Eq. 4), which represents that an agent obtains the highest value when no other agents choose *Car*. We represent $\mathcal{V}_{Bus}(\omega_{Bus})$ as

$$\mathcal{V}_{Bus}(\omega_{Bus}) = \begin{cases} y_{Bus}, & \text{if } \omega_{Bus} \leq \omega^*_{Bus} \\ \frac{1}{\sqrt{2\pi}\omega^*_{Bus}}e^{\frac{-(\omega_{Bus}-\omega^*_{Bus})^2}{2\sigma'^2_{Bus}}}, & \text{otherwise, i.e., } \omega_{Bus} > \omega^*_{Bus}. \end{cases} \tag{12}$$

Table 1. Action costs and sensitivities for each group and each action.

	g_1		g_2		g_3	
	c_{o,g_1}	s_{o,g_1}	c_{o,g_2}	s_{o,g_2}	c_{o,g_3}	s_{o,g_3}
$o = Car$	0	1.3	0.1	1	−0.2	1.4
$o = Bus$	0	1	0.11	1.35	0	0.7
$o = Walk$	0	1	0	1.4	0	0.8

where $\omega^*_{Bus} = 0.4$, $y_{Bus} = 1.14$, and $\sigma'^2_{Bus} = 0.35$, meaning that for the in-capacity case the value is constant, while the over-capacity case is modelled as a uni-model Normal function. These value functions are illustrated in Fig. 1(a), which shows that: (i) the value of choosing $Walk$ is independent of others' choices, (ii) the value of choosing Car reduces as more agents select the Car action, representing an increase in congestion and journey time, and (iii) an agent obtains the highest reward when choosing Bus, provided that only a small proportion of others make the same choice, with the value reducing when higher proportions cause the resource to be over-capacity. From the agents' perspective, the highest utility possible is for 60% of the agents to choose Bus and 40% to choose $Walk$.

We assume that the authority prefers fewer agents to select Car, more agents to select $Walk$, and that there is some preferred proportion of agents who select Bus. This represents a desire to reduce car use, increase active travel, and ensure that investment in providing a bus service is fully utilised (e.g., to cater for groups of individuals with restricted mobility, who might have very high values for $c_{Walk,g}$). From the authority's perspective we represent the utility for the actions as: $\mathcal{U}_{Walk}(\omega_{Walk}) = 1.2$, with $\mathcal{U}_{Car}(\omega_{Car})$ and $\mathcal{U}_{Bus}(\omega_{Bus})$ being uni-modal Normal functions with $\hat{\omega}_{Car} = 0$, $\hat{\sigma}'^2_{Car} = 0.45$ and $\hat{\omega}_{Bus} = 0.3$, $\hat{\sigma}^2_{Bus} = 0.32$, which are illustrated in Fig. 1(b). For the authority, the highest utility occurs when 17% of the agents choose Bus and the remainder choose $Walk$.

We divide the agents into three equal size groups, $G = \{g_1, g_2, g_3\}$, where g_1 corresponds to a baseline agent type, g_2 has strong environmental concerns, and g_3 represents affluent agents. For simplicity, since groups are disjoint, we do not consider affluent agents who also have strong environmental concerns, as this would require an additional group to be defined. An agent's group defines the cost and sensitivity associated with each action which, along with the proportion of other agents choosing the action (in the case of congested actions), determines the reward received for selecting an action.

The costs and sensitivities associated with each action for each group in our simulation are given in Table 1 where $c_{o,g}$ and $s_{o,g}$ denote the cost and sensitivity associated with action o for group g respectively. These costs and sensitivities determine the shape of the reward function (see Eqs. 6 and 7) for each group, as illustrated in Fig. 2. They are not intended to be realistic models of the costs and sensitivities associated with the actions for each group, but rather are intended to illustrate how our framework models congested resources. The baseline group g_1 (Fig. 2(a)) receives the highest reward when choosing Car if few other agents make the same choice. When more agents choose Car the reward decreases. If a

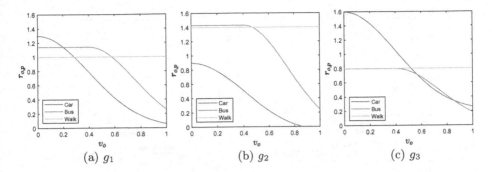

Fig. 2. Reward functions for each group.

high proportion of agents choose *Car*, then agents of type g_1 can obtain a high reward by choosing *Bus*, again provided that not too many others make the same choice. The reward associated with the *Walk* action does not depend on other agents' choices, and if a high proportion of agents choose *Car* or *Bus*, then *Walk* provides the highest reward. Group g_2 (Fig. 2(b)) receives significantly higher rewards from the *Walk* and *Bus* actions, and lower rewards from *Car*, reflecting their environmental concerns. Finally, the affluent agents in g_3 (Fig. 2(c)) receive the highest reward from selecting *Car*, as they have both higher sensitivity and lower (relative) costs associated with this action.

To illustrate our framework, we performed several experiments, the results of which are presented in the following section. First, as a baseline, we consider the effect of the different costs and sensitivities associated with each group, with no interventions from the authority. Second, we consider introducing fixed strategy agents into the population, and show that this is not an effective intervention in our setting. Third, we investigate the impact of manipulating the sensitivity to different actions, allowing us to model, for example, the effect of a targeted behavioural change intervention. Finally, we investigate the effect of modifying the cost associated with different actions, i.e., we consider different values of $\tilde{c}_{o,g}$. This allows us to model interventions such as means-tested charging for private car use, or exemption from congestion charges for certain groups.

5   Results

All results are averaged over 10 runs for each configuration, with $n = 3,000$ agents. In this section, we consider agents' behaviour under different interventions assuming, for illustration, that the authority's aim is to encourage the population to choose *Walk*. Due to space limitations, we discuss representative manipulations, however other alternative manipulations are possible.

5.1   Baseline Setting

As a baseline, we begin by considering agents' behaviour without any intervention. Figure 3 shows that agents' choices in each group are in accordance

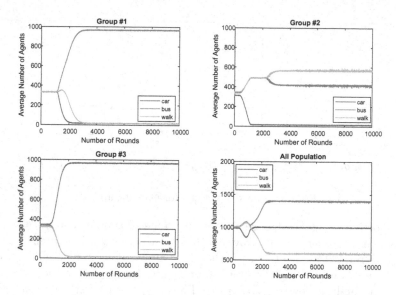

Fig. 3. Average number of agents choosing each of the actions along time. Baseline setting.

with their corresponding reward functions given in Fig. 2. A common measure of norm emergence is the Kittock criteria [21], where a norm is considered to emerge if some proportion of the population (often 90%) adopts a particular action. While this is an effective measure in populations of homogeneous agents playing a coordination or Prisoner's Dilemma game, in our setting of heterogeneous agent groups and congested actions, we do not typically expect to see such large, population wide, adoption. Therefore, for simplicity, rather than specifying a convergence threshold we consider any dominant action in a group (or the population) as being a norm. Thus, we see the norms emerge of choosing *Bus* in group g_1, *Walk* in g_2, *Car* in g_3, and *Bus* being the overall population norm.

5.2 Fixed-Strategy Agents

Fixed-strategy agents perform the same action regardless of others' choices, and small numbers of such agents can cause particular norms to emerge [1]. Fixed strategy agents have been shown to be effective in coordination and Prisoner's Dilemma games, and so it is natural to explore whether they are effective in our setting. Figure 4 shows that introducing 300 fixed-strategy agents (10% of each group selected at random, i.e., 10% of the population) who always select *Walk*, is not sufficient to cause a norm of *Walk* to emerge. Introducing such a set of fixed-strategy agents (Fig. 4(b)) gives similar results to the baseline setting (Fig. 4(a)). While Airiau *et al.* [1] show that it is sufficient for only 1% of the population to be fixed strategy agents to influence the whole population [1], our results show that even a large number of such agents (10% of the population) is not sufficient. We therefore conclude that in our setting there is need for new

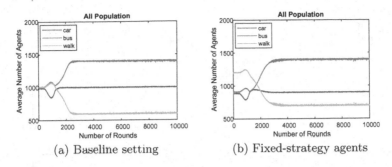

Fig. 4. Average number of agents choosing each of the actions in (a) our baseline setting and (b) with 10% fixed-strategy agents.

interventions, such as manipulating agents' sensitivities or costs (for one or more groups).

5.3   Manipulating Agents' Sensitivities

We now consider the effect of manipulating agents' sensitivities which, for example, can model the impact of an advertising campaign on the health benefits of walking. Suppose that the manipulation is to increase the proportion of agents from g_3 that choose *Walk*, and receive high reward, by reducing the proportion of agents who can choose *Car* and receive maximal reward from 53% in the baseline setting to 19%. We do this by setting $\tilde{s}_{Walk,3} = 1.8 \cdot s_{Walk,3}$.[3] The resulting behaviour, depicted in Fig. 5, shows that agents from g_3 converge to the norm of *Walk* (i.e., fewer agents choose *Car*), which leads to an increase in the number of agents from g_1 choosing *Car* and a decrease in those choosing *Bus*. This consequently leads to more agents in g_2 choosing *Bus* and fewer choosing *Walk*, however at the population level *Walk* increases overall.

Although this basic manipulation has caused a shift in behaviour towards *Walk*, it is not enough to cause the whole population to adopt a norm of *Walk*. For this reason we look at two possible alternatives, each one a combination of the basic intervention (depicted in Fig. 5) with an additional one.

First, suppose that agents from g_1 are able to choose *Walk* and receive a higher reward than *Bus*. This can be modelled by decreasing the sensitivity of g_1 towards *Bus*, i.e., $\tilde{s}_{Bus,1} = 0.86 \cdot s_{Bus,1}$. As can be seen in Fig. 6, applying this intervention, together with reducing the proportion of agents from g_3 who can choose *Car* and receive maximal reward, shifts g_1 towards *Car* (instead of *Bus*), leading agents from g_2 to shift towards *Bus* instead of *Walk*. Overall, the whole population changes its preferences, with many choosing *Walk*.

Second, we decrease the proportion of agents from g_1 that receive a small reward when choosing *Walk* by increasing their sensitivity, such that $\tilde{s}_{Walk,1} =$

---

[3] A similar manipulation (with similar effect) is decreasing the sensitivity of g_3 towards *Car*.

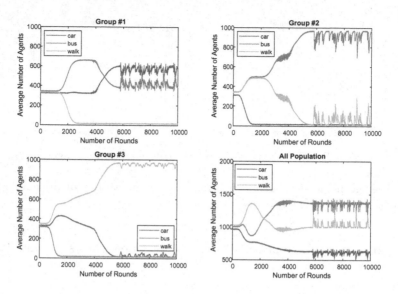

Fig. 5. Average number of agents choosing each of the actions along time. Intervention applied: $\tilde{s}_{Walk,3} = 1.8 \cdot s_{Walk,3}$.

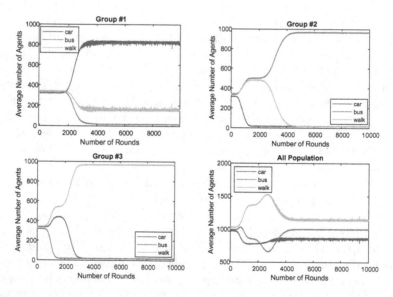

Fig. 6. Average number of agents choosing each of the actions along time. Interventions applied: $\tilde{s}_{Walk,3} = 1.8 \cdot s_{Walk,3}$ and $\tilde{s}_{Bus,1} = 0.86 \cdot s_{Bus,1}$.

$1.14 \cdot s_{Walk,1}$. This manipulation, applied with reducing the proportion of agents from g_3 who can choose *Car* and receive maximal reward, causes agents from g_1 and g_3 to change their behaviour, while g_2 continues to choose *Bus*. Overall, the population shifts towards *Walk*, as can be seen in Fig. 7.

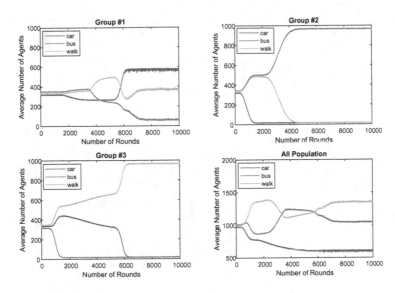

Fig. 7. Average number of agents choosing each of the actions along time. Interventions applied: $\tilde{s}_{Walk,3} = 1.8 \cdot s_{Walk,3}$ and $\tilde{s}_{Walk,1} = 1.14 \cdot s_{Walk,1}$.

5.4   Manipulating Agents' Costs

We now consider manipulating agents' costs, which models interventions such as charging individuals who have polluting vehicles or subsidising the costs of electric vehicles. Suppose that the authority increases the cost of *Car* for g_3 such that other actions have a lower cost (specifically, $\tilde{c}_{Car,3} = 0.8 + c_{Car,3}$). As can be seen in Fig. 8, this results in g_3 adopting a norm of *Walk*, while the population overall still adopts *Bus* as most common action choice.

In order to achieve population wide shift, we consider an alternative manipulation: increasing the cost of g_2 when choosing *Bus* such that a higher reward is associated with *Walk* (specifically, $\tilde{c}_{Bus,2} = 0.03 + c_{Bus,2}$). This manipulation, applied with increasing the cost of g_3 from *Car*, gives a significant change in individuals' preferences with *Walk* emerging as a norm, as depicted in Fig. 9.

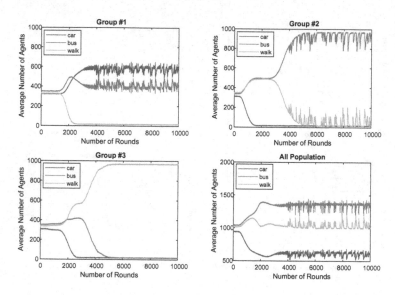

Fig. 8. Average number of agents choosing each of the actions along time. Intervention applied: $\tilde{c}_{Car,3} = 0.8 + c_{Car,3}$.

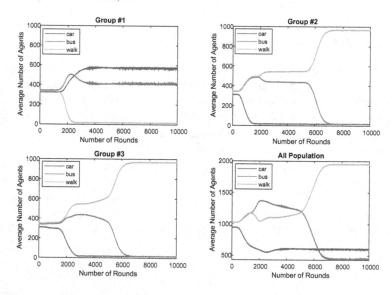

Fig. 9. Average number of agents choosing each of the actions along time. Interventions applied: $\tilde{c}_{Car,3} = 0.8 + c_{Car,3}$ and $\tilde{c}_{Bus,2} = 0.03 + c_{Bus,2}$.

6   Conclusions and Future Work

In this paper, we presented a framework for modeling norm emergence where actions are associated with congested resources. We considered a general setting in which agents are heterogeneous, comprised of groups differing in their preferences regarding actions. Unlike previous research on norm emergence, which typically assumes pairwise interactions, we introduced congested actions with rewards determined exogenously. We also introduced an authority figure which is able to manipulate agents' rewards. Using a simplified transport modality choice illustration, we demonstrated the impact of manipulations on the emergent norms in the population, showing that in the presence of heterogeneous agents different interventions may be required, targeted to the different groups.

There are several directions for future work, including relaxing assumptions about the knowledge available to agents and further exploring agent heterogeneity. We also plan to investigate dynamic populations, and situating agents on an underlying network.

References

1. Airiau, S., Sen, S., Villatoro, D.: Emergence of conventions through social learning. Auton. Agent Multi-Agent Syst. **28**(5), 779–804 (2014). https://doi.org/10.1007/s10458-013-9237-x
2. Amin, K., Kale, S., Tesauro, G., Turaga, D.: Budgeted prediction with expert advice. In: Proceedings of the Twenty-Ninth AAAI Conference on Artificial Intelligence, pp. 2490–2096 (2015)
3. Arce, D.G.: Stability criteria for social norms with applications to the prisoner's dilemma. J. Conflict Resolut. **38**(4), 749–765 (1994)
4. Arthur, W.B.: Inductive reasoning and bounded rationality. Am. Econ. Rev. **84**(2), 406–411 (1994)
5. Auer, P., Cesa-Bianchi, N., Fischer, P.: Finite-time analysis of the multiarmed bandit problem. Mach. Learn. **47**(2–3), 235–256 (2002). https://doi.org/10.1023/A:1013689704352
6. Auer, P., Cesa-Bianchi, N., Freund, Y., Schapire, R.E.: Gambling in a rigged casino: the adversarial multi-armed bandit problem. In: Proceedings of IEEE 36th Annual Foundations of Computer Science, pp. 322–331. IEEE (1995)
7. Auer, P., Cesa-Bianchi, N., Freund, Y., Schapire, R.E.: The nonstochastic multi-armed bandit problem. SIAM J. Comput. **32**(1), 48–77 (2002)
8. Axelrod, R.: An evolutionary approach to norms. Am. Polit. Sci. Rev. **80**(4), 1095–1111 (1986)
9. Beheshti, R., Ali, A.M., Sukthankar, G.: Cognitive social learners: an architecture for modeling normative behavior. In: Proceedings of the 29th AAAI Conference on Artificial Intelligence, pp. 2017–2023 (2015)
10. Bowling, M., Veloso, M.: Multiagent learning using a variable learning rate. Artif. Intell. **136**(2), 215–250 (2002)
11. Conte, R., Paolucci, M.: Intelligent social learning. J. Artif. Soc. Soc. Simul. **4**(1), U61–U82 (2001)
12. Farago, J., Greenwald, A., Hall, K.: Fair and efficient solutions to the Santa Fe bar problem. In: Proceedings of the Grace Hopper Celebration of Women in Computing (2002)
13. Franks, H., Griffiths, N., Jhumka, A.: Manipulating convention emergence using influencer agents. Auton. Agent Multi-Agent Syst. **26**(3), 315–353 (2012). https://doi.org/10.1007/s10458-012-9193-x

14. Granmo, O.-C., Berg, S.: Solving non-stationary bandit problems by random sampling from sibling Kalman filters. In: García-Pedrajas, N., Herrera, F., Fyfe, C., Benítez, J.M., Ali, M. (eds.) IEA/AIE 2010. LNCS (LNAI), vol. 6098, pp. 199–208. Springer, Heidelberg (2010). https://doi.org/10.1007/978-3-642-13033-5_21

15. Granmo, O.C., Glimsdal, S.: Accelerated Bayesian learning for decentralized two-armed bandit based decision making with applications to the Goore game. Appl. Intell. **38**(4), 479–488 (2013). https://doi.org/10.1007/s10489-012-0346-z

16. Haynes, C., Luck, M., McBurney, P., Mahmoud, S., Vítek, T., Miles, S.: Engineering the emergence of norms: a review. Knowl. Eng. Rev. **32**, 1–31 (2017)

17. Heckathorn, D.D.: Collective sanctions and the creations of prisoner's dilemma norms. Am. J. Sociol. **94**(3), 535–562 (1988)

18. Helbing, D., Johansson, A.: Cooperation, norms, and revolutions: a unified game-theoretical approach. PLoS ONE **5**(10), 1–15 (2010)

19. Hu, S., Leung, H.F.: Achieving coordination in multi-agent systems by stable local conventions under community networks. In: Proceedings of the 26th International Joint Conference on Artificial Intelligence (IJCAI), pp. 4731–4737 (2017)

20. Kale, S.: Multiarmed bandits with limited expert advice. In: Conference on Learning Theory, pp. 107–122 (2014)

21. Kittock, J.E.: Emergent conventions and the structure of multi-agent systems. In: Proceedings of the 1993 Santa Fe Institute Complex Systems Summer School, vol. 6, pp. 1–14. Citeseer (1993)

22. Kuleshov, V., Precup, D.: Algorithms for multi-armed bandit problems. J. Mach. Learn. Res. **1**, 1–48 (2000)

23. Li, L., Chu, W., Langford, J., Schapire, R.E.: A contextual-bandit approach to personalized news article recommendation. In: Proceedings of the 19th International Conference on World Wide Web (WWW), pp. 661–670 (2010)

24. Mahmoud, S., Griffiths, N., Keppens, J., Luck, M.: Overcoming omniscience for norm emergence in axelrod's metanorm model. In: Cranefield, S., van Riemsdijk, M.B., Vázquez-Salceda, J., Noriega, P. (eds.) COIN -2011. LNCS (LNAI), vol. 7254, pp. 186–202. Springer, Heidelberg (2012). https://doi.org/10.1007/978-3-642-35545-5_11

25. Mahmoud, S., Griffiths, N., Keppens, J., Luck, M.: Efficient norm emergence through experiential dynamic punishment. In: Proceedings of the 20th European Conference on Artificial Intelligence (ECAI), pp. 576–581 (2012)

26. Malialis, K., Devlin, S., Kudenko, D.: Resource abstraction for reinforcement learning in multiagent congestion problems. In: Proceedings of the 15th International Conference on Autonomous Agents and Multiagent Systems (AAMAS), pp. 503–511 (2016)

27. Marchant, J., Griffiths, N.: Convention emergence in partially observable topologies. In: Sukthankar, G., Rodriguez-Aguilar, J.A. (eds.) AAMAS 2017. LNCS (LNAI), vol. 10642, pp. 187–202. Springer, Cham (2017). https://doi.org/10.1007/978-3-319-71682-4_12

28. Morris-Martin, A., De Vos, M., Padget, J.: Norm emergence in multiagent systems: a viewpoint paper. Auton. Agent Multi-Agent Syst. **33**, 706–749 (2019). https://doi.org/10.1007/s10458-019-09422-0

29. Mukherjee, P., Sen, S., Airiau, S.: Norm emergence under constrained interactions in diverse societies. In: Proceedings of the 7th International Conference on Autonomous Agents and Multiagent Systems (AAMAS), pp. 779–786 (2008)

30. Perreau de Pinninck, A., Sierra, C., Schorlemmer, M.: Distributed norm enforcement via ostracism. In: Sichman, J.S., Padget, J., Ossowski, S., Noriega, P. (eds.)

COIN -2007. LNCS (LNAI), vol. 4870, pp. 301–315. Springer, Heidelberg (2008). https://doi.org/10.1007/978-3-540-79003-7_22

31. Salazar, N., Rodriguez-Aguilar, J.A., Arcos, J.L.: Robust coordination in large convention spaces. AI Commun. **23**, 357–371 (2010)

32. Savarimuthu, B.T.R., Purvis, M., Purvis, M., Cranefield, S.: Social norm emergence in virtual agent societies. In: Baldoni, M., Son, T.C., van Riemsdijk, M.B., Winikoff, M. (eds.) DALT 2008. LNCS (LNAI), vol. 5397, pp. 18–28. Springer, Heidelberg (2009). https://doi.org/10.1007/978-3-540-93920-7_2

33. Schlag, K.H.: Why imitate, and if so, how?: a boundedly rational approach to multi-armed bandits. J. Econ. Theory **78**(1), 130–156 (1998)

34. Seldin, Y., Bartlett, P.L., Crammer, K., Abbasi-Yadkori, Y.: Prediction with limited advice and multiarmed bandits with paid observations. In: Proceedings of the 30th International Conference on Machine Learning (ICML), pp. 280–287 (2014)

35. Sen, O., Sen, S.: Effects of social network topology and options on norm emergence. In: Padget, J., et al. (eds.) COIN -2009. LNCS (LNAI), vol. 6069, pp. 211–222. Springer, Heidelberg (2010). https://doi.org/10.1007/978-3-642-14962-7_14

36. Sen, S., Airiau, S.: Emergence of norms through social learning. In: Proceedings of the 20th International Joint Conference on Artificial Intelligence (IJCAI), pp. 1507–1512 (2007)

37. Shivaswamy, P., Joachims, T.: Multi-armed bandit problems with history. In: Artificial Intelligence and Statistics, pp. 1046–1054 (2012)

38. Shoham, Y., Tennenholtz, M.: On the emergence of social conventions: modeling, analysis, and simulations. Artif. Intell. **94**(1–2), 139–166 (1997)

39. Villatoro, D., Sabater-Mir, J., Sen, S.: Social instruments for robust convention emergence. In: Proceedings of the 22th International Joint Conference on Artificial Intelligence (IJCAI), pp. 420–425 (2011)

40. Vouros, G.A.: The emergence of norms via contextual agreements in open societies. In: Koch, F., Guttmann, C., Busquets, D. (eds.) Advances in Social Computing and Multiagent Systems. CCIS, vol. 541, pp. 185–201. Springer, Cham (2015). https://doi.org/10.1007/978-3-319-24804-2_12

41. Watkins, C.J.C.H., Dayan, P.: Q-learning. Mach. Learn. **8**, 279–292 (1992). https://doi.org/10.1007/BF00992698

42. Yang, A., Yang, G.H.: A contextual bandit approach to dynamic search. In: Proceedings of the ACM International Conference on Theory of Information Retrieval (SIGIR), pp. 301–304 (2017)

43. Yu, C., Zhang, M., Ren, F.: Collective learning for the emergence of social norms in networked multiagent systems. IEEE Trans. Cybern. **44**(12), 2342–2355 (2014)

44. Yu, C., Lv, H., Sen, S., Ren, F., Tan, G.: Adaptive learning for efficient emergence of social norms in networked multiagent systems. In: Booth, R., Zhang, M.-L. (eds.) PRICAI 2016. LNCS (LNAI), vol. 9810, pp. 805–818. Springer, Cham (2016). https://doi.org/10.1007/978-3-319-42911-3_68

45. Zeng, C., Wang, Q., Mokhtari, S., Li, T.: Online context-aware recommendation with time varying multi-armed bandit. In: Proceedings of the 22nd ACM International Conference on Knowledge Discovery and Data Mining (SIGKDD), pp. 2025–2034 (2016)

Aiming for Half Gets You to the Top: Winning PowerTAC 2020

Stavros Orfanoudakis[1]([⊠]), Stefanos Kontos[1], Charilaos Akasiadis[2], and Georgios Chalkiadakis[1]

[1] School of ECE, Technical University of Crete, Chania, Greece
sorfanoudakis@isc.tuc.gr
[2] Institute of Informatics and Telecommunications, NCSR "Demokritos",
Agia Paraskevi, Greece

Abstract. The PowerTAC competition provides a multi-agent simulation platform for electricity markets, in which intelligent agents acting as electricity brokers compete with each other aiming to maximize their profits. Typically, the gains of agents increase as the number of their customers rises, but in parallel, costs also increase as a result of higher transmission fees that need to be paid by the electricity broker. Thus, agents that aim to take over a disproportionately high share of the market, often end up with losses due to being obliged to pay huge transmission capacity fees. In this paper, we present a novel trading strategy that, based on this observation, aims to balance gains against costs; and was utilized by the champion of the PowerTAC-2020 tournament, TUC-TAC. The approach also incorporates a wholesale market strategy that employs Monte Carlo Tree Search to determine TUC-TAC's best course of action when participating in the market's double auctions. The strategy is improved by making effective use of a forecasting module that seeks to predict upcoming peaks in demand, since in such intervals incurred costs significantly increase. A post-tournament analysis is also included in this paper, to help draw important lessons regarding the strengths and weaknesses of the various strategies used in the PowerTAC-2020 competition.

Keywords: Electricity brokers · Trading agents · Bidding strategies

1 Introduction

The rise of renewable energy production in the residential market along with the latest popularization of electric vehicles is gradually creating needs for a "smarter" grid. The necessity of this new Grid is indisputable because of the unique features it will be consisted of. In Smart Grid settings, one of the main purposes is to reduce fossil fuel consumption. This is especially important since fossil fuels will be depleted at some point in the future, so alternative energy sources will be eventually required; and since the burning of fossil fuels has a major negative impact to the climate.

© Springer Nature Switzerland AG 2021
A. Rosenfeld and N. Talmon (Eds.): EUMAS 2021, LNAI 12802, pp. 144–159, 2021.
https://doi.org/10.1007/978-3-030-82254-5_9

Thus, a feature of the new Smart Grid will be an energy market dealing largely in renewable energy, which will consist of a lot of more "prosumer" participants, with most of them being able to buy and sell energy at the same time. Hence, researchers need tools and platforms that will help them to experiment in novel ways to make this new market viable. The Power Trading Agent Competition (PowerTAC) is a rich simulation platform that can provide researchers with efficient ways to try and test different strategies and approaches before actually deploying them in the future Smart Grid. PowerTAC already has most features a smart electricity grid can possess (e.g., interruptible consumption, electric vehicles, renewable energy) so the simulations can be as realistic as possible. Every year, since 2012, a PowerTAC competition is organized. Agents from research teams from around the globe are pitted against each other, and try to generate the highest profit by harnessing the energy supply and demand of the simulation environment. The agent that won PowerTAC 2020 was TUC-TAC.

Now, contemporary MAS research often builds on solid game-theoretic foundations, since game theory provides a compelling framework for strategic decision making in multi-agent environments [8]. TUC-TAC also gets inspiration from a known theoretical result in order to design the winning strategy of the PowerTAC 2020 competition. More specifically, TUC-TAC's basic goal is to get half of the available retail market share, leaving the rest to the others. By so doing, TUC-TAC expects to always have the highest income, while sharing the fees with the other agents. This basic principle underlying TUC-TAC's strategy has certain analogies to the equilibrium strategy used by the winning agent of the 2010 Lemonade Stand Game tournament [10], as will be explained below. TUC-TAC also employs *Monte Carlo Tree Search (MCTS)* for bidding in the double auctions of the wholesale market, similarly to the approach of Chowdhury et al. [1]. Moreover, TUC-TAC's post-competition strategy is enhanced by a consumption forecasting module (using linear regression and neural networks) to predict demand peaks.

In what follows, we first provide the necessary background for the problem domain; next we present TUC-TAC's architecture and strategy in detail; and then proceed to provide an extensive post-tournament analysis, along with an evaluation of the forecasting module built after the PowerTAC 2020 competition.

2   Background and Related Work

In this section we discuss PowerTAC and some past agent approaches.

2.1   The Power Trading Agent Competition

PowerTAC [3] is a rich competitive economic simulation of future energy markets, featuring several Smart Grid components. With the help of this simulator, researchers are able to better understand the behavior of future customer models as well as experiment with retail and wholesale market decision-making, by creating competitive agents and benchmarking their strategies against each other.

In this way, a host of useful information is extracted which can be used by policymakers and industries in order to prepare for the upcoming market changes.

2.2 Past Agent Strategies

In this section, some of the most significant broker-agent strategies will be introduced. Every agent design, in these many years of competition, can be broadly separated into two different, almost distinct, parts. The first part is the Retail Market Module which tries to find the best tariff strategy, i.e. to decide which tariffs to offer to retail customers and to what price; and the second is the wholesale market module, whose main responsibilities are to submit bid and asks in periodic double auctions. Specifically, this module is very important, because the wholesale market is the main place that brokers can buy and sell energy.

Many agents in the past, like COLD [7] used reinforcement learning [9] in order to find the best tariff strategy. Recent agents tried similar strategies. For instance, Mertacor2020 employs Q-Learning techniques in order to maximize the profits from the retail market. The VidyutVanika [2] agent also used a combination of dynamic programming and Q-learning assisted by a Deep Neural Network predictor. However, AgentUDE [5], one of the most successful agents in Power-TAC history, which won the tournaments of 2014, 2017, 2018 and was in the top three brokers in 2016, and 2019, used a much simpler tariff strategy. Specifically, its strategy was based mainly on decision trees and it was being enhanced with some general principles. In addition to that, AgentUDE2017 [6] had a genetic algorithm module to further improve its tariff generation. TUC-TAC 2020 too, uses decision trees in order to find the best tariffs to offer in the retail market; but enhances them with some unique heuristics.

The complexity of the wholesale market actions space, requiring as it does participation in multiple auctions with agent preferences changing dynamically, calls for a very careful design of an agent's respective strategy, in order for it to be profitable. One of the first and most important works in this field was that of TacTex [11] agent in 2013. That team used an MDP price predictor which is the foundation of almost all modern brokers in PowerTAC. Specifically, SPOT [1] agent further improved the previous strategy using MCTS to find the best bids and asks at the best possible times. Another especially efficient wholesale market agent was VidyutVanika [2], which also uses the MDP based price predictor which was firstly implemented by TacTex 2013. Another interesting work, among many, is that of Nativdad et al. (2016) [4], which was using machine learning techniques to reduce the complexity of the wholesale market action space.

3   TUC-TAC's Architecture

TUC-TAC 2020 is an autonomous agent developed to compete in the 2020 Power Trading Agents Competition (PowerTAC-2020). Its main strategy—more specifically, the part of TUC-TAC's strategy that is used in the key for the game retail market—is based on the principle that, acquiring half of the market share will give TUC-TAC half of the total profits, but also only half of the inevitable *transmission capacity fees* (a notion we will explain later) will have to be paid by our agent. Early on in TUC-TAC's development it was realized that greedy strategies would not work in the competitive PowerTAC environment; and the main inspiration for the aforementioned principle came from an interesting equilibrium strategy employed in the context of the "Lemonade Game" competition, and which is briefly presented in Sect. 3.1 below. In order to achieve that, TUC-TAC uses decision trees enhanced with many heuristics and non-heuristics functions that help in the evaluation of the game state. It also employs MCTS for bidding in the double auctions of the wholesale market, adapting it to this setting. In this chapter, we will break down the agent into modules to easier understand how it was designed. Figure 1 below depicts the main components of the agent; these will be analyzed in turn later in this section.

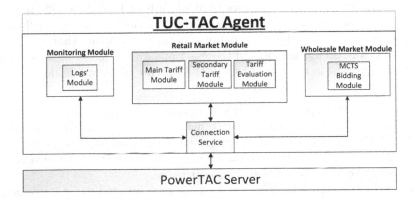

Fig. 1. TUC-TAC's architecture

3.1 An Interesting Equilibrium Strategy for Repeated Multiagent Zero-Sum Game Settings

The *Lemonade Stand Game (LSG)* is a game-theoretic setting with important real-life applications. Specifically, it is a game that can provide important intuitions regarding the choices facing online advertisers, regarding which spot to bid for when participating in real-time online auctions for slots showing up in sponsored search results. In its simplest form, LSG involves N lemonade vendors choosing a location to place their counter at, on the perimeter of a circular island. The utility of each vendor is determined by the distance between her, the neighbor vendors, and the defined space boundaries. In 2010 the first LSG tournament involving artificial intelligent agents took place, sponsored by *Yahoo! Research*, and the strategy of the winning team was shown to be the LSG equilibrium strategy [10]. In short, the strategy demands that one should *always* sit opposite *some* opponent, with the purpose of ensuring that they both maximize their profits via exploiting the third one in this specific iteration; over time, the agent employing this strategy gains most of the profits (across all game iterations), leaving the other two to share the rest of the "pie".

In general, a lesson learned from this equilibrium strategy is that in such settings we should seek to always, at each iteration, claim a *large enough* slice of the pie available, but without being too greedy. This strategy will ensure that any other player will be over time getting lower payoffs than ourselves. In our setting, we are inspired by this equilibrium strategy and develop a strategy for the retail market that seeks to control a high portion of the market share by subscribing a large number of consumers to our services, but also restrain our "greediness" to avoid suffering huge penalties due to transmission capacity fees.

3.2   The Retail Market Module

This component's main responsibility is to publish and revoke tariffs in a way that would be profitable for the agent. Publishing and revoking tariffs alone might sound simple, but there are many aspects of the game that have to be considered before even taking any of these actions. In the following subsections, all these different aspects of the TUC-TAC agent are described in detail.

Preferred Tariff Types. A PowerTAC game has a specified amount of different types of power consumers, thus some distinct types of tariffs should be offered. In TUC-TAC's case, strategies for only 4 different tariff types are implemented. These tariffs are about *Consumption*, *Thermal Storage Consumption*, *Solar Production* and *Wind Production* costumers.

To summarize, simple *Consumption* tariffs were selected to be implemented and offered by our agent, because they provided TUC-TAC with an amount of profit that was in expectation significantly higher than that of other tariff types. Also, the two different sustainable energy production tariffs were selected, not for their potential of making a profit, but for their ability to reduce the transmission capacity fees. This will be further explained later. Finally, Thermal Storage consumption tariffs were selected because they provided a considerable stable income. Specifically, the income from these tariffs were several thousand "euros" from customers and the balancing market. Moreover, these tariffs were considered, because it was necessary to prohibit TUC-TAC's competitors from having an advantage by being uncontested in these non-*Consumption* tariffs.

Objective Value of a Tariff. One of the main problems a PowerTAC agent has to solve, is the evaluation of its opponents' tariffs, with the purpose to offer better ones. (Note that when a broker publishes a new tariff all customers and brokers are notified about its parameters.)

The difficulty of this problem derives from the complexity of the customers' evaluation model itself. A tariff has many parameters to consider while evaluating its objective value. For example some of these parameters are periodic payment, rates, early withdrawal penalties, sign up bonuses and so on.

The average value of rates was calculated using three different methods.[1] The first method tries to find the average value of the rates with the help of the weights which were produced from the time-of-use-technique [5]. In that publication the authors tried to shift the net demand peaks by offering time of use tariffs, so by using their formulas TUC-TAC tried to calculate the objective value of a tariff. The second method calculates the average directly by using the values of the rates without any normalization. The third method calculates the average after normalizing the values of every rate in the tariff. In the end, the second method was selected for the final version of TUC-TAC 2020, because it attracted more customers with the current settings.

Main Tariff Strategy. Since the basics of the game and some "peripheral" strategy aspects have been explained, it is time now to describe in detail the strategy which was responsible for TUC-TAC's success. As mentioned earlier, the basic principle that was applied has certain analogies to the equilibrium strategy used by the winning agent of the 2010 LSG tournament [10]. TUC-TAC's strategy is quite similar to that since its basic goal is to get half the available market share leaving the rest to the others. So by doing that, TUC-TAC expects to always have the highest income, while it shares all the fees with the other agents. Figure 2 below outlines the main TUC-TAC strategy components.

In the beginning, TUC-TAC publishes the initial tariffs and then waits for the assessment timeslots. When it is time for a reassessment of the market state, that agent first checks if any of its current tariffs are exceeding some specific *dynamic* bounds. The tariffs that are out of bounds get revoked, the others remain. Then it checks the number of customers that are subscribed in the total of a tariff type. If the number of subscribed customers is higher than some *MIDDLE-BOUND* value, it instantly revokes its cheapest tariff and creates a new one with the purpose to share the customers with the other brokers. If the amount of the subscribed customers is not higher than *MIDDLE-BOUND*, TUC-TAC checks a *LOWER-BOUND*. The purpose of having a *LOWER-BOUND*, is to remain competitive throughout a game, so, if the amount of the subscribed customers is lower than the *LOWER-BOUND*, it tries to create and publish a tariff that is more attractive than that of its opponents. The aforementioned bounds change dynamically during the games according to weather, time of year, and game state; however, the value of *MIDDLE-BOUND* remains rather close to 50% of the available customers base (more specifically, it ranges between 50% and 62.5%). The whole process is repeated until the game ends.

3.3   The Wholesale Market Module

The second but equally important module of TUC-TAC agent is the Wholesale Market one. Its main responsibilities are to buy and sell energy in the double

---

[1] It has to be clarified that opponent tariffs with unusual features were considered as "baits" and were not evaluated. Such features could be very high early withdrawal penalties, unusually high periodic payments, or values of rates.

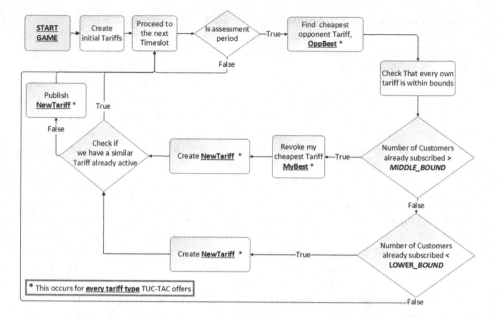

Fig. 2. Main Consumption Tariff strategy flowchart

auctions of the wholesale market. In order to be effective though, it requires finding the best bids so the customers would not have to resort to Balancing Utility to get their energy; in which case TUC-TAC would be charged higher for every single KWh that was not reserved by the agent.

The main algorithm implemented in this module was a variation of the Monte Carlo Tree search method previously developed by Chowdbury et al. [1]. In PowerTAC's case, the double auctions of the wholesale market constitute a complex action-space which requires fast and precise actions in order to be profitable. So, MCTS was selected for its ability to rapidly traverse through huge decision trees and find the best action. Though the concept of this algorithm is indeed suitable for this setting, and can be especially useful, judging by the results of Chowdhury et al. [1], the lack of a proper predictor in TUC-TAC's case makes the current wholesale market approach completely naive. For this reason, we are already working towards creating a limit price predictor for PowerTAC 2021.

3.4 Net Demand Predictor Module

At the beginning of each simulated day, TUC-TAC must decide the amount of energy it has to buy for its customers. However, demand changes dynamically and this information is not available in advance. TUC-TAC's net demand predictor estimates the net demand of the customers for the upcoming 24 timeslots, based on the given weather forecast and the past net demand values. We tested two predictors: a classic linear regression method, and a deep learning one.

Dataset Construction. In order for TUC-TAC to make a good prediction, a dataset with features that are relevant to the target value is required. The features we used according to the information available to the agent during the competition, are *(i)* the hour of day, *(ii)* the day of the week, *(iii)* the month, *(iv)* the year, *(v)* the temperature, *(vi)* the wind speed, *(vii)* the wind direction, and *(viii)* the cloud coverage. Also, we chose to include lags of the target variable (i.e., net demand value) for the previous time slot, as is common in time-series regression tasks; this was shown to improve our results. Formally, the input vector is represented as

$$x = [h_{t+1}, d_{t+1}, m_{t+1}, y_{t+1}, temp_{t+1}, wSpeed_{t+1}, wDirct_{t+1}, cloudCov_{t+1}, mwh_t]$$

denoting the hour, date, and weather forecasts and demand at timeslot t.

All data used for the training datasets arise from the log files of the 2020 PowerTAC final's games. This data was divided into different datasets, one for each geographical area from which weather data originate from, i.e. Denver, Minneapolis, and Phoenix. Note, however, that the particular area is not known to the agent during the game, and thus, data from every site was selected randomly to form a fourth dataset without geographical distinctions.

Linear Regression (LR) Predictor. Our first approach on constructing the predictor was linear regression because it is a classical method for modeling relationships, which in our case is the one between the features in the algorithm's input and the prediction values in the output. To evaluate the method we incorporated the implementation of the scikit learn library in Python.

Deep Learning Regression (DLR) Predictor. This approach uses a neural network to discover hidden patterns between the features and the target value. The neural network consists of 2 hidden layers of 24 neurons each, with 10 epochs of training over the training data. The input dataset consists of the features above, and the target variable is net demand in MWh for the next interval.

4   Experiments and Results

This section presents (a) a post-tournament analysis of the PowerTAC 2020 finals; and (b) experiments evaluating the TUC-TAC's demand predictor module.

4.1   PowerTAC 2020 Post-Tournament Analysis

There were 8 agents participating in the 2020 PowerTAC finals. Each agent participated in 40 eight-player games, 105 five-player games, and 63 three-player games. The scoreboard can be seen in Fig. 3 below[2]. The vertical axis shows

---

[2] The complete results of PowerTAC 2020 are in https://powertac.org/log_archive/ PowerTAC_2020_finals.html. An executable version of the TUC-TAC 2020 agent can be retrieved from https://www.powertac.org/wiki/index.php/TUC_TAC_2020.

the score, while the horizontal axis presents the name of the broker in each of the three different scenarios: games with three, five, and eight players. We now proceed with an overview and details of our post-tournament analysis.

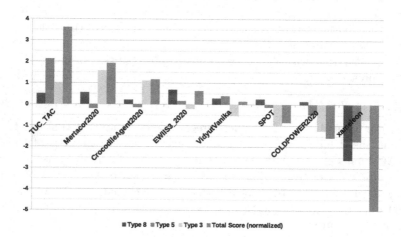

Fig. 3. Final Results of PowerTAC 2020 (Normalized *wrt.* average agent performance)

PowerTAC 2020 Post-tournament Analysis Overview. In PowerTAC 2020, most agents used similar technologies, like Markov Decision Processes or Q-Learning, but in the end they appear to have had strategies that corresponded to different "aggression" levels.[3]

TUC-TAC and Mertacor2020 were quite aggressive in the retail market, regardless of the number of players in the game. Specifically, Mertacor used an aggressive decision-making strategy informed by offline reinforcement learning. In the end, TUC-TAC's adherence to its central, though properly adjusted, strategy principle, its faster response times, and the offering of more attractive tariffs, allowed it to have an advantage over Mertacor, and thus TUC-TAC won most of the games it participated in. CrocodileAgent2020 was especially aggressive in 3-player games, but not so much in the more-than-three player categories. Moreover, ColdPower, Spot, VidyutVanika, and EWIIS3_2020 had a "conservative" behavior in the retail market, judging by their lower average scores in most games. It is also important to note here that apart from the retail market strategy failure of Spot and VidyutVanika, these agents were the ones performing best in the wholesale market, apparently having focused on that market, something that will not be further investigated in this work. On the other hand, Xameleon implemented a greedy strategy that did not perform well, probably because of the high fees it had to pay and some flaws in its design.

---

[3] Some specifics of their strategies were revealed during a post-tournament workshop.

TUC-TAC's Stability with Respect to Transmission Capacity Fees. Transmission capacity fees represent the amount of money a broker should pay for its customers' contribution to demand peaks. This means that when there is a demand peak each broker will have to pay for a portion of the exceeding energy(MWh). In the current PowerTAC competition these fees are the main problem an agent faces when it tries to dominate in the retail market. So after understanding how important those fees are and how these generally affect the game in theory, we present below the results of PowerTAC 2020 for each tier sorted by the total exceeding MWh paid by the brokers as transmission capacity fees. Figure 4 thus demonstrates that TUC-TAC's retail market strategy is the most stable, regardless of the amount of the fees imposed.[4]

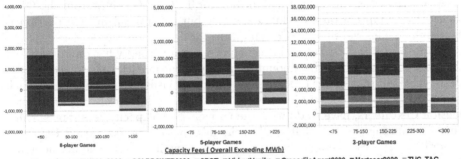

Fig. 4. Categorization by Transmission Capacity Fees: each color bar's area represents the average score for each agent in the games corresponding to different fee levels paid

Thus, we believe one can safely infer that TUC-TAC's retail market strategy achieved its goals. As mentioned earlier in the paper, this strategy was created to mitigate the costs of the transmission capacity fees across more than one agent while TUC-TAC could still take the highest share of the tariff profits. This strategy worked exceptionally well when the majority of agents were in the game, specifically in 8-player and 5-player games. At the same time, this strategy resulted in a very profitable stable performance throughout the 3-player games.

TUC-TAC's Tariff Profits. There are 4 different tariff types offered by TUC-TAC, namely Consumption tariffs, Thermal Storage Consumption Tariffs, Solar Production Tariffs, and Wind Production Tariffs. The left plot of Fig. 5 demonstrates the net profits from Consumption and Thermal Storage Consumption tariffs, while the right plot of Fig. 5 shows the losses deriving from the use of Solar Production and Wind Production tariffs.

---

[4] This and subsequent figures (apart from Fig. 8) exclude the results of "Phoenix games" (see "categorization by balancing fees" below). The extraordinarily high fees paid by the agents in those games would just have added noise to the analysis.

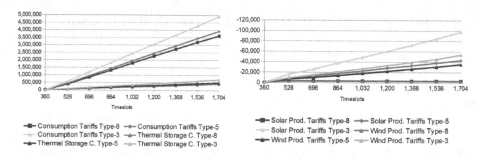

Fig. 5. TUC-TAC's tariffs profits and losses

As observed, the main source of income for TUC-TAC comes from the (electricity) Consumption tariffs, while a smaller but substantial income portion is the result of Thermal Storage Consumption tariffs.

Figure 5 cannot show the real effect that renewable energy has on PowerTAC. The only thing visible is the amount of money spent in each case to acquire the useful effects of that power type; besides that, it is visible that the losses in each case are very small to be considered harmful. Some of these useful effects of Production Costumers, have to do with the transmission capacity fees. Specifically, when calculating the fees that each agent has to pay, the Balancing Utility of PowerTAC charges each agent according to its contribution to the net demand. So, if an agent has customers that produced energy in that timeslot, that will greatly reduce the transmission capacity fees that the agent will have to pay. In addition to that, it was necessary to compete and increase the tariff prices for production customers, especially in 3-player games, because other agents like EWIIS3_2020 had increased amounts of profits when they could get low-cost energy. Also, an agent can sell or provide immediately to its customers the produced energy, but this technique usually does not generate enough profit.

We believe it is clear how important the Consumption Tariffs are for the profitability of a PowerTAC agent. At the same time, there are other sources of income that are not equally important, but can be considered when deciding the tariff types to offer. We found that the Thermal Storage Consumption tariffs can also be key to making substantial profits in a game (Fig. 5).

Interactions Among the Main Competitors. Figure 6 demonstrates how each of the three best (in 3-player games) agents perform when their main competitors are not part of a game. The most impressive graph is that of CrocodileAgent. As it seems when both TUC-TAC and Mertacor are absent, Crocodile's average score is over 1 million higher, while when only one of the main competitors is absent its average score is almost half a million higher. As such, it is fair to say that Crocodile performs better when the competition is weaker, thus that is the reason it got the second place in type 3 games (see Fig. 3).

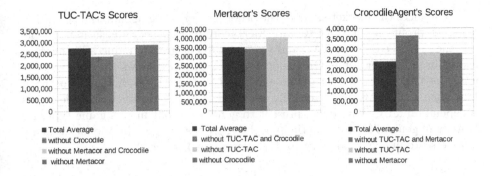

Fig. 6. Impact of TUC-TAC on 3-player games (rewards shown correspond to averages in "regular" games—see Fig. 8).

In addition, Mertacor appears to have a better performance when TUC-TAC was *not* part of a 3 player game (half a million higher than the total average), while its average score dropped by half a million when Crocodile was not part of the game. Still, Mertacor's average score in every case was higher than every other broker in the 3-player games.

However, TUC-TAC's performance was not that much affected by the absence of its main competitors. This of course is a plus in the sense the agent's performance is stable, but at the same time it signifies that TUC-TAC cannot exploit weaker agents that well, unlike CrocodileAgent and Mertacor. Nevertheless, TUC-TAC's stability allowed it to get third place in the 3 player games.

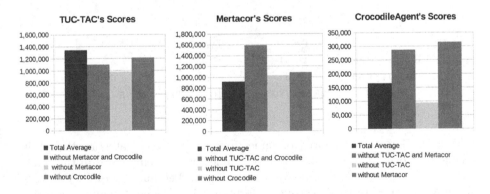

Fig. 7. Impact of TUC-TAC on 5-player games

Figure 7 depicts the performance of the three best agents in the Regular 5-player games when their main competitors are not part of a game. At first, it is visible that TUC-TAC's performance is quite stable. In addition to that, it is inferred that TUC-TAC has better results when Mertacor is part of a game. This happens because the combination of these two highly competitive agents greatly reduces the market share of the other participating agents, thus resulting in higher profits for TUC-TAC and Mertacor. In Mertacor's case it is visible that the presence of TUC-TAC and CrocodileAgent greatly reduces his average income in a 5-player game. On the other hand, this fact shows that Mertacor is better at exploiting the rest of the agents when there is no direct competition (like when TUC-TAC and Crocodile are participating). Lastly, Crocodile seems to depend on TUC-TAC being present to generate profit in this game type. Its strategy in general is problematic in 5-player games, judging by the fact that its average score in every category (of 5-player games) is very low.

Categorization by Balancing Fees. Balancing fees are the fees that are applied to the agents by the *balancing market* when they fail to procure the required energy. The most common reason a broker might fail to accumulate the required by its customers energy, is very high wholesale market prices.

There were two distinct types of games in this year's finals. The "regular games" and the "special Phoenix games". We term as "special Phoenix games" the games that have extended periods of timeslots with unusually high wholesale market prices. In such situations, agents that have not been careful to buy substantial amounts of energy early on, would have to buy energy in very high prices in the wholesale market. As it was observed in PowerTAC 2020, the leading agents were not prepared for this scenario, thus they could not obtain the required energy during these time periods, and resulting in very high balancing fees for each one of them. This phenomenon usually occurred during the summertime of games located in Phoenix.

Table 1. Total wins of TUC-TAC

	Type 8	Type 5	Type 3
"Regular" Games	28/34	81/102	47/57
"Phoenix" Games	0/6	0/3	0/6
Total	**28/40 (70%)**	**81/105 (77%)**	**47/63 (74%)**

TUC-TAC won the majority of games in every "classic" category, though it had the best overall score in the 5-player games, while being third in the other two game types as we have already seen in Fig. 3. The number of TUC-TAC's wins in each game type, depicting performance in "Phoenix" games also, are shown in Table 1.

By comparing the two graphs in Fig. 8 it is clear how different "Phoenix" games are compared to regular ones, for almost all agents but especially for TUC-TAC and Mertacor. The main reason TUC-TAC was under-performing in these games was a flaw in the design of the wholesale module: as mentioned earlier, this flaw rendered TUC-TAC unable to buy enough energy from the wholesale market to provide to its customers, thus resulting in high penalties for the agent. As is apparent in Fig. 8, almost none of the other participants was prepared for

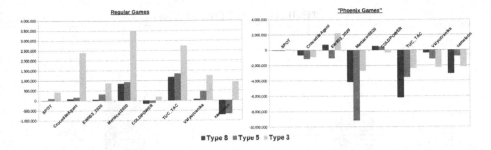

Fig. 8. Differences between Average Scores of "Regular" and "Phoenix" games

these games as well. However, it seems like these exact same scenarios were very profitable for EWIIS3 2020. Even though EWIIS3 was apparently well-prepared for extreme situations, and its performance was generally stable across games, this was not enough to win the tournament. This shows that in order for an agent to win the tournament some aggressive actions should be taken.

4.2   Predictor Evaluation and Impact

In this section we describe experiments that compare our two net demand predictors, with the purpose of identifying the one with the best execution time to error rate ratio. To test the LR and DLR predictors, we perform three types of experiments. In the first one, we take the three geographically divided datasets, fit the 90 % of the datapoints to the linear regression model and predict the rest 10 % of them. In the second one, we combine datasets from 2 out of 3 areas, fit them to the model and predict the target values of the other area. In the third one, we combine all three datasets, shuffle the datapoints, fit 90 % of them to the model and predict the rest 10 % of it. All experiments were performed in a 5-fold validation scheme.

We report that in a preliminary evaluation, we examined the number of lag features that can be used to improve predicting performance. Results (not depicted here due to space restrictions) show that incorporating at least one lag feature leads to lower error rates, but adding more lag features does not help increasing profits significantly.

Now, comparing the two different predictor implementations in terms of execution time is very important, since TUC-TAC is obliged by PowerTAC rules to take decisions within the specific round duration. Results indicate that the execution of the linear regression predictor is about 20 times faster than DLR, which is a significant merit. Specifically, the LR execution time is only 0.69 seconds, as opposed to 655.55 seconds for DLR.

Moreover, the performance of LR in terms of accuracy is very close to that of DLR, as depicted in Fig. 9 which compares the methods in terms of *mean absolute error*, *root mean square error* and *coefficient of determination (R^2)* values. Thus, results indicate that the simpler and faster LR method is the most appropriate to

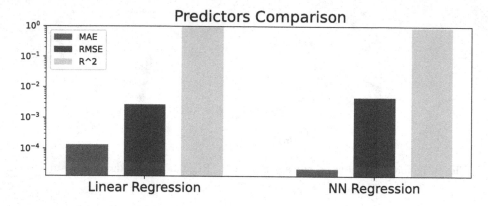

Fig. 9. Error rates comparison between Linear and Deep Learning Regression

incorporate in TUC-TAC. Further experimentation with alternative predictors is in order, and is currently under way.

5   Conclusions and Future Work

The importance of testing the aspects of the emerging Smart Grid before deploying is essential; this is why simulation environments such as PowerTAC are important. This paper presented the strategy of TUC-TAC 2020, the champion of The PowerTAC 2020 competition. A novelty which was arguably key to TUC-TAC's success, is the basic principle underlying its strategy. That principle resembles to some extent the winning, equilibrium strategy of the Lemonade Stand multiagent zero-sum repeated game, in which agents try to acquire approximately half of the market share, leaving the other half to their opponents. However, because of the nature and complexity of PowerTAC, it is next to impossible, in our view, to solve for an actual equilibrium strategy in this domain.

Though TUC-TAC won PowerTAC 2020, there is much room for improvement for the agent. For instance, the wholesale market module has certain drawbacks that need to be overcome. Our first priority is to add a wholesale market limit price predictor. In addition, the MCTS part of the wholesale module needs to be reworked to exploit information accumulated during the 2020 finals. At the same time, it is important to improve the retail market module. Thus, we will look for new ways to improve the agent in the retail market too, having as a first priority to reduce the transmission capacity fees as much as possible. Also, we are looking into ways to support more tariff types to increase profits.

More broadly, we anticipate that the techniques developed for TUC-TAC 2020, can also be applied in a multitude of other multi-agent domains as well. For instance, the generic "equilibrium" strategy for the Retail Market of this competition is conceivably a simple but powerful strategy to use in a host of alternative competitive domains as well.

References

1. Chowdhury, M.M.P., Kiekintveld, C., Tran, S., Yeoh, W.: Bidding in periodic double auctions using heuristics and dynamic Monte Carlo tree search. In: Proceedings of the Twenty-Seventh International Joint Conference on Artificial Intelligence, IJCAI 2018, pp. 166–172 (2018)
2. Ghosh, S., Subramanian, E., Bhat, S.P., Gujar, S., Paruchuri, P.: Vidyutvanika: a reinforcement learning based broker agent for a power trading competition. In: Proceedings of the AAAI Conference on Artificial Intelligence, vol. 33, no. 01, pp. 914 921 (2019)
3. Ketter, W., Collins, J., Reddy, P.: Power TAC: a competitive economic simulation of the smart grid. Energy Econ. **39**, 262–270 (2013)
4. Natividad, F., Folk, R.Y., Yeoh, W., Cao, H.: On the use of off-the-shelf machine learning techniques to predict energy demands of power TAC consumers. In: Ceppi, S., David, E., Hajaj, C., Robu, V., Vetsikas, I.A. (eds.) AMEC/TADA 2015-2016. LNBIP, vol. 271, pp. 112–126. Springer, Cham (2017). https://doi.org/10.1007/978-3-319-54229-4_8
5. Özdemir, S., Unland, R.: The strategy and architecture of a winner broker in a renowned agent-based smart grid competition. In: Web Intelligence, pp. 165–183 (2017)
6. Özdemir, S., Unland, R.: AgentUDE17: a genetic algorithm to optimize the parameters of an electricity tariff in a smart grid environment. In: Demazeau, Y., An, B., Bajo, J., Fernández-Caballero, A. (eds.) PAAMS 2018. LNCS (LNAI), vol. 10978, pp. 224–236. Springer, Cham (2018). https://doi.org/10.1007/978-3-319-94580-4_18
7. Serrano Cuevas, J., Rodriguez-Gonzalez, A.Y., Munoz de Cote, E.: Fixed-price tariff generation using reinforcement learning. In: Fujita, K., et al. (eds.) Modern Approaches to Agent-based Complex Automated Negotiation. SCI, vol. 674, pp. 121–136. Springer, Cham (2017). https://doi.org/10.1007/978-3-319-51563-2_8
8. Shoham, Y., Leyton-Brown, K.: Multiagent systems: algorithmic, game-theoretic, and logical foundations. In: Multiagent Systems: Algorithmic, Game-Theoretic, and Logical Foundations (2008)
9. Sutton, R.S., Barto, A.G.: Reinforcement Learning: An Introduction, 2nd edn. The MIT Press (2018)
10. Sykulski, A., Chapman, A., Munoz de Cote, E., Jennings, N.: The winning strategy for the inaugural lemonade stand game tournament. Front. Artif. Intell. Appl. **215** (2010)
11. Urieli, D., Stone, P.: Tactex'13: a champion adaptive power trading agent. In: Proceedings of the AAAI Conference on Artificial Intelligence, vol. 28, no. 1 (2014)

Parameterized Analysis of Assignment Under Multiple Preferences

Barak Steindl[(✉)] and Meirav Zehavi

Ben Gurion University of the Negev, Beer-Sheva, Israel

Abstract. The ASSIGNMENT problem is a fundamental and well-studied problem in the intersection of Social Choice, Computational Economics and Discrete Allocation. In the ASSIGNMENT problem, a group of agents expresses preferences over a set of items, and the task is to find a *pareto optimal* allocation of items to agents. We introduce a generalized version of this problem, where each agent is equipped with *multiple* incomplete preference lists: each list (called a *layer*) is a ranking of items in a possibly different way according to a different criterion. We introduce the concept of *global optimality*, which extends the notion of pareto optimality to the multi-layered setting, and we focus on the problem of deciding whether a *globally optimal* assignment exists. We study this problem from the perspective of Parameterized Complexity: we consider several natural parameters such as the number of layers, the number of agents, the number of items, and the maximum length of a preference list. We present a comprehensive picture of the parameterized complexity of the problem with respect to these parameters.

1 Introduction

The field of resource allocation problems has been widely studied in recent years. A fundamental and one of the most well-studied problems in this field is the ASSIGNMENT problem[1] [1–3,5,6,9,19,24,35]. In the ASSIGNMENT problem we are given a set of n agents, and a set of m items. Each agent (human, company, or any other entity) has strict preferences over a subset of items, and the objective is to allocate items to agents in an "optimal" way. Different notions of optimality have been considered in the literature, but the one that has received the most attention is *pareto optimality* (see, e.g., [2,5,6]). Intuitively, an assignment p is called *pareto optimal* if there is no other assignment q that is at least good as p for all the agents and also strictly better than p for at least one agent.

Besides its theoretical interest, the problem has also practical importance. Algorithms for the ASSIGNMENT problem have applications in a variety of real-world situations, such as assigning jobs to workers, campus houses to students,

---

[1] The problem is called ASSIGNMENT in all relevant literature. Although this name is somewhat generic, to be consistent with the literature, we use it here as well.

A full version of this paper, including full proofs and examples, can be found in https://arxiv.org/abs/2004.00655.

A. Rosenfeld and N. Talmon (Eds.): EUMAS 2021, LNAI 12802, pp. 160–177, 2021.
https://doi.org/10.1007/978-3-030-82254-5_10

time stamps to users on a common machine, players to sports teams, graduating medical students to their first hospital appointments, and so on [17,23,30,36].

In the ASSIGNMENT problem, each agent has exactly one preference list. The preference lists may represent a single subjective criterion according to which each agent ranks the items. However, they may also represent a combination of different such criteria: each agent associates a score to each item per criterion, and a single preference list is derived from some weighted sum of the scores. In many cases, it is unclear how to combine scores associated with criteria of inherently incomparable nature - that is like "comparing apples with oranges". Additionally, even if a single list can be forcefully extracted, most data is lost.[2]

Thus, the classic model seems somewhat restrictive in real world scenarios where people rely on highly *varied* aspects to rank other entities. For example, suppose that there are n candidates who need to be assigned to n positions. The recruiters may rank the candidates for each position according to different criteria, such as academic background, experience, impression, and so on [4,22]. Moreover, when assigning campus houses to students, the students may rank the houses by multiple criteria such as their location, rent, size etc. [33]. This motivates the employment of multiple preference lists where each preference list (called a *layer*) is defined by a different criterion.

In many real-world scenarios, the preferences of the agents may sometimes depend on external circumstances that may not be completely known in advance such as growth of stocks in the market, natural phenomena, outbreak of pandemics [32,34] and so on. In such cases, each layer in our generalized model can represent a possible "state" of the world, and we may seek an assignment that is optimal in as many states as possible. For instance, suppose that there is a taxi company with n taxis and m costumers ($n > m$) that want to be picked at a specific time in future. The "cost" of each taxi depends on the time taken to reach the costumer from the starting location of the taxi. Many factors (that may not be completely known a-priori) may affect the total cost such as road constructions, weather, car condition and the availability of the drivers [15,29]. The firm may suggest different possible scenarios (each represents a layer). For each scenario, the costumers may be ranked differently by the taxis, and an assignment that is pareto optimal in as many layers as possible will cover most of the scenarios and will give the lowest expected total cost.

Furthermore, it is not always possible to completely take hold of preferences of some (or all) agents due to lack of information or communication, as well as security and privacy issues [10,27]. In addition, even if it is technically and ethically feasible, it may be costly in terms of money, time, or other resources to gather all information from all the agents [26]. In these cases, we can "complete the preferences" using different assumptions on the agents. As a result, we will have a list of preference profiles that represent different possible states of the world. An assignment that is pareto optimal in as many preference profiles as possible will be pareto optimal with high probability.

---

[2] Our new generalized model allows us to limit the amount of data that can be ignored using the parameter α.

Table 1. Summary of our results. Results marked with † are proved to be optimal under the exponential-time hypothesis.

Parameter	Complexity class	Running time	Polynomial kernel?
$\ell + d$	para-NP-hard [Theorem 8]	–	–
$\ell + (m - d)$	para-NP-hard [Theorem 8]	–	–
n	FPT	$\mathcal{O}^*(n!)^†$ [Theorem 1 + Theorem 5]	No [Theorem 9]
m	XP, W[1]-hard [Theorem 6]	$(nm)^{\mathcal{O}(m)}$ [Theorem 4]	–
$m + \alpha$	XP, W[1]-hard [Theorem 6]	$(nm)^{\mathcal{O}(m)}$ [Theorem 4]	–
$n + m + \alpha$	FPT	$\mathcal{O}^*(n!)^†$ [Theorem 1 + Theorem 5]	No [Theorem 9]
$m + (\ell - \alpha)$	XP, W[1]-hard [Theorem 6]	$(nm)^{\mathcal{O}(m)}$ [Theorem 4]	–
$n + m + (\ell - \alpha)$	FPT	$\mathcal{O}^*(n!)^†$ [Theorem 1 + Theorem 5]	No [Theorem 9]
$m + \ell$	FPT	$\mathcal{O}^*(((m!)^{\ell+1})!)$ [C.1]	No [Theorem 9]
$n + \ell$	FPT	$\mathcal{O}^*(n!)$ [Theorem 1]	Yes [Theorem 2]
$n + m + \ell$	FPT	$\mathcal{O}^*(n!)$ [Theorem 1]	Yes [Theorem 2]

Our work is inspired by that of Chen et al. [12], who studied the STABLE MARRIAGE problem under multiple preferences.[3] Chen et al. [12] considered an extension where there are ℓ layers of preferences, and adapted the definition of stability accordingly. Specifically, three notions of stability were defined: α-*global stability*, α-*pair stability*, and α-*individual stability*. The authors studied the algorithmic complexity of finding matchings that satisfy each of these stability notions. Their notion of α-global stability extends the original notion of stability in a natural way, by requiring the sought matching to be stable in (at least) some α layers. Our notion of α-*global optimality* extends pareto optimality in the same way, by requiring an assignment to be pareto optimal in some α layers.

Although the ASSIGNMENT problem can be solved in polynomial time using a mechanism called "serial dictatorship" [2], we show that the problem becomes much harder when multiple preference lists are taken into account. So, in this paper, we study the parameterized complexity of deciding whether a globally optimal assignment exists with respect to various parameters.

Our Contributions. One important aspect of our contribution is conceptual: we are the first to study pareto optimality (in the ASSIGNMENT problem) in the presence of multiple preference lists. This opens the door to many future studies (both theoretical and experimental) of our concept, as well as refinements or extensions thereof (see Sect. 6). In this work, we focus on the classical and parameterized complexity of the problem.

We consider several parameters such as the number of layers ℓ, the number of agents n (also denoted by #agents), the number of items m (also denoted by #items), the maximum length of a preference list d, and the given number of layers α for which we require an assignment to be pareto optimal. The choice of these parameters is sensible because in real-life scenarios such as those mentioned earlier, some of these parameters may be substantially smaller than the

---

[3] In the full version, we further argue that the ASSIGNMENT and STABLE MARRIAGE problems, being based on different concepts of stability, are very different problems.

input size. For instance, ℓ, α and $\ell - \alpha$ are upper bounded by the number of criteria according to which the agents rank the items. Thus, they are likely to be small in practice: when ranking other entities, people usually do not consider a substantially large number of criteria (further, up until now, attention was only given to the case where $\ell = \alpha = 1$). For instance, when sports teams rank candidate players, only a few criteria such as the player's winning history, his impact on his previous teams, and physical properties are taken into account [18]. In addition, the parameter $\ell - \alpha$ may be small particularly in cases where we want to find an assignment that is optimal with respect to as many criteria as possible. Moreover, in various cases concerning ranking of people, jobs, houses etc., people usually have a limited number of entities that they want or are allowed to ask for [14]. In these cases, the parameter d is likely to be small. Moreover, in small countries (such as Israel), the number of universities, hospitals, sports teams and many other facilities and organizations is very small [13,31]. Thus, in scenarios concerning these entities, at least one among n and m may be small. A summary of our results is given in Table 1.

Fixed-Parameter Tractability and ETH Based Lower Bounds. We prove that α-GLOBALLY OPTIMAL ASSIGNMENT is *fixed-parameter tractable* (FPT) with respect to n by providing an $\mathcal{O}^*(n!)$ time algorithm that relies on the connection between pareto optimality and serial dictatorship. We then prove that the problem admits a polynomial kernel with respect to $n + \ell$ and that it is FPT with respect to #items$+\ell$ by providing an exponential kernel. We also prove that the problem is *slice-wise polynomial* (XP) with respect to #items by providing an $m^{\mathcal{O}(m)} \cdot n^{\mathcal{O}(n)}$ time algorithm. In addition, we prove that $\mathcal{O}^*(2^{\mathcal{O}(t \log t)})$ is a tight lower bound on the running time (so, our $\mathcal{O}^*(n!)$ time algorithm is essentially optimal) under ETH (defined in Sect. 2) for even larger parameters such as $t = n+m+\alpha$ and $t = n+m+(\ell-\alpha)$ using two linear parameter reductions from the $k \times k$ PERMUTATION CLIQUE problem. Lastly, we prove that the problem is W[1]-hard with respect to $m + \alpha$ and $m + (\ell - \alpha)$ using two parameterized reductions from MULTICOLORED INDEPENDENT SET.

NP-Hardness. We prove that the problem is NP-hard for any fixed α and ℓ such that $2 \leq \alpha \leq \ell$ using a polynomial reduction from the SERIAL DICTATORSHIP FEASIBILITY problem that relies on a reduction by Aziz el al. [6]. We also define three polynomial-time constructions of preference profiles given an instance of 3-SAT, and we rely on them in two polynomial reductions from 3-SAT, such that in the resulting instances $\ell + d$ and $\ell + (m - d)$ are bounded by fixed constants. This proves that the problem is para-NP-hard for $\ell + d$ and $\ell + (m - d)$.

Non-existence of Polynomial Kernels. We prove that the problem does not admit polynomial kernels unless $\mathsf{NP} \subseteq \mathsf{coNP/poly}$ w.r.t. $n+m+\alpha$, $n+m+(\ell-\alpha)$, and $m + \ell$ using three *cross-compositions* (defined in Sect. 2) from 3-SAT that rely on the aforementioned reduction to prove para-NP-hardness.

2   Preliminaries

For any natural number t, we denote $[t] = \{1, \ldots, t\}$. We use the $\mathcal{O}^*$ and the Ω^* notations to suppress polynomial factors in the input size, that is, $\mathcal{O}^*(f(k)) = f(k) \cdot n^{\mathcal{O}(1)}$ and $\Omega^*(f(k)) = \Omega(f(k)) \cdot n^{\mathcal{O}(1)}$.

The Assignment Problem. An instance of the ASSIGNMENT problem is a triple (A, I, P) where A is a set of n agents $\{a_1, \ldots, a_n\}$, I is a set of m items $\{b_1, \ldots, b_m\}$, and $P = (<_{a_1}, \ldots, <_{a_n})$, called the *preference profile*, contains the preferences of the agents over the items, where each $<_{a_i}$ is a linear order over a *subset* of I. We refer to such linear orders as *preference lists*. If $b_j <_{a_i} b_r$, we say that agent a_i *prefers* item b_r over item b_j, and we write $b_j \leq_{a_i} b_r$ if $b_j <_{a_i} b_r$ or $b_j = b_r$. Item b is ac *We use the $\mathcal{O}^*$ and the Ω^* notations to suppress polynomial factors in the input size, that is, $\mathcal{O}^*(f(k)) = f(k) \cdot n^{\mathcal{O}(1)}$ and $\Omega^*(f(k)) = \Omega(f(k)) \cdot n^{\mathcal{O}(1)}$.ceptable* by agent a if b appears in $<_a$. An *assignment* is an allocation of items to agents such that each agent is allocated at most one item, and each item is allocated to at most one agent. We define a special item $b_\emptyset$, seen as the least preferred item of each agent, and will be used as a sign that an agent is not assigned to an item. We assume that $b_\emptyset$ is not part of the input item set, and that it appears at the end of every preference list (we will not write it explicitly). Formally, an assignment $p : A \to I \cup \{b_\emptyset\}$ is a mapping between agents to items, s.t. for each $i \in [n]$: (1) $p(a_i) = b_\emptyset$, or (2) both $p(a_i) \in I$ and for each $j \in [n] \setminus \{i\}$, $p(a_i) \neq p(a_j)$. We refer to p as *legal* if each item is assigned to an agent who accepts it. For brevity, we will usually omit the term "legal".[4] Moreover, when we write a set in a preference list, we assume that its elements are ordered arbitrarily, unless stated otherwise.

Optimality. An assignment p is *pareto optimal* if there does not exist another assignment q such that both $p(a_i) \leq_{a_i} q(a_i)$ for every $i \in [n]$, and there exists $i \in [n]$ such that $p(a_i) <_{a_i} q(a_i)$; p admits a *trading cycle* $(a_{i_0}, b_{j_0}, a_{i_1}, b_{j_1}, \ldots, a_{i_{k-1}}, b_{j_{k-1}})$ if for each $r \in \{0, \ldots, k-1\}$, we have that $p(a_{i_r}) = b_{j_r}$ and $b_{j_r} <_{a_{i_r}} b_{j_{r+1} \pmod{k}}$. We say that p admits a *self loop* if there exist an agent a_i and an item b_j such that b_j is not allocated to any agent, and a_i prefers b_j over its own item. We now provide a simple characterization of pareto optimality that is defined with respect to trading cycles and self loops:

Proposition 1 (Folklore; see, e.g., Aziz et al. [5,6]). *An assignment is pareto optimal if and only if it does not admit trading cycles and self loops.*

For an instance (A, I, P) and an assignment p, the corresponding *trading graph* is the directed graph over $A \cup I$, constructed as follows: (1) for each $a \in A$ s.t. $p(a) \neq b_\emptyset$, $p(a)$ points to a; (2) each $a \in A$ points to all the items it prefers over its assigned item $p(a)$; (3) each $b \in I$ with no owner points to all the agents that accept it. An assignment is pareto optimal if and only if its corresponding trading graph does not contain cycles (see, e.g., Aziz et al. [5,6]).

---

[4] All the "optimal" assignments that we construct in this paper will be legal in a sufficient number of layers, where they are claimed to be pareto optimal.

A simple assignment mechanism is the greedy *serial dictatorship* mechanism. For a given permutation over the agents, the agent ordered first allocates its most preferred item, then the agent ordered second allocates its most preferred item among the remaining items, and so on. If at some point, an agent has no available item to allocate, it allocates $b_\emptyset$. We say that an assignment p is a *possible outcome* of serial dictatorship if there exists a permutation π such that applying serial dictatorship with respect to π results in p.

Proposition 2 (Abdulkadiroglu and Tayfun [2]). *An assignment is pareto optimal if and only if it is a possible outcome of serial dictatorship.*

This implies that the ASSIGNMENT problem is solvable in polynomial time.

Generalization of the Assignment Problem. We introduce a generalized version of the ASSIGNMENT problem where there are ℓ layers of preferences. For each $j \in [\ell]$, we refer to $<_{a_i}^{(j)}$ as a_i's preference list in layer j. The *preference profile in layer j* is the collection of all the agents' preference lists in layer j, namely, $P_j = (<_{a_1}^{(j)}, \ldots, <_{a_n}^{(j)})$.

Definition 1. *An assignment p is α-globally optimal for an instance $(A, I, P_1, \ldots, P_\ell)$ if there exist α layers $i_1, \ldots, i_\alpha \in [\ell]$ such that p is pareto optimal in layer i_j for each $j \in [\alpha]$.*

α-GLOBALLY OPTIMAL ASSIGNMENT
Input: $(A, I, P_1, \ldots, P_\ell, \alpha)$, where A is a set of n agents, I is a set of m items, P_i is the preference profile in layer i for each $i \in [\ell]$, and $\alpha \in [\ell]$.
Question: Does an α-globally optimal assignment exist?

Notice that this problem is solvable in polynomial time when $\alpha = 1$ by applying serial dictatorship in some arbitrary layer. We study α-GLOBALLY OPTIMAL ASSIGNMENT from the perspective of parameterized complexity.

Parameterized Complexity. In the framework of parameterized complexity, each instance of a problem Π is associated with a *parameter* k. We say that Π is *fixed-parameter tractable* (FPT) or *slice-wise polynomial* (XP) if any instance (I, k) of Π is solvable in time $f(k) \cdot |I|^{\mathcal{O}(1)}$ or $|I|^{f(k)}$, respectively, where f is an arbitrary computable function of k. We say that a problem is W[1]-hard if it is unlikely to be FPT, and the main technique to prove so is by using parameterized reductions. A *polynomial compression* from Π to Π' is a polynomial-time algorithm that given an instance (I, k) of Π, outputs an equivalent instance I' of Π' such that $|I'| \leq poly(k)$. If $\Pi' = \Pi$, we say that Π admits a *polynomial kernel*. A *cross-composition* from Π to Π' is a polynomial-time algorithm that given instances $I_1, I_2, \ldots, I_t$ of Π for some $t \in \mathbb{N}$ that are of the same size $s \in \mathbb{N}$, outputs an instance (I, k) of Π' such that (1) $k \leq poly(s + \log t)$; and (2) (I, k) is a Yes-instance of Π' if and only if at least one of $I_1, I_2, \ldots, I_t$ is a Yes-instance of Π. By [7,8], the existence of a cross-composition from an NP-hard problem Π to a parameterized problem Π' implies that Π' does not admit a polynomial compression, unless NP $\subseteq$ coNP/poly. To obtain (essentially) tight conditional lower bounds for the running times of algorithms, we rely on the *Exponential-Time Hypothesis (ETH)* [11,20,21]. Informally, ETH asserts that 3-SAT cannot be solved in time $2^{o(n)}$ where n is the number of variables.

3   Fixed-Parameter Tractability and ETH Based Bounds

We first prove that α-GLOBALLY OPTIMAL ASSIGNMENT is FPT with respect to the parameter $n = \#$agents.

Theorem 1 (*).[5] *There exists an $\mathcal{O}^*(n!)$ algorithm for α-*GLOBALLY OPTIMAL ASSIGNMENT.

Proof (sketch). We provide a brute-force algorithm. The algorithm enumerates all possible pareto optimal assignments in each layer, using serial dictatorship with respect to all possible permutations on the agents. For each assignment p, it constructs the corresponding trading graphs for all the layers with respect to p, and checks whether there exist α graphs with no cycles. The running time of the algorithm is $\mathcal{O}^*(n!)$, since it iterates over $\mathcal{O}(\ell n!)$ assignments (each layer may have at most $n!$ different pareto optimal assignments by Proposition 2), and for each assignment, it takes polynomial time to construct the trading graphs, and to count how many contain no cycles. □

We now provide a simple lemma that will help us to design a polynomial kernel for α-GLOBALLY OPTIMAL ASSIGNMENT with respect to $n + \ell$.

Lemma 1. *Let (A, I, P) be an instance of the* ASSIGNMENT *problem where $|A| = n$. Then, for any agent $a \in A$ and pareto optimal assignment, a is assigned to $b_\emptyset$ or to one of the n most preferred items in its preference list.*

Proof. By Proposition 2, each pareto optimal assignment is a possible outcome of serial dictatorship. Observe that for each $i \in [n]$, when the mechanism is in the i-th step, it has already allocated at most $i - 1$ items. Thus, the i-th allocated item must be either: (i) $b_\emptyset$ (if all the items in the current preference list has already been allocated); or (ii) one of the i first ranked items in the current preference list. □

Theorem 2 (*). α-GLOBALLY OPTIMAL ASSIGNMENT *admits a kernel of size $\mathcal{O}(\ell n^2)$. Thus, it admits a polynomial kernel w.r.t. $n + \ell$.*

Proof (sketch). Given an instance of α-GLOBALLY OPTIMAL ASSIGNMENT $I_1 = (A, I, P_1, \ldots, P_\ell, \alpha)$, the kernel reduces each preference profile P_i to a preference profile P_i' by keeping only the (at most) n first-ranked items in each preference list. Let I' be a set containing the items ranked in the first n positions in some preference list in I_1. The resulting instance is $I_2 = (A, I', P_1', \ldots, P_\ell', \alpha)$, which satisfies $|I_2| = \mathcal{O}(\ell n^2)$. We prove that I_1 is equivalent to I_2 using Lemma 1. □

---

[5] Proofs of statements marked by * are omitted due to lack of space; full proofs can be found in the full version.

Before we present an exponential kernel for α-GLOBALLY OPTIMAL ASSIGNMENT with respect to the parameter $m + \ell$, let us define the following.

Definition 2. *Let* $Q = (A, I, P_1, \ldots, P_\ell, \alpha)$ *be an instance of* α-GLOBALLY OPTIMAL ASSIGNMENT *and* $u \in A$. *The agent class of* u *in* Q, $\mathcal{C}(u, Q)$, *is the tuple that contains the preference lists of* u *in all the layers, namely,* $\mathcal{C}(u, Q) = (<_u^1, \ldots, <_u^\ell)$. *Define* $D = \{B \subseteq I \times I | B \text{ is a linear order}\}$. *For a given tuple of length* ℓ *consisting of linear orderings on subsets of* I, $C \subseteq D^\ell$, *define* $A(C, Q) = \{a \in A \mid \mathcal{C}(a, Q) = C\}$.

Theorem 3 (*). α-GLOBALLY OPTIMAL ASSIGNMENT *admits a kernel of size* $\mathcal{O}((m!)^{\ell+1})$. *Thus, it is FPT with respect to* $m + \ell$.

Proof (sketch). Given an instance of α-GLOBALLY OPTIMAL ASSIGNMENT $Q = (A, I, P_1, \ldots, P_\ell, \alpha)$, the kernelization algorithm works as follows (formally described in the full version): It removes from A agents which share the same agent class together with all their preference lists, such that in the resulting instance there will be at most $m + 1$ agents in the set $A(\mathcal{C}(a, Q), Q)$, for each $a \in A$. Intuitively, since there are m items, at most m agents in $A(\mathcal{C}(a, Q), Q)$ will be assigned to items; we keep at most $m + 1$ agents (rather than m) in each agent class to cover the case where an agent is assigned to $b_\emptyset$ and admits a self-loop.

Assume that we run the kernel on $I_1 = (A_1, I, P_1, \ldots, P_\ell, \alpha)$ to obtain an instance $I_2 = (A_2, I, Q_1, \ldots, Q_\ell, \alpha)$. We first show that $|I_2| = \mathcal{O}((m!)^{\ell+1})$. There exist $\sum_{j=0}^{m} \binom{m}{j} \cdot j! = \sum_{j=0}^{m} \frac{m!}{j!(m-j)!} j! = m! \sum_{j=0}^{m} \frac{1}{j!} \leq e \cdot m! = \mathcal{O}(m!)$ possible orderings of subsets of I. Then, there exist $\mathcal{O}((m!)^\ell)$ different combinations of such ℓ orderings, implying that there exist $\mathcal{O}((m!)^\ell)$ possible agent classes over the item set I. Since for each agent class C, $|A_2(C, I_2)| \leq m + 1$, we have that $|A_2| = \Sigma_{\text{agent class } C} |A_2(C, I_2)| \leq (m!)^\ell \cdot (m+1)$. Thus, $|I_2| = \mathcal{O}((m!)^\ell \cdot (m+1)) = \mathcal{O}((m!)^{\ell+1})$.

We now prove that I_1 is a Yes-instance if and only if I_2 is a Yes-instance.

($\Rightarrow$): Assume that there exists an α-globally optimal assignment p for I_1. Then, there exist α layers $i_1, \ldots, i_\alpha$ of I_1 in which p is pareto optimal. We create an assignment $q : A_2 \to I \cup \{b_\emptyset\}$ for the reduced instance as follows: For each $a \in A_2$, let $p(A_1(\mathcal{C}(a, I_1), I_1))$ denote the set of items allocated to the agents from $A_1(\mathcal{C}(a, I_1), I_1)$ by p. We allocate the items in $p(A_1(\mathcal{C}(a, I_1), I_1))$ to agents in $A_2(\mathcal{C}(a, I_2), I_2)$ arbitrarily (observe that $\mathcal{C}(a, I_1) = \mathcal{C}(a, I_2)$). Agents that do not have available items are assigned to $b_\emptyset$. First, observe that q allocates all the items which are allocated by p since there are at most m items, and the algorithm keeps all or exactly $m + 1$ agents from each set $A_1(\mathcal{C}(a, I_1), I_1)$. As a result, q cannot admit self loops in layers $i_1, \ldots, i_\alpha$ of I_2. Formally, the sets $A_1(\mathcal{C}(a, I_1), I_1)$ and $A_2(\mathcal{C}(a, I_2), I_2)$ satisfy $|A_2(\mathcal{C}(a, I_2), I_2)| \leq |A_1(\mathcal{C}(a, I_1), I_1)|$. Since the agents in these sets are allocated the same number of items by p and q, if there exists an agent in $A_2(\mathcal{C}(a, I_2), I_2)$ that admits a self loop in I_2, there must exist an agent in $A_1(\mathcal{C}(a, I_1), I_1)$ that admits a self loop in I_1. Second, we claim that q does not admit trading cycles in these layers. For the sake of contradiction, suppose there exists a layer i_j in I_2, and t agents $a'_1, \ldots, a'_t \in A_2$ that admit a trading cycle $(a'_1, q(a'_1), \ldots, a'_t, q(a'_t))$ in Q_{i_j}. By the construction of q, notice that there exist t agents $a_1, \ldots, a_t \in A_1$, such that for each $i \in [t]$, $\mathcal{C}(a_i, I_1) = \mathcal{C}(a'_i, I_2)$, and $q(a'_i) = p(a_i)$. Then, p admits the trading cycle $(a_1, p(a_1), \ldots, a_t, p(a_t))$ in P_{i_j}. This gives a contradiction to Proposition 1.

($\Leftarrow$): Assume that there exists an α-globally optimal assignment q for I_2. Then there exist α layers $i_1, \ldots, i_\alpha$ in I_2 in which q is pareto optimal. We denote an assignment p for I_1 by $p(a) = \begin{cases} q(a) & a \in A_2 \\ b_\emptyset & \text{otherwise} \end{cases}$, and we claim that p is pareto optimal in layers $i_1, \ldots, i_\alpha$ in I_1. By the construction of p, for each $a_1 \in A_1 \setminus A_2$, there exists an agent $a_2 \in A_2$ such that $\mathcal{C}(a_1, I_1) = \mathcal{C}(a_2, I_2)$ and $p(a_1) = q(a_2)$. Namely, there exists a mapping f from agents in A_1 to agents in A_2 such that for each $a_1 \in A_1$, $\mathcal{C}(a_1, I_1) = \mathcal{C}(f(a_1), I_2)$ and $p(a_1) = q(f(a_1))$. If p admits a trading cycle $(a_1, p(a_1), \ldots, a_r, p(a_r))$ in some layer i_j of I_1, then q admits the trading cycle $(f(a_1), q(f(a_1)), \ldots, f(a_r), q(f(a_r)))$ in layer i_j of I_2. If p admits a self loop in layer i_j of I_1 with agent $a_1 \in A_1$, then q admits a self loop with agent $f(a_1)$ in layer i_j of I_2. Thus by Proposition 1, we conclude that p is α-globally optimal in I_1. $\qquad\square$

Corollary 1 (of Theorems 1 and 3). α-GLOBALLY OPTIMAL ASSIGNMENT *is solvable in time* $\mathcal{O}^*(((m!)^{\ell+1})!)$.

Theorem 4. α-GLOBALLY OPTIMAL ASSIGNMENT *is solvable in time* $(nm)^{\mathcal{O}(m)}$. *Thus, it is XP with respect to* m.

Proof. We present a simple brute-force algorithm. The algorithm simply iterates over all subsets of items $I' \subseteq I$. For each subset, it iterates over all subsets $A' \subseteq A$ such that $|A'| = |I'|$. For each $a \notin A'$, the algorithm allocates $b_\emptyset$, and it tries all possible $|I'|!$ different ways to allocate the items in I' to the agents in A' (it skips allocations that allocate items that are not acceptable by their owners in more than $\ell - \alpha + 1$ layers). The algorithm constructs the corresponding trading graphs, and verifies in polynomial time whether the current assignment is α-globally optimal. Hence, the running time of the algorithm is $\sum_{t=0}^{m} \binom{m}{t} \cdot \binom{n}{t} \cdot t! \cdot (n+m)^{\mathcal{O}(1)} \le m \cdot 2^m \cdot n^{\frac{m}{2}} \cdot m! \cdot (n+m)^{\mathcal{O}(1)} = (nm)^{\mathcal{O}(m)}$. $\qquad\square$

Before we continue with our next results, let us discuss a simple property that will help in many of our proofs.

Definition 3. *Let* (A, I, P) *be an instance of the* ASSIGNMENT *problem and suppose that* $P = \{<_a | \; a \in A\}$. *We say that agents* $a_1, a_2 \in A$ *respect each other if there exists a linear order on a subset of* I, $\lhd \subseteq I \times I$, *such that both* $<_{a_1} \subseteq \lhd$ *and* $<_{a_2} \subseteq \lhd$.

Lemma 2. *Let* (A, I, P) *be an instance of the* ASSIGNMENT *problem such that there exist agents* $a_1, \ldots, a_r \in A$ *where for each* $i, j \in [r]$, a_i *and* a_j *respect each other. Then, for every assignment* $p : A \to I \cup \{b_\emptyset\}$, p *does not admit a trading cycle among the agents* $a_1, \ldots, a_r$.

Proof. Towards a contradiction, suppose there exist an assignment p which admits a trading cycle $(a_1, p(a_1), \ldots, a_r, p(a_r))$ whose agents pairwise respect each other. Then, there exists a linear order $\vartriangleleft \subseteq I \times I$, such that for each $i \in [r]$, $<_{a_i} \subseteq \vartriangleleft$. This implies that $p(a_1) \vartriangleleft p(a_2) \vartriangleleft \ldots \vartriangleleft p(a_r)$. Since $p(a_r) <_{a_r} p(a_1)$, we have that $p(a_r) \vartriangleleft p(a_1)$, a contradiction to $\vartriangleleft$ being a linear order. $\square$

We now prove that $\Omega^*(k!)$ is a (tight) lower bound on the running time of any algorithm for α-GLOBALLY OPTIMAL ASSIGNMENT under the ETH, even for larger parameters than n such as $k = n + m + \alpha$ and $k = n + m + (\ell - \alpha)$. So, the algorithm in Theorem 1 is optimal (in terms of running time).

Theorem 5 (*). *Unless ETH fails, there does not exist an algorithm for α-GLOBALLY OPTIMAL ASSIGNMENT with running time $\mathcal{O}^*(2^{o(k \log k)})$ where $k = n + m + \alpha$ or $k = n + m + (\ell - \alpha)$.*

Proof (sketch). We provide a proof sketch for the parameter $k = n + m + \alpha$ (the proof for the second parameter is provided in the full version). We use the technique of linear parameter reduction (for more information, see the proposition by Cygan et al. [16] in the full version) from $k \times k$ PERMUTATION CLIQUE to α-GLOBALLY OPTIMAL ASSIGNMENT. In $k \times k$ PERMUTATION CLIQUE, we are given a graph G where the vertices are elements of a $k \times k$ table $(V(G) = [k] \times [k])$. The task is to decide whether there exists a $k \times k$-*permutation clique* in G, which is a clique of size k in G that contains exactly one vertex from each row and exactly one vertex from each column, i.e. there exists a permutation π on $[k]$ such that the vertices of the clique are $(1, \pi(1)), \ldots, (k, \pi(k))$. Lokshtanov et al. [25] proved that there is no $\mathcal{O}^*(2^{o(k \log k)})$-time algorithm for $k \times k$ PERMUTATION CLIQUE, unless ETH fails.

Let (G, k) be an instance of $k \times k$ PERMUTATION CLIQUE. We create an agent a_i for each row $i \in [k]$, and an item b_j for each column $j \in [k]$. We construct an instance of α-GLOBALLY OPTIMAL ASSIGNMENT with k^2 layers, each corresponds to a row-column pair (i, j), containing the preference profile $P_{(i,j)}$ defined as follows: (i) $a_i : b_j$ (ii) $a_r : \{b_q \mid \{(i, j), (r, q)\} \in E(G), q \neq j\}$ (sorted in ascending order by q) $\forall r \in [k] \setminus \{i\}$.

We finally set $\alpha = k$. We prove that there exists a $k \times k$-permutation clique in G if and only if there exists a k-globally optimal assignment for the instance.

$(\Rightarrow)$ Suppose there exists a permutation π for $[k]$ such that $(1, \pi(1)), \ldots, (k, \pi(k))$ form a clique in G. We define an assignment p by $p(a_i) = b_{\pi(i)}$ for each $i \in [k]$ (each row agent is assigned to its corresponding column item). Observe that for each $i \in [k]$, $b_{\pi(i)}$ is acceptable by a_i in $P_{(i, \pi(i))}$ and in all profiles $P_{(j, \pi(j))}$ such that $j \in [k] \setminus \{i\}$ since there is an edge between $(i, \pi(i))$ and each $(j, \pi(j))$. Moreover, each $P_{(j, \pi(j))}$ contains no self loops because all the items are allocated. Since we sorted each preference list in an ascending order by the item indices, all the agents respect each other in each preference profile and by Lemma 2, p does not admit trading cycles in any layer.

$(\Leftarrow)$ Suppose there exists a k-globally optimal assignment p for the constructed instance. Note that if p is pareto optimal in some profile $P_{(i,j)}$, it must satisfy $p(a_i) = b_j$, as otherwise, a_i would admit a self loop. Hence, we have that for each $i \in [k]$, p is pareto optimal in at most one profile among $P_{(i,1)}, \ldots, P_{(i,k)}$ and in at most one profile among $P_{(1,i)}, \ldots, P_{(k,i)}$. Since $\alpha = k$, we have that there exists a permutation π on $[k]$ such that p is pareto optimal in $P_{(i,\pi(i))}$ for each $i \in [k]$. It can be proved that $\{(i, \pi(i)) \mid i \in [k]\}$ is the vertex set of a $k \times k$-permutation clique in G.

It holds that $n + m + \alpha = \mathcal{O}(k)$. Thus, by Cygan et al. [16], we conclude that there is no $\mathcal{O}^*(2^{o(k \log k)})$-time algorithm for α-GLOBALLY OPTIMAL ASSIGN-MENT, unless ETH fails.   □

Theorem 6 (*). α-GLOBALLY OPTIMAL ASSIGNMENT *is W[1]-hard for the parameters* $m + \alpha$ *and* $m + (\ell - \alpha)$.

Proof (sketch). We provide a proof sketch for $m + (\ell - \alpha)$ (the proof for the parameter $m + \alpha$ is provided in the full version). We present a parameterized (and also polynomial) reduction from the W[1]-hard problem MULTICOLORED INDEPENDENT SET to α-GLOBALLY OPTIMAL ASSIGNMENT. The input of MUL-TICOLORED INDEPENDENT SET consists of an undirected graph $G = (V, E)$, and a coloring $c : V \rightarrow [k]$ that colors the vertices in V with k colors. The task is to decide whether G admits a *multicolored* independent set of size k, which is an independent set $V' \subseteq V$ that satisfies $\{c(v') \mid v' \in V'\} = [k]$ and $|V'| = k$.

Given an instance $(G = (V, E), c)$, assume that $V = \{v_1, \ldots, v_n\}$. We con-struct an instance of α-GLOBALLY OPTIMAL ASSIGNMENT with the agent set $A = \{a_1, \ldots, a_n\}$ and the item set $I = \{b_1, \ldots, b_k\}$, consisting of $\ell = n + 1$ layers. Informally, the agents that will allocate the items from I in an ℓ-globally optimal assignment will correspond to vertices that form a multicolored inde-pendent set in G. The first layer enforces each agent to allocate either the item that corresponds to its color, or $b_\emptyset$ and it is defined by: $a_i : b_{c(i)} \; \forall i \in [k]$. For each $i \in [n]$, the goal of layer $1 + i$ is to admit trading cycles if both v_i and one of its neighbors are included in the independent set (this happens when both of their agents allocate items). It is defined as follows:

(i) $a_i : \{b_j \mid j \in [k]\} \backslash \{b_{c(v_i)}\}$ (ordered arbitrarily) $> b_{c(v_i)}$ (ii) $a_j : b_{c(v_j)} \; \forall j \in [n] \backslash \{i\}$ such that (1) $\{v_i, v_j\} \in E$ and $c(v_j) = c(v_i)$ or (2) $\{v_i, v_j\} \notin E$ (iii) $a_j : b_{c(v_i)} > b_{c(v_j)} \; \forall j \in [n] \backslash \{i\}$ such that $\{v_i, v_j\} \in E$ and $c(v_j) \neq c(v_i)$. We finally set $\alpha = \ell$. We claim that G admits a multicolored independent set of size k if and only if there exists an ℓ-globally optimal assignment for the constructed instance.

($\Rightarrow$): Suppose that G admits a multicolored independent set of size k, $V' = \{v_{i_1}, \ldots, v_{i_k}\}$. Denote an assignment p by $p(a_{i_j}) = b_{c(v_{i_j})}$ for each $j \in [k]$, and $p(a_i) = b_\emptyset$ for each $i \notin \{i_1, \ldots, i_k\}$. Observe that for each $i \in [k]$, $p(a_i)$ is acceptable by a_i in each layer, and each layer cannot admit self loops since all the items are allocated. Moreover, notice that p is pareto optimal in the first layer since no trading cycles can be performed. We prove that p is pareto-optimal in layer $1 + i$ for each $i \in [n]$. Towards a contradiction, suppose that there exists $i \in [n]$ such that p is not pareto optimal in layer $1 + i$. Observe that the only possible trading cycle in this layer consists of the agent a_i and an agent a_r such that $p(a_i) = b_{c(v_i)}$, $c(v_i) \neq c(v_r)$, $\{v_i, v_r\} \in E$, and $p(a_r) = b_{c(v_r)}$. Then, we have that $v_i, v_r \in V'$, a contradiction.

($\Leftarrow$): Provided in the full version. $\square$

4 NP Hardness

Theorem 7 (*). *For any $2 \leq \alpha \leq \ell$, α-Globally Optimal Assignment is NP-hard.*

Proof (sketch). We extend a polynomial reduction by Aziz et al. [6] from the Serial Dictatorship Feasibility problem, which was proved to be NP-hard by Saban and Sethuraman [28]. In the Serial Dictatorship Feasibility problem, the input is a tuple (A, I, P, a, b) where A is a set of n agents, I is a set of n items, P is the preference profile in which each agent has a complete linear order on the items, $a \in A$, and $b \in I$. The task is to decide whether there exists a permutation for which serial dictatorship (defined in Sect. 2) allocates item b to agent a. Given such (A, I, P, a, b), Aziz et al. [6] constructed two preference profiles, P_1 and P_2, such that (A, I, P, a, b) is a Yes-instance if and only if there exists an assignment that is pareto optimal in both P_1 and P_2.

We add $\ell - \alpha$ additional new items $c_1, \ldots, c_{\ell-\alpha}$ and we define $I' = I \cup \{c_1, \ldots, c_{\ell-\alpha}\}$. We construct an instance of α-Globally Optimal Assignment over A and I', consisting of ℓ layers. The first two layers are P_1 and P_2, the next $\alpha - 2$ layers are copies of P_1, and the next $\ell - \alpha$ layers are $P'_1, \ldots, P'_{\ell-\alpha}$, where for each $i \in [\ell-\alpha]$, P'_i is defined as follows: (i) $a : c_i$ (ii) $a' : \emptyset \; \forall a' \in A \backslash \{a\}$. Notice that the only pareto optimal assignment for P'_i is the assignment that allocates c_i to a, and $b_\emptyset$ to each $a' \in A \backslash \{a\}$. Using this observation, we prove that an assignment is α-globally optimal for the constructed instance if and only if it is pareto optimal in both P_1 and P_2. $\square$

We define three constructions of preference profiles given an instance of 3-SAT and we consider their connections to the satisfiability of the formula. We will rely on these connections to design a polynomial reduction from 3-SAT to α-Globally Optimal Assignment that shows that α-Globally Optimal Assignment is para-NP-hard with respect to $\ell + d$. We will also rely on these results in Sect. 5 to prove that the problem is unlikely to admit polynomial kernels with respect to $n + m + \alpha$, $n + m + (\ell - \alpha)$, and $m + \ell$.

Let $n, m \in \mathbb{N}$ be positive integers. Denote the agent set $A(m, n) = \{a_{i,j}, \overline{a_{i,j}} \mid i \in [m], j \in [n]\}$, and the item set $I(m, n) = \{b_{i,j}, \overline{b_{i,j}} \mid i \in [m], j \in [n]\}$. We provide two preference profiles over $A(m, n)$ and $I(m, n)$: $P_1(m, n)$ and $P_2(m, n)$. Intuitively, given a 3-SAT instance with n variables and m clauses, the way the agents and the items are assigned to each other in an assignment that is pareto optimal in both $P_1(m, n)$ and $P_2(m, n)$ will encode a boolean assignment for the variable set of the instance. $P_1(m, n)$ is defined as follows: $\forall i \in [m], j \in [n]$: (i) $a_{i,j} : b_{i,j} > \overline{b_{i,j}}$ (ii) $\overline{a_{i,j}} : b_{i,j} > \overline{b_{i,j}}$. $P_2(m, n)$ is defined as follows:

- $\forall j \in [n]$: (i) $a_{m,j} : b_{m,j} > b_{m-1,j} > \overline{b_{m,j}}$ (ii) $\overline{a_{m,j}} :\ b_{m,j} > b_{m-1,j} > \overline{b_{m,j}}$
- $\forall i \in \{2, \ldots, m-1\}$, $j \in [n]$: (i) $a_{i,j} : b_{i-1,j} > \overline{b_{i,j}} > \overline{b_{i+1,j}} > b_{i,j}$ (ii) $\overline{a_{i,j}} :$
  $b_{i-1,j} > \overline{b_{i,j}} > \overline{b_{i+1,j}} > b_{i,j}$
- $\forall j \in [n]$: (i) $a_{1,j} : \overline{b_{1,j}} > \overline{b_{2,j}} > b_{1,j}$ (ii) $\overline{a_{1,j}} : \overline{b_{1,j}} > \overline{b_{2,j}} > b_{1,j}$

Claim 1 (*). An assignment $p : A(m,n) \to I(m,n) \cup \{b_\emptyset\}$ is pareto optimal in $P_1(m,n)$ if and only if $\{p(a_{i,j}), p(\overline{a_{i,j}})\} = \{b_{i,j}, \overline{b_{i,j}}\}$ for each $i \in [m]$ and $j \in [n]$.

We denote $P_j^{\text{true}} = \{(a_{i,j}, b_{i,j}), (\overline{a_{i,j}}, \overline{b_{i,j}}) \mid i \in [m]\}$, and $P_j^{\text{false}} = \{(a_{i,j}, \overline{b_{i,j}}), (\overline{a_{i,j}}, b_{i,j}) \mid i \in [m]\}$. Intuitively, P_j^{true} and P_j^{false} will correspond to setting the variable x_j to true or false, respectively.

Claim 2 (*). An assignment $p : A(m,n) \to I(m,n) \cup \{b_\emptyset\}$ is pareto optimal in both $P_1(m,n)$ and $P_2(m,n)$ if and only if for each $j \in [n]$, either $P_j^{\text{true}} \subseteq p$ or $P_j^{\text{false}} \subseteq p$.

Proof (sketch). ($\Rightarrow$): Assume that p is pareto optimal in both $P_1(m,n)$ and $P_2(m,n)$. Towards a contradiction, suppose that there exists $j \in [n]$ satisfying that both $P_j^{\text{true}} \not\subseteq p$ and $P_j^{\text{false}} \not\subseteq p$. By Claim 1, there exist $i_1, i_2 \in [m]$ such that $i_1 < i_2$, satisfying that either (1) $p(a_{i_1,j}) = b_{i_1,j}$ and $p(a_{i_2,j}) = \overline{b_{i_2,j}}$, or (2) $p(a_{i_1,j}) = \overline{b_{i_1,j}}$ and $p(a_{i_2,j}) = b_{i_2,j}$. We have that there must exist $i_1 \le i < i_2$ such that either (1) $p(a_{i,j}) = b_{i,j}$ and $p(a_{i+1,j}) = \overline{b_{i+1,j}}$, or (2) $p(a_{i,j}) = \overline{b_{i,j}}$ and $p(a_{i+1,j}) = b_{i+1,j}$. This implies that p admits the trading cycles $(a_{i,j}, b_{i,j}, a_{i+1,j}, \overline{b_{i+1,j}})$ or $(\overline{a_{i,j}}, b_{i,j}, \overline{a_{i+1,j}}, \overline{b_{i+1,j}})$ in $P_2(m,n)$, a contradiction.

($\Leftarrow$): Assume that for each $j \in [n]$, either $P_j^{\text{true}} \subseteq p$ or $P_j^{\text{false}} \subseteq p$. By Claim 1, p is pareto optimal in $P_1(m,n)$. Then by the construction of $P_2(m,n)$, observe that every possible trading cycle in $P_2(m,n)$ has one of the forms: (1) $(a_{i,j}, \overline{b_{i,j}}, a_{i-1,j}, b_{i-1,j})$ or (2) $(\overline{a_{i,j}}, \overline{b_{i,j}}, \overline{a_{i-1,j}}, b_{i-1,j})$, where $i \in \{2, \ldots, m\}$. Then, there exist $j \in [n]$ and $i \in \{2, \ldots, m\}$ such that either (1) $p(a_{i,j}) = b_{i,j}$ and $p(a_{i-1,j}) = \overline{b_{i,j}}$ or (2) $p(a_{i,j}) = b_{i,j}$ and $p(a_{i-1,j}) = b_{i,j}$. Thus, both $P_j^{\text{true}} \subsetneq p$ and $P_j^{\text{false}} \subsetneq p$, a contradiction. $\qquad\square$

Let $D = (\mathcal{X}, \mathcal{C})$ be an instance of 3-SAT where $\mathcal{X} = \{x_1, \ldots, x_n\}$ is the set of variables, and $\mathcal{C} = \{C_1, \ldots, C_m\}$ is the set of clauses, each of size 3. In order to construct the third preference profile $P_3(D)$, order the literals in each clause arbitrarily, such that $C_i = \ell_i^1 \vee \ell_i^2 \vee \ell_i^3$ for each $i \in [m]$. The third preference profile is responsible for the satisfiability of the formula. We define $\text{ind}_D(i,j)$ as the index of the variable which appears in the j-th literal in C_i for each $j \in [3]$, and

we define $b_D(i,j) = \begin{cases} \overline{b_{i,\text{ind}_D(i,j)}} & \ell_i^j \text{ is negative} \\ b_{i,\text{ind}_D(i,j)} & \ell_i^j \text{ is positive} \end{cases}$. Intuitively, when $a_{i,\text{ind}_D(i,j)}$

gets $b_D(i,j)$ and $\overline{a_{i,\text{ind}_D(i,j)}}$ gets $\overline{b_D(i,j)}$, it means that ℓ_i^j is "satisfied". Define the preference profile $P_3(D)$ as follows:

- $\forall i \in [m]$: (i) $a_{i,\text{ind}_D(i,3)}$: $b_D(i,3) > \overline{b_D(i,2)} > \overline{b_D(i,3)}$
  (ii) $a_{i,\text{ind}_D(i,2)} :\ b_D(i,2) > \overline{b_D(i,1)} > \overline{b_D(i,2)}$
  (iii) $a_{i,\text{ind}_D(i,1)} :\ b_D(i,1) > \overline{b_D(i,3)} > \overline{b_D(i,1)}$
  (iv) $\overline{a_{i,\text{ind}_D(i,r)}} :\ b_D(i,r) > \overline{b_D(i,r)}\ \forall r \in [3]$

- $\forall i \in [m], j \in [n]$ such that x_j does not appear in C_i: (i) $a_{i,j} : b_{i,j} > \overline{b_{i,j}}$ (ii) $\overline{a_{i,j}} : b_{i,j} > \overline{b_{i,j}}$

Claim 3 (*). An assignment $p : A(m,n) \to I(m,n) \cup \{b_{\emptyset}\}$ is pareto optimal in $P_1(m,n), P_2(m,n),$ and $P_3(D)$ if and only if: (1) for each $j \in [n]$, either $P_j^{\text{true}} \subseteq p$ or $P_j^{\text{false}} \subseteq p$; and (2) for each clause $C_i = \ell_i^1 \vee \ell_i^2 \vee \ell_i^3 \in \mathcal{C}$, there exists at least one $j \in [3]$ such that $p(a_{i,\text{ind}_D(i,j)}) = b_D(i,j)$.

Proof (sketch). ($\Rightarrow$): Assume that p is pareto optimal in $P_1(m,n), P_2(m,n)$ and $P_3(D)$. By Claim 2, p satisfies the first condition. Observe that the only possible trading cycles in $P_3(D)$ are of the form $(a_{i,\text{ind}_D(i,3)}, \overline{b_D(i,3)}, a_{i,\text{ind}_D(i,2)}, \overline{b_D(i,2)}, a_{i,\text{ind}_D(i,1)}, \overline{b_D(i,1)})$. Then by Claim 1, for each $i \in [m]$, there must exists $j \in [3]$ such that $p(a_{i,\text{ind}_D(i,j)}) = b_D(i,j)$. The opposite direction is provided in the full version. □

Lemma 3 (*). *An instance $D = (\mathcal{X}, \mathcal{C})$ of 3-SAT such that $|\mathcal{X}| = n$ and $|\mathcal{C}| = m$, is a Yes-instance if and only if there exists an assignment $p : A(m,n) \to I(m,n) \cup \{b_{\emptyset}\}$ that is pareto optimal in $P_1(m,n), P_2(m,n),$ and $P_3(D)$.*

Theorem 8 (*). *3-SAT is polynomial-time reducible to α-GLOBALLY OPTIMAL ASSIGNMENT where $\alpha = \ell = 3$ and $d = 3$ or where $\alpha = \ell = 4$ and $d = m$.*

5 Non-existence of Polynomial Kernels

In this section, we prove (using three cross-compositions) that α-GLOBALLY OPTIMAL ASSIGNMENT is unlikely to admit polynomial kernels with respect to $n + m + \alpha$, $n + m + (\ell - \alpha)$, and $m + \ell$.

Theorem 9 (*). *There does not exist a polynomial kernel for α-GLOBALLY OPTIMAL ASSIGNMENT with respect to $n + m + \alpha$, $n + m + (\ell - \alpha)$, and $m + \ell$ unless NP $\subseteq$ coNP/poly.*

Proof (sketch). We provide a proof sketch for the parameter $m + \ell$ (the proofs for the other parameters are provided in the full version). We provide a cross-composition from 3-SAT to α-GLOBALLY OPTIMAL ASSIGNMENT. Given instances of 3-SAT $D_0 = (\mathcal{X}_0, \mathcal{C}_0), \ldots, D_{t-1} = (\mathcal{X}_{t-1}, \mathcal{C}_{t-1})$ of the same size $n \in \mathbb{N}$ for some $t \in \mathbb{N}$, we first modify each instance D_i to have $\mathcal{X}_i = \{x_1, \ldots, x_n\}$ and $|\mathcal{C}_i| = n$. We define an agent set $A_i(n,n) = \{a_{r,j}^i, \overline{a_{r,j}^i} \mid r, j \in [n]\}$ for each $i \in \{0, \ldots, t-1\}$. The constructed instance is defined over the agent set $A = \bigcup_{i=0}^{t-1} A_i(n,n)$ and the item set $I = I(n,n)$ (defined in Sect. 4); and it consists of $2\lceil \log t \rceil + 2$ layers. Intuitively, the goal of the first $2\lceil \log t \rceil$ layers is to enforce each α-globally optimal assignment to allocate all the items only to agents that correspond to the same Yes-instance (if one exists). Let $i \in [\lceil \log t \rceil]$, the preference profile in layer i (or $\lceil \log t \rceil + i$) requires an assignment to assign the items in I only to agents whose corresponding instance is D_j such that the i-th bit in the binary representation of j is 0 (or 1), and to assign $b_{\emptyset}$ to all other agents. These layers are constructed as a composition of $P_1(n,n)$ over $A_r(n,n)$ and $I(n,n)$ for every $r \in \{0, \dots t-1\}$ such that the i-th bit in the binary representation of r is 0 (or 1), together with empty preferences for all the other agents. Layer $2\lceil \log t \rceil + 1$ is constructed as a composition of the profile $P_2(n,n)$ over $A_i(n,n)$ and $I(n,n)$ for each $i \in \{0, \dots, t-1\}$, and the last layer is a composition of the profiles $P_3(D_i)$ over $A_i(n,n)$ and $I(n,n)$ for each $i \in \{0, \dots, t-1\}$. We finally set $\alpha = \lceil \log t \rceil + 2$. Notice that every assignment can be pareto optimal in at most one among layers i and $\lceil \log t \rceil + i$ for each $i \in [\lceil \log t \rceil]$. Then, each α-globally optimal assignment is pareto optimal in exactly $\lceil \log t \rceil$ layers among the first $2\lceil \log t \rceil$ layers, and must be pareto optimal in the last two layers. Therefore, we have that each such assignment "encodes" some $i \in \{0, \dots, t-1\}$ in the first $2\lceil \log t \rceil$ layers (if it is pareto optimal in layer j or $\lceil \log t \rceil + j$, then the j-th bit of i is 0 or 1, respectively). The optimality in the last two layers implies that p is pareto optimal in both $P_2(n,n)$ and $P_3(n,n)$ over $A_i(n,n)$ and $I(n,n)$. Thus, by Lemma 3, D_i is a Yes-instance. The opposite direction follows from Lemma 3 as well.   □

6   Conclusion and Future Research

In this paper, we introduced a new variant of the ASSIGNMENT problem where each agent is equipped with multiple incomplete preference lists, and we defined the notion of global optimality, that naturally extends pareto optimality. We considered several natural parameters, and presented a comprehensive picture of the parameterized complexity of the problem with respect to them.

The results show that the problem of finding an α-globally optimal assignment is, in general, computationally hard, but that it admits more positive results when the parameter depends on $n = \#$agents (and α or ℓ) than when it depends on $m = \#$items (and α or ℓ). We proved that the problem admits an XP algorithm with respect to m, but is unlikely to admit one with respect to $\ell + d$ and $\ell + (m-d)$. We provided an $\mathcal{O}^*(n!)$-time algorithm and an exponential kernel with respect to $m + \ell$. Both results showed that the problem is FPT with respect to these parameters. In addition, we proved that $\mathcal{O}^*(k!)$ is essentially a tight lower bound on the running time under ETH for even larger parameters than n such as $k = n + m + \alpha$ and $k = n + m + (\ell - \alpha)$. Moreover, we proved that the problem admits a polynomial kernel with respect to $n + \ell$, but is unlikely to admit one with respect to all the other parameters that we considered. We also proved that the problem is W[1]-hard with respect to $m + \alpha$ and $m + (\ell - \alpha)$. However, two questions are still open: (1) Is it possible to obtain a (not polynomial) better kernel for $m + \ell$ with size *substantially* smaller than $\mathcal{O}^*((m!)^{\ell+1})$? (2) Is it possible to obtain a better running time than $\mathcal{O}^*(k!)$ for $k = n + m + \ell$?

Continuing our research, it might be interesting to study "weaker" definitions of optimality, for example: finding an assignment such that every group of k agents has some α layers where they (1) do not admit trading cycles; (2) are not parts of larger trading cycles; or (3) do not admit the same trading cycle. Verification variants of these problems can also be suggested, i.e. given an assignment p, check whether it is optimal.

Another direction is to study the particular case where the preferences of the agents are complete since it may provide more positive algorithmic results under some parameterizations. In addition, notice that a solution to α-GLOBALLY OPTIMAL ASSIGNMENT can be seen as an approximation to the "optimal" solution in which an assignment is pareto optimal in a maximum number of layers (this is similar to the VERTEX COVER problem, where the parameter k is somewhat an "approximation" to the size of the minimum vertex cover). In this approach, we can define the problem as an approximation problem and study it from the perspective of parameterized approximability.

In this paper, we considered the basic "unweighed" model of the problem (since this is the first study of this kind). Another direction is to consider a weighted version in which some criteria (layers) may have higher importance than others. A straightforward way to model this is by having several copies of layers. However, if weights are high and varied, this might lead to inefficiency.

References

1. Abdulkadirog, A.: House allocation with existing tenants 1 (1999)
2. Abdulkadiroglu, A., Sonmez, T.: Random serial dictatorship and the core from random endowments in house allocation problems. Econometrica **66**(3), 689–702 (1998). https://ideas.repec.org/a/ecm/emetrp/v66y1998i3p689-702.html
3. Abraham, D.J., Cechlárová, K., Manlove, D.F., Mehlhorn, K.: Pareto optimality in house allocation problems. In: Fleischer, R., Trippen, G. (eds.) ISAAC 2004. LNCS, vol. 3341, pp. 3–15. Springer, Heidelberg (2004). https://doi.org/10.1007/978-3-540-30551-4_3
4. Alderfer, C.P., McCord, C.G.: Personal and situational factors in the recruitment interview. J. Appl. Psychol. **54**(4), 377 (1970)
5. Aziz, H., Biro, P., de Haan, R., Rastegari, B.: Pareto optimal allocation under compact uncertain preferences. In: Thirty Third AAAI Conference on Artificial Intelligence, 01 February 2019, October 2018. https://eprints.soton.ac.uk/425734/
6. Aziz, H., de Haan, R., Rastegari, B.: Pareto optimal allocation under uncertain preferences. In: Proceedings of the Twenty-Sixth International Joint Conference on Artificial Intelligence, IJCAI-17, pp. 77–83 (2017). https://doi.org/10.24963/ijcai.2017/12
7. Bodlaender, H.L., Downey, R.G., Fellows, M.R., Hermelin, D.: On problems without polynomial kernels. J. Comput. Syst. Sci. **75**(8), 423–434 (2009). https://doi.org/10.1016/j.jcss.2009.04.001
8. Bodlaender, H.L., Jansen, B.M.P., Kratsch, S.: Kernelization lower bounds by cross-composition. SIAM J. Discrete Math. **28**(1), 277–305 (2014). https://doi.org/10.1137/120880240
9. Bogomolnaia, A., Moulin, H.: A new solution to the random assignment problem. J. Econ. Theory **100**, 295–328 (2001)
10. Browne, A.: Lives ruined as NHS leaks patients' notes. The Observer, 25 June 2000
11. Calabro, C., Impagliazzo, R., Paturi, R.: The complexity of satisfiability of small depth circuits. In: Chen, J., Fomin, F.V. (eds.) IWPEC 2009. LNCS, vol. 5917, pp. 75–85. Springer, Heidelberg (2009). https://doi.org/10.1007/978-3-642-11269-0_6

12. Chen, J., Niedermeier, R., Skowron, P.: Stable marriage with multi-modal preferences. In: Proceedings of the 2018 ACM Conference on Economics and Computation, EC 2018, pp. 269–286. Association for Computing Machinery, New York (2018). https://doi.org/10.1145/3219166.3219168
13. Chernichovsky, D., Kfir, R.: The state of the acute care hospitalization system in Israel (2019)
14. Clinedinst, M.: State of college admission (2019)
15. Cools, M., Moons, E., Wets, G.: Assessing the impact of weather on traffic intensity. Weather Clim. Soc. **2**(1), 60–68 (2010)
16. Cygan, M., et al.: Parameterized Algorithms. Springer, Cham (2015). https://doi.org/10.1007/978-3-319-21275-3
17. Faudzi, S., Abdul-Rahman, S., Abd Rahman, R.: An assignment problem and its application in education domain: a review and potential path. Adv. Oper. Res. **2018** (2018)
18. Fearnhead, P., Taylor, B.M.: On estimating the ability of NBA players. J. Quant. Anal. Sports **7**(3) (2011)
19. Gourvès, L., Lesca, J., Wilczynski, A.: Object allocation via swaps along a social network. In: 26th International Joint Conference on Artificial Intelligence (IJCAI 2017), Melbourne, Australia, pp. 213–219 (2017). https://doi.org/10.24963/ijcai.2017/31. https://hal.archives-ouvertes.fr/hal-01741519
20. Impagliazzo, R., Paturi, R.: On the complexity of k-SAT. J. Comput. Syst. Sci. **62**(2), 367–375 (2001). https://doi.org/10.1006/jcss.2000.1727
21. Impagliazzo, R., Paturi, R., Zane, F.: Which problems have strongly exponential complexity? J. Comput. Syst. Sci. **63**(4), 512–530 (2001). https://doi.org/10.1006/jcss.2001.1774
22. Kinicki, A.J., Lockwood, C.A.: The interview process: an examination of factors recruiters use in evaluating job applicants. J. Vocat. Behav. **26**(2), 117–125 (1985)
23. Kolasa, T., Krol, D.: A survey of algorithms for paper-reviewer assignment problem. IETE Tech. Rev. **28**(2), 123–134 (2011). https://doi.org/10.4103/0256-4602.78092
24. Lian, J.W., Mattei, N., Noble, R., Walsh, T.: The conference paper assignment problem: using order weighted averages to assign indivisible goods (2018). https://www.aaai.org/ocs/index.php/AAAI/AAAI18/paper/view/17396
25. Lokshtanov, D., Marx, D., Saurabh, S.: Slightly superexponential parameterized problems. SIAM J. Comput. **47**(3), 675–702 (2018). https://doi.org/10.1137/16M1104834
26. Mulder, J., de Bruijne, M.: Willingness of online respondents to participate in alternative modes of data collection. Surv. Pract. **12**(1), 1–11 (2019)
27. Nass, S.J., Levit, L.A., Gostin, L.O., et al.: The value and importance of health information privacy. In: Beyond the HIPAA Privacy Rule: Enhancing Privacy, Improving Health Through Research. National Academies Press (US) (2009)
28. Saban, D., Sethuraman, J.: The complexity of computing the random priority allocation matrix. Math. Oper. Res. **40**(4), 1005–1014 (2015). https://EconPapers.repec.org/RePEc:inm:ormoor:v:40:y:2015:i:4:p:1005--1014
29. Saleh, S.M., Sugiarto, S., Hilal, A., Ariansyah, D.: A study on the traffic impact of the road corridors due to flyover construction at surabaya intersection, banda aceh of indonesia. In: AIP Conference Proceedings, vol. 1903, p. 060005. AIP Publishing LLC (2017)
30. Singh, S., Dubey, G., Shrivastava, R.: A comparative analysis of assignment problem. IOSR J. Eng. **2**(8), 01–15 (2012)

31. The Council for Higher Education and The Planning and Budgeting Committee: The higher education system in Israel (2014)
32. Topcu, M., Gulal, O.S.: The impact of COVID-19 on emerging stock markets. Financ. Res. Lett. **36**, 101691 (2020)
33. Wu, K., DeVriese, A.: How students pick their housing situations: factors and analysis (2016)
34. Zeren, F., Hizarci, A.: The impact of COVID-19 coronavirus on stock markets: evidence from selected countries. Muhasebe Finans İncelemeleri Dergisi **3**(1), 78–84 (2020)
35. Zhou, L.: On a conjecture by gale about one-sided matching problems. J. Econ. Theory **52**(1), 123–135 (1990). https://EconPapers.repec.org/RePEc:eee:jetheo:v:52:y:1990:i:1:p:123-135
36. Öncan, T.: A survey of the generalized assignment problem and its applications. INFOR: Inf. Syst. Oper. Res. **45**(3), 123–141 (2007). https://doi.org/10.3138/infor.45.3.123

Solid Semantics for Abstract Argumentation Frameworks and the Preservation of Solid Semantic Properties

Xiaolong Liu[1,2] and Weiwei Chen[1(✉)]

[1] Institute of Logic and Cognition and Department of Philosophy,
Sun Yat-sen University, Guangzhou, China
{liuxlong6,chenww26}@mail2.sysu.edu.cn
[2] IRIT, University of Toulouse, Toulouse, France

Abstract. In this paper, we propose solid admissibility that is a strengthened version of Dung's admissibility to obtain the most acceptable set of arguments. Besides, other solid extensions based on solid admissibility are defined. Such extensions not only include all defenders of its elements but also exclude all arguments indirectly attacked and indirectly defended by some argument(s). Furthermore, we characterize solid extensions with propositional formulas. Using these formulas, we aggregate solid extensions by using approaches from judgment aggregation. Especially, although no quota rule preserves Dung's admissibility for any argumentation framework, we show that there exist quota rules that preserve solid admissibility for any argumentation framework.

Keywords: Abstract argumentation · Solid semantics · Social choice theory

1 Introduction

In Dung's work [12], an argumentation framework (AF) is a directed graph, where nodes represent arguments and edges represent elements of a binary relation. It has been studied widely over the last decades. One of the core notions of AFs is *admissibility*. An *admissible extension* is a set of arguments that contains no internal conflict and defends its elements against any attacker.

In this paper, we mainly focus on obtaining the most acceptable arguments in AFs by strengthening Dung's admissibility. Before discussing this idea, we first illustrate two problems (or drawbacks) observed from the literature. The first one is observed from *graded acceptability* [14] which provides an approach to rank arguments from the most acceptable to the weakest one(s) by parameterizing the numbers of attackers and counter-attackers. Hence, we can require that a set of arguments is graded-acceptable if it contains at least n counter-attackers for each attacker of its elements. Graded acceptability is flexible as we can tune

Supported by the China Postdoctoral Science Foundation Grant, No. 2019M663352.

A. Rosenfeld and N. Talmon (Eds.): EUMAS 2021, LNAI 12802, pp. 178–193, 2021.
https://doi.org/10.1007/978-3-030-82254-5_11

the parameter n. What if we want to find out in an AF the sets of arguments such that they exactly contain all counter-attackers for each attacker of their elements? It is impossible to achieve this goal by tuning the parameter n, as different attackers may have different numbers of counter-attackers. Consider the following example.

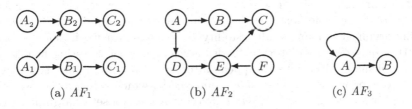

(a) AF_1 (b) AF_2 (c) AF_3

Fig. 1. Three problematic argumentation frameworks

Example 1. In Fig. 1a, $\{A_1, C_1\}, \{A_2, C_2\}$ and $\{A_1, A_2, C_2\}$ are acceptable under graded semantics when we require that a set of arguments is acceptable if it contains at least one counter-attacker for each attacker of its elements. We should notice that although $\{A_1, A_2, C_2\}$ contains all counter-attackers when its elements are attacked, $\{A_2, C_2\}$ fails to contain all counter-attackers whenever its elements are attacked. When the requirement is more demanding in the sense that a set of arguments is acceptable if it contains at least two counter-attackers for each attacker of its elements, $\{A_1, A_2, C_2\}$ is still acceptable under this requirement. Although $\{A_1, C_1\}$ contains all counter-attackers when its elements are attacked, it fails to satisfy this requirement.

The other problem is observed from the situation where some argument indirectly attacks and indirectly defends some argument. There are other semantics [1,7] that also provide approaches to rank arguments. But their approaches rely on conjectures regarding the processing of cycles. However, Dung indicates in [12] that the presence of cycles could be a problem. In this work, an argument A is *controversial* w.r.t. an argument B if A indirectly attacks and indirectly defends B. Such arguments could lead to problematic situations. Consider the following example.

Example 2. In Fig. 1b, A is controversial w.r.t. C as A indirectly attacks and indirectly defends C. From a skeptical view, A and C should not occur in the same set of acceptable arguments. But $\{A, C, F\}$ is admissible in Dung's semantics.

There is no consensus on whether to accept or reject such arguments. Note that any argument in an odd-length cycle is controversial w.r.t. any argument in this cycle. There are many articles aiming to address this problem [3,4,6,11]. For example, Baumann et al. [4] argue that in Fig. 1c, A should be rejected while B should be accepted, since the attack from the self-defeat argument A

is not valid. However, Jakobovits and Vermeir [15] state that A and B can be labeled as "undecided" and "rejected", resp. They argue that since A is "strong enough" to attack A, surely it is strong enough to do the same with B. Compared with these approaches directly facing these disputable situations, our approach is more like bypassing such situations.

Considering the emergence of the problems above, we argue that the most acceptable arguments should satisfy two criteria: (i) they should have defenders as many as possible, and (ii) they should avoid the undesirable interference of some arguments. Dung's admissibility only requires a weak defense in the sense that only one mandatory defender is enough. An interesting fact is that some problematic situations disappear after Dung's admissibility is strengthened. In this paper, we propose *solid admissibility* which satisfies the two criteria. Roughly speaking, a *solidly admissible extension* is a set of arguments that contains no internal conflict, defends its elements against any attackers, and contains all the defenders. We will show that if an argument A is controversial w.r.t. an argument B, then B will never occur in any solid extension based on solid admissibility. To sum up, such extensions not only contain all defenders of their elements, but also avoid the interference of any argument that is indirectly attacked and indirectly defended by some argument. This conforms to the intuition in practical reasoning or real life in the sense that if an argument has more defenders, then surely it has less controversy.

We apply solid semantics in the field of *judgment aggregation*, a branch of social choice theory. When a group of agents evaluates which arguments are acceptable in an AF, each of them may report a different extension under a specific solid semantics that represents a individual viewpoint about which arguments are acceptable. We study whether their collective outcome is also a solid extension under this semantics when quota rules are applied. Especially, we show that there exist quota rules that preserve solid admissibility for any AF.

Contribution. Firstly, we propose a family of new semantics for abstract argumentation. Such semantics provide an approach to circumvent a controversial situation in AFs and also capture a feature that graded semantics fail to capture. Secondly, the new semantics have more possibility results for extension aggregation than Dung's semantics do.

Paper Outline. The rest of this paper is organized as follows. Section 2 reviews the background of abstract argumentation and judgment aggregation. Section 3 defines solid admissibility and shows how the problems are addressed. Section 4 develops more solid semantics and shows the connections among them. Besides, we compare solid semantics with Dung's semantics. Furthermore, we present propositional formulas that characterize the solid semantics and pave the way for solid extensions aggregation. Section 5 shows preservation results for the solid semantics. Section 6 mainly compares solid semantics with other related semantics. Section 7 concludes this paper and points out future work.

2 Preliminary

2.1 Abstract Argumentation

This part reviews some notions of abstract argumentation [12]. Some definitions are adopted from [14].

Definition 1 (Argumentation framework). *An* argumentation framework *is a pair $AF = \langle Arg, \rightharpoonup \rangle$, where Arg is a finite and non-empty set of arguments, and $\rightharpoonup$ is a binary relation on Arg.*

For any $A, B \in Arg$, $A \rightharpoonup B$ (or *A* attacks *B*) denotes that $(A, B) \in \rightharpoonup$. For any $B \in Arg$, $\overline{B} = \{A \in Arg \mid A \rightharpoonup B\}$, namely, $\overline{B}$ denotes the set of the attackers of *B*. *A* is an *initial argument* iff $\overline{A} = \emptyset$. For any $\Delta \subseteq Arg$ and any $B \in Arg$, $\Delta \rightharpoonup B$ denotes that there exists an argument $A \in \Delta$ such that $A \rightharpoonup B$. For any $\Delta \subseteq Arg$ and any $A \in Arg$, $A \rightharpoonup \Delta$ denotes that there exists an argument $B \in \Delta$ such that $A \rightharpoonup B$. For any $A, C \in Arg$, *A* is a *defender* of *C* iff there exists an argument $B \in Arg$ such that $A \rightharpoonup B$ and $B \rightharpoonup C$.

An argument *A* *indirectly attacks* an argument *B* iff there exists a finite sequence $A_0, \ldots, A_{2n+1}$ such that (*i*) $B = A_0$ and $A = A_{2n+1}$, and (*ii*) for each i, $0 \leqslant i \leqslant 2n$, $A_{i+1} \rightharpoonup A_i$. An argument *A* *indirectly defends* an argument *B* iff there exists a finite sequence $A_0, \ldots, A_{2n}$ such that (*i*) $B = A_0$ and $A = A_{2n}$, and (*ii*) for each i, $0 \leqslant i < 2n$, $A_{i+1} \rightharpoonup A_i$. An argument *A* is *controversial* w.r.t. an argument *B* iff *A* indirectly attacks and indirectly defends *B*. Note that direct attackers (resp. defenders) are also indirect attackers (resp. defenders).

Definition 2 (Dung's defense). *Given $AF = \langle Arg, \rightharpoonup \rangle$. $\Delta \subseteq Arg$ defends $C \in Arg$ iff for any $B \in Arg$, if $B \rightharpoonup C$ then $\Delta \rightharpoonup B$.*

Definition 3 (Defense function). *Given $AF = \langle Arg, \rightharpoonup \rangle$. The* defense function *$d: 2^{Arg} \longrightarrow 2^{Arg}$ of AF is defined as $d(\Delta) = \{C \in Arg \mid \Delta \text{ defends } C\}$.*

Definition 4 (Neutrality function). *Given $AF = \langle Arg, \rightharpoonup \rangle$. The* neutrality function *$n: 2^{Arg} \longrightarrow 2^{Arg}$ of AF is defined as $n(\Delta) = \{B \in Arg \mid \text{not } \Delta \rightharpoonup B\}$.*

Definition 5 (Dung's semantics). *Given $AF = \langle Arg, \rightharpoonup \rangle$. For any $\Delta \subseteq Arg$, (i) Δ is a* conflict-free *extension iff $\Delta \subseteq n(\Delta)$; (ii) Δ is a* self-defending *extension iff $\Delta \subseteq d(\Delta)$; (iii) Δ is an* admissible *extension iff $\Delta \subseteq n(\Delta)$ and $\Delta \subseteq d(\Delta)$; (iv) Δ is a* complete *extension iff $\Delta \subseteq n(\Delta)$ and $\Delta = d(\Delta)$; (v) Δ is a* preferred *extension iff Δ is a maximal admissible extension; (vi) Δ is a* stable *extension iff $\Delta = n(\Delta)$; (vii) Δ is the* grounded *extension iff Δ is the least fixed point of the defense function d.*

Theorem 1 (Dung, 1995). *Given $AF = \langle Arg, \rightharpoonup \rangle$. (i) If $\Delta \subseteq Arg$ is a preferred extension, then Δ is complete extension, but not vice versa; (ii) If $\Delta \subseteq Arg$ is an admissible extension, then there exists a preferred extension Γ such that $\Delta \subseteq \Gamma$.*

2.2   Integrity Constraints and Judgment Aggregation

Given $AF = \langle Arg, \rightarrow \rangle$, Dung's semantics can be captured by propositional language (denoted as $\mathcal{L}_{AF}$), whose literals are arguments in Arg [5]. A model is represented by the set of the literals which it satisfies. In other words, a model of a formula is a subset of Arg: (i) for any $A \in Arg$, $\Delta \vDash A$ iff $A \in \Delta$; (ii) $\Delta \vDash \neg\varphi$ iff $\Delta \vDash \varphi$ does not hold; (iii) $\Delta \vDash \varphi \wedge \psi$ iff $\Delta \vDash \varphi$ and $\Delta \vDash \psi$.

A *property* σ of extensions can be regarded as a subset of 2^{Arg}, namely, $\sigma \subseteq 2^{Arg}$. Then the set of the extensions under a semantics is a property, e.g., completeness is the set of the complete extensions of AF. For any formula φ in $\mathcal{L}_{AF}$, we let $\mathrm{Mod}(\varphi) = \{\Delta \subseteq Arg \mid \Delta \vDash \varphi\}$, namely, $\mathrm{Mod}(\varphi)$ denotes the set of all models of φ. Obviously, $\sigma = \mathrm{Mod}(\varphi)$ is a property. When using a formula φ to characterize such a property, φ is referred to as an *integrity constraint*.

We next introduce a model for the aggregation of extensions [10,13]. Given $AF = \langle Arg, \rightarrow \rangle$. Let $N = \{1, \cdots, n\}$ be a finite set of *agents*. Imagining that each agent $i \in N$ reports an extension $\Delta_i \subseteq Arg$. Then $\boldsymbol{\Delta} = (\Delta_1, \cdots, \Delta_n)$ is referred to as a *profile*. An *aggregation rule* is a function $F: (2^{Arg})^n \longrightarrow 2^{Arg}$, mapping any given profile of extensions to a subset of Arg.

Definition 6 (Quota rules). *Given $AF = \langle Arg, \rightarrow \rangle$, let N be a finite set of n agents, and let $q \in \{1, \cdots, n\}$. The* quota rule *with quota q is defined as the aggregation rule mapping any given profile $\boldsymbol{\Delta} = (\Delta_1, \cdots, \Delta_n) \in (2^{Arg})^n$ of extensions to the set including exactly those arguments accepted by at least q agents: $F_q(\boldsymbol{\Delta}) = \{A \in Arg \mid \#\{i \in N \mid A \in \Delta_i\} \geqslant q\}$.*

The quota rule F_q for n agents with $q = \lceil \frac{n+1}{2} \rceil$ (resp., $q = 1$, $q = n$) for AF is called the *strict majority* (resp., *nomination*, *unanimity*) rule.

Definition 7 (Preservation). *Given $AF = \langle Arg, \rightarrow \rangle$. Let $\sigma \subseteq 2^{Arg}$ be a property of extensions. An aggregation rule $F: (2^{Arg})^n \longrightarrow 2^{Arg}$ for n agents is said to* preserve σ *if $F(\boldsymbol{\Delta}) \in \sigma$ for every profile $\boldsymbol{\Delta} = (\Delta_1, \cdots, \Delta_1) \in \sigma^n$.*

Lemma 1 (Grandi and Endriss, 2013). *Given $AF = \langle Arg, \rightarrow \rangle$. Let φ be a clause (i.e., disjunctions of literals) in $\mathcal{L}_{AF}$ with k_1 positive literals and k_2 negative literals. Then a quota rule F_q for n agents preserves the property $\mathrm{Mod}(\varphi)$ for AF iff the following inequality holds: $q \cdot (k_2 - k_1) > n \cdot (k_2 - 1) - k_1$.*

Lemma 2 (Grandi and Endriss, 2013). *Given $AF = \langle Arg, \rightarrow \rangle$. Let φ_1 and φ_2 be integrity constraints in $\mathcal{L}_{AF}$. If an aggregation rule F preserves both $\mathrm{Mod}(\varphi_1)$ and $\mathrm{Mod}(\varphi_2)$, then F preserves $\mathrm{Mod}(\varphi_1 \wedge \varphi_2)$, but not vice versa.*

3   Solid Admissibility

To obtain the most acceptable arguments that satisfy the two criteria proposed in the introduction, we formally introduce solid admissibility in this section. Arguments in admissible extensions satisfy the criteria. Firstly, we strengthen Dung's defense. Definition 8 states that a set of arguments *solidly defends* an argument iff this set defends (in Dung's sense) this argument and contains all the defenders of each element of this set.

Definition 8 (Solid defense). *Given $AF = \langle Arg, \rightarrowtail \rangle$. $\Delta \subseteq Arg$ solidly defends (or s-defends) $C \in Arg$ iff for any $B \in Arg$, if $B \rightarrowtail C$, then $\Delta \rightarrowtail B$ and $\overline{B} \subseteq \Delta$.*

Definition 9 (Solid defense function). *Given $AF = \langle Arg, \rightarrowtail \rangle$. The solid defense function $d_s \colon 2^{Arg} \longrightarrow 2^{Arg}$ of AF is defined as follows. For any $\Delta \subseteq Arg$,*

$$d_s(\Delta) = \{ C \in Arg \mid \Delta \text{ s-defends } C \} \tag{1}$$

Next we show an important property of the solid defense function. It is easy to see that, if a set of arguments s-defends an argument, then any superset of this set also s-defends this argument by Definition 8.

Theorem 2. *The solid defense function d_s is monotonic.*

Proposition 1. *Given $AF = \langle Arg, \rightarrowtail \rangle$. For any $\Delta \subseteq Arg$, $d_s(\Delta) \subseteq d(\Delta)$, but not vice versa.*

Proposition 1 states that solid defense strengthens Dung's defense since, if a set of arguments s-defends an argument, then this set also defends this argument. To show the converse does not hold, consider AF_1 in Fig. 2a. Δ defends C. But the attackers of B are not fully included in Δ. So Δ does not s-defend C.

Definition 10. *Given $AF = \langle Arg, \rightarrowtail \rangle$. For any $\Delta \subseteq Arg$, Δ is a s-self-defending extension iff $\Delta \subseteq d_s(\Delta)$.*

In graded semantics [14], a set of arguments Δ *mn-defends* an argument C iff there are at most $m - 1$ attackers of C that are not counterattacked by at least n arguments in Δ, where m and n are positive integers. A set of arguments is *mn-self-defending* iff it mn-defends each element. We can tune the parameters to obtain defenses with different levels of strength. For example, when $n = 1$, the larger m is, the stronger the defense is. In Fig. 1a, $\{A_1, C_1\}$, $\{A_2, C_2\}$ and $\{A_1, A_2, C_2\}$ are 11-self-defending. But $\{A_2, C_2\}$ fails to contain all defenders of C_2. One might be tempted to tune the parameters to obtain a stronger defense. Then only $\{A_1, A_2, C_2\}$ is 12-self-defending. Although $\{A_1, C_1\}$ contains all defenders of C_1, it is not 12-self-defending. Hence, graded defense can not capture sets of arguments that exactly contain all defenders of their elements by tuning the parameters. However, solid defense can accomplish this, since it is identified that $\{A_2, C_2\}$ is not s-self-defending while $\{A_1, C_1\}$ and $\{A_1, A_2, C_2\}$ are s-self-defending.

Definition 11. *Given $AF = \langle Arg, \rightarrowtail \rangle$. For any $\Delta \subseteq Arg$, Δ is a s-admissible extension iff $\Delta \subseteq n(\Delta)$ and $\Delta \subseteq d_s(\Delta)$.*

Definition 11 states that a set of arguments is a s-admissible extension iff the set is a conflict-free and s-self-defending extension. Next we show that Dung's Fundamental Lemma has a counterpart in our semantics. The following lemma states that whenever we have a s-admissible extension, if we put into this extension an argument that is s-defended by this extension, then the new set is still a s-admissible extension. The proof is similar to Dung's proof [12].

Lemma 3 (s-fundamental lemma). *Given $AF = \langle Arg, \rightharpoonup \rangle$, a s-admissible extension $\Delta \subseteq Arg$, and two arguments C, $C' \in Arg$ which are s-defended by Δ. Then (i) $\Delta' = \Delta \cup \{C\}$ is s-admissible and (ii) Δ' s-defends C'.*

As we have strengthened Dung's admissibility, the second problem mentioned in the introduction can be addressed now. From a skeptical view, it is not cautious to accept an argument that is indirectly attacked and indirectly defended by some argument. The following theorem states that such arguments never occur in s-admissible extensions.

Theorem 3. *Given $AF = \langle Arg, \rightharpoonup \rangle$ and a s-admissible extension $\Delta \subseteq Arg$. If an argument $A \in Arg$ is controversial w.r.t. an argument $B \in Arg$, then $B \notin \Delta$.*

Proof. Assume that A is controversial w.r.t. B. Suppose for the sake of a contradiction that $B \in \Delta$. Since A indirectly defends B and Δ is s-self-defending, we also have $A \in \Delta$. Besides, since A indirectly attacks B, there exists a finite sequence $A_0, \ldots, A_{2n+1}$ such that (i) $B = A_0$ and $A = A_{2n+1}$, and (ii) for each i, $0 \leqslant i \leqslant 2n$, $A_{i+1} \rightharpoonup A_i$. If $n = 0$, then $A_1 \rightharpoonup A_0$, namely, $A \rightharpoonup B$. This contradicts the conflict-freeness of Δ. If $n \neq 0$, then A_{2n} indirectly defends B. Since Δ is s-self-defending, $A_{2n} \in \Delta$. Again, the fact $A_{2n+1} \rightharpoonup A_{2n}$ (i.e., $A \rightharpoonup A_{2n}$) contradicts the conflict-freeness of Δ. So we conclude that $B \notin \Delta$. □

Note that in Theorem 3, A is not excluded from Δ, since A could be an initial argument. It is not reasonable to reject an unattacked argument. Consider AF_2 in Fig. 1b. We can see that $\{A, C, F\}$ is admissible. However, since A is controversial w.r.t. C, $\{A, C, F\}$ is not s-admissible. $\{A\}$ is still s-admissible. The problem of odd-length cycles has been widely studied. It is thorny to assign a status to an argument in an odd-length cycle, since any argument in an odd-length cycle is controversial w.r.t. any argument in this cycle. There is no consensus on this problem. Interestingly, the following corollary states that such arguments never occur in s-admissible extensions. Moreover, once there is a path from an odd-length cycle to some argument, this argument will never occur in any s-admissible extension since any argument in the odd-length cycle is controversial w.r.t. it.

Corollary 1. *Given $AF = \langle Arg, \rightharpoonup \rangle$ and a s-admissible extension $\Delta \subseteq Arg$. If an argument $A \in Arg$ is in an odd-length cycle, then $A \notin \Delta$.*

4   Solid Semantics

We start by developing some solid semantics based on solid admissibility in this section. These semantics strengthen Dung's semantics in the sense that for a *solid extension* Δ, there exists a Dung's extension Γ such that Δ is a subset of Γ. Moreover, we will show connections among solid extensions and compare solid extensions with Dung's extensions. These solid semantics can be characterized by propositional formulas.

Definition 12 (Solid semantics). *Given $AF = \langle Arg, \rightarrow \rangle$. For any $\Delta \subseteq Arg$, (i) Δ is a s-complete extension iff $\Delta \subseteq n(\Delta)$ and $\Delta = d_s(\Delta)$; (ii) Δ is a s-preferred extension iff Δ is a maximal s-admissible extension; (iii) Δ is a s-stable extension iff $\Delta = n(\Delta)$ and for any argument $A \notin \Delta$, $\overline{A} \subseteq \Delta$; (iv) Δ is the s-grounded extension iff Δ is the least fixed point of d_s.*

Here are some comments for the definition above. We define these solid extensions by using the neutrality function n and the solid defense function d_s, like Dung's extension in Definition 5. A s-complete extension is a fixed point of d_s which is also a conflict-free extension. In other words, a s-complete extension is a s-admissible extension that contains all arguments s-defended by it. A s-preferred extension has maximality and solid admissibility. A set of arguments Δ is a s-stable extension whenever it is a fixed point of n and all attackers of any argument outside of Δ are in Δ. The s-grounded extension is unique.

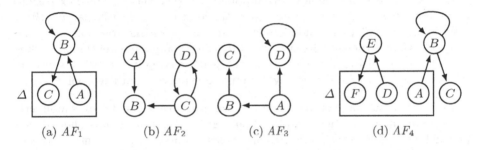

(a) AF_1 (b) AF_2 (c) AF_3 (d) AF_4

Fig. 2. Four argumentation frameworks

Next we present some connections among solid semantics. A s-stable extension is a s-preferred extension. And a s-preferred extension is a s-complete extension. Besides, the s-grounded extension is the least s-complete extension.

Theorem 4. *Given $AF = \langle Arg, \rightarrow \rangle$. For any $\Delta \subseteq Arg$, (i) if Δ is a s-preferred extension, then Δ is a s-complete extension, but not vice versa; (ii) if Δ is a s-stable extension, then Δ is a s-preferred extension, but not vice versa; (iii) The s-grounded extension is the least s-complete extension.*

Proof. Take a set of arguments $\Delta \subseteq Arg$. (i) Suppose that Δ is a s-preferred extension. Then according to Definition 11 and the second item of Definition 12, we have $\Delta \subseteq n(\Delta)$ and $\Delta \subseteq d_s(\Delta)$. It suffices to show $d_s(\Delta) \subseteq \Delta$. Suppose that an argument $C \in d_s(\Delta)$, namely, Δ s-defends C. Then $\Delta \cup \{C\}$ is s-admissible by Lemma 3. Suppose for the sake of a contradiction that $C \notin \Delta$. This contradicts the maximality of Δ. Hence, $C \in \Delta$. It follows that $\Delta = d_s(\Delta)$. So Δ is s-complete extension by the first item of Definition 12. Next we show the converse does not hold. Consider AF_2 in Fig. 2b. Take two sets $\Delta = \{A\}$ and $\Gamma = \{A, C\}$. Then Δ is a s-complete extension. However, we can see that Γ is s-admissible and $\Delta \subset \Gamma$. Hence, Δ is not a maximal s-admissible extension (i.e., not s-preferred).

(ii) Suppose that Δ is a s-stable extension. Then applying the third item of Definition 12 yields $\Delta = n(\Delta)$. We next verify $\Delta \subseteq d_s(\Delta)$. Assume that an argument $C \in \Delta$. To demonstrate $C \in d_s(\Delta)$, suppose that an argument $B \in Arg$ attacks C. Then $B \notin \Delta$ as Δ is conflict-free. It follows that $B \notin n(\Delta)$. Thus, $\Delta \rightharpoonup B$ by Definition 4. Again, using the third item of Definition 12 yields $\overline{B} \subseteq \Delta$. Hence, Δ s-defends C by Definition 8. Then $C \in d_s(\Delta)$ by Definition 9. It follows that Δ is a s-admissible extension. At last, we prove the maximality of Δ. Suppose for the sake of a contradiction that there exists a s-admissible set Γ such that $\Delta \subset \Gamma$. Then there exists an argument C' such that $C' \in \Gamma$ but $C' \notin \Delta$. Immediately, we have $\Delta \rightharpoonup C'$ as $C' \notin \Delta$. This contradicts conflict-freeness of Γ. So Δ is a maximal s-admissible extension. To show that the converse does not hold, let us consider AF_3 in Fig. 2c. Let $\Delta = \{A, C\}$. Then Δ is a s-preferred extension. We can see that $D \notin \Delta$. But the attackers of D are not fully included in Δ. Hence, Δ is not a s-stable extension.

(iii) As Arg is finite, the least fixed point of d_s (i.e., the grounded extension) can be computed as $d_s^{i_{min}}(\emptyset)$ where i_{min} is the least integer i such that $d_s^{i+1}(\emptyset) = d_s^i(\emptyset)$. Moreover, $d_s^i(\emptyset)$ is s-admissible by induction on natural number i and Lemma 3. Hence, the least fixed point of d_s is a s-complete extension according to the first item of Definition 12. Thus, the least fixed point of d_s is a subset of any s-complete extension as as any s-complete extension is a fixed point of d_s.

Recall that any s-admissible extension contains no argument that is indirectly attacked and indirectly defended by some argument. Since we have showed that the solid extensions in Definition 12 are also s-admissible, they contain no such argument either, according to Theorem 3. Next we present an interesting property that the set of arguments outside of a s-stable extension is conflict-free.

Proposition 2. *Given $AF = \langle Arg, \rightharpoonup \rangle$. For any $\Delta \subseteq Arg$, if Δ is a s-stable extension, then $Arg \setminus \Delta$ is a conflict-free extension.*

In the following, we show that solid semantics can be interpreted as a class of strengthenings of Dung's semantics. In other words, for any solid extension, there exists a Dung's counterpart such that it is a superset of the solid extension.

Proposition 3. *Given $AF = \langle Arg, \rightharpoonup \rangle$. For any $\Delta \subseteq Arg$, (i) if Δ is a s-self-defending extensions, then Δ is self-defending extension; (ii) if Δ is a s-admissible extension, then Δ is an admissible extension; (iii) if Δ is a s-complete extension, then there exists a complete extension Γ such that $\Delta \subseteq \Gamma$; (iv) if Δ is a s-preferred extension, then there exists a preferred extension Γ such that $\Delta \subseteq \Gamma$; (v) if Δ is a s-stable extension, then Δ is a stable extension; (vi) if Δ is the s-grounded extension, then Δ is a subset of the grounded extension.*

Proof. Take a set of arguments $\Delta \subseteq Arg$. (i) Suppose Δ is s-self-defending. Then from Definition 10 we have $\Delta \subseteq d_s(\Delta)$. We also have $d_s(\Delta) \subseteq d(\Delta)$ by Proposition 1. It follows that $\Delta \subseteq d(\Delta)$. ($ii$) This item is easily obtained from the first item. (iii) Suppose that Δ is s-complete. Then Δ is s-admissible. Hence, Δ is admissible. Therefore, there exists a preferred extension Γ such that $\Delta \subseteq \Gamma$ by

Theorem 1. Besides, Γ is also a complete extension by Theorem 1. (iv) Suppose that Δ is s-preferred. Then Δ is s-admissible. Hence, Δ is admissible. Therefore, there exists a preferred extension Γ such that $\Delta \subseteq \Gamma$ by Theorem 1. (v) This item follows from the third item of Definition 12 and the fifth item of Definition 5. (vi) Recall that the least fixed point of d_s (resp., d) is found by iterating the application of d_s (resp., d) from the empty set. Besides, we have $d_s^i(\emptyset) \subseteq d^i(\emptyset)$ by induction on natural number i. And we also have $d^i(\emptyset) \subseteq d^{i+1}(\emptyset)$. Therefore, during the process of iteration, the s-grounded extension will be found no later than the grounded extension. So the former is a subset of the latter.

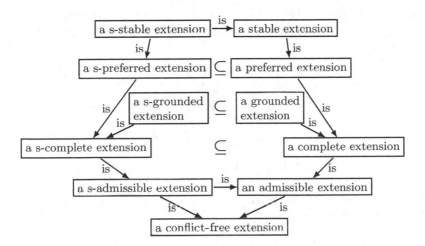

Fig. 3. An overview of solid semantics and Dung's semantics. We can see that for any solid extension, there exists a superset that is also a Dung's extension.

To gain a better understanding of differences between Dung's extensions and solid extensions, we provide two examples. Example 3 shows that if a set of arguments is a self-defending (resp., a complete, a preferred, a stable, or the grounded) extension, then it may fail to be a s-self-defending (resp., s-complete, a s-preferred, a s-stable or the s-grounded) extension. Example 4 shows that if a set of arguments is a s-complete (resp., a s-preferred or the s-grounded) extension, then it may fail to be a complete (resp., a preferred or the grounded) extension. However, it is easy to see that a s-stable extension must be a stable extension by Definition 5 and Definition 12. We illustrate in Fig. 3 an overview of how the solid extensions are related to each other and Dung's extensions.

Example 3. Let us consider AF_1 in Fig. 2a. Take a set of arguments $\Delta = \{A, C\}$. Then it is easy to see that Δ is a self-defending extension but not a s-self-defending extension. Besides, Δ is a complete, a preferred, a stable and the grounded extension. However, according to Theorem 3, C can not be included in any s-admissible extension, since B is controversial w.r.t. C. Hence, Δ is neither a s-complete, a s-preferred, a s-stable, nor the s-grounded extension.

Example 4. Let us consider AF_4 in Fig. 2d. Let $\Delta = \{A, D, F\}$. Then Δ is a s-complete, a s-preferred and the s-grounded extension. However, we can see that argument C which is defended by Δ is not included in Δ. Hence, Δ is neither a complete, a preferred, a stable nor the grounded extension.

Before moving to the next section, we characterize the solid semantics in terms of integrity constraints (i.e., propositional formulas) expressed in $\mathcal{L}_{AF}$. We say that a set of arguments is a *s-reinstating* extension iff each argument s-defended by this set belongs to this set. It is worth mentioning that the integrity constrain of conflict-freeness [5] is $\mathrm{IC}_{CF} \equiv \bigwedge_{\substack{A,B \in Arg \\ A \rightarrow B}} (\neg A \vee \neg B)$.

Proposition 4. *Given $AF = \langle Arg, \rightarrow \rangle$. $\Delta \subseteq Arg$ is a s-self-defending, s-reinstating, s-stable, s-admissible, s-complete, s-preferred and s-grounded extension, resp. iff*

- $\Delta \models \mathrm{IC}_{SS}$ *where* $\mathrm{IC}_{SS} \equiv \bigwedge_{C \in Arg} \left[C \rightarrow \bigwedge_{\substack{B \in Arg \\ B \rightarrow C}} \left(\left(\bigvee_{\substack{A \in Arg \\ A \rightarrow B}} A \right) \wedge \left(\bigwedge_{\substack{A \in Arg \\ A \rightarrow B}} A \right) \right) \right]$;
- $\Delta \models \mathrm{IC}_{SR}$ *where* $\mathrm{IC}_{SR} \equiv \bigwedge_{C \in Arg} \left[\bigwedge_{\substack{B \in Arg \\ B \rightarrow C}} \left(\left(\bigvee_{\substack{A \in Arg \\ A \rightarrow B}} A \right) \wedge \left(\bigwedge_{\substack{A \in Arg \\ A \rightarrow B}} A \right) \right) \rightarrow C \right]$;
- $\Delta \models \mathrm{IC}_{SST}$ *where* $\mathrm{IC}_{SST} \equiv \bigwedge_{B \in Arg} \left[\left(B \leftrightarrow \bigwedge_{\substack{A \in Arg \\ A \rightarrow B}} \neg A \right) \wedge \left(\neg B \rightarrow \bigwedge_{\substack{A \in Arg \\ A \rightarrow B}} A \right) \right]$;
- $\Delta \models \mathrm{IC}_{SA}$ *where* $\mathrm{IC}_{SA} \equiv \mathrm{IC}_{CF} \wedge \mathrm{IC}_{SS}$;
- $\Delta \models \mathrm{IC}_{SC}$ *where* $\mathrm{IC}_{SC} \equiv \mathrm{IC}_{SA} \wedge \mathrm{IC}_{SR}$;
- Δ *is a maximal model of* IC_{SA};
- Δ *is the least model of* IC_{SC}.

5   Preservation of Solid Semantic Properties

Quota rules are natural rules to be considered when contemplating mechanisms to perform aggregation. They have low computational complexity and satisfy some appealing properties. For instance, they are monotonic and strategy-proof as studied in judgment aggregation. The problem of aggregating extensions submitted by several agents on a given AF is an important and interesting topic. Especially, no quota rule preserves Dung's admissibility for all AFs [10]. So we wonder what admissible extensions can be preserved. In light of the integrity constraints for solid semantics in Proposition 4, we can investigate the preservation results for solid semantic properties by using the model defined in Sect. 2.2 and quota rules. We analyze that in the scenarios where a set of agents each provides us with a set of arguments that satisfies a specific solid semantics, under what circumstance such solid semantic property will be preserved under aggregation.

5.1   Preserving Solid Self-defence and Solid Admissibility

We start by exploring the circumstances where the s-self-defending property can be preserved. Theorem 5 presents a positive result that every quota rule preserves the s-self-defending property for all AFs.

Theorem 5. *Given $AF = \langle Arg, \rightarrow \rangle$. Every quota rule F_q for n agents preserves the property of being s-self-defending for AF.*

Proof. Recall from Proposition 4 that IC_{SS} is a conjunction of formulas of the form: $\varphi \equiv C \rightarrow \bigwedge_{\substack{B \in Arg \\ B \rightarrow C}} \left(\left(\bigvee_{\substack{A \in Arg \\ A \rightarrow B}} A \right) \wedge \left(\bigwedge_{\substack{A \in Arg \\ A \rightarrow B}} A \right) \right)$. Note that this formula is indexed by argument C, let us study the preservation of such formula. If C is an initial argument (an argument not receiving attacks in AF), then $\varphi \equiv C \rightarrow \top$, which can be simplified to $\varphi \equiv \top$. It follows that in this case, every quota rule F_q for n agents preserves $\text{Mod}(\varphi)$ for AF. If C has at least one attacker, then we need to take into account the following two cases. The first case is that there exists an attacker B of C such that B is an initial argument. In this case, we have $\varphi \equiv \neg C$ (this can be easily obtained as $\bigwedge_{\substack{B \in Arg \\ B \rightarrow C}} \left(\left(\bigvee_{\substack{A \in Arg \\ A \rightarrow B}} A \right) \wedge \left(\bigwedge_{\substack{A \in Arg \\ A \rightarrow B}} A \right) \right)$ is always false if there is an attacker B of C that has no attacker). Then, according to Lemma 1, every quota rule F_q for n agents preserves $\text{Mod}(\varphi)$ for AF, as the inequality $q \cdot (1 - 0) > n \cdot (1 - 1) - 0$, which can be simplified to $q > 0$, always holds. The other case is that all attackers of C are not initial. Then, we let $\{B_1, \ldots, B_p\}$ be the set of attackers of C, and let $\{A_1^i, \ldots, A_{\ell_i}^i\}$ be the set of attackers of B_i where $1 \leqslant i \leqslant p$ and $\ell_i = |\overline{B_i}|$. Then φ can be rewritten as follows: $\varphi \equiv \left((\neg C \vee A_1^1) \wedge \cdots \wedge (\neg C \vee A_{\ell_1}^1) \right) \wedge \cdots \wedge \left((\neg C \vee A_1^p) \wedge \cdots \wedge (\neg C \vee A_{\ell_p}^p) \right)$. Thus, in this case, φ is a conjunction of clauses with one negative literal and one positive literal. We take one such clause $\psi = \neg C \vee A_{l_j}^i$. According to Lemma 1, every quota rule F_q preserves ψ in this case. Thus, every quota rule for n agents preserves φ. It follows that all clauses of IC_{SS} can be preserved by all quota rules. We conclude that every quota rule F_q for n agents preserves the property $\text{Mod}(IC_{SS})$ for AF by Lemma 2.

Obviously, the strict majority rule, the nomination rule and the unanimity rule as specific quota rules, will preserve s-self-defense. Note that different from the property of being s-self-defending, Dung's self-defense cannot be preserved by some quota rule. One example is the strict majority rule [10].

We now turn to consider the preservation of solid admissibility. Recall that a set of arguments is s-admissible if it satisfies conflict-freeness and s-self-defense. With Lemma 2, we know that if an aggregation rule preserves both conflict-freeness and s-self-defense, then solid admissibility will be preserved by such rule. The following proposition restates a result for conflict-freeness in [10].

Proposition 5. *Given $AF = \langle Arg, \rightarrow \rangle$. A quota rule F_q for n agents preserves conflict-freeness for AF if $q > \frac{n}{2}$.*

Theorem 6. *Given $AF = \langle Arg, \rightarrow \rangle$. Any quota rule F_q for n agents with $q > \frac{n}{2}$ preserves solid admissibility for AF.*

Applying Theorem 5 and Proposition 5 immediately yields Theorem 6, which shows that any quota rule higher than or equal to the strict majority rule can preserve solid admissibility for arbitrary AF. Recall that no quota rule preserves Dung's admissibility for all AFs [10]. Thus, we have obtained a positive result, i.e., we know that there exist quota rules that preserve solid admissibility for all AFs. Notably, Chen [9] uses a different model to show that the majority rule guarantees Dung's admissibility on profiles of solid admissible sets during aggregation of extensions. Theorem 6 entails this result, but not vice versa.

5.2   Preserving Solid Reinstatement and Solid Completeness

We turn to explore solid reinstatement. For convenience, we provide three notations. Given $AF = \langle Arg, \rightarrow \rangle$. Firstly, for any $C \in Arg$, $\mathscr{D}_{AF}(C)$ denotes the set of C's defenders, i.e., $\mathscr{D}_{AF}(C) = \{A \in Arg \mid A \text{ is a defender of } C\}$. Secondly, we let $\mathcal{E}(AF)$ denote the set of arguments which are not initial arguments and whose attackers are not initial arguments either, i.e., $\mathcal{E}(AF) = \{C \in Arg \mid \overline{C} \neq \emptyset$ and for any $B \in \overline{C}, \overline{B} \neq \emptyset\}$. Thirdly, we let $\mathcal{M}(AF)$ denote the maximal number of the defenders of an argument in $\mathcal{E}(AF)$, i.e., $\mathcal{M}(AF) = \max\limits_{C \in \mathcal{E}(AF)} |\mathscr{D}_{AF}(C)|$.

Theorem 7. *Given $AF = \langle Arg, \rightarrow \rangle$. A quota rule F_q for n agents preserves the property of being s-reinstating for AF if $q \cdot (\mathcal{M}(AF) - 1) > n \cdot (\mathcal{M}(AF) - 1) - 1$.*

Proof. Assume that $q \cdot (\mathcal{M}(AF) - 1) > n \cdot (\mathcal{M}(AF) - 1) - 1$. IC_{SR} is a conjunction of formulas of the form of $\varphi \equiv \bigwedge_{\substack{B \in Arg \\ B \rightarrow C}} \left(\left(\bigvee_{\substack{A \in Arg \\ A \rightarrow B}} A \right) \wedge \left(\bigwedge_{\substack{A \in Arg \\ A \rightarrow B}} A \right) \right) \rightarrow C$ from Proposition 4. Take an argument $C \in Arg$. If C is an initial argument, then $\varphi \equiv C$, which can be regarded as a 1-clause (with 1 positive literal and no negative literal). Applying Lemma 1, any quota rule F_q for n agents preserves $\text{Mod}(\varphi)$ for AF in this case, as the inequality $q \cdot (0 - 1) > n \cdot (0 - 1) - 1$ (which can be simplified to $q < n + 1$) always holds.

If C is not an initial argument, then we need to consider two cases. The first case is that there exists a C's attacker B such that B is an initial argument, then $\varphi \equiv \top$. It follows that in this case, any quota rule F_q for n agents preserves $\text{Mod}(\varphi)$ for AF. The second case is that any C's attacker B is not an initial argument. Then we can let $\{B_1, \cdots, B_p\}$ be the set of C's attackers, and let $\{A_1^i, \cdots, A_{\ell_i}^i\}$ be the set of B_i's attackers where $1 \leqslant i \leqslant p$ and $\ell_i = |\overline{B_i}|$. we can reformulate φ as follows: $\varphi \equiv \left((\neg A_1^1 \vee \cdots \vee \neg A_{\ell_1}^1) \vee \cdots \vee (\neg A_1^p \vee \cdots \vee \neg A_{\ell_p}^p) \right) \vee C$.

Hence, φ is a $(\sum\limits_{i=1}^{p} \ell_i + 1)$-clause (with $\sum\limits_{i=1}^{p} \ell_i$ negative literals and 1 positive literal). By Lemma 1, a quota rule F_q for n agents preserves $\text{Mod}(\varphi)$ if the following inequality holds: $q \cdot (\sum_{i=1}^{p} \ell_i - 1) > n \cdot (\sum_{i=1}^{p} \ell_i - 1) - 1$. Doing so becomes harder as $\sum_{i=1}^{p} \ell_i$ increases. Note that $C \in \mathcal{E}(AF)$ in this case and $\sum_{i=1}^{p} \ell_i$ is the number of the defenders of C. Recall that the maximal number of defenders of an argument in $\mathcal{E}(AF)$ is $\mathcal{M}(AF)$. Hence, the maximal value of $\sum_{i=1}^{p} \ell_i$ is $\mathcal{M}(AF)$. Thus, by Lemma 1, a quota rule F_q for n agents preserve $\text{Mod}(\varphi)$ for AF in this case, if the inequality holds for the maximal value of $\sum_{i=1}^{p} \ell_i$ (i.e., $\mathcal{M}(AF)$). As we have assumed that $q \cdot (\mathcal{M}(AF) - 1) > n \cdot (\mathcal{M}(AF) - 1) - 1$, it follows that a quota rule F_q for n agents preserves $\text{Mod}(\varphi)$ for AF. Finally, using Lemma 2, we can conclude that a quota rule F_q for n agents preserves $\text{Mod}(\text{IC}_{SR})$ for AF if $q \cdot (\mathcal{M}(AF) - 1) > n \cdot (\mathcal{M}(AF) - 1) - 1$.

Recall that the unanimity rule is a quota rule F_q for n agents with $q = n$. It is easy to see that the inequality $n \cdot (\mathcal{M}(AF) - 1) > n \cdot (\mathcal{M}(AF) - 1) - 1$ always holds. Then according to Theorem 7, the unanimity rule preserves the property of being s-reinstating for any AF. The theorem below for s-completeness is a direct consequence of Theorem 6 and Theorem 7.

Theorem 8. *Given $AF = \langle Arg, \rightarrow \rangle$. A quota rule F_q for n agents preserves s-completeness for AF if $q > \frac{n}{2}$ and $q \cdot (\mathcal{M}(AF) - 1) > n \cdot (\mathcal{M}(AF) - 1) - 1$.*

5.3 Preserving Solid Groundedness, Solid Preferredness and Solid Stability

As the s-grounded extension is unique in any AF, any quota rule preserves s-groundedness for any AF. We say that a property σ is *inclusion maximal* if for any Δ_1, $\Delta_2 \in \sigma$, if $\Delta_1 \subseteq \Delta_2$ then $\Delta_1 = \Delta_2$. It is easy to see that both the solid preferredness and solid stability are inclusion maximal. Hence, we can investigate these two properties together. Given $AF = \langle Arg, \rightarrow \rangle$, let σ be an inclusion maximal property of extensions such that $|\sigma| \geqslant 2$, and let n be the number of agents. If n is even, then no quota rule preserves σ for AF. If n is odd, then no quota rule different from the strict majority rule preserves σ for AF. Such results are highly analogous to Theorem 15 in [10]. We omit the proof for this reason.

6 Related Work

Various notions of admissibility are proposed since Dung's admissibility was introduced in [12]. Baroni and Giacomin introduce the notion of strong admissibility [2] which is stronger than Dung's admissibility. It captures the idea that any argument in a strongly admissible set neither defend itself nor involve in its own defense. Grossi and Modgil propose *Graded admissibility* [14], whereby Dung's admissibility can be strengthened or weakened by parameterizing the numbers of attackers and defenders. Chen [8] proposes *concrete* admissibility. Differently from solid admissibility, concrete admissibility does not require the existence of defenders, although both of them require containing all defenders. Prudent semantics [11] is another semantics that aims at dealing with controversial arguments. Whenever an argument A is controversial w.r.t. an argument B, both prudent semantics and solid semantics can prevent A and B from occurring in the same extension. But there is a difference between these two semantics: both A and B can occur in a prudent extension independently, however, B is excluded from any s-admissible extension, while A might occur in some s-admissible extension (e.g., A is an initial argument).

7 Conclusion and Future Work

This paper mainly makes contributions to the field of abstract argumentation theory. To address the problems observed in ranking-based argumentation and controversial arguments, we develop solid semantics by strengthening Dung's semantics. By applying the technique in [5], we capture solid semantics by using propositional formulas. Finally, in virtue of these formulas, we aggregate solid extensions by using quota rules and obtain positive preservation results.

Recall that solid defense requires that all the defenders of an argument C are included in a set of arguments Δ. It would be interesting to characterize the idea that any percent of the defenders of C are included in a set of arguments Δ. Moreover, we can also allow a part of attackers to be not attacked. For example, we can try to capture the idea that Δ defends C if more than fifty percent of C's attackers have more than fifty percent of their attackers in Δ (i.e., if the majority of C's attackers have the majority of their attackers in Δ). Future work could focus on introducing proportionality to the defense of arguments of abstract argumentation. Furthermore, the complexity of reasoning tasks involving solid semantics should be studied.

References

1. Amgoud, L., Ben-Naim, J.: Ranking-based semantics for argumentation frame-works. In: Liu, W., Subrahmanian, V.S., Wijsen, J. (eds.) SUM 2013. LNCS (LNAI), vol. 8078, pp. 134–147. Springer, Heidelberg (2013). https://doi.org/10.1007/978-3-642-40381-1_11
2. Baroni, P., Giacomin, M.: On principle-based evaluation of extension-based argumentation semantics. Artif. Intell. **171**(10–15), 675–700 (2007)
3. Baroni, P., Giacomin, M., Guida, G.: SCC-recursiveness: a general schema for argumentation semantics. Artif. Intell. **168**(1–2), 162–210 (2005)
4. Baumann, R., Brewka, G., Ulbricht, M.: Revisiting the foundations of abstract argumentation-semantics based on weak admissibility and weak defense. In: Proceedings of the AAAI Conference on Artificial Intelligence, vol. 34, pp. 2742–2749 (2020)
5. Besnard, P., Doutre, S.: Checking the acceptability of a set of arguments. In: NMR, vol. 4, pp. 59–64. Citeseer (2004)
6. Bodanza, G.A., Tohmé, F.A.: Two approaches to the problems of self-attacking arguments and general odd-length cycles of attack. J. Appl. Log. **7**(4), 403–420 (2009)
7. Cayrol, C., Lagasquie-Schiex, M.C.: Graduality in argumentation. J. Artif. Intell. Res. **23**, 245–297 (2005)
8. Chen, W.: Preservation of admissibility with rationality and feasibility constraints. In: Dastani, M., Dong, H., van der Torre, L. (eds.) CLAR 2020. LNCS (LNAI), vol. 12061, pp. 245–258. Springer, Cham (2020). https://doi.org/10.1007/978-3-030-44638-3_15
9. Chen, W.: Guaranteeing admissibility of abstract argumentation frameworks with rationality and feasibility constraints. J. Log. Comput. (2021, forthcoming)
10. Chen, W., Endriss, U.: Aggregating alternative extensions of abstract argumentation frameworks: preservation results for quota rules. In: COMMA, pp. 425–436 (2018)
11. Coste-Marquis, S., Devred, C., Marquis, P.: Prudent semantics for argumentation frameworks. In: 17th IEEE International Conference on Tools with Artificial Intelligence (ICTAI 2005), pp. 568–572. IEEE (2005)

12. Dung, P.M.: On the acceptability of arguments and its fundamental role in non-monotonic reasoning, logic programming and n-person games. Artif. Intell. **77**(2), 321–357 (1995)
13. Grandi, U., Endriss, U.: Lifting integrity constraints in binary aggregation. Artif. Intell. **199**, 45–66 (2013)
14. Grossi, D., Modgil, S.: On the graded acceptability of arguments in abstract and instantiated argumentation. Artif. Intell. **275**, 138–173 (2019)
15. Jakobovits, H., Vermeir, D.: Robust semantics for argumentation frameworks. J. Log. Comput. **9**(2), 215–261 (1999)

Verification of Multi-layered Assignment Problems

Barak Steindl$^{(\boxtimes)}$ and Meirav Zehavi

Ben Gurion University of the Negev, Beer-Sheva, Israel

Abstract. The class of assignment problems is a fundamental and well-studied class in the intersection of Social Choice, Computational Economics and Discrete Allocation. In a general assignment problem, a group of agents expresses preferences over a set of items, and the task is to allocate items to agents in an "optimal" way. A verification variant of this problem includes an allocation as part of the input, and the question becomes whether this allocation is "optimal". In this paper, we generalize the verification variant to the setting where each agent is equipped with *multiple* incomplete preference lists: Each list (called a *layer*) is a ranking of items in a possibly different way according to a different criterion.

In particular, we introduce three multi-layer verification problems, each corresponds to an optimality notion that weakens the notion of global optimality (that is, pareto optimality in multiple layers) in a different way. Informally, the first notion requires that, for each group of agents whose size is exactly some input parameter k, the agents in the group will not be able to trade their assigned items among themselves and benefit in at least α layers; the second notion is similar, but it concerns all groups of size at most k rather than exactly k; the third notion strengthens these notions by requiring that groups of k agents will not be part of possibly larger groups that benefit in at least α layers. We study the three problems from the perspective of parameterized complexity under several natural parameterizations such as the number of layers, the number of agents, the number of items, the number of allocated items, the maximum length of a preference list, and more. We present an almost comprehensive picture of the parameterized complexity of the problems with respect to these parameters.

1 Introduction

The field of resource allocation problems has been widely studied in recent years. A central class of problems in this field is the class of *assignment problems* [1–3,6,7,10,19,21,26]. In the most general, abstract formulation of an assignment problem (to which we will refer as the *general assignment problem*), an instance consists of a set of n agents and a set of m items. Each agent (human, company, or

---

A full version of this paper, including an extended preliminaries, full proofs and examples, can be found in https://arxiv.org/abs/2105.10434.

© Springer Nature Switzerland AG 2021
A. Rosenfeld and N. Talmon (Eds.): EUMAS 2021, LNAI 12802, pp. 194–210, 2021.
https://doi.org/10.1007/978-3-030-82254-5_12

any other entity) expresses preferences over a subset of items, and the objective is to allocate items to agents in an "optimal" way. A verification variant of the general assignment problem includes, in addition, some allocation as part of the input, and the question becomes whether this allocation is "optimal".

Different notions of optimality have been considered in the literature, but the one that has received the most attention is *pareto optimality* (see, e.g., [2, 6,7]). Intuitively, an assignment p is called *pareto optimal* if there is no other assignment q that is at least good as p for all agents and also strictly better than p for at least one agent. An equivalent requirement for an assignment to be pareto optimal is to admit no *trading cycle* (see, e.g., Aziz et al. [6,7]). Intuitively, an assignment admits a trading cycle if there exists a set of agents who all benefit by exchanging their allocated items among themselves (as indicated by the cycle). It is known to imply that the problem of verifying whether an assignment is pareto optimal can be solved efficiently in polynomial time (see, e.g., Aziz et al. [6,7]). Even the seemingly more difficult problem of finding a pareto optimal assignment can be solved in polynomial time by Abdulkadiroglu and Sönmez [2].

Besides their theoretical interest, these problems (both decision and verification variants) have also practical importance. Algorithms for both variants are applied in a variety of real-world situations, such as assigning jobs to workers, campus houses to students, time stamps to users on a common machine, players to sports teams, graduating medical students to their first hospital appointments, and so on. In particular, algorithms for verifying whether an assignment is optimal are useful in cases where we already have an assignment and we want to check whether it is pareto optimal; if it is not, we may seek a "strategy" to improve the assignment (e.g., a trading cycle). For example, when the input is large, finding an optimal assignment may be computationally expensive, so a better choice will be to use some heuristic to find an initial assignment, verify whether it is optimal or not, and proceed accordingly.

In the general assignment problem, each agent has exactly one preference list. The preference lists may represent a single subjective criterion according to which each agent ranks the items. However, they may also represent a combination of different such criteria: each agent associates a score to each item per criterion, and a single preference list is derived from some weighted sum of the scores. In many cases, it is unclear how to combine scores associated with criteria of inherently incomparable nature - that is like "comparing apples with oranges". Even if a single list can be forcefully extracted, most data is lost.[1]

Thus, the classic model seems somewhat restrictive in real world scenarios where people rely on highly *varied* aspects to rank other entities. For example, suppose that there are n candidates who need to be assigned to n positions. The recruiters may rank the candidates for each position according to different criteria, such as academic background, experience, impression by the interview, and so on [4,20]. Moreover, when assigning campus houses to students, the student may rank the houses by multiple criteria such as their location (how close the

---

[1] Our new generalized model allows us to limit the amount of data that can be ignored for each agent group using the parameter α.

house is to their faculty), rent, size etc. [25]. This motivates the employment of multiple preference lists where each preference list (called a *layer*) is defined by a different criterion.

Our work is inspired by the work of Chen et al. [11], who studied the STABLE MARRIAGE problem under multiple preference lists. In our recent work [23], we defined the notion of *global optimality*, which (similarly to global stability defined by Chen et al. [11]) extends the notion of pareto optimality to the case where there are multiple layers by requiring an assignment to be pareto optimal in a given number of layers. They studied the parameterized complexity of the problem of finding a globally optimal assignment (in the presence of multiple preference lists), and they showed that it is an extremely hard computational task with no efficient parameterized algorithms (with respect to almost any parameter combination). Two factors cause this hardness: First, in general, finding an optimal assignment is harder than verifying whether an assignment is optimal. Second, the concept of global optimality, which requires "global agreement" among the agents on the layers where beneficial trading cannot be performed, may seem too strong. Thus, a natural direction is to consider an adaptation of the verification variant to the multi-layer model, and to weaken the notion of global optimality.

We define three new notions of optimality: (k, α)-*optimality*, (k, α)-*upper-bounded optimality*, and (k, α)-*subset optimality*. Intuitively, the first notion requires that each subset of agents of size k does not admit trading cycles (without additional agents) in at least α layers. The second notion is similar, but it additionally applies this condition on all subsets of size at most k rather than only exactly k. The third notion requires that each subset of k agents does not appear in trading cycles, together with possibly other agents, in at least α layers. In contrast to global optimality, these notions do not require having the same α layers where all agents cannot trade and benefit - each "small" subset of agents may have different α layers where the its agents do not admit trading cycles.

The consideration of the parameter k is reasonable: indeed, suppose that some assignment can be improved but only if a large group of agents would exchange their items among themselves. In many cases, such trading may not be feasible since it may require a lot of efforts and organization [14,15]. Thus, we define k as a fixed size or as an upper bound on the size of agent groups for which trading can be performed (in (k, α)-optimal and (k, α)-upper-bounded optimal). In contrast, in the definition of (k, α)-subset optimality, the parameter k is, essentially, a "lower bound" on the size of subsets which do not admit trading cycles. This notion was designed to represent real scenarios where (i) we are not interested in finding short trading cycles but only in finding large ones since they would gain the most benefit and only they might justify changing the status quo, and where (ii) large and complicated cycles can be performed [5].

Although the verification variant of the assignment problem can be solved in polynomial time in the single-layer model (see, e.g., Aziz et al. [6,7]), similarly to the decision variant in [23], the problem becomes harder when multiple preference lists are taken into account. However, we show that, while some verification variants are still hard with respect to various parameters, they also admit fixed-parameter algorithms rather than mainly hardness results (as in [23]). A comparison between running times of algorithms is included in the full version.

Table 1. Summary of our results for the problems VERIFY OPTIMAL ASSIGNMENT, VERIFY UPPER-BOUNDED OPTIMAL ASSIGNMENT, and VERIFY SUBSET OPTIMAL ASSIGNMENT. The results are applicable to the three problems, unless stated otherwise.

Parameter	Complexity class	Running time	Polynomial kernel?
α	para-coNP-hard (Theorem 6)	–	–
	VUOA: P when $\alpha = \ell$	Polynomial	Yes
ℓ	para-coNP-hard (Theorem 6)	–	–
k	coW[1]-hard (Theorem 5)	$\mathcal{O}^*(n^{\mathcal{O}(k)})$ (Theorem 3)	–
	VOA, VUOA: XP (Theorem 3)	$\mathcal{O}^*(n^{\mathcal{O}(k)})$ (Theorem 3)	–
$k + \ell$	coW[1]-hard (Theorem 5)	$\mathcal{O}^*(n^{\mathcal{O}(k)})$ (Theorem 3)	–
	VOA,VUOA: XP (Theorem 3)	$\mathcal{O}^*(n^{\mathcal{O}(k)})$ (Theorem 3)	–
$k + d$	VOA,VUOA: FPT (Theorem 4)	$\mathcal{O}^*(d^k)$ (Theorem 4)	No (Theorem 7)
$(n - k) + \ell + d$	para-coNP-hard (Theorem 6)	–	–
#alloc	FPT (Theorem 2)	$\mathcal{O}^*(2^{\#\mathrm{alloc}})$ (Theorem 2)	No (Theorem 7)
#alloc $+ \ell$	FPT (Theorem 2)	$\mathcal{O}^*(2^{\#\mathrm{alloc}})$ (Theorem 2)	Yes (Theorem 1)
$n + m + \alpha$	FPT (Theorem 2)	$\mathcal{O}^*(2^{\#\mathrm{alloc}})$ (Theorem 2)	No (Theorem 7)
$n + m + (\ell - \alpha)$	FPT (Theorem 2)	$\mathcal{O}^*(2^{\#\mathrm{alloc}})$ (Theorem 2)	No (Theorem 7)

Our Contributions. We consider several parameters such as the number of layers ℓ, the number of agents $n = \#$agents, the number of items $m = \#$items, the maximum length of a preference list d, the number of allocated items #alloc, and the parameters α and k that are related to the optimality concepts (see Sect. 2 for the formal definitions). In particular, we present an almost comprehensive picture of the parameterized complexity of the problems with respect to these parameters. The choice of these parameters is sensible because in real-life scenarios such as those mentioned earlier, some of these parameters may be substantially smaller than the input size. For instance, ℓ, α and $\ell - \alpha$ are upper bounded by the number of criteria according to which the agents rank the items. Thus, they are likely to be small in practice: when ranking other entities, people usually do not consider a substantially large number of criteria. For instance, when sports teams rank candidate players, only a few criteria such as the player's winning history, his impact on his previous teams, and physical properties are taken into account [16]. In addition, the parameter $\ell - \alpha$ may be small particularly in cases where we want each group of agents to admit no conflicts in a large number of layers. Moreover, in various cases concerning ranking of people, jobs, houses etc., people usually have a limited number of entities that they want or are allowed to ask for [13]. In these cases, the parameter d is likely to be small. In addition, in small countries (such as Israel), the number of universities, hospitals, sports teams and many other facilities and organizations is very small [12,24]. Thus, in scenarios concerning these entities, at least one among n and m (and thus also #alloc) may be small. Furthermore, when assigning students to universities, workers to companies, and players to sports teams since the number of universities, companies and sports teams are usually substantially smaller than the number of students, workers and players, respectively. The consideration of k is justified by previous arguments. A summary of our results is given in Table 1.

Fixed-Parameter Tractability. We first provide some simple properties of the problems VERIFY OPTIMAL ASSIGNMENT (VERIFY-OA), VERIFY UPPER-BOUNDED OPTIMAL ASSIGNMENT (VERIFY-UOA), and VERIFY SUBSET OPTIMAL ASSIGNMENT (VERIFY-SOA). We then prove that the three problems are in coNP and that VERIFY-UOA is solvable in polynomial time when $\alpha = \ell$. Afterward, we prove that the problems admit polynomial kernels when parameterized by #alloc $+ \ell$ and that they are *fixed-parameter tractable (FPT)* with respect to #alloc by providing $\mathcal{O}^*(2^{\#\text{alloc}})$-time dynamic programming algorithms that are inspired by Björklund et al. [9] and by the Floyd–Warshall algorithm [18]. We then prove that VERIFY-OA and VERIFY-UOA are *slice-wise polynomial (XP)* with respect to k by providing an $\mathcal{O}^*(n^{\mathcal{O}(k)})$-time algorithm, and that they are FPT with respect to $k + d$ by providing an $\mathcal{O}^*(d^k)$-time algorithm. Finally, we prove that the three problems are coW[1]-hard when parameterized by $k + \ell$ using a parameterized reduction from MULTICOLORED INDEPENDENT SET.

coNP-Hardness. We prove that the problems are para-coNP-hard with respect to $\ell + d + (n - k)$. This is done using a polynomial reduction from the HAMILTONIAN CYCLE problem on directed graphs with maximum degree 3 (proved to be NP-hard by Plesník [22]) to the complements of the problems.

Non-existence of Polynomial Kernels. We prove that VERIFY-OA and VERIFY-SOA do not admit polynomial kernels with respect to $n + m + \alpha$ and $n + m + (\ell - \alpha)$ using two cross-compositions from HAMILTONIAN CYCLE on directed graphs with maximum degree 3, which rely on the aforementioned reduction to prove para-coNP-hardness. We then extend these cross-compositions to have the same results for VERIFY-UOA.

2   Preliminaries

For any $t \in \mathbb{N}$, let $[t] = \{1, \ldots, t\}$. The $\mathcal{O}^*$-notation suppresses polynomial factors in the input size, that is, $\mathcal{O}^*(f(k)) = f(k) \cdot n^{\mathcal{O}(1)}$.

Assignment Problems. An instance of the (general) assignment problem is a triple (A, I, P) where A is a set of n agents $\{a_1, \ldots, a_n\}$, I is a set of m items $\{b_1, \ldots, b_m\}$, and $P = (<_{a_1}, \ldots, <_{a_n})$, called the *preference profile*, contains the (possibly incomplete) preferences of the agents over the items, where each $<_{a_i}$ encodes the preferences of a_i and is a linear order over a *subset* of I. We refer to such linear orders as *preference lists*. If $b_j <_{a_i} b_r$, we say that agent a_i *prefers* item b_r over item b_j, and we write $b_j \leq_{a_i} b_r$ if $b_j <_{a_i} b_r$ or $b_j = b_r$. An *assignment* is an allocation of items to agents such that each agent is allocated at most one item, and each item is allocated to at most one agent. Since the preferences of the agents may be incomplete, or the number of items may be smaller than the number of agents, some agents may not have available items to be assigned to. To deal with this case, a special item $b_\emptyset$ is defined, seen as the least preferred item of each agent, and will be used as a sign that an agent is not allocated an item. Thus, a mapping $p : A \to I \cup \{b_\emptyset\}$ is called an *assignment* if for each $i \in [n]$, it satisfies (i) $p(a_i) = b_\emptyset$, or (ii) both $p(a_i) \in I$ and for each $j \in [n] \setminus \{i\}$, $p(a_i) \neq p(a_j)$. We refer to p as *legal* if it satisfies $p(a_i) = b_\emptyset$ or that $p(a_i) \in I$ appears in a_i's preference list for each layer $i \in [n]$. Throughout this paper, we assume that $b_\emptyset$ is not part of the input item set, and that it appears at the end of every preference list (we will not write $b_\emptyset$ explicitly in the preference lists). We will omit the term "legal" and refer to a legal assignment just as an assignment.[2] Moreover, when we write a set in a preference list, we assume that its elements are ordered arbitrarily, unless stated otherwise. In the general assignment problem, given such a triple (A, I, P), we seek an assignment which is "optimal" according to some criterion.

Pareto Optimality. An assignment $p : A \to I \cup \{b_\emptyset\}$ is *pareto optimal* if there does not exist another assignment $q : A \to I \cup \{b_\emptyset\}$ that satisfies: (i) $p(a_i) \leq_{a_i} q(a_i)$ for every $i \in [n]$, and (ii) there exists $i \in [n]$ such that $p(a_i) <_{a_i} q(a_i)$. That is, there does not exist another assignment q that is "at least as good" as p for all the agents, and is "better" for at least one agent. The ASSIGNMENT problem is a special case of the general assignment problem where the criterion of optimality is pareto optimality.

An assignment admits a *trading cycle* $(a_{i_0}, b_{j_0}, a_{i_1}, b_{j_1}, \ldots, a_{i_{k-1}}, b_{j_{k-1}})$ if for each $r \in \{0, \ldots, k-1\}$, we have that $p(a_{i_r}) = b_{j_r}$ and $b_{j_r} <_{a_{i_r}} b_{j_{r+1} \pmod{k}}$. Moreover, we say that p admits a *self loop* if there exist an agent a_i and an item b_j such that b_j is not allocated to any agent by p, and $p(a_i) <_{a_i} b_j$. It is known that an assignment is pareto optimal if and only if it does not admit trading cycles and self loops (see, e.g., Aziz et al. [6,7]). The problem of checking whether an assignment admits trading cycles or self loops can be reduced to checking whether a directed graph contains cycles. For an instance (A, I, P) and an assignment p, the corresponding *trading graph* is the directed graph over $A \cup I$, containing three types of edges: (i) For each $a \in A$ such that $p(a) \neq b_\emptyset$, $p(a)$ points to a; (ii) each agent $a \in A$ points to all the items it prefers over its item $p(a)$; (iii) each item with no owner points to all the agents that accept it. It is known that an assignment is pareto optimal if and only if its corresponding trading graph does not contain cycles (see, e.g., Aziz et al. [6,7]).

Generalization of the Assignment Problem. We introduce a generalized assignment problem where there are ℓ layers of preferences. For each $j \in [\ell]$, we refer to $<_{a_i}^{(j)}$ as a_i's preference list in layer j. The *preference profile in layer j* is the collection of the agents' preference lists in the layer, namely, $P_j = (<_{a_1}^{(j)}, \ldots, <_{a_n}^{(j)})$. Thus, the new problem is defined as follows.

---

[2] All the "optimal" assignments that we construct in this paper will be legal for each agent group in a sufficient number of layers.

MULTI-LAYERED ASSIGNMENT (ML-ASSIGNMENT)
Input: $(A, I, P_1, \ldots, P_\ell)$, where A is a set of n agents, I is a set of m items, P_i is the preference profile in layer i for each $i \in [\ell]$.
Question: Does an "optimal" assignment exist?

New Concepts of Optimality. In [23], we introduced a new concept of optimality that naturally extends pareto optimality by requiring an assignment to be pareto optimal in a given number of layers. It is defined as follows: For an instance $(A, I, P_1, \ldots, P_\ell)$, we say that an assignment p is α-*globally optimal* if there exist α layers $i_1, \ldots, i_\alpha \in [\ell]$ such that p is pareto optimal in layer i_j, for each $j \in [\alpha]$. Thus, in the new problem, α-GLOBALLY OPTIMAL ASSIGNMENT, we are given ℓ preference profiles and a parameter α, and we ask whether there exists an α-globally optimal assignment. Here, we "weaken" this notion. Notice that global optimality requires that there exist α layers with no trading cycles or self loops. That is, there is a "global agreement" among the agents on the layers where they cannot trade and benefit. This requirement seems too strong, thus, instead of requiring the same α layers for all the agents, we will require that each group of agents of a bounded size will have its own α layers where the group cannot exchange their items and benefit. We say that a subset of agents K admits a trading cycle in layer $j \in [\ell]$ if all the agents in K appear (without additional agents) in a trading cycle in P_j. Then, we define three new concepts of optimality as follows.

Definition 1 ((k, α)-*optimality*). *An assignment is (k, α)-optimal for an instance $(A, I, P_1, \ldots, P_\ell)$ if it satisfies that: (i) If $k \geq 2$, then for each subset of agents $K \subseteq A$ such that $|K| = k$, there exist α layers $i_1, \ldots, i_\alpha$ such that K does not admit a trading cycle in layer i_j, for each $j \in [\alpha]$; and (ii) if $k = 1$, then for each $a \in A$, there exist α layers where a does not admit a self loop.*

The definition for (k, α)-upper-bounded optimality is similar, but it applies the first condition on all subsets K such that $|K| \leq k$; and the second condition is always required. Intuitively, these concepts require that each group of (at most) k agents cannot trade and benefit in at least α layers (that may depend on the specific group). In order to show that an assignment p is not (k, α)-optimal (or not (k, α)-upper-bounded optimal), we will provide a set $K \subseteq A$ of (at most) k agents which admits "conflicts" (trading cycles or self loops) in at least $\ell - \alpha + 1$ layers. The third definition further does not allow small groups of agents to be part of larger trading cycles:

Definition 2 ((k, α)-*subset optimality*). *An assignment is (k, α)-subset optimal for an instance $(A, I, P_1, \ldots, P_\ell)$ if it satisfies that: (i) For each subset of agents $K \subseteq A$ such that $|K| = k$, there exist α layers $i_1, \ldots, i_\alpha$ such that, for each $j \in [\alpha]$, there does not exist $K' \subseteq A$ that contains K ($K \subseteq K' \subseteq A$) and admits a trading cycle in layer i_j; and (ii) if $k = 1$, then for each $a \in A$, there exist α layers where it does not admit a self loop.*

Notice that when $k = 1$, both conditions need to be satisfied (we mentioned them separately since the notions of trading cycle and self loop are different).

Clearly, a (k, α)-upper-bounded optimal assignment is also (k', α)-optimal for every $k' \in [k]$, and a (k, α)-subset optimal assignment is also (k, α)-optimal. In the new decision problems, OPTIMAL ASSIGNMENT, UPPER-BOUNDED OPTIMAL ASSIGNMENT, and SUBSET OPTIMAL ASSIGNMENT, we are given an input as in the ML-ASSIGNMENT problem and we ask whether an optimal assignment exist with respect to each one of the definitions above.

Verification Variants. In this paper, we focus on the verification variants of these problems, in which we are additionally given an assignment, and we ask whether it is optimal.

VERIFY OPTIMAL ASSIGNMENT (VERIFY-OA)
Input: $(A, I, P_1, \ldots, P_\ell, \alpha, k, p)$, where A is a set of n agents, I is a set of m items, P_i is the preference profile in layer i for each $i \in [\ell]$, $\alpha \in [\ell]$, $k \in [n]$ and p is an assignment $p : A \to I \cup \{b_\emptyset\}$.
Question: Is p (k, α)-optimal?

The other verification problems, VERIFY UPPER-BOUNDED OPTIMAL ASSIGNMENT (VERIFY-UOA) and VERIFY SUBSET OPTIMAL ASSIGNMENT (VERIFY-SOA), are defined analogously. We study these problems from the perspective of parameterized complexity.

3   Properties of the Concepts of Optimality

We start with some simple properties regarding the notions of (k, α)-optimality, (k, α)-upper-bounded optimality, and (k, α)-subset optimality. Additionally, we prove that VERIFY-OA, VERIFY-UOA, and VERIFY-SOA are in coNP, and that VERIFY-UOA is solvable in polynomial time when $\alpha = \ell$.

Observation 1. *Let $(A, I, P_1, \ldots, P_\ell)$ be an instance of ML-ASSIGNMENT with ℓ layers, and let $p : A \to I \cup \{b_\emptyset\}$ be an assignment. Then, for every $k \in [\|A\|]$ and $\alpha \in [\ell]$, p is (k', α)-optimal for all $k' \in [k]$ (simultaneously) if and only if p is (k, α)-upper-bounded optimal.*

Lemma 1 (*).[3] *Let $(A, I, P_1, \ldots, P_\ell)$ be an instance of ML-ASSIGNMENT with ℓ layers. Let $p : A \to I \cup \{b_\emptyset\}$ be an assignment. Then, the following properties are equivalent: (i) p is (k, ℓ)-optimal for all $k \in [n]$ (simultaneously); (ii) p is (n, ℓ)-upper-bounded optimal; (iii) p is $(1, \ell)$-subset optimal; (iv) p is ℓ-globally optimal.*

Lemma 2 (*). *The problems VERIFY-OA, VERIFY-UOA, and VERIFY-SOA are in coNP.*

Observation 2 (*). *Let $(A, I, P_1, \ldots, P_\ell)$ be an instance of ML-ASSIGNMENT with ℓ layers, and let $p : A \to I \cup \{b_\emptyset\}$ be an assignment. Assume that for each $i \in [\ell]$, P_i does not contain trading cycles containing more than k agents with respect to p. Then, p is (k, α)-optimal if and only if it is (k, α)-subset optimal.*

---

[3] Proofs of statements marked by * are (partially or completely) omitted due to lack of space; full proofs can be found in the full version.

Lemma 3 (*). *Let $(A, I, P_1, \ldots, P_\ell)$ be an instance of* ML-ASSIGNMENT, *let p be an assignment, and let $k \in [n]$. Then: (i) deciding whether p is (k, ℓ)-upper-bounded optimal takes a polynomial time; (ii) deciding whether p is (k', ℓ)-subset optimal for all $k' \in [k]$ (simultaneously) takes a polynomial time.*

4 Fixed-Parameter Tractability

Theorem 1 (*). VERIFY-OA, VERIFY-UOA, *and* VERIFY-SOA *admit kernels of size $\mathcal{O}(\ell \cdot (\#\text{alloc})^2)$.*

Proof (Sketch). The kernels rely on the fact that only agents assigned to items different than $b_\emptyset$ can appear in trading cycles. If $k = 1$, or the input is an instance of VERIFY-UOA, the kernels start with a preprocessing step to verify whether each agent does not admit self loops in (at least) α layers. If some agent admits self loops in $\ell - \alpha + 1$ layers, they return No. Afterwards, the kernels remove from the input all the agents and the items that are unmatched by the assignment. Notice that the resulting instance cannot contain self loops and it is equivalent to the original instance since the trading cycles in each layer remains the same. □

Theorem 2. VERIFY-OA *and* VERIFY-SOA *are solvable in time $\mathcal{O}^*(2^{\#\text{alloc}})$.*

Proof. We provide dynamic programming algorithms. Each begins by running the kernel in Theorem 1, and then it constructs ℓ tables with boolean values. We first define the following:

Definition 3. *Let $(A, I, P_1, \ldots, P_\ell, \alpha, k, p)$ be an instance of* VERIFY-OA, VERIFY-UOA *or* VERIFY-SOA, *and let $s, t \in A$. We say that there is a* trading path *from s to t in layer i if there exist agents $a_1, \ldots, a_r \in A$ such that the trading graph of P_i with respect to p contains the path $p(s) \to s \to p(a_1) \to a_1 \to \ldots \to p(a_r) \to a_r \to p(t) \to t$.*

Notice that a trading cycle is a trading path from an agent to itself. For an agent $s \in A$, we denote $N_i(s) = \{a \in A | (s, p(a)) \text{ is an edge in the trading graph of} P_i\}$. Notice that the trading graph of P_i contains the path $p(s) \to s \to p(a) \to a$ for each $a \in N_i(s)$. We now describe each algorithm separately.

Verify-OA and Verify-UOA: Given an instance $(A, I, P_1, \ldots, P_\ell, \alpha, k, p)$, the algorithm first performs the kernelization algorithm in Theorem 1 to reduce the number of agents to $\#\text{alloc}$. If the kernel returns No, then the algorithm returns false. It initializes ℓ tables with boolean values $M_1, \ldots, M_\ell$, defined as follows. For each $i \in [\ell]$, agents $s, t \in A$ and a subset of agents $X \subseteq A$: $M_i[s, t, X]$ = true if there exists a trading path from s to t that contains only the agents from $X \cup \{s, t\}$ and their assigned items; and $M_i[s, t, X]$ = false otherwise. Notice that $M_i[s, t, \emptyset] = \begin{cases} \text{true if } (s, p(t)) \text{ is an edge in} G_i \\ \text{false otherwise} \end{cases}$, where

G_i is the trading graph of P_i, and that for each $X \subseteq A$ such that $X \neq \emptyset$, $M_i[s,t,X] = \bigvee_{s' \in N_i(s)} M_i[s',t,X \setminus \{s'\}]$. This is because each trading path from s to t must start with an item of some agent from $N_i(s)$. Each table M_i contains $(\#\text{alloc})^2 \cdot 2^{\#\text{alloc}}$ entries and can be constructed in the same running time. The algorithm constructs the ℓ tables, then, it verifies if for each subset of agents $K \subseteq A$ of size k (or at most k for VERIFY-UOA), there exist α layers where it does not admit trading cycles. To perform this, for each such subset K, the algorithm picks a random agent $a \in K$ and verifies whether at least α values among $M_1[a,a,K\setminus\{a\}], \ldots, M_\ell[a,a,K\setminus\{a\}]$ are true. In this case, the algorithm returns true, otherwise, it returns false. The total running time is $\mathcal{O}^*(2^{\#\text{alloc}})$.

Verify-SOA: Here, we first run the algorithm for VERIFY-OA. If it returns false, then we return false as well. Otherwise, we have the ℓ tables $M_1, \ldots, M_\ell$. We need to verify that for each $K \subseteq A$ such that $|K| = k$, the agents from K do not admit trading cycles possibly together with other agents in at least α layers. To adapt to this notion of subset optimality, we define ℓ new tables $N_1, \ldots, N_\ell$. For each $i \in [\ell]$, agents $s, t \in A$, and subset $X \subseteq A$, $N_i[s,t,X] = \text{true}$ if there exists a trading path in layer i from s to t that containing all the agents from $X \cup \{s,t\}$ with their assigned items and possibly additional agents with their assigned items; and $N_i[s,t,X] = \text{false}$ otherwise. Notice that for each $i \in [\ell]$: $N_i[s,t,X] = \bigvee_{Y \subseteq A \text{ s.t. } X \subseteq Y} M_i[s,t,Y] = \bigvee_{Z \subseteq A \setminus X} M_i[s,t,X \cup Z]$. To construct the tables efficiently, we perform the following. Assume that $A = \{a_1, \ldots, a_r\}$ where $r = \#\text{alloc}$. We represent each subset $X \subseteq A$ as a vector of r bits $(x_1, \ldots, x_r)$ such that for each $i \in [r]$, $x_i = 1$ if $a_i \in X$, and $x_i = 0$ otherwise. Observe that $X = (x_1, \ldots, x_r)$ and $Y = (y_1, \ldots, y_r)$ satisfy $X \subseteq Y$ if and only if for each $i \in [r]$: $x_i \leq y_i$. Thus, for every subset $X = (x_1, \ldots, x_r) \subseteq A$, and agents $s, t \in A$, we have that: $N_i[s,t,(x_1, \ldots, x_r)] = \bigvee_{y_1, \ldots, y_r \in \{0,1\}} \delta[x_1 \leq y_1 \wedge \ldots \wedge x_r \leq y_r] \cdot M_i[s,t,(y_1, \ldots, y_r)]$, where δ is an indicator that equals 1 if the expression in it is true, and 0 otherwise. For each $j \in [r]$, we define: $N_i^{(j)}[s,t,(x_1, \ldots, x_r)] = \bigvee_{y_1, \ldots, y_j \in \{0,1\}} \delta[x_1 \leq y_1 \wedge \ldots \wedge x_j \leq y_j] \cdot M_i[s,t,(y_1, \ldots, y_j, x_{j+1}, \ldots, x_r)]$. We also define: $N_i^{(0)}[s,t,(x_1, \ldots, x_r)] = M_i[s,t,(x_1, \ldots, x_r)]$.

Notice that $N_i[s,t,(x_1, \ldots, x_r)] = N_i^{(r)}[s,t,(x_1, \ldots, x_r)]$. We can compute the values $N_i^{(j)}[s,t,(x_1, \ldots, x_r)]$ efficiently by the following observation:

$$N_i^{(j)}[s,t,(x_1, \ldots, x_r)] = \begin{cases} N_i^{(j-1)}[s,t,(x_1, \ldots, x_r)] & \text{if } x_j = 1 \\ N_i^{(j-1)}[s,t,(x_1, \ldots, x_{j-1}, 1, x_{j+1}, \ldots, x_r)] \vee & \text{if } x_j = 0 \\ \quad N_i^{(j-1)}[s,t,(x_1, \ldots, x_{j-1}, 0, x_{j+1}, \ldots, x_r)] \end{cases}$$

Each table N_i^j can be constructed in time $\mathcal{O}(2^{\#\text{alloc}+2})$, thus the total running time is $\mathcal{O}(\ell \cdot \#\text{alloc} \cdot 2^{\#\text{alloc}}) = \mathcal{O}^*(2^{\#\text{alloc}})$. Then, the algorithm verifies whether each subset K does not admit trading cycles with possible other agents similarly as in the algorithm for VERIFY-OA and returns an answer accordingly. Since the parameter #alloc is smaller or equal than $\min\{n, m\}$, we conclude that the problems are FPT w.r.t #alloc, n and m. □

Theorem 3 (*). VERIFY-OA *and* VERIFY-UOA *are solvable in time* $\mathcal{O}^*(n^{\mathcal{O}(k)})$.

Theorem 4 (*). VERIFY-OA *and* VERIFY-UOA *are solvable in time* $\mathcal{O}^*(d^k)$.

Proof (Sketch). The algorithm is based on the observation that, since each agent prefers at most $d - 1$ items over its own assigned item (or at most d if it not allocated an item), the number of possible trading cycles with exactly k agents (or at most k agents if the input is an instance of VERIFY-UOA) is at most $\mathcal{O}(n \cdot d^k)$. The algorithm first performs the kernelization algorithm in Theorem 1 to test whether each agent does not admit self loops in at least α layers, and to reduce the instance size to $\mathcal{O}(\ell \cdot (\#\text{alloc})^2)$. Then, for each $i \in [\ell]$, it considers all the trading cycles in layer i with k (or at most k) agents. For each such trading cycle C, it checks in which other layers the agents in C admit trading cycles (using an $\mathcal{O}^*(2^n)$-time algorithm for HAMILTONIAN CYCLE on directed graphs by Bellman [8]). If it finds that there are at least $\ell - \alpha + 1$ layers where the agents admit trading cycles, then it returns No. □

Theorem 5 (*). VERIFY-OA *and* VERIFY-UOA *are* coW[1]*-hard with respect to the parameter* $k + \ell$.

Proof (Sketch). We provide a parameterized reduction from MULTICOLORED INDEPENDENT SET (proved to be W[1]-hard by Fellows et al. [17]) to the complements of VERIFY-OA and VERIFY-UOA. The input of MULTICOLORED INDEPENDENT SET consists of an undirected graph $G = (V, E)$, an integer $2 \leq \tilde{k} \leq |V|$, and a coloring $c : V \to [\tilde{k}]$ that colors the vertices in G with $\tilde{k}$ colors. The task is to decide whether G admits a *multicolored independent set* of size $\tilde{k}$, which is an independent set of size $\tilde{k}$ whose vertices are colored with all the colors. Given an instance $(G = (V, E), \tilde{k}, c)$, denote $V = \{v_1, \ldots, v_n\}$. We construct an instance with n agents, n items, $\binom{\tilde{k}}{2}$ layers, $\alpha = 1$, $k = \tilde{k}$, and an assignment p. We will prove that there exists a subset of agents of size k that admits trading cycles in all the the layers with respect to p if and only if G contains a multicolored independent set of size $\tilde{k}$. We first create an agent a_i and an item b_i for each vertex $v_i \in V$. Thus, the agent set and the item set of the constructed instance are $A = A_n$ and $I = I_n$, respectively. We also set $p = p_n$ (recall that $p(a_i) = b_i$ for each $i \in [n]$). Intuitively, if there exists a multicolored independent set in G, then the agents corresponding to the vertices in the multicolored independent set will admit trading cycles in all the layers. Each layer corresponds to a pair of colors $\{u, w\}$, and ensures that (i) every trading cycle contains exactly k agents which correspond to vertices colored by all the colors; and (ii) the vertices with the colors u and w whose agents appear in a trading cycle will not be adjacent in G. For each $s \in [\tilde{k}]$, denote $A(s) = \{a_i \in A | c(v_i) = s\}$ and $I(s) = \{b_i \in I | c(v_i) = s\}$, namely, the agents and the items that correspond to vertices colored with s by c. Let $u, w \in [\tilde{k}]$ be two different colors such that $u < w$; and assume that $s_1, \ldots, s_{\tilde{k}-2} \in [\tilde{k}] \setminus \{u, w\}$ such that

$s_1 < \ldots < s_{\widetilde{k}-2}$ (i.e. we sort the colors different than u and w). The preference profile $P^{MCIS}_{\{u,w\}}$ is defined as follows: (i) a_r : $I(s_{j+1}) > b_r \; \forall v_r \in V, j \in [\widetilde{k}-3]$ s.t. $c(v_r) = s_j$; (ii) a_r : $I(u) > b_r \; \forall v_r \in V$ s.t. $c(v_r) = s_{\widetilde{k}-2}$; (iii) a_r : $I(w) \cap \{a_i | \{v_i, v_r\} \notin E\} > b_r \; \forall v_r \in V$ s.t. $c(v_r) = u$; (iv) a_r : $I(s_1) > b_r \; \forall v_r \in V$ s.t. $c(v_r) = w$. We prove that every trading cycle (if exists) in $P^{MCIS}_{\{u,w\}}$ must begin with a sequence $(a_{i_1}, b_{i_1}, \ldots, a_{i_{\widetilde{k}-2}}, b_{i_{\widetilde{k}-2}})$, such that a_{i_j} corresponds to a vertex colored with s_j for each $j \in [\widetilde{k}-2]$; and after that, it contains a sequence $(a_{i_{\widetilde{k}-1}}, b_{i_{\widetilde{k}-1}}, a_{i_{\widetilde{k}}}, b_{i_{\widetilde{k}}})$ such that $a_{i_{\widetilde{k}-1}}$ and $a_{i_{\widetilde{k}}}$ correspond to non-adjacent vertices colored with u and w, respectively. By this claim, we show that a subset of agents of size (at most) k admits trading cycles in all the layers if and only if the corresponding vertices of these agents admit a multicolored independent set of size $\widetilde{k}$ in G (by the form of the trading cycles, this subset must contain agents that correspond to vertices colored with all the colors, and each pair of agents correspond to a non-adjacent pair of vertices of different colors). This proves the correctness of the reduction. Since $k + \ell$ depends only on the parameter $\widetilde{k}$, we have that the two problems are W[1]-hard with respect to $k + \ell$. □

5   coNP-Hardness

In this section, we prove that the problems VERIFY-OA, VERIFY-UOA, and VERIFY-SOA are para-coNP-hard for $\ell + d + (n - k)$. Before that, let us define two preference profiles that we will use in our next proofs. Let $G = (V, E)$ be a directed graph, and suppose that $V = \{v_1, \ldots, v_n\}$. For each vertex in G, we create one agent and one item. We denote the agent set $A_n = \{a_1, \ldots, a_n\}$, the item set $I_n = \{b_1, \ldots, b_n\}$, and the assignment p_n by $p_n(a_i) = b_i$ for each $i \in [n]$. We construct the first preference profile, $P_1(G)$, over A_n and I_n, so that its trading graph with respect to p_n will be derived from the graph G. For each $i \in [n]$, the preference list of a_i in $P_1(G)$ is: a_i : $\{b_j | (v_i, v_j) \in E\}$ (in arbitrary order) $> b_i$.

Lemma 4. *A directed graph G contains a cycle $(v_{i_1}, \ldots, v_{i_t})$ if and only if $P_1(G)$ contains the trading cycle $(a_{i_1}, b_{i_1}, \ldots, a_{i_t}, b_{i_t})$ with respect to p_n.*

Proof. $\Rightarrow$: Suppose that $(v_{i_1}, \ldots, v_{i_t})$ is a cycle in G. Note that there exists a directed edge from v_{i_j} to $v_{i_{j+1}}$ for each $j \in [t-1]$ and from v_t to v_1. Thus, by the construction of $P_1(G)$, a_{i_j} prefers $b_{i_{j+1}}$ over its assigned item $p_n(a_{i_j}) = b_{i_j}$, and a_{i_t} prefers b_{i_1} over its assigned item $p_n(a_{i_t}) = b_{i_t}$. This yields the trading cycle $(a_{i_1}, b_{i_1}, \ldots, a_{i_t}, b_{i_t})$.

$\Leftarrow$: Suppose that $(a_{i_1}, b_{i_1}, \ldots, a_{i_t}, b_{i_t})$ is a trading cycle in $P_1(G)$ with respect to p_n. Then, for each $j \in [t-1]$, a_{i_j} prefers $b_{i_{j+1}}$ over b_{i_j}, and a_{i_t} prefers b_{i_1} over b_{i_t}. By the construction of $P_1(G)$, $(v_{i_j}, v_{i_{j+1}}) \in E$ for each $j \in [t-1]$, and $(v_{i_t}, v_{i_1}) \in E$. This implies that G contains the cycle $(v_{i_1}, \ldots, v_{i_t})$. □

The second preference profile, $P_2(n)$, is constructed so that its trading graph with respect to p_n will contain a single trading cycle over all the agents in A_n.

For each $i \in [n-1]$, the preference list of a_i in $P_2(n)$ is $a_i : b_{i+1} > b_i$, and the preference list of a_n in $P_2(n)$ is $a_n : b_1 > b_n$. Observe that the only trading cycle in $P_2(n)$ is $(a_1, b_1, \ldots, a_n, b_n)$. Intuitively, the goal of $P_2(n)$ is to ensure that if there exists a subset of agents that admit trading cycles in both $P_1(G)$ and $P_2(n)$, then this subset must be equal to A_n. Thus, by Lemma 4, we will conclude that G contains a cycle over all the vertices, i.e. a Hamiltonian cycle.

Lemma 5 (*). *A set $K \subseteq A_n$ admits trading cycles in both $P_1(G)$ and $P_2(n)$ with respect to p_n if and only if $K = A_n$ and G contains a Hamiltonian cycle.*

Proof (Sketch). Since the only trading cycle in $P_2(n)$ consists of all the agents in A_n, we have that $K = A_n$. Lemma 4 implies that G contains a cycle on all the vertices, i.e. a Hamiltonian cycle. □

Using these constructions, we provide a polynomial reduction from HAMILTONIAN CYCLE on directed graphs with maximum degree 3 (NP-hard by Plesník [22]) to the complements of the three problems. This proves the following result.

Theorem 6 (*). VERIFY-OA, VERIFY-UOA, *and* VERIFY-SOA *are coNP-hard when $k = n$, $\ell = 1$ ($\ell = 2$ for VERIFY-UOA), $\alpha = 1$, and $d = 3$.*

6   Non-existence of Polynomial Kernels

In this section, we prove that the three problems are unlikely to admit polynomial kernels with respect to $n+m+\alpha$ and $n+m+(\ell-\alpha)$. So, considering α or $(\ell-\alpha)$ rather than ℓ, even while considering the larger parameter $n + m$ rather than #alloc, yields negative results. So, our classification is complete in this sense.

Theorem 7 (*). VERIFY-OA, VERIFY-UOA, *and* VERIFY-SOA *do not admit polynomial kernels with respect to $n + m + \alpha$ and $n + m + (\ell - \alpha)$, unless* NP $\subseteq$ coNP/poly.

Proof (Sketch). For VERIFY-OA and VERIFY-SOA, we provide a cross-composition from HAMILTONIAN CYCLE on directed graphs with maximum degree 3 to the complements of the problems. Given t directed graphs with the same number of vertices n and maximum degree 3, $G_1, \ldots, G_t$. Suppose that $V(G_i) = \{v_1, \ldots, v_n\}$ for each $i \in [t]$. We construct an instance of $\overline{\text{VERIFY-OA}}$ (or $\overline{\text{VERIFY-UOA}}$) with $\ell = t$ layers over the agent set A_n and the item set I_n, such that for each $i \in [t]$, layer i contains the preference profile $P_1(G_i)$ (defined in Sect. 5). By Lemma 4, a subset of k agents admits a trading cycle in some layer $i \in [t]$ if and only if G_i is a Yes-instance. So, for the parameter $n + m + \alpha$, we set $k = n$ and $\alpha = 1$, and we treat the cross-composition as an AND-cross-composition. Notice that there exists a subset of k agents that admits trading cycles in all the layers if and only if all the input graphs are Yes-instances. For the parameter $n + m + (\ell - \alpha)$, we set $k = n$, $\alpha = \ell$, and we treat the cross-composition as an OR-cross-composition since there exists a subset of k agents that admits trading cycles in at least one layer if and only if at least one input graph is a Yes-instance. Since the parameters $n + m + \alpha$ (in the first cross-composition) and $n + m + (\ell - \alpha)$ (in the second cross-composition) are polynomial in $\max_{i=1}^{t} |G_i|$, we conclude that VERIFY-OA and VERIFY-SOA do not admit polynomial kernels with respect to them, unless $\mathsf{NP} \subseteq \mathsf{coNP/poly}$.

Verify-UOA: We focus on the parameter $n + m + (\ell - \alpha)$. We provide an OR-cross-composition from HAMILTONIAN CYCLE on directed graphs with maximum degree 3 to $\overline{\text{VERIFY-UOA}}$, which extends the previous cross-compositions. Given t directed graphs with n vertices and maximum degree 3, $G_1, \ldots, G_t$, we construct an instance of $\overline{\text{VERIFY-UOA}}$ that is a Yes-instance if and only if at least one of the input graphs admits a Hamiltonian cycle. Assume that $V(G_i) = V = \{v_1, \ldots, v_n\}$ for each $i \in [t]$. Denote the agent set $C = \{c_i | i \in [\lfloor \log t \rfloor + 1]\} \cup \{\overline{c_i} | i \in [\lfloor \log t \rfloor + 1]\}$ and the item set $D = \{d_i | i \in [\lfloor \log t \rfloor + 1]\} \cup \{\overline{d_i} | i \in [\lfloor \log t \rfloor + 1]\}$. Intuitively, these sets will "encode" the index of each input graph, and will be parts of unique trading cycles for each input graph. The agent set and the item set of the constructed instance are $A = A_n \cup C$ and $I = B_n \cup D$, respectively. We define the assignment $p : A \to I$ by $p(a_i) = b_i$ for each $i \in [n]$; and $p(c_i) = d_i$, $p(\overline{c_i}) = \overline{d_i}$ for each $i \in [\lfloor \log t \rfloor + 1]$. Notice that p restricted to A_n is equal to p_n. We construct $2t$ layers: informally, each input graph G_i will have two corresponding layers, $2i - 1$ and $2i$, which are compositions of the preference profiles $P_1(G_i)$ or $P_2(n)$ for each graph G_i together with unique $2(\lfloor \log t \rfloor + 1)$ preference lists for the agents in C. Intuitively, the goal of the agents and items in $C \cup D$ is to ensure that for each $i \in [t]$, there is a unique subset $C' \subseteq C$ of size $\lfloor \log t \rfloor + 1$ that is part of trading cycles in both layers $2i - 1$ and $2i$. This will imply that if there exists a subset of agents from $A_n \cup C$ that admits trading cycles in both trading graphs of these layers, then this subset is a unique subset of size $n + \lfloor \log t \rfloor + 1$ that does not admit trading cycles in the rest of the layers. If G_i contains a Hamiltonian cycle, then we will have in layers $2i - 1$ and $2i$ similar trading cycles as in the trading graphs of $P_1(G_i)$ and $P_2(n)$, but appended with a chain of $\lfloor \log t \rfloor + 1$ agents from C. For $i \in [t]$, we denote by $i[j]$ the j'th bit in the binary representation of i, for each $j \in [\lfloor \log t \rfloor + 1]$. For each $i \in [t]$ and $j \in [\lfloor \log t \rfloor + 1]$, denote $c_j^i = c_j$ if $i[j] = 1$ and $c_j^i = \overline{c_j}$ if $i[j] = 0$. Similarly, $d_j^i = d_j$ if $i[j] = 1$ and $d_j^i = \overline{d_j}$ if $i[j] = 0$. Notice that $p(c_j^i) = d_j^i$. Assume that $\overline{\overline{c_j}} = c_j$ for each $j \in [\lfloor \log t \rfloor + 1]$. For each $i \in [t]$, we create two preference profiles Q_{2i-1} and Q_{2i}, appearing in layers $2i - 1$ and $2i$, respectively (the preference profiles are given formally in the full version). We finally set $k = n + \lfloor \log t \rfloor + 1$ and $\alpha = \ell - 1 = 2n - 1$, so $\ell - \alpha + 1 = 2$. We prove that $W = (a_{j_1}, b_{j_1}, \ldots, a_{j_n}, b_{j_n})$ is a trading cycle in $P_1(G_i)$ with respect to p_n (when $j_n = n$) if and only if $W' = (a_{j_1}, b_{j_1}, \ldots, a_{j_n}, b_{j_n}, c_1^i, d_1^i, \ldots, c_{\lfloor \log t \rfloor + 1}^i, d_{\lfloor \log t \rfloor + 1}^i)$ is a trading cycle in Q_{2i-1} with respect to p; and that the only trading cycle in Q_{2i} with respect to p is $(a_1, b_1, \ldots, a_n, b_n, c_1^i, d_1^i, \ldots, c_{\lfloor \log t \rfloor + 1}^i, d_{\lfloor \log t \rfloor + 1}^i)$. The correctness of the cross composition is derived by using these claims. The construction can be clearly implemented in polynomial time in $\sum_{i=1}^{t} |G_i|$. Notice that $n + m + (\ell - \alpha) = 2n + 4(\lfloor \log t \rfloor + 1) + 1 = poly(\max_{i=1}^{t} |G_i| + \log(t))$ for the constructed instance. Thus, VERIFY-UOA does not admit a polynomial kernel with respect to $n + m + (\ell - \alpha)$, unless $\mathsf{NP} \subseteq \mathsf{coNP/poly}$. $\qquad\square$

7   Conclusion and Future Research

In this paper, we introduced a generalization of the verification variant of the general assignment problem where each agent is equipped with multiple incomplete preference lists. We defined three natural concepts of optimality, we considered several natural parameters and we presented an almost comprehensive picture of the parameterized complexity of the corresponding problems with respect to them. We proved that the problems are para-coNP-hard with respect to $\ell+d+(n-k)$. We also proved that the three problems admit polynomial kernels when parameterized by #alloc $+ \ell$, but that they are unlikely to admit polynomial kernels with respect to $n+m+\alpha$ and $n+m+(\ell-\alpha)$. Additionally, we proved that the problems are coW[1]-hard with respect to $k + \ell$. However, we showed that VERIFY-OA and VERIFY-UOA admit XP algorithms with respect to k, and even FPT algorithms with respect to $k + d$. We also provided $\mathcal{O}^*(2^{\#\text{alloc}})$-time algorithms for the three problems. This proved that the problems are FPT with respect to the parameters #alloc, n, and m. Still, two questions remained open: (1) Is it possible to obtain an $\mathcal{O}^*((2 - \varepsilon)^{\#\text{alloc}})$-time algorithm, for some fixed $\varepsilon > 0$, for each one of the problems? (2) Does VERIFY-UOA admit XP algorithms with respect to the parameters k, $k + \ell$, and $k + d$?

Additional Directions for Future Research. Continuing our research, it may be interesting to consider a new concept of optimality: in the full version, we formally define the new notion of (k, α)-*ordered optimality*, which weakens the notion of (k, α)-optimality as follows. Consider an instance $(A, I, P_1, \ldots, P_\ell, k, \alpha, p)$ of VERIFY-OA for which p is not (k, α)-optimal. Thus, there exists a group of k agents which admits trading cycles (where agents may appear in any order) in some $\ell - \alpha + 1$ layers. Since the trading cycles in these layers are not necessarily the same, there may not exist one "strategy" that solves all these conflicts and improves the status of the agents in K at once. In particular, if the agents in the group perform a possible beneficial trade in one layer, their status may get worse in other layers. Thus, one can claim that p can be "optimal" since each "small" group cannot benefit in some $\ell - \alpha + 1$ layers in parallel. Informally, (k, α)-ordered optimality considers the *order* of the trading cycles and requires that for each subset of agents of size k, there exist some α layers where the agents in the subset cannot perform *the same* beneficial trade. Thus, as a direction for future research we propose to study the new decision and verification problems: ORDERED OPTIMAL ASSIGNMENT and VERIFY ORDERED OPTIMAL ASSIGNMENT (which correspond to (k, α)-ordered optimality).

We remark that no notion of optimality is better or worse, but the choice depends on the scenario at hand. For example, will a subset of k agents rebel if it finds many layers where it is dissatisfied, or only if it actually has a strategy that improves its situation? More philosophically, how do we know if our assignment is good or bad? From a public opinion point of view, the unordered variant may make more sense, but from a practitioner's point of view (who should actually improve an assignment if need be), the ordered variant might make more sense.

We also remark that when $k = n$, the unordered version corresponds to global optimality, while the ordered version does not.

Another direction is to consider weighted versions of the problems. In this paper, we considered the basic "unweighed" model of the problems (since this is the first study of this kind). That is, all the criteria (layers) have the same importance. There are cases where some criteria may have higher importance than others, and we would like to give them a higher weight. A straightforward way to model these cases is by having several copies of layers. However, if weights are high and varied, this might lead to inefficiency.

Lastly, we suggest to test our results practically, i.e. implementing the algorithms for the problems, and testing them on real data sets. Besides the analysis of running times in practice, we find it interesting to see how much effect does using different notions of optimality has on the solutions.

References

1. Abdulkadiroğlu, A., Sönmez, T.: House allocation with existing tenants. J. Econ. Theory **88**(2), 233–260 (1999)
2. Abdulkadiroglu, A., Sonmez, T.: Random serial dictatorship and the core from random endowments in house allocation problems. Econometrica **66**(3), 689–702 (1998). https://ideas.repec.org/a/ecm/emetrp/v66y1998i3p689-702.html
3. Abraham, D.J., Cechlárová, K., Manlove, D.F., Mehlhorn, K.: Pareto optimality in house allocation problems. In: Fleischer, R., Trippen, G. (eds.) ISAAC 2004. LNCS, vol. 3341, pp. 3–15. Springer, Heidelberg (2004). https://doi.org/10.1007/978-3-540-30551-4_3
4. Alderfer, C.P., McCord, C.G.: Personal and situational factors in the recruitment interview. J. Appl. Psychol. **54**(4), 377 (1970)
5. Ashlagi, I., Gamarnik, D., Rees, M.A., Roth, A.E.: The need for (long) chains in kidney exchange. Technical report, National Bureau of Economic Research (2012)
6. Aziz, H., Biro, P., de Haan, R., Rastegari, B.: Pareto optimal allocation under compact uncertain preferences. In: Thirty Third AAAI Conference on Artificial Intelligence, 01 February 2019 (2018). https://eprints.soton.ac.uk/425734/
7. Aziz, H., de Haan, R., Rastegari, B.: Pareto optimal allocation under uncertain preferences. In: Proceedings of the Twenty-Sixth International Joint Conference on Artificial Intelligence, IJCAI-17, pp. 77–83 (2017). https://doi.org/10.24963/ijcai.2017/12
8. Bellman, R.: Dynamic programming treatment of the travelling salesman problem. J. ACM **9**(1), 61–63 (1962)
9. Björklund, A., Husfeldt, T., Kaski, P., Koivisto, M.: Fourier meets möbius: Fast subset convolution. In: Proceedings of the Thirty-Ninth Annual ACM Symposium on Theory of Computing, STOC 2007, pp. 67–74. Association for Computing Machinery, New York (2007). https://doi.org/10.1145/1250790.1250801
10. Bogomolnaia, A., Moulin, H.: A new solution to the random assignment problem. J. Econ. Theory **100**, 295–328 (2001)
11. Chen, J., Niedermeier, R., Skowron, P.: Stable marriage with multi-modal preferences. In: Proceedings of the 2018 ACM Conference on Economics and Computation, EC 2018, pp. 269–286. Association for Computing Machinery, New York (2018). https://doi.org/10.1145/3219166.3219168

12. Chernichovsky, D., Kfir, R.: The state of the acute care hospitalization system in Israel. State of the Nation Report (2019)
13. Clinedinst, M.: State of college admission (2019)
14. Dickerson, J.P., Manlove, D.F., Plaut, B., Sandholm, T., Trimble, J.: Position-indexed formulations for kidney exchange. In: Proceedings of the 2016 ACM Conference on Economics and Computation, pp. 25–42 (2016)
15. Dickerson, J.P., Procaccia, A.D., Sandholm, T.: Optimizing kidney exchange with transplant chains: theory and reality. In: Proceedings of the 11th International Conference on Autonomous Agents and Multiagent Systems, vol. 2, pp. 711–718 (2012)
16. Fearnhead, P., Taylor, B.M.: On estimating the ability of NBA players. J. Quant. Anal. Sports **7**(3) (2011)
17. Fellows, M., Hermelin, D., Rosamond, F., Vialette, S.: On the parameterized complexity of multiple-interval graph problems. Theor. Comput. Sci. **410**, 53–61 (2009). https://doi.org/10.1016/j.tcs.2008.09.065
18. Floyd, R.W.: Algorithm 97: shortest path. Commun. ACM **5**(6), 345 (1962)
19. Gourvès, L., Lesca, J., Wilczynski, A.: Object allocation via swaps along a social network. In: 26th International Joint Conference on Artificial Intelligence (IJCAI2017), Melbourne, Australia, pp. 213–219 (2017). https://doi.org/10.24963/ijcai.2017/31. https://hal.archives-ouvertes.fr/hal-01741519
20. Kinicki, A.J., Lockwood, C.A.: The interview process: an examination of factors recruiters use in evaluating job applicants. J. Vocat. Behav. **26**(2), 117–125 (1985). https://doi.org/10.1016/0001-8791(85)90012-0. https://www.sciencedirect.com/science/article/pii/0001879185900120
21. Lian, J.W., Mattei, N., Noble, R., Walsh, T.: The conference paper assignment problem: using order weighted averages to assign indivisible goods (2018). https://www.aaai.org/ocs/index.php/AAAI/AAAI18/paper/view/17396
22. Plesník, J.: The np-completeness of the hamiltonian cycle problem in planar digraphs with degree bound two. Inf. Process. Lett. **8**(4), 199–201 (1979)
23. Steindl, B., Zehavi, M.: Parameterized analysis of assignment under multiple preferences. arXiv preprint arXiv:2004.00655 (2020)
24. The Council for Higher Education and The Planning and Budgeting Committee: the higher education system in Israel (2014)
25. Wu, K., DeVriese, A.: How students pick their housing situations: factors and analysis (2016)
26. Zhou, L.: On a conjecture by gale about one-sided matching problems. J. Econ. Theory **52**(1), 123–135 (1990). https://EconPapers.repec.org/RePEc:eee:jetheo:v:52:y:1990:i:1:p:123-135

Logic and Model Checking by Imprecise Probabilistic Interpreted Systems

Alberto Termine[1]([⊠]), Alessandro Antonucci[2], Giuseppe Primiero[1], and Alessandro Facchini[2]

[1] Department of Philosophy, University of Milan, Milan, Italy
{alberto.termine,giuseppe.primiero}@unimi.it
[2] Istituto Dalle Molle di Studi sull'Intelligenza Artificiale (IDSIA), USI-SUPSI, Lugano, Switzerland
{alessandro,alessandro.facchini}@idsia.ch

Abstract. Stochastic multi-agent systems raise the necessity to extend probabilistic model checking to the epistemic domain. Results in this direction have been achieved by epistemic extensions of Probabilistic Computation Tree Logic and related Probabilistic Interpreted Systems. The latter, however, suffer of an important limitation: they require the probabilities governing the system's behaviour to be *fully* specified. A promising way to overcome this limitation is represented by *imprecise probabilities*. In this paper we introduce imprecise probabilistic interpreted systems and present a related logical language and model-checking procedures based on recent advances in the study of imprecise Markov processes.

Keywords: Probabilistic Interpreted Systems · Imprecise Markov chains · Imprecise probabilities · Model checking

1 Introduction

Probabilistic model checking arises in connection with the specification and verification of computational systems of stochastic nature. Broadly speaking, it includes a series of languages for specifying probabilistic properties of stochastic systems and relative semantics based on Markov models [3]. Notable examples of logical languages for property specification are PCTL [14], its extensions (PCTL*, PRCTL) and CSL [3]. Probabilistic model checking has been applied to many different fields, such as software verification [7], communication protocols [6], and even computational biology [5,8].

In recent years, the increasing relevance of stochastic multi agent systems (MAS for short) has raised the necessity of extending probabilistic model checking to languages endowed with epistemic modalities. Given its popularity, it has

G. Primiero—Supported by the project "Departments of Excellence 2018–2022", Ministry of Education, University and Research (MIUR).
A. Facchini—Supported by the Hasler foundation grant n. 20061.

A. Rosenfeld and N. Talmon (Eds.): EUMAS 2021, LNAI 12802, pp. 211–227, 2021.
https://doi.org/10.1007/978-3-030-82254-5_13

been natural to propose *epistemic* extensions of probabilistic model checking, in particular within the field of MAS verification. Regarding property specification, these extensions result in a series of languages merging PCTL and standard epistemic operators for both single and multi-agent knowledge and belief (e.g. in [9,26]). Regarding model specification, these extensions exploit the formalism of so-called *Probabilistic Interpreted Systems* (PIS), a class of structures obtained by merging standard interpreted systems [24] with Markov models [3]. For example, [26] introduces the logic PCTLK to represent probabilistic knowledge in stochastic MASs. The logic is conceived to merge PCTL and epistemic operators, the former modelled through a probabilistic state-transition matrix, as in standard PCTL, the latter modelled by epistemic accessibility relations as in canonical interpreted systems. Furthermore, the paper proves the reducibility of relevant model-checking tasks for PCTLK to more standard model-checking procedures implementable in *PRISM*, the canonical software tool to model-check probabilistic systems [18].

Despite their success, standard probabilistic model-checking and its epistemic extensions suffer the limitation of requiring the probabilities describing the system behaviour to be precisely defined. This represents a problem especially for epistemic domains, because it is tantamount to assuming that an agent *always* knows *precisely* all the probability values describing each possible state-transition of the system. In other words, it is impossible to model agents with an high-order uncertainty about transition probabilities. This is the case, for instance, when agents in a MAS (partially) ignore the stochastic behaviour of other agents in the system. A possible way to overcome this limitation is represented by so-called parametric Markov models [2,10], which replace precise probabilities with unknown parameters. In [2] for instance, the authors introduce an extension of PCTL specific for parametric Markov chains. The complexity of the corresponding model-checking procedure, based on *fraction-free Gaussian elimination*, is however exponential in the number of states of the models, hence limiting its applicability only to models of small size.

An alternative, but poorly explored, approach is offered by the formalism of imprecise probabilities [25] and, for what interests us here, related imprecise Markov models such as imprecise Markov chains (IMC) [13,16,23]. Roughly, IMCs are the imprecise counterparts of precise Markov chains obtained by replacing precise probability distributions with so-called Credal sets, i.e., sets of probability distributions describing the model and compatible with some specific constraints given by the agents [11].

A first attempt to extend probabilistic model-checking to imprecise probabilities has been proposed in [23], which introduces an *imprecise* PCTL with a semantics based on discrete-time imprecise Markov chains (IMC). The language for properties specification is obtained by replacing the standard probability operator with an operator for representing lower and upper bounds of imprecise probability distributions. Model checking with respect to the new probability operators is reduced to the computation of lower and upper bounds of marginal probabilities on an IMC. These bounds are computed efficiently by means of specific transition operators whose applicability is an optimisation task solvable through linear programming. This approach enables the authors to verify that shifting from precise to imprecise probabilistic models does not affect the overall complexity of the most relevant model-checking procedures. Another example of imprecise probabilistic model-checking is offered in [21], which proposes a semantics and corresponding model-checking procedures based on imprecise Markov reward models. Differently from [23], the model-checking procedures outlined by [21] are based on an algorithm proposed by [22] for computing, among others, lower and upper bounds of *hitting probabilities*. The present work extends the results presented in [21] with the as yet unexplored application of model-checking with *imprecise* probabilistic models to the *epistemic domain*.

The paper is structured as follows. In Sect. 2 we recap some background knowledge about Markov models and their imprecise counterparts. In Sect. 2.2 we introduce *imprecise probabilistic interpreted systems*, a new kind of structures conceived as the imprecise counterparts of the probabilistic interpreted systems proposed in [26]. In Sect. 3 we introduce a new language, called *epistemic imprecise* PCTL (EIPCTL) extending standard PCTL with new *imprecise-probabilistic*, *epistemic* and *doxastic* operators. In Sect. 3.2 we introduce a proper semantics for EIPCTL based on imprecise probabilistic interpreted systems. In Sect. 4 we discuss relevant procedures for model checking imprecise probabilistic interpreted systems against EIPCTL formulae. Interestingly, we verify that shifting to imprecise probabilities does not affect the overall computational complexity of the relevant model-checking tasks, which therefore remains polynomial in the number of states of the models. In Sect. 5, we propose a simple illustrative example. Finally, in Sect. 6 we underline some conclusive remarks about future extensions.

2   Background

Let $\mathcal{S}$ denote a finite non-empty set of possible states and S a variable taking its values from $\mathcal{S}$. A *probability mass-function* (PMF) over S, denoted as $P(S)$, is a non-negative normalized real map defined over $\mathcal{S}$. Furthermore, given a real-values function f of S, its *expectation* based on $P(S)$, denoted $E_P[f]$, is defined as: $E[f] := \sum_{s \in \mathcal{S}} f \cdot P(S)$. A *joint* PMF $P(S', S)$ is a PMF that gives for each pair of states s, s' the probability that s and s' jointly occur. A *conditional* PMF instead, defined as $P(S'|s) := \{P(s', s)/P(s)\}_{\forall s' \in \mathcal{S}}$, is a PMF that assigns to each $s' \in \mathcal{S}$ the probability of s' to occur given that s occurred. Furthermore, if $P(s'|s) = P(s')$ for each $s' \in \mathcal{S}$, we say that S' is (stochastically) *irrelevant* to s. It is easy to check that stochastic irrelevance and independence are equivalent.

A *Credal Set* (CS) over S, denoted by $K(S)$, is a collection of PMFs over S compatible with some given constraints. We consider here only finitely generated CSs, i.e., CSs whose convex hull has only a finite number of extreme points. Given a function f of S, its *upper expectation* with respect to $K(S)$ is defined as $\overline{E}_P[f] := \sup_{P(S) \in K(S)} E_P[f]$ while the lower expectation is defined as $\underline{E} := \inf_{P(S) \in K(S)} E_P[f]$. Furthermore, as stated by [11], suprema (infima) of upper (lower) expectations can be equivalently reduced to maxima (mimima) over the extreme points of the CS convexification. Consequently, we can identify a CS with the extreme points of its convex hull. Given a joint CS $K(S, S')$, defined as a collection of joint PMFs $P(S, S')$, the (marginal) CS $K(S')$ is obtained by element-wise marginalization of S on its elements. At the same time, if $P(s) > 0$ for each $P(S) \in K(S)$, the conditional CS $K(S'|s)$ can be obtained by element-wise conditioning. Finally, we say that S is *epistemically* irrelevant to S' if and only if $K(S'|s) = K(S')$ for each $s \in S$. It is easy to check that epistemic irrelevance is the generalization to the formalism of CSs of the standard notion of stochastic irrelevance. Although in the present paper we decide to adopt *epistemic irrelevance* as the standard generalization of stochastic irrelevance, other possible ways of representing it are based on stochastic independence of the CS elements, or of the CS extreme points (usually called, respectively, *strict* and *strong* irrelevance) [12]. All these notions are equivalent for unconditional queries [17], as it is the case for most of the inferential tasks considered in this work.

2.1   Markovian Models

Precise Markov Chains. A precise discrete-time Markov Chain (MC, for short) is a family of categorical stochastic variables $\{S_t\}_{t \in \mathbf{N}}$ taking their values from S, that satisfies the *Markov* property, i.e., $P(S_{t+1}|S_t) = P(S_{t+1}|S_t, \ldots, S_0)$, and the *stationarity* assumption, i.e. $P(S_{t+1}|S_t)$ is the same for each $t \in \mathbf{N}$. Given the Markov property and the stationarity assumption, a MC can be fully described by a single *transition matrix* $T : S^2 \mapsto [0, 1]$ such that $T(s, s') := P(S_{t+1} = s'|S_t = s)$ for each $(s, s') \in S^2$ and a $t \in \mathbf{N}$ whose choice is arbitrary because of stationarity.

To compute relevant inferences in MCs it is useful to introduce a *transition operator* $\hat{T}$ and its *dual* $\hat{T}^\dagger$. The former maps a non-negative real function f defined over S to its left scalar product, i.e.:

$$(\hat{T}f)(s) := \sum_{s' \in S} T(s', s) \cdot f(s'); \tag{1}$$

for each $s \in S$; while the latter maps the same function on the right scalar product, i.e.:

$$(\hat{T}^\dagger f)(s) := \sum_{s' \in S} T(s, s') \cdot f(s'); \tag{2}$$

for each $s \in S$. It is easy to check that $\hat{T}P(S_t) = P(S_{t+1})$ hence, by the well-known total probability theorem, $\hat{T}^t P(S_0) = P(S_t)$. Similarly, it is also easy to check that $\hat{T}^\dagger f(S_t) = E[f(S_{t+1})|S_t]$ hence, by definition of conditional expectation, $((\hat{T}^\dagger))^t f(S_0))(s) = E[f(S_t)|S_0 = s]$.

Notice that, given an *event* $B \subseteq S$ and the indicator vector $\mathbf{I}_B$ of B, the $\hat{T}$ operator allows to efficiently compute the marginal probability of B, i.e., $P(S_t \in B) := \hat{T}^t \mathbf{I}_B$. Similarly, its dual $\hat{T}^\dagger$ is useful for computing the *hitting probability* vector h_B, i.e. the vector that provides for each $s \in S$ the probability of reaching a given event $B \subseteq S$ from s *eventually* in the future. According to standard literature [3,19], h_B is defined as the vector of the *minimal* solutions, for each $s \in S$, of the following system of linear equations:

$$h_B(s) := \begin{cases} 1 \text{ if } s \in B, \\ \sum_{s' \in S} h_B(s') \text{ otherwise} \end{cases} \tag{3}$$

For MCs with a finite time-horizon $t \in \mathbf{N}$ an efficient algorithm to solve the above system in time polynomial in $|S|$ is the following. Let h_B^t denote the *bounded-time* hitting probability vector providing, for each $s \in S$, the probability of reaching B until a number of time-steps less than or equal to t. Let $\mathbf{I}_B$ denote the indicator function of B returning, for each $s \in S$, 1 if $s \in B$ and 0 otherwise. For $t = 0$, h_B^t is given by

$$h_B^{t=0} = \mathbf{I}_B. \tag{4}$$

The probability of reaching B in 0 time-steps can corresponds only to 1 or 0 depending on whether the actual state is included in the event B or not. Given $\mathbf{I}_B$ and $\mathbf{I}_{B^c}$, respectively the indicator vector of B and of the complement of B, the algorithm proceeds by computing h_B^τ for increasing values of $\tau := 0, 1, \ldots, t$ as follows:

$$h_B^\tau = \mathbf{I}_B + \mathbf{I}_{B^c} \cdot [\hat{T}^\dagger h_B^{\tau-1}], \tag{5}$$

where the sums and the products are intended as element-wise operations on the vector arrays.

Obviously, this procedure allows to compute h_B^t only for finite time horizons $t \in \mathbf{N}$. The standard definition of hitting probability, however, is conceived for MCs of possibly infinite time-length and refers to the probability of reaching B *eventually* in the future. Intuitively, the computation of h_B corresponds to compute $\lim_{\tau \to +\infty} h_B^\tau$. As under the *stationary* hypothesis it has been proved that $\lim_{\tau \to +\infty} h_B^\tau$ is always defined [19], it is possible to approximate the values of h_B through Eq. 5 by iterating h_B^τ over increasing values of τ until convergence.

Imprecise Markov Chains. An *imprecise Markov chain* (IMC) is the imprecise counterpart of a MC. It is obtained replacing the initial PMF $P(S_0)$ with a CS $K(S_0)$ and all the conditional PMFs $\{P(S_{t+1}|s_t)\}_{s_t \in S}$ with conditional CSs $\{K(S_{t+1}|s_t)\}_{s \in S}$. The imprecise counterpart of the *stationarity* hypothesis consists of assuming the specification of the collections of CSs $K(S_{t+1}|S_t)$ independent of t. As for standard MCs, under the stationarity hypothesis, a compact specification of the CSs can be achieved in terms of an initial CS $K(S_0)$ and a collection $\{K(S'|s)\}_{s \in S}$ of *transition* CSs. The collection of CSs can be seen as an *imprecise* transition matrix $\mathcal{T} := \{K(S'|s)\}_{s \in S}$ whose rows consist of the transition CSs $K(S'|s)$ for each $s \in S$. This matrix provides a full specification of the stochastic behaviour of the system modelled by the IMC [12]. Similarly, the linear transition operator in Eqs. (1) and its dual in (2) are replaced in IMCs with analogous *non-linear* operators for modelling, respectively, the *lower* and *upper* bounds of transition probabilities. Following [23, Definition 14], in particular, the *upper* transition operator, denoted by $\overline{\mathcal{T}}$, is defined as follows:

$$(\overline{\mathcal{T}} f)(s) := \sup_{T(S',s) \in K(S'|s)} \sum_{\forall s' \in \mathcal{S}} T(s', s) \cdot f(s') \tag{6}$$

while its dual [22, Eq. 1], denoted by $\overline{\mathcal{T}}^{\dagger}$, is defined as follows:

$$(\overline{\mathcal{T}}^{\dagger} f)(s) := \sup_{T(s,S') \in K(S'|s)} \sum_{\forall s' \in \mathcal{S}} T(s, s') \cdot f(s') \tag{7}$$

The analogous *lower* operators, denoted respectively by $\underline{\mathcal{T}}$ and $\underline{\mathcal{T}}^{\dagger}$ can be defined by replacing the *supremum* in Eqs. (6) and (7) with an *infimum*. Notice that, the optimization for (7) is a linear programming task whose feasible region is the convex hull generated by $K(S'|s)$ that can be described by a finite number of linear constraints, see [25].

Similarly to precise MCs, these operators can be used to compute lower and upper bounds of, respectively, *marginal* and *hitting* probabilities. In particular, as recently proved in [23, Eq. 34, 35], the lower $\underline{P}(S_t \in B)$ and upper $\overline{P}(S_t \in B)$ bounds of the marginal probability $P(S_t \in B)$ for a number $t \in \mathbf{N}$ of time-steps can be computed by t application of the lower (upper) transition operator to the indicator vector $\mathbf{I}_B$ of B, i.e.:

$$\underline{P}(S_t \in B) := \underline{\mathcal{T}}^t \mathbf{I}_B \tag{8}$$

$$\overline{P}(S_t \in B) := \overline{\mathcal{T}}^t \mathbf{I}_B \tag{9}$$

Similarly, [16, Lemma 14] and [22] proved that a recursive schema analogous to 5 can be used to compute, respectively, the *lower* $\underline{h}_B^t$ and the *upper* $\overline{h}_B^t$ hitting probability vectors for IMCs of a finite time length $t \in \mathbf{N}$. As in the precise case, the initialization for both $\underline{h}_B^{t=0}$ and $\overline{h}_B^{t=0}$ is given by the indicator vector of B, while the recursive steps are defined as follows:

$$\underline{h}_B^{\tau} = \mathbf{I}_B + \mathbf{I}_{B^c} \underline{\mathcal{T}}^{\dagger} \underline{h}_B^{\tau-1}, \tag{10}$$

$$\overline{h}_B^{\tau} = \mathbf{I}_B + \mathbf{I}_{B^c} \overline{\mathcal{T}}^{\dagger} \overline{h}_B^{\tau-1}; \tag{11}$$

These definitions, similarly to their analogous for precise MCs in Eq. (5), allow to compute the lower and upper hitting probability vectors only for IMCs of finite time length. As in the precise case, however, the generalization to IMCs of infinite time length can be obtained by computing the respective limits: $\lim_{\tau \to +\infty} \underline{h}_B^{\tau}$ and $\lim_{\tau \to +\infty} \overline{h}_B^{\tau}$. As proved in [16, Prop 16], these limits are defined. Consequently, the values of the lower $\underline{h}_B$ and the upper $\overline{h}_B$ hitting probability vectors for IMCs of infinite time length can be approximated by iterating both (10) and (11) for increasing values of τ until converge.

Labelled Markov Chains. When dealing with model-checking tasks, we need to refer to *labelled* MCs (respectively, labelled IMCs), which are standard MCs (respectively, IMCs) augmented with a set of atomic propositions $AP := \{p, q, \ldots\}$ and a labelling function $l : \mathcal{S} \mapsto 2^{AP}$ that assigns to each $s \in \mathcal{S}$ a set $l(s) \subseteq AP$. From now on, when talking about MCs (respectively, IMCs) we always refer to their labelled extensions.

2.2 Probabilistic Interpreted Systems

Precise PISs. In computational logic, *probabilistic interpreted systems* (PIS) are usually considered the reference formalism for representing knowledge and beliefs in stochastic MASs [26]. A PIS is a tuple:

$$M_{\text{PIS}} := \langle \mathcal{S}, \mathcal{A}, \{\sim^i\}_{i \in \mathcal{A}}, \{T^i\}_{i \in \mathcal{A}}, AP, l(s) \rangle; \tag{12}$$

consisting of a finite non-empty set of states $\mathcal{S}$, a finite non-empty set of agents $\mathcal{A} := \{i, j, \ldots, n\}$, a set of atomic propositions AP, a labelling function $l : \mathcal{S} \mapsto 2^{AP}$, a transition matrix T^i for each $i \in \mathcal{A}$ describing the stochastic behaviour of the single agent i and an *epistemic equivalence relation* (EER) $\sim^i \subseteq 2^{\mathcal{S} \times \mathcal{S}}$ for each agent $i \in \mathcal{A}$ such that $\sim^i$ associates to each $s \in \mathcal{S}$ all the states $s' \in \mathcal{S}$ that are *epistemically equivalent* (or *indistinguishable*) from s according to i. Given a state $s \in \mathcal{S}$, the set of all the states $s' \in \mathcal{S}$ such that $s \sim^i s'$ is called the *equivalence class* of s for i, denoted as $Eq^i(s)$. Given a group of agents $\Gamma \subseteq \mathcal{A}$, specific EERs for different kinds of multi-agent knowledge can be defined, including:

- *Everybody Knows:* $\sim_E^\Gamma := \bigcup_{\forall i \in \Gamma} \sim^i$
- *Common Knowledge:* $\sim_C^\Gamma := it(\bigcup_{\forall i \in \Gamma} \sim^i)$, where *it* denotes the *iterative closure*
- *Distributed Knowledge:* $\sim_D^\Gamma := \bigcap_{\forall i \in \Gamma} \sim^i$.

Each EER induces a respective epistemic equivalence class (EEC) for Γ. In the following, by Eq_E^Γ, Eq_C^Γ, Eq_D^Γ, we denote the equivalence classes respectively for *Everybody Knows*, *Common Knowledge* and *Distributed Knowledge*. Finally, while each individual transition matrix $T^i, i \in \mathcal{A}$ describes the stochastic behaviour of a single agent, a global transition matrix T_{PIS} describing the stochastic behaviour of the whole MAS can be generated computing, for each $s, s' \in \mathcal{S} \times \mathcal{S}$, the *logarithmic pooling* of the transitions:

$$T_{\text{PIS}}(s, s') := \eta \prod_{i \in \mathcal{A}} T^i(s, s') \tag{13}$$

where η is a *normalizing factor* given by

$$\eta := \frac{1}{\sum_{s'' \in \mathcal{S}: s'' \neq s'} T^i(s, s'')}$$

that forces the transitions to satisfy the condition: $\sum_{\forall s' \in S} T_{\mathsf{PIS}}(s, s') = 1$ for each $s \in S$. The global transition matrix T_{PIS} also describes a specific MCs. This is typically called the *embedded* MC of the PIS and describes the overall stochastic behaviour of the whole MAS.

Imprecise Probabilistic Interpreted Systems. An imprecise probabilistic interpreted systems (IPIS) is the imprecise counterpart of a PIS. For each agent $i \in \mathcal{A}$, let $\{K^i(S'|s)\}_{s \in S}$ denote a family of (credal) sets including, for each $s \in S$, all the transition PMFs $P^i(S'|s)$ that are compatible with some agent's beliefs. By replacing in a standard PIS, for each $i \in \mathcal{A}$, the transition matrices T^i with the imprecise transition matrices $\mathcal{T}^i := \{K^i(S'|s)\}_{s \in S}$, whose rows correspond to the transition CSs: $K^i(S'|s), s \in S$, we obtain an IPIS. Since transition CSs are *sets* of PMFs, admitting such sets is tantamount to admit agents' *high-order* (non-quantified) uncertainty about transition probabilities.

Similarly to PISs, in the case of IPISs a global *imprecise* transition matrix $\mathcal{T}_{\mathsf{IPIS}}$ can be obtained computing, for each transition $s, s' \in S \times S$, the *credal logarithmic pooling* of the family of conditional CSs $\{K^i(S'|s) : i \in \mathcal{A}\}$ defined as the element-wise application of the standard logarithmic pooling to the elements of the credal sets. This element-wise approach, however, might comport exponential complexity with respect to the number of agents in the model. A similar problem also occurs when considering alternative strategies, such as the one proposed in [1] within the framework of general credal networks. An efficient way to overcome the problem, here adopted, consists of considering a so-called *outer approximation* of the lower and upper bounds of the credal logarithmic pooling. This is achieved by defining:

$$\underline{\mathcal{T}}_{\mathsf{IPIS}}(s, s') := \frac{\prod_{i \in \mathcal{A}} \underline{\mathcal{T}}_{\mathsf{IPIS}}(s, s')}{\prod_{i \in \mathcal{A}} \underline{\mathcal{T}}_{\mathsf{IPIS}}(s, s') + \sum_{s'' \neq s'} \prod_{i \in \mathcal{A}} \underline{\mathcal{T}}_{\mathsf{IPIS}}(s, s'')}; \tag{14}$$

and similarly for the upper bound:

$$\overline{\mathcal{T}}_{\mathsf{IPIS}}(s, s') := \frac{\prod_{i \in \mathcal{A}} \overline{\mathcal{T}}_{\mathsf{IPIS}}(s, s')}{\prod_{i \in \mathcal{A}} \overline{\mathcal{T}}_{\mathsf{IPIS}}(s, s') + \sum_{s'' \neq s'} \prod_{i \in \mathcal{A}} \overline{\mathcal{T}}_{\mathsf{IPIS}}(s, s'')}; \tag{15}$$

The obtained global transition matrix $\mathcal{T}_{\mathsf{IPIS}}$ consists of an *interval-valued* transition matrix $\mathcal{T}_{\mathsf{IPIS}}$ whose entries are intervals $(a, b) \subseteq [0, 1]$ with a and b representing, respectively, the lower $\underline{\mathcal{T}}_{\mathsf{IPIS}}(s, s')$ and the upper $\overline{\mathcal{T}}_{\mathsf{IPIS}}(s, s')$ bounds of the transition probabilities. Similarly to the precise case, the global matrix describes a specific IMC called the *embedded* IMC of the IPIS. As we show in the following, this can be used to compute inferences arising with the overall stochastic behaviour of the whole MAS modelled by the IPIS.

3 Imprecise Epistemic PCTL

3.1 EIPCTL Syntax

The EIPCTL syntax is defined as follows:

$$\mathcal{A} := \{i, j, \ldots, n\},$$
$$\nabla := \{<, \leqslant, =, \geqslant, >\},$$
$$\phi := \top \mid p \mid \neg\phi \mid \phi_1 \wedge \phi_2 \mid P_J\psi \mid \underline{P}_{\nabla b}\psi \mid \overline{P}_{\nabla b}\psi \mid K^i\phi \mid E^\Gamma\phi \mid C^\Gamma\phi \mid D^\Gamma\phi,$$
$$\psi := \bigcirc\phi \mid \phi_1 \bigcup^{\leqslant t} \phi_2 \mid \phi_1 \bigcup \phi_2,$$
$$\epsilon := B^i_{\nabla \underline{b}}\phi \mid B^i_{\nabla \overline{b}}\phi;$$

The language is an epistemic extension of the well-known PCTL able to cope with agents' *high-order* uncertainty about transition probabilities. To this aim, the canonical PCTL probability operator is replaced with three new operators, for the following formulas with $b \in [0,1], J \subseteq [0,1]$:

1. $\underline{P}_{\nabla b}\psi$: *The lower bound of the probability of reaching a path that satisfies ψ is ∇b;*
2. $\overline{P}_{\nabla b}\psi$: *The upper bound of the probability of reaching a path that satisfies ψ is ∇b;*
3. $P_J\psi$: *The probability of reaching a path that satisfies ψ belongs to the interval J.*

In addition, we extend standard PCTL language including a (single-agent) knowledge operator and canonical multi-agent operators for *Everybody Knows*, *Common Knowledge* and *Distributed Knowledge*. Finally, we also include in the language two weighted-belief operators:

- $B^i_{\nabla \underline{b}}\phi$: *The agent i believes that the lower bound of the probability to reach ϕ eventually in the future is ∇b;*
- $B^i_{\nabla \overline{b}}\phi$: *The agent i believes that the upper bound of the probability to reach ϕ eventually in the future is ∇b.*

In the following, the doxastic formulae including these operators are called *imprecise probabilistic beliefs*.

3.2 Semantics of EIPCTL

Semantics of Boolean Formulae. Given an IPIS $\mathcal{M}_{\mathsf{IPIS}}$ and a state $s \in \mathcal{S}$, the following conditions hold:

$$\mathcal{M}_{\mathsf{IPIS}}, s \models p \text{ iff } p \in l(s),$$
$$\mathcal{M}_{\mathsf{IPIS}}, s \models \neg\phi \text{ iff } \mathcal{M}_{\mathsf{IPIS}}, s \not\models \phi,$$
$$\mathcal{M}_{\mathsf{IPIS}}, s \models \phi_1 \wedge \phi_2 \text{ iff } \mathcal{M}_{\mathsf{IPIS}}, s \models \phi_1 \text{ and } \mathcal{M}_{\mathsf{IPIS}}, s \models \phi_2.$$

Semantics of ψ formulae. Given an IPIS $\mathcal{M}_{\mathsf{IPIS}}$ and a path π, the following conditions hold:

$$\mathcal{M}_{\mathsf{IPIS}}, \pi \models \bigcirc\phi \text{ iff } M, \pi(1) \models \phi,$$

$$\mathcal{M}_{\mathsf{IPIS}}, \pi \models \phi_1 \overset{\leqslant t}{\bigcup} \phi_2 \text{ iff } \exists \tau \leqslant t : \begin{array}{l} \mathcal{M}_{\mathsf{IPIS}}, \pi(\tau) \models \phi_2 \\ \forall \tau' : 0 \leqslant \tau' < \tau : \mathcal{M}_{\mathsf{IPIS}}, \pi(\tau) \models \phi_1 \end{array},$$

$$\mathcal{M}_{\mathsf{IPIS}}, \pi \models \phi_1 \bigcup \phi_2 \text{ iff } \exists \tau \geqslant 0 : \begin{array}{l} \mathcal{M}_{\mathsf{IPIS}}, \pi(\tau) \models \phi_2 \\ \forall \tau' : 0 \leqslant \tau' < \tau \ \mathcal{M}_{\mathsf{IPIS}}, \pi(\tau') \models \phi_1 \end{array}.$$

Semantics of Probabilistic Formulae. Given a model $\mathcal{M}_{\mathsf{IPIS}}$ and a state $s \in \mathcal{S}$, let Paths(s) denote the set of all the paths $\pi := (\pi(0), \pi(1), \dots)$ such that $\pi(0) = s$. We denote by $P_{\mathsf{IPIS}}(\pi \in \text{Paths}(s)|\pi \models \psi)$ the *overall*[1] probability that a path π satisfying the property ψ belongs to Paths(s). Similarly, we denote by $\underline{P}_{\mathsf{IPIS}}(\pi \in \text{Paths}(s)|\pi \models \psi)$ and $\overline{P}_{\mathsf{IPIS}}(\pi \in \text{Paths}(s)|\pi \models \psi)$, respectively the *lower* and *upper* bounds of $P_{\mathsf{IPIS}}(\pi \in \text{Paths}(s)|\pi \models \psi)$.

The satisfiability conditions for *probabilistic-until* formulae are hence defined as follows:

$$\mathcal{M}_{\mathsf{IPIS}}, s \models \underline{P}_{\nabla b}\psi \text{ iff } \underline{P}_{\mathsf{IPIS}}(\pi \in \text{Paths}(s)|\pi \models \psi)\nabla b,$$

$$\mathcal{M}_{\mathsf{IPIS}}, s \models \overline{P}_{\nabla b}\psi \text{ iff } \overline{P}_{\mathsf{IPIS}}(\pi \in \text{Paths}(s)|\pi \models \psi)\nabla b,$$

$$\mathcal{M}_{\mathsf{IPIS}}, s \models P_J\psi \text{ iff } \mathcal{M}_{\mathsf{IPIS}}, s \models \underline{P}_{=(\inf J)}\psi \text{ and } \mathcal{M}_{\mathsf{IPIS}}, s \models \overline{P}_{=(\sup J)}\psi.$$

Notice that, similarly to standard PCTL [3], the computation of the lower and upper bounds of $P_{\mathsf{IPIS}}(\pi \in \text{Paths}(s)|M, \pi \models \psi)$ varies depending on ψ. We analyse further this point in the next section focused on model-checking procedures.

Semantics of Epistemic Formulae. Given an IPIS $\mathcal{M}_{\mathsf{IPIS}}$, an agent $i \in \mathcal{A}$ or a group of agents $\Gamma \subseteq \mathcal{A}$ and a state $s \in S$, the following conditions hold:

$$\mathcal{M}_{\mathsf{IPIS}}, s \models K^i\phi \text{ iff } \forall s', s \sim^i s' : s' \models \phi,$$

$$\mathcal{M}_{\mathsf{IPIS}}, s \models E^\Gamma\phi \text{ iff } \forall s', s \sim^\Gamma_E s' : s' \models \phi,$$

$$\mathcal{M}_{\mathsf{IPIS}}, s \models C^\Gamma\phi \text{ iff } \forall s', s \sim^\Gamma_C s' : s' \models \phi,$$

$$\mathcal{M}_{\mathsf{IPIS}}, s \models D^\Gamma\phi \text{ iff } \forall s', s \sim^\Gamma_D s' : s' \models \phi.$$

Semantics of Imprecise Probabilistic Beliefs. The weighted-belief operators of EIPCTL model the lower and upper bounds of the probability that a single agent $i \in \mathcal{S}$ eventually reaches a state satisfying ϕ. Following the *probabilistic until* semantics (Sect. 3.2), this probability can be written as $P^i(\pi \in \text{Paths}(s)|\pi \models \top \bigcup \phi)$, that is, the probability that ϕ is satisfied eventually in the future according to agent i. This probability is computed analogously to $P(\pi \in \text{Paths}(s)|\pi \models \top \bigcup \phi)$, see Sect. 3.2, but replacing the global imprecise transition matrix $\mathcal{T}_{\mathsf{IPIS}}$, describing the overall stochastic behaviour of the whole MAS, with the transition matrix $\mathcal{T}^i$ that describes the specific behaviour of the agent $i \in \mathcal{A}$. As here

---

[1] i.e., computed through the global transition matrix $\mathcal{T}_{\mathsf{IPIS}}$.

we consider imprecise models, as usual, we are interested in computing the lower and upper bounds of $P^i(\pi \in \text{Paths}(s)|\pi \models \top \bigcup \phi)$ that we denote, respectively, by $\underline{P}(\pi \in \text{Paths}(s)|\pi \models \top \bigcup \phi)$ and $\overline{P}(\pi \in \text{Paths}(s)|\pi \models \top \bigcup \phi)$. The procedure to compute those bounds is further detailed in Sect. 4. Here we limit to introduce the satisfiability conditions for imprecise probabilistic belief formulae as follows:

$$\mathcal{M}_{\text{IPIS}}, s \models B^i_{\nabla_b} \phi \text{ iff } \forall s' : s \sim^i s' \ \underline{P}^i(\pi \in \text{Paths}(s')|\pi \models \top \bigcup \phi)\nabla b,$$

$$\mathcal{M}_{\text{IPIS}}, s \models B^i_{\nabla_{\overline{b}}} \phi \text{ iff } \forall s' : s \sim^i s' \ \overline{P}^i(\pi \in \text{Paths}(s')|\pi \models \top \bigcup \phi)\nabla b.$$

4   Model Checking

The present section describes specific procedures to model-check an IPIS against properties specified in the EIPCTL language. In particular, it aims to prove that relevant model-checking tasks can be solved using slightly modified versions of the algorithms described in Sect. 2.1. Here we consider only procedures relevant for probabilistic and epistemic formulae of EIPCTL. The checking procedures against Boolean and CTL formulae are standard and a detailed explanation of them can be found in [3].

Probabilistic Formulae. Given the semantics introduced in Sect. 3.2, to check whether a model satisfies a given probabilistic formula requires to compute the lower and upper bounds of $P_{\text{IPIS}}(\pi \in \text{Paths}(s)|M, \pi \models \psi)$. These, in turn, vary depending on ψ.

Probabilistic Next. We first consider the case when $\psi := \bigcirc \phi$. Let Φ denote the set of all the states satisfying ϕ. Thus, $P_{\text{IPIS}}(\pi \in \text{Paths}(s)|M, \pi \models \psi)$ corresponds to the marginal probability $P_{\text{IPIS}}(S_1 \in \Phi|S_0 = s)$. The first step for determining such probability consists in generating the indicator vector $\mathbf{I}_\Phi$ computing, for each $s \in \mathcal{S}$, the indicator function

$$\mathbf{I}_\Phi(s) := \begin{cases} 1 & \text{if } s \in \Phi, \\ 0 & \text{else.} \end{cases}$$

This step requires a time linear in $|\mathcal{S}|$. The second step requires to introduce the lower $\underline{\mathcal{T}}_{\text{IPIS}}$ or the upper $\overline{\mathcal{T}}_{\text{IPIS}}$ transition operator. Given the global transition matrix $\mathcal{T}_{\text{IPIS}}$, these can be defined following Eq. (6) and used for computing the lower and upper bounds of $P_{\text{IPIS}}(S_1 \in \Phi|S_0 = s)$ as follows:

$$\underline{P}_{\text{IPIS}}(S_1 \in \Phi|S_0 = s) = (\underline{\mathcal{T}}_{\text{IPIS}}\mathbf{I}_\Phi)(s). \tag{16}$$

$$\overline{P}_{\text{IPIS}}(S_1 \in \Phi|S_0 = s) = (\overline{\mathcal{T}}_{\text{IPIS}}\mathbf{I}_\Phi)(s). \tag{17}$$

As stated in Sect. 2.1, each application of either the lower or the upper transition operator requires to solve, for each $s \in \mathcal{S}$, a linear programming task whose feasible region is the convex hull obtained by convex closure of the local CS $K(S'|s)$. By definition, the time complexity of each linear programming task is, at most, polynomial in $|\mathcal{S}|$. Hence, since the computation requires to solve at most $|\mathcal{S}|$ linear programming tasks, the overall time complexity is at most polynomial in $|\mathcal{S}|$.

Probabilistic Bounded Until. For $\psi = \phi_1 \bigcup^{\leqslant t} \phi_2$, let us first define Φ_1 and Φ_2 as the subsets of $\mathcal{S}$ satisfying, respectively, ϕ_1 and ϕ_2. The probability in Eqs. (16) and (17) can be seen as a bounded-time hitting probability of Φ_2 with the additional condition that all the states visited before reaching Φ_2 are in Φ_1. We denote such *conditional* hitting probability by $h_{\Phi_2|\Phi_1}^t(s), s \in \mathcal{S}$. A recursive algorithm analogous to Eqs. (10) and (11) can be formulated to compute the values of the lower $\underline{h}_{\Phi_2|\Phi_1}^t$ and upper $\overline{h}_{\Phi_2|\Phi_1}^t$ hitting probability vectors. Let $\mathbf{I}_{\Phi_2}$ denote the indicator vector of Φ_2. Let $\mathbf{I}_{\Phi_1 \setminus \Phi_2}$ denote the indicator vector giving 1 to all the states that are in Φ_1 but not in Φ_2 and 0 otherwise. Finally, let $\mathcal{T}_{\mathsf{IPIS}}$ denote the *global* transition matrix describing the overall behaviour of the whole MAS, and let $\underline{\mathcal{T}}_{\mathsf{IPIS}}^\dagger, \overline{\mathcal{T}}_{\mathsf{IPIS}}^\dagger$ denote, respectively, the lower and the upper *dual* transition operators obtained as by definitions (10) and (11). A slightly modified version of the algorithms in (10), (11) for computing, for each $0 < \tau \leqslant t$, the above lower and upper hitting probability vectors can be achieved as follows:

$$\underline{h}_{\Phi_2|\Phi_1}^\tau := \mathbf{I}_{\Phi_2} + \mathbf{I}_{\Phi_1 \setminus \Phi_2}(\underline{\mathcal{T}}_{\mathsf{IPIS}}^\dagger \, \underline{h}_{\Phi_2|\Phi_1}^{\tau-1}), \tag{18}$$

$$\overline{h}_{\Phi_2|\Phi_1}^\tau := \mathbf{I}_{\Phi_2} + \mathbf{I}_{\Phi_1 \setminus \Phi_2}(\overline{\mathcal{T}}_{\mathsf{IPIS}}^\dagger \, \overline{h}_{\Phi_2|\Phi_1}^{\tau-1}). \tag{19}$$

Notice that, exactly as in Eqs. (10) and (11) the initialization is given by the indicator function of Φ_2 while the recursive steps consist of iterated applications of the lower (upper) transition operator to the hitting vector computed at the precedent time-step $\tau - 1$, for each $0 < \tau \leqslant t$. The only relevant difference with the analogous scheme presented in Sect. 2.1 consists of the indicator vector $\mathbf{I}_{\Phi_1 \setminus \Phi_2}$ that replaces $\mathbf{I}_{B^c}$, i.e., the indicator vector of the complement of the hitting event B. In the general scheme, $\mathbf{I}_{B^c}$ limits the iteration considering only paths that have not already visited an $s \in B$. Here, by $\mathbf{I}_{\Phi_1 \setminus \Phi_2}$ we limit the iteration considering only paths whose actual and previous states are all in Φ_1 and that have not already reached a state $s \in \Phi_2$. This constraint follows from the semantics of probabilistic until, see Sect. 4.

The time complexity remains polynomial with respect to $|\mathcal{S}|$. In fact, the solution of the schema (18) requires: (i) to generate the indicator vectors for Φ_2 and $\Phi_1 \setminus \Phi_2$, (ii) to execute element-wise sums and products on the vectors arrays, (iii) to execute $t - 1$ applications of the lower (respectively, upper) transition operator. (i) requires a number of time-steps linear in $|\mathcal{S}|$ and (ii) requires a number of time-steps linear in $|\mathcal{S}|$ for each recursive step $0 < \tau \leqslant t$. Both, hence, do not affect the overall time complexity of the procedure. Finally, remember that each application of the lower (upper) dual operator has a time complexity at most polynomial in $|\mathcal{S}|$, see Sect. 2.1. As the overall procedure requires a finite number $t - 1 \in \mathbf{N}$ of successively recursive applications of the respective transition operator, one for each recursive step $0 < \tau \leqslant t$, the overall time complexity results being polynomial in $|\mathcal{S}|$. To conclude, notice that here we consider the CSs $K_{\mathsf{IPIS}}(S'|s), s \in \mathcal{S}$ describing the *global* transitions of the whole MAS. By the definition of *global* transition matrix $\mathcal{T}_{\mathsf{IPIS}}$ in Sect. 2.2, these CSs are given by the rows of $\mathcal{T}_{\mathsf{IPIS}}$.

Probabilistic Until. The strategy to solve model-checking tasks for probabilistic (unbounded) until formulae, i.e. formulae composed by a probabilistic operator ranging over $\psi := \phi_1 \bigcup \phi_2$, is the same as for probabilistic bounded until but considering, in place of IMCs of a finite time length $t \in \mathbf{N}$, IMCs of infinite time length. Recall that the existence of the limits $\lim_{\tau \to +\infty} \underline{h}_B^\tau$ and $\lim_{\tau \to +\infty} \overline{h}_B^\tau$ defined in Sect. 2.1 has been proved, see [16, Lemma 14]. The slightly modification introduced in 10 and 11, consisting of replacing $\mathbf{I}_B$ in the general schema with the indicator vector $\mathbf{I}_{\Phi_1 \backslash \Phi_2}$, does not affect the validity of the proof outlined in [16]. Consequently, the values of the lower and upper hitting probability vectors $\underline{h}_{\Phi_2 | \Phi_1}$ and $\overline{h}_{\Phi_2 | \Phi_1}$ can be approximated by iterating the schema 10, respectively, the schema 11, over increasing values of τ until convergence. Regarding the overall time complexity of the procedure, the same reasoning outlined above for probabilistic bounded until formulae holds.

Epistemic Formulae. The model-checking for epistemic formulae requires an iterative procedure. In practice, it consists of computing the *epistemic equivalence class* (EEC) relative to the specified agent (respectively, group of agents) and the actual state of the system, hence checking for each state in the EEC whether it satisfies the formula nested by the epistemic operator.

Let $\kappa := K^i, E^\Gamma, C^\Gamma, D^\Gamma, \kappa\phi$ and let $Eq_{E,C,D}^{i,\Gamma}$ be a generic notation for one of the possible EEC $Eq^i(s), Eq_E^\Gamma(s), Eq_C^\Gamma(s), Eq_D^\Gamma(s)$. Given a state $s \in \mathcal{S}$, our task consists of defining a procedure for checking whether $s \models \kappa\phi$. Step (i) consists of deciding which states $s' \in \mathcal{S}$ belong to the EEC $Eq_{E,C,D}^{i,\Gamma}(s)$. This can be obtained in time linear in $|\mathcal{S}|$ by simply computing the *characteristic function* of $Eq_{E,C,D}^{i,\Gamma}$, i.e.:

$$\mathbf{I}_{Eq_{E,C,D}^{i,\Gamma}}(s) := \begin{cases} 1 & \text{if } s' \in Eq_{E,C,D}^{i,\Gamma}(s), \\ 0 & \text{otherwise.} \end{cases} \tag{20}$$

Step (ii) consists of selecting the appropriate model-checking procedure for ϕ, else check, for each $s' \in Eq_{E,C,D}^{i,\Gamma}(s)$, whether $s' \models \phi$. If ϕ is an epistemic formula, (i.e., $\phi := \kappa'\phi'$) we return to step (i) and repeat the same procedure for each $s' \in Eq_{E,C,D}^{i,\Gamma}$. Steps (i) and (ii) are successively iterated until all the resting nested formulae ϕ are all non-epistemic formulae. The time complexity of the whole procedure is polynomial in $|\mathcal{S}|$. In fact, (i) consists of computing an EEC, a task that can be solved in time linear in $|\mathcal{S}|$ while (ii) requires the execution of a checking procedure for each state in the EEC. As all the checking tasks relative to any kind of EIPCTL non-epistemic formulae are solvable in time polynomial in $|\mathcal{S}|$, also (ii) will be solvable in time at most polynomial in $|\mathcal{S}|$.

Imprecise Probabilistic Belief. The model-checking procedure for imprecise probabilistic beliefs formulae requires to compute $\underline{P}^i(\pi \in \text{Paths}(s) | \pi \models \top \bigcup \phi)$ and $\overline{P}^i(\pi \in \text{Paths}(s) | \pi \models \top \bigcup \phi)$. As the semantics of *imprecise probabilistic belief* formulae is analogous to the semantics of *probabilistic until* formulae, we can reduce the computation of $\underline{P}^i(\pi \in \text{Paths}(s) | \pi \models \top \bigcup \phi)$ and

$\overline{P}^i(\pi \in \text{Paths}(s)|\pi \models \top \bigcup \phi)$ to the computation of, respectively, $\underline{h}^i_\Phi$ and $\overline{h}^i_\Phi$. These are the lower and upper bounds of the hitting probability of Φ computed through the i's transition matrix T^i instead of the *global* transition matrix T_{IPIS}. Let $\underline{\mathcal{T}}^\dagger_i$ and $\overline{\mathcal{T}}^\dagger_i$ denote respectively the lower and the upper dual transition operators obtained from T^i as by definitions (10), (11). The model-checking procedure is analogous to (18) with the only difference that we replace the dual transition operators $\underline{\mathcal{T}}^\dagger_{\text{IPIS}}$, $\overline{\mathcal{T}}^\dagger_{\text{IPIS}}$ with the analogous dual transition operators $\underline{\mathcal{T}}^\dagger_i$ $\overline{\mathcal{T}}^\dagger_i$. Regarding the time complexity of the procedure, the same reasoning outlined above for probabilistic until formulae holds.

5　Example

We now validate the applicability of the proposed model-checking tasks on a simple example. Consider an IPIS $\mathcal{M}_{\text{IPIS}}$ made of three agents $\mathcal{A} := \{i, j, k\}$ and three states $\mathcal{S} := \{1, 2, 3\}$ labelled as: $p := \{1, 2\}$, $q := \{3\}$. The EER for each agent are defined as:

$$\sim^i: \{1, 2\}, \{3\}; \quad \sim^j: \{1, 2\}, \{3\}; \quad \sim^k: \{1\}, \{2\}, \{3\}. \tag{21}$$

while the stochastic behaviours of the single agents are described by the following *imprecise*, interval-valued, transition matrices:

$$i := \begin{bmatrix} 0 & 0.4-0.9 & 0.1-0.6 \\ 0.2-0.8 & 0 & 0.2-0.8 \\ 0.3-0.5 & 0.7-0.5 & 0 \end{bmatrix}, \quad j := \begin{bmatrix} 0 & 0.45-0.95 & 0.05-0.55 \\ 0.25-0.88 & 0 & 0.12-0.75 \\ 0.32-0.5 & 0.5-0.78 & 0 \end{bmatrix},$$

$$k := \begin{bmatrix} 0 & 0.55-0.95 & 0.05-0.45 \\ 0.15-0.95 & 0 & 0.05-0.85 \\ 0.32-0.5 & 0.5-0.78 & 0 \end{bmatrix}.$$

The task consists in checking whether the following formula holds for $s = 1$:

$$\mathcal{M}, s \models K^i P_{0.99-1} \top \overset{\leqslant 150}{\bigcup} (3); \tag{22}$$

First, we derive the global transition matrix T_{IPIS} from the subjective transition matrices stated above. Applying Eqs. (14) and (15) to each row of the matrix, and rounding to the fourth digit, we obtain:

$$\begin{bmatrix} 0 & 0.4-0.9997 & 0.0003-0.6 \\ 0.0145-0.9982 & 0 & 0.0018-0.9855 \\ 0.0673-0.5 & 0.5-0.9327 & 0 \end{bmatrix}.$$

Second, we compute for each $s' \in \mathcal{S} : 1 \sim^i s'$ whether:

$$\mathcal{M}_{\text{IPIS}}, s' \models \underline{P}_{\geqslant 0.99} \top \overset{\leqslant 150}{\bigcup} (3).$$

Since the only states equivalent to 1 for i are 1 and 2, we check the above formula with respect to both these two states. Following Eq. (16), this corresponds to calculate the lower $\underline{h}^{150}_{(3)}$ and upper $\overline{h}^{150}_{(3)}$ bounded-time hitting probability vectors

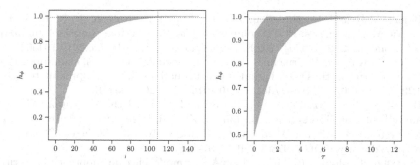

Fig. 1. Hitting probability ranges w.r.t. increasing time horizon $0 < \tau \leqslant 150$ for starting state 1 (left) and 2 (right). The horizontal dotted line denote the threshold level $\underline{h}_{(3)} = 0.99$, while the vertical dotted line show the first time step for which such threshold is exceeded.

relative to event $\{3\}$ by means of the recursive scheme in Eqs. (10) and (11) for a time horizon $t = 150$. These lower and upper bounds are reported in Fig. 1. Finally, we extract from the vector the respective values for states 1 and 2 and check for both if the probability conditions specified in the formula are satisfied. As showed in Fig. 1, both for states 1 and 2 the lower bound reached value 0.99 as well as the upper bounds converges to 1 before $t = 150$. The above formula is hence satisfied for $s = 1$.

6   Conclusions

In this paper we define a logic and relative model-checking procedures to model-check stochastic MASs characterized by agents' high-order (not quantified) uncertainty about transition probabilities. Here we limit to consider agents whose stochastic behaviour can be described by discrete-time models. Recent developments [15] in the study of imprecise *continuous-time* Markov chains (ICTMC) strongly suggest that an analogous extension for agents whose behaviour is described by continuous-time models is possible. These models are particularly relevant for applications in fields like computational and systems biology, see [5,8]. Other important extensions we would consider are multi-agent imprecise Markov decision-processes because they offer a natural connection with the field of Reinforcement Learning [20]. Finally, we aim to consider possible connections with other logical formalism developed within the theory of imprecise probabilities, such as depth-bounded belief functions [4].

References

1. Antonucci, A., Huber, D., Zaffalon, M., Luginbühl, P., Chapman, I., Ladouceur, R.: Credo: a military decision-support system based on credal networks. In: Proceedings of the 16th Conference on Information Fusion (FUSION 2013), Istanbul, Turkey (2013)

2. Baier, C., Hensel, C., Hutschenreiter, L., Junges, S., Katoen, J., Klein, J.: Parametric Markov chains: PCTL complexity and fraction-free Gaussian elimination. Inf. Comput. **272**, 104504 (2020). https://doi.org/10.1016/j.ic.2019.104504
3. Baier, C., Katoen, J.: Principles of Model Checking. MIT Press, Cambridge (2008)
4. Baldi, P., Hosni, H.: Depth-bounded belief functions. Int. J. Approximate Reason. **123**, 26–40 (2020). https://doi.org/10.1016/j.ijar.2020.05.001
5. Beneš, N., Brim, L., Pastva, S., Šafránek, D.: Model checking approach to the analysis of biological systems. In: Liò, P., Zuliani, P. (eds.) Automated Reasoning for Systems Biology and Medicine. CB, vol. 30, pp. 3–35. Springer, Cham (2019). https://doi.org/10.1007/978-3-030-17297-8_1
6. Bentahar, J., Moulin, B., Meyer, J.C.: A new model checking approach for verifying agent communication protocols. In: Proceedings of the Canadian Conference on Electrical and Computer Engineering, CCECE 2006, Ottawa Congress Centre, Ottawa, Canada, 7–10 May 2006, pp. 1586–1590. IEEE (2006). https://doi.org/10.1109/CCECE.2006.277640
7. Bérard, B., et al.: Systems and Software Verification, Model-Checking Techniques and Tools. Springer, Heidelberg (2001)
8. Brim, L., Češka, M., Šafránek, D.: Model checking of biological systems. In: Bernardo, M., de Vink, E., Di Pierro, A., Wiklicky, H. (eds.) SFM 2013. LNCS, vol. 7938, pp. 63–112. Springer, Heidelberg (2013). https://doi.org/10.1007/978-3-642-38874-3_3
9. Chen, T., Primiero, G., Raimondi, F., Rungta, N.: A computationally grounded, weighted doxastic logic. Stud. Logica. **104**(4), 679–703 (2016)
10. Daws, C.: Symbolic and parametric model checking of discrete-time Markov chains. In: Liu, Z., Araki, K. (eds.) ICTAC 2004. LNCS, vol. 3407, pp. 280–294. Springer, Heidelberg (2005). https://doi.org/10.1007/978-3-540-31862-0_21
11. De Cooman, G., De Bock, J., Lopatatzidis, S.: Imprecise stochastic processes in discrete time: global models, imprecise Markov chains and ergodic theorems. Int. J. Approx. Reason. **76**, 18–46 (2016)
12. De Cooman, G., Hermans, F., Quaeghebeur, E.: Imprecise Markov chains and their limit behavior. Probab. Eng. Inf. Sci. **23**(4), 597–635 (2009)
13. Delgado, K.V., De Barros, L.N., Dias, D.B., Sanner, S.: Real-time dynamic programming for Markov decision processes with imprecise probabilities. Artif. Intell. **230**, 192–223 (2016)
14. Hansson, H., Jonsson, B.: A logic for reasoning about time and reliability. Formal Aspects Comput. **6**(5), 512–535 (1994)
15. Krak, T., De Bock, J., Siebes, A.: Imprecise continuous-time Markov chains. Int. J. Approximate Reason. **88**, 452–528 (2017)
16. Krak, T.E., T'Joens, N., Bock, J.D.: Hitting times and probabilities for imprecise Markov chains. In: Bock, J.D., de Campos, C.P., de Cooman, G., Quaeghebeur, E., Wheeler, G.R. (eds.) International Symposium on Imprecise Probabilities: Theories and Applications, ISIPTA 2019, Thagaste, Ghent, Belgium, 3–6 July 2019. Proceedings of Machine Learning Research, vol. 103, pp. 265–275. PMLR (2019). http://proceedings.mlr.press/v103/krak19a.html
17. Mauá, D.D., de Campos, C.P., Benavoli, A., Antonucci, A.: Probabilistic inference in credal networks: new complexity results. J. Artif. Intell. Res. **50**, 603–637 (2014)
18. Parker, D., Norman, G., Kwiatkowska, M.: Prism: probabilistic symbolic model checker, 4.6 version (2020). https://www.prismmodelchecker.org
19. Revuz, D.: Markov Chains. Elsevier (2008)
20. Sutton, R.S., Barto, A.G.: Reinforcement Learning - An Introduction. Adaptive Computation and Machine Learning. MIT Press, Cambridge (1998)

21. Termine, A., Antonucci, A., Facchini, A., Primiero, G.: Robust model checking with imprecise Markov reward models. In: International Symposium on Imprecise Probabilities: Theories and Applications, ISIPTA 2021, Granada, Spain, 6–9 July 2021. Proceedings of Machine Learning Research, PMLR (2021)
22. T'Joens, N., Krak, T., Bock, J.D., Cooman, G.: A recursive algorithm for computing inferences in imprecise Markov chains. In: Kern-Isberner, G., Ognjanović, Z. (eds.) ECSQARU 2019. LNCS (LNAI), vol. 11726, pp. 455–465. Springer, Cham (2019). https://doi.org/10.1007/978-3-030-29765-7_38
23. Troffaes, M.C.M., Skulj, D.: Model checking for imprecise Markov chains. In: Cozman, F., Denoeux, T., Dcstercke, S., Seidenfeld, T. (eds.) Proceedings of the Eighth International Symposium on Imprecise Probability: Theories and Applications, ISIPTA 2013, Compiègne, France, 2–5 July 2013, pp. 337–344. Society for Imprecise Probability: Theories and Applications (SIPTA), July 2013
24. van Ditmarsch, H., van der Hoek, W., Halpern, J., Kooi, B. (eds.): Handbook of Epistemic Logic. College Publications (2015)
25. Walley, P.: Statistical Reasoning with Imprecise Probabilities. Chapman and Hall (1991)
26. Wan, W., Bentahar, J., Hamza, A.B.: Model checking epistemic-probabilistic logic using probabilistic interpreted systems. Knowl. Based Syst. 50, 279–295 (2013). https://doi.org/10.1016/j.knosys.2013.06.017

On the Complexity of Predicting Election Outcomes and Estimating Their Robustness

Dorothea Baumeister$^{(\boxtimes)}$ and Tobias Hogrebe

Institut für Informatik, Heinrich-Heine-Universität Düsseldorf, Düsseldorf, Germany
{d.baumeister,tobias.hogrebe}@uni-duesseldorf.de

Abstract. When dealing with election data it is reasonable to assume that the votes are incomplete or noisy. The reasons are manifold and range from cost-intensive elicitation to manipulation. We study the problems of evaluating elections with incomplete data and determining the robustness of elections with noisy data from a computational point of view. To capture a wide variety of motivations, we consider three different models for the distribution of preferences: the uniform distribution over the completions of incomplete preferences inspired by the possible winner problem, the dispersion around complete preferences, also called Mallows noise model, and a model in which the distribution over the votes of each voter is explicitly given. We consider both approval vector preferences and linear order preferences and show that the complexity of the problems can vary greatly depending on the voting rule, the distribution model, and the parameterization. We investigate the problems both in terms of counting complexity as well as decision complexity and discuss the effects of the winner model and tie-breaking on the results.

Keywords: Probabilistic social choice · Computational complexity · Voting · Election robustness · Election prediction

1 Introduction

Elections are an integral part of any democracy, be it for the collective decision-making of a whole country or just for any group of people, a sports club or employees of a company. In addition to these classic applications, elections are also considered in connection with software agents and automation. Here, the applications of elections range from multi-agent planning (see, e.g., Ephrati and Rosenschein [16]) and meta-search engines (see, e.g., Dwork et al. [15]) to recommender systems (see, e.g., Ghosh et al. [18]) and email classification (see, e.g., Cohen et al. [11]). In the classic case, we assume that we have perfect knowledge about the preferences of the voters and are able to use a voting rule to determine the rightful winners with respect to the specific rule.

A preliminary version of this work was published as an extended abstract in the proceedings of AAMAS 2020 (see Baumeister and Hogrebe [3]).

A. Rosenfeld and N. Talmon (Eds.): EUMAS 2021, LNAI 12802, pp. 228–244, 2021.
https://doi.org/10.1007/978-3-030-82254-5_14

However, in many realistic scenarios, we can not assume that we have perfect information about voter preferences. Nevertheless, a decision must often be made or at least in some way a result of the election must be presented, for example in the form of the winning probabilities considered here. The reasons for imperfect election data are manifold. First, we often cannot assume that the election data we receive is complete. In the case of actual elections, the collection of complete election data is often cost-intensive, complicated, or simply not possible under the given circumstances. The same holds for the creation of election forecasts based on partial data aggregated from social networks or polls, where a complete collection of election data is not appropriate. On the other hand, even if we receive complete election data, in many situations we cannot assume that it has not been corrupted in transmission, by manipulation, or through the elicitation itself. In these situations the question arises how robust and thereby justified a candidate's victory is if the data has been corrupted to a certain degree.

Therefore, we study the problem of determining the probability that a particular candidate wins an election for a given distribution over the preferences of the voters. Conitzer and Sandholm [12] were the first to study this problem and referred to it as the evaluation problem. The relevance of the problem is immense, as it captures many different, and in particular the previously presented, scenarios, such as the winner determination on incomplete data, the creation of election forecasts, and the examination of the justification or robustness of a candidate's victory if corruption of the data is possible. To cover those different motivations, we consider three models for the distribution of preferences: the uniform distribution over the completions of incomplete preferences inspired by the possible winner problem, the dispersion around complete preferences, also called Mallows noise model, and a model in which the distribution over the votes of each voter is explicitly given. The basic definitions of formal elections as well as the formal definition of the evaluation problem, the preference distributions, and computational complexity will be introduced in Sect. 2. In Sect. 3, we study the computational complexity of the evaluation problem regarding those distributions and consider both voting rules on approval vector preferences and linear order preferences, namely positional scoring rules. Our results include both hardness results for #P as well as polynomial-time algorithms. We show that the complexity of the problem can vary greatly depending on the voting rule, the distribution model, and the parameterization. Especially, we investigate the problem both in terms of counting complexity as well as decision complexity in Sect. 3.4. Finally, we will examine the relation between our and related work in Sect. 4 and discuss our results in Sect. 5.

2   Preliminaries

Formally an election is given by a tuple $E = (C, V)$, with $C = \{c_1, \ldots, c_m\}$ with $m \geq 2$ denoting the set of *candidates* and $V = (v_1, \ldots, v_n)$ with $n \geq 1$ denoting the *preference profile* consisting of n votes over C. We consider the two most prominent types of votes: approval vectors and linear orders. In the case of *approval vectors*, each vote is represented by a vector $v_i \in \{0,1\}^m$ in which voter i expresses approval for the candidate c_j by setting the respective entry, denoted by $\text{app}_{v_i}(c_j)$, to 1. In the case of *linear orders*, each vote v_i is represented by a complete strict linear order $>_i$ over C. By $\mathcal{L}(C)$ we denote the set of all strict linear orders over C.

We consider the following voting rules for winner determination. For approval vectors, we use the canonical *approval voting* (AV). That is, the candidates with the most approvals win. The common variant in which the voters must distribute exactly k approvals is denoted by k-AV with fixed $k \geq 1$ for $m > k$. For linear orders, we focus on positional scoring rules. A *positional scoring rule* (or *scoring rule* for short) is characterized by a scoring vector $\boldsymbol{\alpha} = (\alpha_1, \ldots, \alpha_m) \in \mathbb{N}_0^m$ with $\alpha_1 \geq \alpha_2 \geq \cdots \geq \alpha_m$ and $\alpha_1 > \alpha_m$, where α_j denotes the number of points a candidate receives for being placed on position j by one of the voters. Those candidates with the maximum number of points are the winners of the election. A scoring rule covering an arbitrary number of candidates is given by an efficiently evaluable function determining a scoring vector for each number of candidates above a certain minimum. Note that without loss of generality of our results we assume that $\alpha_m = 0$ holds. The most prominent scoring rules are *Borda* with $\boldsymbol{\alpha} = (m-1, m-2, \ldots, 1, 0)$, the scoring rule characterized by $\boldsymbol{\alpha} = (2, 1, \ldots, 1, 0)$, k-*approval* with fixed $k \geq 1$ for $m > k$ characterized by $\boldsymbol{\alpha} = (\alpha_1, \ldots, \alpha_m)$ with $\alpha_1 = \cdots = \alpha_k = 1$ and $\alpha_{k+1} = \cdots = \alpha_m = 0$, and k-*veto* with fixed $k \geq 1$ for $m > k$ characterized by $\boldsymbol{\alpha} = (\alpha_1, \ldots, \alpha_m)$ with $\alpha_1 = \cdots = \alpha_{m-k} = 1$ and $\alpha_{m-k+1} = \cdots = \alpha_m = 0$. More specifically, 1-approval is also refereed to as *plurality* and 1-veto as *veto*. Note, that k-AV and k-approval essentially describe the same voting rule and differ only in the amount of information we are given about the preferences of the voters. Interestingly, this very distinction leads to differing complexity results in some cases, as we will see later.

In the course of this work we will also encounter elections with partial information. A *partial profile* $\tilde{V} = (\tilde{v}_1, \ldots, \tilde{v}_n)$, in contrast to a normal profile, may contain *partial votes*. In the case of approval vectors, a partial vote is represented by a *partial approval vector* $\tilde{v}_i \in \{0, 1, \bot\}^m$, where $\bot$ indicates that the approval for the respective candidate is undetermined. An approval vector v_i is a completion of a partial approval vector $\tilde{v}_i$ if for all $j \in \{1, \ldots, m\}$ it holds $\text{app}_{\tilde{v}_i}(c_j) \in \{0, 1\} \Rightarrow \text{app}_{v_i}(c_j) = \text{app}_{\tilde{v}_i}(c_j)$. In the case of linear orders, a partial vote consists of a *partial order* $\tilde{v}_i : \succ_i$ over C that is, an irreflexive and transitive, but on the contrary to linear orders, not necessarily connex relation. A linear order $>_i$ is a completion of a partial order $\succ_i$ if for all $c_s, c_t \in C$ it holds $c_s \succ_i c_t \Rightarrow c_s >_i c_t$. For both types of votes, a profile $V = (v_1, \ldots, v_n)$ is a completion of a partial profile $\tilde{V} = (\tilde{v}_1, \ldots, \tilde{v}_n)$, if v_i is a completion of $\tilde{v}_i$ for $1 \leq i \leq n$. The set of all completions of a vote $\tilde{v}_i$ or a profile $\tilde{V}$ is denoted by $\Lambda(\tilde{v}_i)$ or $\Lambda(\tilde{V})$ respectively.

As mentioned earlier, there may be uncertainty about the votes in elections due to several reasons. Thus we assume some distribution over possible profiles, and investigate the problem of determining the winning probability of a certain candidate. This is formalized in the problem $\mathcal{E}$-EVALUATION for a given voting rule $\mathcal{E}$ as follows.

$\mathcal{E}$-EVALUATION

Given: Set of candidates C, profile distribution $\mathcal{P}$ over C, and candidate $p \in C$.
Question: What is the probability Φ that p is a winner of the election with respect to $\mathcal{E}$ assuming $\mathcal{P}$?

Here we mainly focus on the *non-unique winner* case where p is considered a winner of election (C, V) with respect to voting rule $\mathcal{E}$, if and only if p is contained in the set of winners $\mathcal{E}(C, V)$. In the *unique winner* case, we require $\mathcal{E}(C, V) = \{p\}$ for p to be considered a winner of the election. In addition, we also consider *random* and *lexicographic tie-breaking*, where in the former the victory of a candidate is weighted according to the total number of winners and in the latter a tie is resolved according to a given order. Unless stated otherwise, the results presented here hold for all four models. Note that regarding the definition of EVALUATION, the distribution as part of the input means that the respective distribution is specified by the necessary parameters as part of the input.

In the following we will present the three distribution models for profiles considered in this paper. Note that all the models presented here are products of independent distributions over the preferences for each voter. For a discussion of the properties and relevance of those models considered here and comparable models, we refer to the overview by Boutilier and Rosenschein [8].

PPIC. The first model we consider is the normalized variant of the possible winner motivated model of Bachrach et al. [2]. We will refer to this model as *partial profile impartial culture model* (PPIC). Given a set of candidates C, a partial profile $\tilde{V} = (\tilde{v}_1, \ldots, \tilde{v}_n)$ over C. The probability of a profile $V = (v_1, \ldots, v_n)$ over C according to PPIC is given by $\Pr_{\mathrm{PPIC}}(V \mid \tilde{V}) = 1/|\Lambda(\tilde{V})|$. Thereby, each completion of the partial profile is equally likely, hence the name 'impartial culture'. Note, that for partial linear orders, the computation of the probability of a given profile is #P-hard, since the calculation of the normalization $|\Lambda(\tilde{V})|$ itself is already a #P-hard problem as shown by Brightwell and Winkler [9] whereby the normalized variant and the variant considered by Bachrach et al. [2] are not immediately equivalent under polynomial-time reduction. For AV and k-AV, on the other hand, the probability of a given profile can be calculated in polynomial time. For AV it holds that $|\Lambda(\tilde{V})| = 2^{N_\perp}$ where $N_\perp$ denotes the total number of undetermined approvals in $\tilde{V}$. For k-AV it holds that $|\Lambda(\tilde{V})| = \prod_{i=1}^{n} \binom{u(\tilde{v}_i)}{k - a(\tilde{v}_i)}$ where $u(\tilde{v}_i) = |\{c \in C \mid \mathrm{app}_{\tilde{v}_i}(c) = \perp\}|$ and $a(\tilde{v}_i) = |\{c \in C \mid \mathrm{app}_{\tilde{v}_i}(c) = 1\}|$. For EVALUATION under PPIC the parameter is the partial profile $\tilde{V}$. Referring back to the motivations stated at the beginning, PPIC can be used in relation to the evaluation problem to create election forecasts based on partial data about the preferences aggregated from social networks or polls. In terms of robustness, PPIC can be motivated by the possibility that data was partially lost during the collection or transmission. In both scenarios there is a reasonable interest in finding out with which probability which candidate is the winner of the election.

Example 1. Suppose we are in the run-up to a plurality (1-approval) election over the set of candidates $C = \{a, b, c\}$ and we have received the partial profile $\tilde{V}$ over C shown in Fig. 1 from aggregating social network data. The evaluation problem assuming PPIC with distinguished candidate a asks for the probability that a is a winner, when all possible completions are considered with equal probability. In this case a is only a winner in one of the six possible completions of $\tilde{V}$, whereby the answer to the EVALUATION instance is $\Phi = 1/6$.

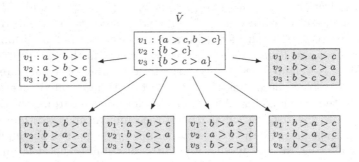

Fig. 1. Example for an EVALUATION instance assuming PPIC with distinguished candidate a. All possible completions of $\tilde{V}$, each with probability $1/6$. Profiles for which a is not a winner are grayed out.

We now use Example 1 to illustrate the difference between k-approval and k-AV regarding EVALUATION. They are essentially the same voting rule and differ only in the amount of information we are given about the preferences and thereby in the expressiveness of the partial preferences. For v_1 with partial preference $\{a > c, b > c\}$ an equivalent partial 1-AV preference could be given by $(\bot, \bot, 0)$ over (a, b, c). However, for v_2 with partial preference $\{b > c\}$ it is not possible to construct a partial approval vector such that b receives the approval with a probability of $2/3$ and a with a probability of $1/3$. It is precisely this difference in the underlying preferences that leads to different complexities for the evaluation problem in Theorem 1 and Theorem 3 for the essentially one and the same voting rule described by k-approval and k-AV.

Mallows. The second model we are considering is the *Mallows noise model* [28] which is hereinafter mostly referred to as Mallows for short. The basic idea is that some reference profile is given, and the probability of another profile is measured according to its distance to the reference profile. Since the Mallows model is originally defined for linear orders, we will also present a version that applies to approval vectors. Given a set of candidates C, a profile $\hat{V} = (\hat{v}_1, \ldots, \hat{v}_n)$ over C and dispersion $\varphi \in (0, 1)$. The probability of a profile $V = (v_1, \ldots, v_n)$ over C according to the Mallows model is given by $\mathrm{Pr}_{\mathrm{Mallows}}(V \mid \hat{V}, \varphi) = \varphi^{d(V, \hat{V})}/Z^n$ with distance d and normalization constant Z chosen according to the vote type. Note, that it is assumed that the dispersion is the same for all voters. In the original case of linear orders, the total swap distance (also known as the Kendall tau distance) $d(V, \hat{V}) = \sum_{i=1}^{n} \text{sw}(v_i, \hat{v}_i)$ is used, where $\text{sw}(v_i, \hat{v}_i)$ is the minimum number of swaps of pairwise consecutive candidates that are needed to transform v_i into $\hat{v}_i$. The normalization can be written as $Z = Z_{m,\varphi} = 1 \cdot (1 + \varphi) \cdot (1 + \varphi + \varphi^2) \cdots (1 + \cdots + \varphi^{m-1})$ (see, e.g., Lu and Boutilier [27]). In the case of approval vectors, we propose to use the total Hamming distance $d(V, \hat{V}) = \sum_{i=1}^{n} H(v_i, \hat{v}_i)$ with $H(v_i, \hat{v}_i) = |\{c \in C \mid \text{app}_{v_i}(c) \neq \text{app}_{\hat{v}_i}(c)\}|$. The normalization factor is $Z = Z_{m,\varphi} = \sum_{j=0}^{m} \binom{m}{j} \cdot \varphi^j$. Additionally, for k-AV vectors, the normalization becomes $Z = Z_{m,k,\varphi} = \sum_{j=0}^{\lfloor m/2 \rfloor} \binom{k}{j} \cdot \binom{m-k}{j} \cdot \varphi^{2j}$. For EVALUATION under Mallows, the parameters are the reference profile $\hat{V}$ over C and dispersion φ. Referring to the motivations, Mallows model captures the scenarios in which the data was corrupted in transmission, by small-scale manipulation, through the elicitation, or the preferences of the voters have changed over time. While the profile obtained in this scenario is the most likely, we have to assume that there is a statistical dispersion. Again, it is natural that, in such scenario, we are interested in how likely and thereby justified and robust the victory of a candidate is.

Example 2. Suppose we perform a 1-AV election over the set of candidates $C = \{a, b\}$ and the profile $\hat{V}$ over C shown in Fig. 2. We assume that it has been slightly corrupted in transmission with dispersion $\varphi = 1/2$. Now, EVALUATION assuming Mallows with distinguished candidate b asks for the probability that b is a winner of the election. The profile $\hat{V}$ over (a, b) and the surrounding profiles with their respective total Hamming distance to $\hat{V}$ and probabilities are shown in Fig. 2. The probability that b is a winner, and thereby the answer to the EVALUATION instance, is $\Phi = (0.25+0.25+0.0625+0.015625)/Z^3 = 0.296$ with $Z^3 = 1.953125$. Whereby, candidate b or the voters could have legitimate concerns about the robustness and thereby the legitimacy of the victory of candidate a under those circumstances.

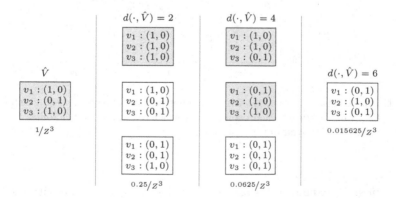

Fig. 2. Example for an EVALUATION instance assuming Mallows with distinguished candidate b. The probability for each profile is given with respect to its Hamming distance to $\hat{V}$. Profiles for which b is not a winner are grayed out.

EDM. Finally, we consider the model introduced by Conitzer and Sandholm [12] and later studied by Hazon et al. [19]. Due to its nature, we refer to it as the *explicit distribution model* (EDM). Given a set of candidates C, for each voter $i \in \{1, \ldots, n\}$ we are given a probability distribution π_i over the votes over C through a list of votes paired with their non-zero probabilities. Each unspecified vote has probability 0. The probability of a profile $V = (v_1, \ldots, v_n)$ over C according to EDM for $\pi = (\pi_1, \ldots, \pi_n)$ is given by $\mathrm{Pr}_{\mathrm{EDM}}(V \mid \pi) = \prod_{i=1}^{n} \pi_i(v_i)$. The parameters needed for EVALUATION under EDM is the list of votes over C paired with their probabilities for each voter. In practice, it can be quite difficult to determine meaningful probabilities for the individual preferences required for EDM. On the other hand, using EDM, one can replicate both PPIC, Mallows and other models by explicitly stating the respective probability distribution for each voter. However, this may require high computational effort as well as a list of exponential length depending on the number of candidates for each voter. Nevertheless, EDM in its generality and flexibility covers the motivations and scenarios of the other models.

Example 3. Suppose we focus on a Borda election over the set of candidates $C = \{a, b, c\}$ and the probability distribution π shown in Fig. 3. The evaluation problem assuming EDM with distinguished candidate b asks for the probability that b is a winner of the election. Here b wins in two profiles with positive probability, $12/20$ and $3/20$, so the answer to the EVALUATION instance is $\Phi = 3/5$.

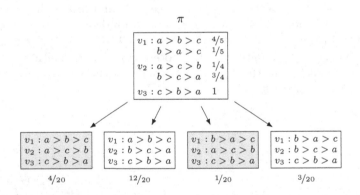

Fig. 3. Example for an EVALUATION instance assuming EDM with distinguished candidate b. The probability for each profile is given with respect to π. Profiles for which b is not a winner are grayed out.

Computational Complexity. We assume that the reader is familiar with the basics of computational complexity, such as the classes P, NP, FP, and #P. For further information, we refer to the textbooks by Arora and Barak [1] and Papadimitriou [30]. We examine the complexity of the problems presented here mainly in

Table 1. Complexity results for $\mathcal{E}$-EVALUATION in the non-unique winner case. The number of voters is denoted by n. For a constant number of candidates, see Theorem 11.

	PPIC		Mallows		EDM	
	General	Const. n	General	Const. n	General	Const. n
AV	FP, Theorem 2		FP, Theorem 9		#P-hard, Theorem 10	FP, Theorem 10
k-AV ($k \geq 1$)	#P-hard, Theorem 3	FP, Theorem 3	?	FP, Theorem 9	#P-hard, Theorem 10	FP, Theorem 10
k-appr. ($k \geq 1$), k-veto ($k \geq 1$), $(2, 1, \ldots, 1, 0)$	#P-hard, Theorem 1	#P-hard $(n - 1)$, Theorem 1	#P-hard, Theorem 6, 7	FP, Theorem 5	#P-hard, Theorem 10	FP, Theorem 10
Borda			#P-hard, Theorem 6	FP ($n = 1$), Theorem 4		

terms of *counting complexity* as introduced by Valiant [34] using polynomial-time Turing reductions from #P-hard counting problems to show the hardness of the problems or by presenting polynomial-time algorithms to verify their membership in FP. Comparing the complexity of #P-hard problems to the complexity of decision problems in the polynomial hierarchy, we recognize the immense complexity of just those. According to the theorem of Toda [33], the whole polynomial hierarchy is contained in $P^{\#P}$. Therefore, a polynomial-time algorithm for a #P-hard problem would implicate the collapse of the whole polynomial hierarchy, including NP, to P.

3 Results

In this section we present our results regarding the evaluation problem. Table 1 summarizes our main results for the non-unique winner case. Note that we have omitted several proofs due to the length restrictions but briefly address the ideas.

3.1 PPIC

In the following, we present our results regarding PPIC. We start with the results for profiles consisting of linear order votes. Bachrach et al. [2] have shown that the evaluation problem for the non-normalized variant of PPIC is #P-hard for plurality and veto, even though each preference has at most two completions. It is precisely the latter limitation that makes it possible to easily transfer this result to the normalized variant considered here. Furthermore, by using the circular block votes lemma of Betzler and Dorn [6] it is possible to extend the result to all scoring rules. Note, however, that all these proofs require a variable number of voters. Therefore, we start by showing that $\mathcal{E}$-EVALUATION assuming PPIC is #P-hard for all scoring rules in the non-unique winner case, even if only one voter is participating in the election.

Theorem 1. $\mathcal{E}$-EVALUATION *is #P-hard for each scoring rule assuming PPIC, even for one voter.*

Proof. We show the #P-hardness by a polynomial-time Turing reduction from the problem #LINEAR-EXTENSION, the problem of counting the number of completions (also referred to as linear extensions) of a partial order $\succ_X$ over a set of elements X, which was shown to be #P-hard by Brightwell and Winkler [9]. Assume we are given a #LINEAR-EXTENSION instance consisting of a set $X = \{x_1, \ldots, x_t\}$ and a partial order $\succ_X$ over X. First, we determine one completion $>_X^*$ of $\succ_X$ through topological sorting. Set $X_0 = X$. For $i = 0, \ldots, t-2$ we perform the following routine.

In the following, we construct an instance for a query to the $\mathcal{E}$-EVALUATION oracle. Note that X_i contains $t-i$ elements. Set $C = X_i \cup \{b_j \mid 1 \leq j \leq t+i\}$ with $m = 2t$. We assume that the given scoring rules is defined for $2t$ candidates. If not, the given linear extension instance can be enlarged using padding elements. Let $\boldsymbol{\alpha} = (\alpha_1, \ldots, \alpha_m)$ with $\alpha_m = 0$ be the scoring vector for m candidates and $k = \min\{j \in \{1, \ldots, m-1\} \mid \alpha_j > \alpha_{j+1}\}$. We distinguish between two cases.

Case 1 $(k < t-1)$: Let $\tilde{V}$ be a partial profile over C consisting of one partial vote $\tilde{v} : b_1 \succ \cdots \succ b_{k-1} \succ X_i^{\succ_X} \succ b_k \succ \cdots \succ b_{t+i}$ with $X_i^{\succ_X}$ being the elements in X_i partially ordered by $\succ_X$. Let x_s be the element in X_i for which $\forall x_j \in X_i \setminus \{x_s\} : x_s >_X^* x_j$ holds.

Case 2 $(k \geq t-1)$: Let $\tilde{V}$ be a partial profile over C consisting of one partial vote $\tilde{v} : b_1 \succ \cdots \succ b_{k-t+1} \succ X_i^{\succ_X} \succ b_{k-t+2} \succ \cdots \succ b_{t+i}$ with $X_i^{\succ_X}$ being the elements in X_i partially ordered by $\succ_X$. Let x_s be the element in X_i for which $\forall x_j \in X_i \setminus \{x_s\} : x_j >_X^* x_s$ holds.

We subsequently set $\Theta_i = \Phi$ (Case 1) or $\Theta_i = 1 - \Phi$ (Case 2) with Φ denoting the answer of the $\mathcal{E}$-EVALUATION oracle regarding the previously constructed instance consisting of the set of candidates C, partial profile $\tilde{V}$, and candidate $p = x_s$. The routine ends with setting $X_i = X_i \setminus \{x_s\}$.

Finally, after considering each value of i, we return $\prod_{i=0}^{t-2} \Theta_i^{-1}$ as the number of completions of $\succ_X$. We now show the correctness of the reduction. By $\succ_{X_i}$ we denote the partial order over X_i induced by $\succ_X$. We show that $\Theta_i = |\Lambda(\succ_{X_{i+1}})|/|\Lambda(\succ_{X_i})|$ for $i \in \{0, \ldots, t-2\}$ holds. For this we consider an arbitrary step i. It holds that $\alpha_1 = \cdots = \alpha_k > \alpha_{k+1}$. Note that in both cases, the partiality of $\tilde{v}$ is limited to the partial order $\succ_{X_i}$ embedded in it. In Case 1, x_s is a winner of the election regarding completion $V = (v)$ of $\tilde{V} = (\tilde{v})$ if and only if x_s is placed in position k in v. Candidate x_s being placed in position k in v is equivalent to $\forall x_j \in X_i \setminus \{x_s\} : x_s >_v x_j$. Thereby, $\Theta_i = |\{>^* \in \Lambda(\succ_{X_i}) \mid \forall x_j \in X_i \setminus \{x_s\} : x_s >^* x_j\}|/|\Lambda(\succ_{X_i})|$ holds. But if x_s is fixed to the top position regarding X_i, it holds that the remaining number of completions equals the number of completions regarding $X_{i+1} = X_i \setminus \{x_s\}$ whereby $|\{>^* \in \Lambda(\succ_{X_i}) \mid \forall x_j \in X_i \setminus \{x_s\} : x_s >^* x_j\}| = |\Lambda(\succ_{X_{i+1}})|$ holds. Thereby, $\Theta_i = |\Lambda(\succ_{X_{i+1}})|/|\Lambda(\succ_{X_i})|$ follows. In Case 2, x_s is not a winner of the election regarding completions $V = (v)$ of $\tilde{V} = (\tilde{v})$ if and only if x_s is placed in position $k + 1$ in v. The proportion of completions in which x_s is not a winner and thus fixed to the last position regarding X_i is given by $\Theta_i = 1 - \Phi$ with Φ denoting the probability that x_s wins. Thereby, $\Theta_i = |\Lambda(\succ_{X_{i+1}})|/|\Lambda(\succ_{X_i})|$ can be shown analogous to Case 1.

Finally, it holds that $|X_{t-1}| = 1$ whereby $|\Lambda(\succ_{X_{t-1}})| = 1$. Thus, by repeatedly applying $|\Lambda(\succ_{X_i})| = \Theta_i^{-1} \cdot |\Lambda(\succ_{X_{i+1}})|$ for $i \in \{0, \ldots, t-2\}$, $|\Lambda(\succ_X)| = |\Lambda(\succ_{X_0})|$ $| = \prod_{i=0}^{t-2} \Theta_i^{-1}$ follows. As the reduction can be performed in polynomial time, the #P-hardness follows.   □

Note that the complexity in the unique winner case is much more diverse. For scoring rules fulfilling $\alpha_1 > \alpha_2$ for each number of candidates, for example plurality, $(2, 1, \ldots, 1, 0)$, and Borda, the #P-hardness of the problem in the case of one voter can be shown using the previous reduction. For 2-approval, the problem is trivial for one voter, but can be shown to be #P-hard for two voters using a slightly adjusted version of the previous reduction. Finally, for veto, the problem is not hard for any constant number of voters, since the problem is trivial if the number of candidates exceeds the number of voters by more than one.

We now turn to the results regarding approval voting. We start with the result for approval voting with a variable number of approvals per voter, for which the complexity is significantly lower than for scoring rules.

Theorem 2. $\mathcal{E}$-EVALUATION *is in* FP *for AV assuming PPIC.*

Proof. We show that the problem is in FP using a dynamic programming approach. Assume we are given an AV-EVALUATION instance assuming PPIC consisting of a set of candidates $C = \{p, c_1, \ldots, c_{m-1}\}$, partial profile $\tilde{V} = (\tilde{v}_1, \ldots, \tilde{v}_n)$ and candidate p.

First, we define some shorthand notations. By $d(c)$, $a(c)$, and $u(c)$ we denote the number of votes $\tilde{v}_i$ in $\tilde{V}$ with $\mathrm{app}_{\tilde{v}_i}(c) = 0$, 1, or $\perp$ respectively. For a candidate $c \in C$, by $R(i, c)$ for $0 \le i \le n$ we denote the number of combinations to extend the partial entries in $\tilde{V}$ for candidate c such that c has exactly i approvals. It holds that $R(i, c) = \binom{u(c)}{i-a(c)}$ for $0 \le i - a(c) \le u(c)$ and 0 otherwise. By $N(s, j, k)$ we denote the number of combinations to extend the partial entries in $\tilde{V}$ for the candidates $c_1, \ldots, c_j$ in a way that exactly k candidates in $\{c_1, \ldots, c_j\}$ receive exactly s approvals each while each other candidate in $\{c_1, \ldots, c_j\}$ receives less than s approvals. Set $N(s, 0, 0) = 1$ for $0 \le s \le n$ and $N(s, j, k) = 0$ for $k > j$ or negative s, j, or k. The following relationship applies. $N(s, j, k) = \left[\sum_{i=0}^{s-1} R(i, c_j)\right] \cdot N(s, j-1, k) + R(s, c_j) \cdot N(s, j-1, k-1)$ for $0 \le s \le n$, $1 \le j \le m-1$, and $0 \le k \le m-1$. The factor in the first term of the formula equals the number of different possibilities for c_j to receive less than s approvals in a completion. The factor in the second term corresponds to the number of different possibilities for c_j in a completion to obtain exactly s approvals, which increases the number of candidates with exactly s approvals by one. Therefore, by summing over all possible numbers of co-winners and each score of p that p could receive considering the different ways p may receive this score we obtain $H = \sum_{k=0}^{m-1} \sum_{s=0}^{n} (R(s, p) \cdot N(s, m-1, k))$ denoting the number of completions for which p is a winner of the election. Thereby the probability Φ that p is a winner of the election is given by $H/2^{N_\perp}$ with $N_\perp$ denoting the total number of undetermined approvals in $\tilde{V}$. We have to determine $\mathcal{O}(n \cdot m^2)$ different entries with each one requiring at most $\mathcal{O}(n^2)$ steps whereby the whole approach only requires a polynomial bounded number of steps. In the unique winner case we receive the number of completions in which p is the winner of the elections by excluding the possibility of co-winners: $H = \sum_{s=0}^{n} R(s,p) \cdot N(s, m-1, 0)$. $\square$

On the other hand, if the number of approvals is fixed for each voter, the problem becomes hard for approval voting. Interestingly, and contrary to the result for scoring rules, this hardness does not hold for a constant number of voters. This leads to the apparently contradictory result that the complexity of the problem for one and the same voting rule described by k-approval and k-AV is differing. This difference can be traced back to the differing degree of information which was addressed in the explanation after Example 1.

Theorem 3. $\mathcal{E}$-EVALUATION *is #P-hard for k-AV for any fixed $k \geq 1$ assuming PPIC, but lies in FP for a constant number of voters.*

The first statement can be shown by a reduction from #PERFECT-BIPARTITE-MATCHING which was shown to be #P-hard by Valiant [34]. The second statement follows from the observation that there is only a polynomially bounded number of votes per voter and thus for a constant number of voters there is only a polynomially bounded number of profiles with non-zero probability.

3.2 Mallows

In the following, we present our results regarding the Mallows noise model. Note that the Mallows model is generalized by the *repeated insertion model* (RIM). Therefore, the hardness results in this section also hold for RIM. Again, we first present the results for profiles consisting of linear order votes. Note that our main tool for the hardness results presented here is the observation that the evaluation problem regarding Mallows is equivalent to the counting variant of the *unit-cost swap bribery problem* (see Dorn and Schlotter [14]) under polynomial-time Turing reduction. We omitted the proof for this result due to the length restrictions. The main idea is to choose the dispersion factor in such a way that it is possible to recalculate the exact number of profiles in a certain total swap distance in which the respective candidate is a (non-)unique winner.

Theorem 4. $\mathcal{E}$-EVALUATION *is in FP for all scoring rules assuming Mallows for one voter.*

We show that Kendall's approach (see Kendall [22]) of calculating the number of linear orders with an exact given swap distance to a given vote can be formulated as dynamic programming and extended to take into account the position of p.

This result can also be extended to any constant number of voters for a certain class of scoring rules. We call a scoring rule *almost constant* if the number of different values in its scoring vectors is bounded by a constant, and additionally only one value has an unbounded number of entries. This class of scoring rules was considered by Baumeister et al. [5] and later by Kenig and Kimelfeld [23], the latter of which coined the name. This class contains, for example, scoring rules like k-approval, k-veto and $(2, 1, \ldots, 1, 0)$.

Theorem 5. $\mathcal{E}$-EVALUATION *is in* FP *for all almost constant scoring rules assuming Mallows for a constant number of voters.*

The result is based on the fact that the number of combinations of relevant prefixes and suffixes of the votes in the profile is bounded by a polynomial with the degree including the number of positions covered by the values with a bounded number of entries and the number of voters. As we will see in Theorem 8, there also exist scoring rules beyond this class for which the problem is hard for a constant number of voters. We proceed with our results for an unbounded number.

Theorem 6. $\mathcal{E}$-EVALUATION *is #P-hard for* $(2, 1, \ldots, 1, 0)$ *and Borda assuming Mallows.*

Baumeister et al. [5] showed the NP-hardness of the unit-cost swap bribery problem for $(2, 1, \ldots, 1, 0)$ and Borda through a polynomial-time many-one-reduction from the NP-complete problem X3C. As the respective counting problem #X3C is #P-hard as shown by Hunt et al. [20] and the previously mentioned reductions by Baumeister et al. are also parsimonious, the counting version of the unit-cost swap bribery problem is #P-hard for $(2, 1, \ldots, 1, 0)$ and Borda. Therefore, by the results stated at the beginning of this section regarding the polynomial-time Turing equivalence of the problems, the #P-hardness of $\mathcal{E}$-EVALUATION for $(2, 1, \ldots, 1, 0)$ and Borda assuming Mallows follows.

Contrary to Borda and $(2, 1, \ldots, 1, 0)$, it is known that the unit-cost swap bribery problem is in P for plurality and veto (Dorn and Schlotter [14]). As we see in the following, however, the respective counting variants and evaluation problems assuming Mallows are #P-hard.

Theorem 7. $\mathcal{E}$-EVALUATION *is #P-hard for k-approval and k-veto with fixed $k \geq 1$ assuming Mallows.*

The proof consists of a reduction from #PERFECT-BIPARTITE-MATCHING for 3-regular graphs which was shown to be #P-hard by Dagum and Luby [13].

Considering Theorem 4 and Theorem 5, the question arises as to whether a scoring rule exists and, if so, whether a natural scoring rule exists, for which the evaluation problem assuming Mallows is #P-hard even for a constant number of voters. For this we consider *top-$\lfloor m/2 \rfloor$ Borda* characterized by the scoring vector $\alpha = (k, k - 1, \ldots, 1, 0, \ldots, 0)$ for $k = \lfloor m/2 \rfloor$ and m candidates.

Theorem 8. $\mathcal{E}$-EVALUATION *is #P-hard for top-$\lfloor m/2 \rfloor$ Borda assuming Mallows, even for a constant number voters.*

Again, the proof consists of a reduction from #PERFECT-BIPARTITE-MATCHING for 3-regular graphs using König's Line Coloring Theorem (König [24]). The number of voters here is 13. We expect that the problem is already hard for a lower number of voters for scoring rules similar to top-$\lfloor m/2 \rfloor$ Borda and Borda.

We now turn to the results regarding approval voting.

Theorem 9. $\mathcal{E}$-EVALUATION *is in* FP *for AV assuming Mallows and for k-AV assuming Mallows and a constant number of voters.*

The proof for the first case consists of a dynamic programming approach similar to that in the proof of Theorem 2. The second case follows from the fact that only a polynomial bounded number of possible profiles exist.

3.3   EDM

We now present our results regarding EDM. Since EDM generalizes both PPIC and Mallows, and, under certain restrictions, even through a polynomial-time Turing reduction, many of the previous results can be transferred to EDM for both scoring rules and approval voting. Note that some results for individual scoring rules and EDM were already known through Hazon et al. [19].

Theorem 10. $\mathcal{E}$-EVALUATION *is #P-hard for AV, k-AV, and all scoring rules assuming EDM, but lies in* FP *for a constant number of voters.*

The hardness results follow from the proofs of the hardness results regarding PPIC (see the note on the complexity regarding an unbounded number of voters above Theorem 1 and Theorem 3) in which for the constructed instances the number of completions of a vote is at most two and thus the instance can be efficiently transformed into an EDM instance. The efficiency result follows from the fact that the number of possible profiles is polynomially bounded.

Finally, we present our results for a constant number of candidates.[1]

Theorem 11. $\mathcal{E}$-EVALUATION *is in* FP *for AV, k-AV, and all scoring rules assuming PPIC, Mallows, or EDM for a constant number of candidates.*

The result follows by slight adjustments from the approach for a constant number of candidates by Hazon et al. [19] and the fact that Mallows and PPIC instances can be efficiently transformed to EDM instances for a constant number of candidates.

3.4   Corresponding Decision Problem

Conitzer and Sandholm [12] defined the evaluation problem as a decision problem instead of a weighted counting problem. Assume we are given a rational number r with $0 \leq r \leq 1$ as part of the input. Here we ask whether the probability that the given candidate is a winner of the election is greater than r. We refer to this problem as $\mathcal{E}$-EVALUATION-DEC. The question arises whether the decision problem in some cases is easier to answer than the weighted counting problem. The following result shows that this is not the case for the cases considered here, namely AV, k-AV and scoring rules assuming PPIC, Mallows, and EDM. This result holds for all winner models and parameterized cases considered here.

---

[1] Theorem 11 covers the case of classical scoring rules with a fixed-size scoring vector.

Theorem 12. *For the cases considered here, the problems $\mathcal{E}$-EVALUATION and $\mathcal{E}$-EVALUATION-DEC are equivalent under polynomial-time Turing reduction.*

While the reduction of the decision variant to the probability variant is straightforward, the reduction in the opposite direction uses the decision problem as oracle for the search algorithm of Kwek and Mehlhorn [25]. It follows that $\mathcal{E}$-EVALUATION is in FP, if and only if $\mathcal{E}$-EVALUATION-DEC is in P. On the other hand, $\mathcal{E}$-EVALUATION is #P-hard, if and only if $\mathcal{E}$-EVALUATION-DEC is #P-hard. While it is unusual to speak of #P-hardness of decision problems, it is possible to show just that using Turing reductions. The #P-hardness makes the NP-membership of such a problem unlikely (Toda [33]).

An interesting special case of the decision problem is to ask if the probability that the given candidate wins is greater than $r = 0$. By the previous theorem it follows that if the problem for $r = 0$ is NP-hard, the NP-hardness of the evaluation problem under Turing reduction follows, but not the stronger #P-hardness. Regarding EDM, the problem is referred to as the CHANCE-EVALUATION problem by Hazon et al. [19]. Regarding PPIC, the problem is equivalent to the well studied possible winner problem (for a recent overview, see Lang [26]). Regarding Mallows, the problem is trivial for the voting rules considered here as each candidate has a non-zero winning probability.

4 Further Related Work

In the following we discuss the related work which has not been sufficiently covered in the paper so far. For a comprehensive overview regarding elections with probabilistic or incomplete preferences, we refer to the overview by Boutilier and Rosenschein [8] and the survey by Walsh [35].

Subsequently to the polynomial-time randomized approximation algorithm with additive error for calculating a candidates' winning probability assuming PPIC by Bachrach et al. [2], Kenig and Kimelfeld [23] recently presented such an algorithm with multiplicative error for calculating the probability that a candidate loses assuming PPIC or RIM including Mallows.

Wojtas and Faliszewski [37] and recently Imber and Kimelfeld [21] have studied the problem of determining the winning probability for elections in which the participation of candidates or voters is uncertain by examining the complexity of the counting variants of election control problems.

Shiryaev et al. [31] studied the robustness of elections by considering the minimum number of swaps in the profile necessary to replace the current winner for which the evaluation problem under Mallows forms the probabilistic variant. Very recently, Boehmer et al. [7] have further built on these studies and thoroughly investigated the corresponding counting variant considering the parameterized complexity and by experiments based on the election map dataset by Szufa et al. [32], to investigate the practical complexity as well as the actual stability measurement considered by the problem. In comparison to the Mallows model, not all profiles are taken into account, weighted according to their distance, but all profiles up to a given distance limit are equally weighted.

In many cases the Mallows model is used to describe the distribution of votes based on a true general underlying ranking. If one assumes that the assumption regarding the existence of such a ranking is correct, it seems a reasonable approach to determine the winner by determining the most likely underlying ranking or to ask for a voting rule with the output as close as possible to such an underlying ranking. This approach has been examined, beside others, by Caragiannis et al. [10] and de Weerdt et al. [36].

The evaluation problem is also considered in other contexts. For example, in sports, the evaluation problem was studied by Mattei et al. [29] for various tournament formats and subsequently by Baumeister and Hogrebe [4] with a particular focus on predicting the outcome of round-robin tournaments.

5   Conclusion

We studied the computational complexity of the evaluation problem for approval voting and positional scoring rules regarding PPIC, the Mallows noise model, and EDM. We showed that the complexity of the problem varies greatly depending on the voting rule, the distribution model, and the parameterization. While in the general case, and partially even in very restricted cases, the evaluation problem is quite hard, we also identified general cases in which the probability that the given candidate wins the election can be calculated efficiently. Finally, in addition to the more practical motivations we have presented at the beginning, the evaluation problem is essential for the theoretical investigations of probabilistic variants of election interference problems such as manipulation, bribery, and control. As introduced by Conitzer and Sandholm [12] the decision variant of the evaluation problem is essentially the verification problem for just those problems. They show NP-hardness for several cases, but also finally point out that these problems do not necessarily lie in NP. In Sect. 3.4 we show that this assumption is probably correct by proving the #P-hardness for several cases. For just those NP- and #P-hard cases, it is unlikely that the interference problem itself lies in NP, as the problem of verifying the success of a given intervention is probably not contained in P.

Besides solving the open cases, namely the complexity regarding Mallows and k-AV in general and Borda for a constant number of voters, it may be interesting to consider multi-winner elections, further distribution models, and the fine-grained parameterized counting complexity as introduced by Flum and Grohe [17]. Of course, the worst-case, and the slightly more practical parameterized worst-case, analysis is only the first but an indispensable step in the complexity analysis of the problems and should, especially for the here identified hard cases, be followed by an average-case or typical-case analysis.

Acknowledgment. We thank the anonymous reviewers for their helpful suggestions for improving this paper. This work is supported by the DFG-grant BA6270/1-1.

References

1. Arora, S., Barak, B.: Computational Complexity: A Modern Approach. Cambridge University Press, Cambridge (2009)
2. Bachrach, Y., Betzler, N., Faliszewski, P.: Probabilistic possible winner determination. In: Proceedings of the 24th AAAI Conference on Artificial Intelligence, pp. 697–702. AAAI Press (2010)
3. Baumeister, D., Hogrebe, T.: Complexity of election evaluation and probabilistic robustness. In: Proceedings of the 19th International Conference on Autonomous Agents and Multiagent Systems, pp. 1771–1773. IFAAMAS (2020)
4. Baumeister, D., Hogrebe, T.: Complexity of scheduling and predicting round-robin tournaments. In: Proceedings of the 20th International Conference on Autonomous Agents and Multiagent Systems, pp. 178–186. IFAAMAS (2021)
5. Baumeister, D., Hogrebe, T., Rey, L.: Generalized distance bribery. In: Proceedings of the 33rd AAAI Conference on Artificial Intelligence, pp. 1764–1771. AAAI Press (2019)
6. Betzler, N., Dorn, B.: Towards a dichotomy of finding possible winners in elections based on scoring rules. J. Comput. Syst. Sci. **76**(8), 812–836 (2010)
7. Boehmer, N., Bredereck, R., Faliszewski, P., Niedermeier, R.: On the robustness of winners: counting briberies in elections. arXiv preprint arXiv:2010.09678 (2020)
8. Boutilier, C., Rosenschein, J.: Incomplete information and communication in voting. In: Brandt, F., Conitzer, V., Endriss, U., Lang, J., Procaccia, A. (eds.) Handbook of Computational Social Choice, chap. 10, pp. 223–257. Cambridge University Press (2016)
9. Brightwell, G., Winkler, P.: Counting linear extensions. Order **8**(3), 225–242 (1991)
10. Caragiannis, I., Procaccia, A., Shah, N.: When do noisy votes reveal the truth? ACM Trans. Econ. Comput. **4**(3), 15 (2016)
11. Cohen, W., Schapire, R., Singer, Y.: Learning to order things. In: Advances in Neural Information Processing Systems, pp. 451–457 (1998)
12. Conitzer, V., Sandholm, T.: Complexity of manipulating elections with few candidates. In: Proceedings of the 18th National Conference on Artificial Intelligence, pp. 314–319. AAAI Press (2002)
13. Dagum, P., Luby, M.: Approximating the permanent of graphs with large factors. Theor. Comput. Sci. **102**(2), 283–305 (1992)
14. Dorn, B., Schlotter, I.: Multivariate complexity analysis of swap bribery. Algorithmica **64**(1), 126–151 (2012)
15. Dwork, C., Kumar, R., Naor, M., Sivakumar, D.: Rank aggregation methods for the web. In: Proceedings of the 10th International Conference on World Wide Web, pp. 613–622. ACM (2001)
16. Ephrati, E., Rosenschein, J.: Multi-agent planning as a dynamic search for social consensus. In: Proceedings of the 13th International Joint Conference on Artificial Intelligence, pp. 423–429 (1993)
17. Flum, J., Grohe, M.: The parameterized complexity of counting problems. SIAM J. Comput. **33**(4), 892–922 (2004)
18. Ghosh, S., Mundhe, M., Hernandez, K., Sen, S.: Voting for movies: the anatomy of a recommender system. In: Proceedings of the 3rd Annual Conference on Autonomous Agents, pp. 434–435. ACM (1999)
19. Hazon, N., Aumann, Y., Kraus, S., Wooldridge, M.: On the evaluation of election outcomes under uncertainty. Artif. Intell. **189**, 1–18 (2012)

20. Hunt, H., Marathe, M., Radhakrishnan, V., Stearns, R.: The complexity of planar counting problems. SIAM J. Comput. **27**(4), 1142–1167 (1998)
21. Imber, A., Kimelfeld, B.: Probabilistic inference of winners in elections by independent random voters. In: Proceedings of the 20th International Conference on Autonomous Agents and Multiagent Systems, pp. 647–655. IFAAMAS (2021)
22. Kendall, M.G.: Rank Correlation Methods. Theory & Applications of Rank Order-Statistics, 3rd edn. C. Griffin (1962)
23. Kenig, B., Kimelfeld, B.: Approximate inference of outcomes in probabilistic elections. In: Proceedings of the 33rd AAAI Conference on Artificial Intelligence, vol. 33, pp. 2061–2068. AAAI Press (2019)
24. König, D.: Graphok és alkalmazásuk a determinánsok és a halmazok elméletére. Mathematikai és Természettudományi Ertesito **34**, 104–119 (1916)
25. Kwek, S., Mehlhorn, K.: Optimal search for rationals. Inf. Process. Lett. **86**(1), 23–26 (2003)
26. Lang, J.: Collective decision making under incomplete knowledge: possible and necessary solutions. In: 29th International Joint Conference on Artificial Intelligence and 17th Pacific Rim International Conference on Artificial Intelligence, pp. 4885–4891. International Joint Conferences on Artificial Intelligence Organization (2020)
27. Lu, T., Boutilier, C.: Effective sampling and learning for Mallows models with pairwise-preference data. J. Mach. Learn. Res. **15**(1), 3783–3829 (2014)
28. Mallows, C.: Non-null ranking models. Biometrika **44**, 114–130 (1957)
29. Mattei, N., Goldsmith, J., Klapper, A., Mundhenk, M.: On the complexity of bribery and manipulation in tournaments with uncertain information. J. Appl. Log. **13**(4), 557–581 (2015)
30. Papadimitriou, C.: Computational Complexity. Addison-Wesley, Boston (1994)
31. Shiryaev, D., Yu, L., Elkind, E.: On elections with robust winners. In: Proceedings of the 12th International Conference on Autonomous Agents and Multiagent Systems, pp. 415–422. IFAAMAS (2013)
32. Szufa, S., Faliszewski, P., Skowron, P., Slinko, A., Talmon, N.: Drawing a map of elections in the space of statistical cultures. In: Proceedings of the 19th International Conference on Autonomous Agents and Multiagent Systems, pp. 1341–1349. IFAAMAS (2020)
33. Toda, S.: PP is as hard as the polynomial-time hierarchy. SIAM J. Comput. **20**(5), 865–877 (1991)
34. Valiant, L.: The complexity of computing the permanent. Theor. Comput. Sci. **8**(2), 189–201 (1979)
35. Walsh, T.: Uncertainty in preference elicitation and aggregation. In: Proceedings of the 22nd AAAI Conference on Artificial Intelligence, pp. 3–8 (2007)
36. de Weerdt, M., Gerding, E., Stein, S.: Minimising the rank aggregation error. In: Proceedings of the 15th International Conference on Autonomous Agents and Multiagent Systems, pp. 1375–1376. IFAAMAS (2016)
37. Wojtas, K., Faliszewski, P.: Possible winners in noisy elections. In: Proceedings of the 26th AAAI Conference on Artificial Intelligence, pp. 1499–1505. AAAI Press (2012)

Point Based Solution Method
for Communicative IPOMDPs

Sarit Adhikari[✉] and Piotr Gmytrasiewicz

University of Illinois at Chicago, Chicago, IL 60607, USA
{sadhik6,piotr}@uic.edu

Abstract. Communicative interactive POMDPs (CIPOMDPs) provide
a principled framework for optimal interaction and communication in
multi-agent settings by endowing agents with nested models (theories
of mind) of others and with the ability to communicate with them. In
CIPOMDPs, agents use Bayes update to process their observations and
messages without the usual assumption of cooperative discourse. We propose a variant of the point-based value iteration method, called IPBVI-
Comm, to compute the approximate optimal policy of a CIPOMDP
agent. We then use the IPBVI-Comm to study the optimal communicative behavior of agents in cooperative and competitive scenarios.
Unsurprisingly, it is optimal for agents to attempt to mislead if their
preferences are not aligned. But it turns out the higher depth of reasoning allows an agent to detect insincere communication and to guard
against it. Specifically, in some scenarios, the agent is able to distinguish
a truthful friend from a deceptive foe based on the message received.

Keywords: Decision-theoretic planning · Multi agent systems ·
Deception

1 Introduction

The Communicative Interactive Partially Observable Markov Decision Process
(CIPOMDP) provides a principled framework for rational interaction and communication in a multi-agent environments [19]. CIPOMDP framework is an
extension of interactive POMDP [18] to include the exchange of messages among
the agents. IPOMDP, in turn, extends Partially Observable Markov Decision
Process (POMDP) [39] to include other agents by incorporating their models
into its state space. As in POMDPs, the value function of CIPOMDPs is represented in terms of max over linear segments called alpha-vectors. Each alpha
vector corresponds to a policy and each component of alpha vector ascribes value
to an interactive state. Value iteration proceeds by backing up alpha-vectors to
a higher time horizon starting from horizon 1. POMDPs suffer from the curse
of dimensionality and the curse of history. Naturally, These curses are carried
over to IPOMDPs and CIPOMDPs, which require solving of nested POMDPs
and CIPOMDPs. The curse of history is more prominent in CIPOMDPs because

© Springer Nature Switzerland AG 2021
A. Rosenfeld and N. Talmon (Eds.): EUMAS 2021, LNAI 12802, pp. 245–263, 2021.
https://doi.org/10.1007/978-3-030-82254-5_15

the policy is now conditional on both observation and message received. Since computing optimal policies for POMDPs by exact solution methods are proven to be PSPACE-complete for finite time horizon and undecidable for an infinite time horizon [25], a large amount of work has been done in computing approximate solution. [31] introduced a point-based value iteration (PBVI) algorithm to approximate exact value iteration by selecting a fixed set of representative belief points and maintaining alpha vectors that are optimal at those points only. Our work builds on the interactive point-based value iteration [11] which showed improvement in runtime over other IPOMDP solution methods like [10]. Exact value iteration quickly becomes intractable in PODMPs and IPOMDPs due to generation of large number of alpha-vectors which is exponential in observation space $|A||\nu^{t+1}|^{|\Omega|}$, where ν^{t+1} denote set of alpha vectors being backed-up from $t+1$ to t. In the case of CIPOMDP, the size is further exploded due to the inclusion of message space in the policy. The exact number of alpha-vectors generated at time t will be $|A||\nu^{t+1}|^{|\Omega||\mathsf{M}|}$. To keep the size of the alpha-set in each iteration tractable, we can use the point-based method, which only retains the vectors which are optimal at the fixed set of belief points. As in IPOMDP, we need to solve the lower-level model to compute the alpha vectors. Accordingly, we limit the initial model of other agents to a finite set.

The study of communication and interaction among self-interested agents in a partially observable and stochastic domain has application in several fields ranging from military [3,17] to social robotics [4]. The communicative behavior among the agents in multi-agent systems has been studied in cognitive science [2], economics [13] and artificial intelligence [22,43]. With the advancement of artificial intelligence, the topic of machine deception has become more important. In particular, since communication among agents is becoming ubiquitous, malicious agents trying to exploit the vulnerabilities in other AI systems and humans might be a common problem of the future. Thus it is important to lay the foundation for deception-resistant AI systems. Further, as more AI agents are becoming part of our social life, the study of emergent social behavior among communicating agents (both artificial and human) with varied preferences is vital.

Although vast literature exists on the topic of machine fooling humans through fake content [37] and human fooling machines with adversarial attacks [24], the study of deception in a sequential decision-making scenario, by modeling other agents have rarely been explored. As argued in [23], AI needs to guard itself against malevolent humans and sometimes be able to deceive as well. On the other hand, when the agents' preferences align, then they benefit from sincere communication. Like physical actions, communicative actions are guided by the expected utility obtained in a particular state. Agents sometimes benefit from being sincere and sometimes it is in their best interest to deceive. To be able to cooperate, deceive or guard against deception, the agent needs to model the belief, intention, and preference of the other agent [5]. While POMDPs provide a theoretically sound framework to model uncertainty about the state of the world, the Theory of Mind (ToM) approach of IPOMDPs and CIPOMDPs

allows modeling of uncertainty about other agents, including their beliefs about
the world and other agents. Figure 1 shows the theory of mind (ToM) of the
decision-making agent which is uncertain about the type of another agent and
how it may model others including the original agent. At the bottom of the
hierarchy of models could be a random agent, or a rational agent that does not
model others, i.e., a classical POMDP agent. A great deal of research in psychology establishes a connection of deception to the recursive theory of mind
reasoning, which starts at an early age in humans [9, 32, 38]. More recently, [29]
provides a comprehensive quantitative analysis of the role of rationality and
theory of mind in deception and detecting deception.

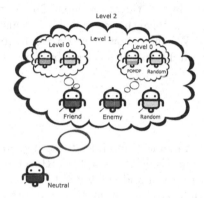

Fig. 1. Theory of Mind (ToM) reasoning from the perspective of agent i interacting
with agent j when there is uncertainty about the opponent type. Level is indicative of
cognitive sophistication. The neutral agent i thinks j might be enemy, friend or random
agent. Further, i thinks j thinks i might be a sincere and gullible agent or a random
agent. The behavior of j is simulated by i by putting itself in j's shoes. Within that
simulation, i needs to reason how j simulates i's behavior.

In order to advance the usefulness of CIPOMDPs in multiagent planning,
particularly in non-cooperative setting, we proceed to fill in missing gaps in current CIPOMDP literature. First, we propose an offline solution method called
interactive point based value iteration with communication (IPBVI-Comm) to
solve for the optimal communicative behavior. Then, we use IPBVI-Comm to
study communicative behaviors of CIPOMDP agents in various cooperative and
deceptive scenarios. Further, compared to [19], we provide more formal definition of the message space in terms of discretized interactive belief space, and
specify how the missing variables are marginalized. We also formalize the definition of sincerity and deception in terms of the message sent by the agent and
its belief about the state of the world. The proposed point-based offline solution
technique is used to compute the policy which finds the optimal action-message
pair to send at each time-step of interaction with the other agent. The subsequent policies are conditional on not only the observation but also the message
received from the other agent. Based on the preference of the agent and what is

known about the preferences of the modeled agent, the agent may benefit from incorporating the message from another agent into its belief, but discounting it if it thinks the other agent has an incentive to lie. The policy of POMDP agent on the bottom of a ToM hierarchy is augmented with a sincere message using a look-ahead reachability tree from the initial belief in the interactive state of the modeling agent. Similarly, we propose a way for an agent modeled as a POMDP to receive messages by augmenting its observation space. We apply IPBVI-Comm to agents interacting in the multi-agent tiger game and show that communication is valuable to agents and results in superior policies compared to its no communication counterpart. In cooperative scenarios, the agent can take advantage of messages from a sincere agent as additional observations, and can send sincere messages that inform the other agent. In competitive scenarios, the agent not only attempts to deceive the other agent but also ignores the message it knows to be deceitful. We then show how Bayesian update allows an agent higher in a cognitive hierarchy to tell a friend from foe based on the message received and its own observation.

2   Related Work

The problem of agents communicating and interacting simultaneously has been addressed in several decision-theoretic as well as RL settings. [14] uses DDRQN to learn communication protocol and solve a riddle by coordination. [15] combines multiagent RL with a bayesian update to compute communication protocols and policies in cooperative, partially observable multi-agent settings. [40] uses a neural model that learns communication along with the policy. In the planning and control setting, [28] uses communication for controllers to share part of their observation and control history at each step. More recently, [41] used POMDP with communication for human-robot collaboration task. Other work in HRI include [6,8,42]. [7] uses a theory of mind approach for the execution of a shared plan.

Communication has been studied extensively in other multi-agent decision theoretic frameworks [26,27,30,44]. In [33], agents use extended belief state that contain approximation of other agents' beliefs. But these works assume fully cooperative interactions and mostly involve central planning. CIPOMDPs, on the other hand, provide subjective theory of mind reasoning during communication, and follows Bayesian approaches to pragmatics.

Deception has been widely studied across multiple disciplines including game theory [12,35], psychology [16] and economics [21]. When it comes to a sequential decision process to study attacker's and defender's approaches in cybersecurity research, decision theoretic framework of POMDP [1] and IPOMDP [36] has been used. [34] combines ToM with components from deception theory and implements an epistemic agent using Agent-Oriented Programming Language.

3   Background

3.1   Communicative Interactive POMDPs

CIPOMDP [19] is the first general framework for an autonomous self-interested agent to communicate and interact with other agents in the environment based on Bayesian decision theory. A finitely nested communicative interactive POMDP of agent i in an environment with agent j, is defined as:

$$CIPOMDP_i = \langle IS_{i,l}, A_i, \mathbb{M}, \Omega_i, T_i, O_i, R_i \rangle \tag{1}$$

where $IS_{i,l}$ is a set of interactive states, defined as $IS_{i,l} = S \times M_{j,k}, l \geq 1$, where S is the set of physical states and $M_{j,k}$ is the set of possible models of agent j, l is the strategy (nesting) level, and $k < l$. The set of possible models $M_{j,k}$ consists of intentional models, Θ_j, or sub-intentional ones, SM_j. While the intentional models ascribe beliefs, preferences and rationality in action selection to the modeled agent, the sub-intentional models do not. We consider kth (less than l) level intentional models of agent j defined as $\theta_{j,k} = \langle b_{j,k}, A_j, \Omega_j, T_j, O_j, R_j \rangle$, where $b_{j,k}$ is agent j's belief nested to the level k, $b_{j,k} \in \Delta(IS_{j,k})$. The intentional model $\theta_{j,k}$, is sometimes called *type*, can be rewritten as $\theta_{j,k} = \langle b_{j,k}, \hat{\theta}_j \rangle$, where $\hat{\theta}_j$ includes all elements of the intentional model other than the belief and is called the agent j's frame. Among the classes of sub-intentional models, we consider no-information model [20] which randomly selects action to execute and message to send in each time-step. The random models are possible in each level starting with level-0.

In contrast to classical POMDPs and similar to IPOMDPs, the transition, observation and reward functions in CIPOMDPs take actions of other agents into account. $A = A_i \times A_j$ is the set of joint actions of all agents, Ω_i is the set of agent i's possible observations, $T_i : S \times A \times S \rightarrow [0,1]$ is the state transition function, $O_i : S \times A \times \Omega_i \rightarrow [0,1]$ is the observation function, $R_i : S \times A \rightarrow R$ is the reward function.

The $IS_{i,l}$ can be defined inductively

$$IS_{i,0} = S, \qquad\qquad \Theta_{j,0} = \{\langle b_{j,0}, \hat{\theta}_j \rangle : b_{j,0} \in \Delta(S)\}$$
$$M_{j,0} = \Theta_{j,0} \cup SM_j$$

$$IS_{i,1} = S \times M_{j,0}, \qquad \Theta_{j,1} = \{\langle b_{j,1}, \hat{\theta}_j \rangle : b_{j,1} \in \Delta(IS_{j,1})\}$$
$$M_{j,1} = \Theta_{j,1} \cup SM_j$$

$$\ldots\ldots$$

$$IS_{i,l} = S \overset{l-1}{\underset{k=0}{\times}} M_{j,k}, \qquad \Theta_{j,l} = \{\langle b_{j,l}, \hat{\theta}_j \rangle : b_{j,l} \in \Delta(IS_{j,l})\}$$

$$M_{j,l} = \Theta_{j,l} \cup SM_j$$

The above defines the 0-level model, $\theta_{j,0}$ as having beliefs only over the physical state space, S. The level 1 agent model maintains beliefs over the physical states and 0-level models of the opponent. A level l agent, $\theta_{j,l}$, maintains beliefs over S and over models of the opponent nested up to $l - 1$.

M is a set of messages the agents can send to and receive from each other, i.e., it is a communication language the agents share. Since agents' beliefs are probability distributions and communication is intended to share beliefs, it is natural to interpret a message in M as a marginal probability distribution over a subset of variables in the agents' interactive state spaces IS_i and IS_j, which overlap. That way M is a set of probabilistic statements about the interactive state space. The message nil, i.e., silence, contains no variables. Note that we do not assume that messages reflect agents' actual beliefs. We will further discretize M below.

3.2 Belief Update in CIPOMDPs

Belief update in CIPOMDPs is analogous to belief update in IPOMDPs when it comes to actions and observations. At any particular time step agents i and j can not only perform physical actions and observe but also send and receive messages. Call the message i sent at time $t-1$ $m_{i,s}^{t-1}$, and one i received at time t $m_{i,r}^t$, and analogously for j. We assume all messages are in M and that message transmission is perfect. We provide precise definition of message space in our formulation in Sect. 4.1. The belief update in CIPOMDPs has to update the probability of interactive state given the previous belief, action and observation, and given the message sent (at the previous time step) and received (at the current time): $P(is^t|b_i^{t-1}, a_i^{t-1}, m_{i,s}^{t-1}, o_i^t, m_{i,r}^t)$:

$$b_i^t(is^t) = P(is^t|b_i^{t-1}, a_i^{t-1}, m_{i,s}^{t-1}, o_i^t, m_{i,r}^t) = \eta \sum_{is^{t-1}} b_i^{t-1}(is^{t-1}) \sum_{a_j^{t-1}} P(m_{j,s}^{t-1}, a_j^{t-1}|\theta_j^{t-1})$$

$$\times O_i(s^t, a^{t-1}, o_i^t) T_i(s^{t-1}, a^{t-1}, s^t) \sum_{o_j^t} \tau_{\theta_j^t}(b_j^{t-1}, a_j^{t-1}, m_{j,s}^{t-1}, o_j^t, m_{j,r}^t, b_j^t) O_j(s^t, a^{t-1}, o_j^t)$$

The term $P(m_{j,s}^{t-1}, a_j^{t-1}|\theta_j^{t-1})$ quantifies the relation between the message i received from j and the model, θ_j, of agent j that generated the message.[1] This term is the measure of $j's$ sincerity, i.e., whether the message j sent reflects j's beliefs which are part of the model θ_j. η is the normalizing constant.

3.3 Planning in CIPOMDPs

The utility of interactive belief of agent i, contained in i's type θ_i, is:

$$U_i(\theta_i) = \max_{(m_{i,s}, a_i)} \left\{ \sum_{is \in IS} b_{is}(s) ER_i(is, m_{i,s}, a_i) \right.$$

$$\left. + \gamma \sum_{(m_{i,r}, o_i)} P(m_{i,r}, o_i|b_i, a_i) U_i(\langle SE_{\theta_i}(b_i, a_i, m_{i,s}, o_i, m_{i,r}), \hat{\theta}_i \rangle) \right\} \quad (2)$$

---

[1] Note that $m_{j,s}^{t-1} = m_{i,r}^t$ because message transmission is assumed to be perfect.

$ER_i(is, m_{i,s}, a_i)$ above is the immediate reward to i for sending $m_{i,s}$ and executing action a_i given the interactive state is and is equal to $\Sigma_{a_j} R_i(is, a_i, a_j, m_{i,s}) P(a_j|\theta_j)$. The planning in CIPOMDP makes use of Eq. 2, which is based on the Bellman optimality principle. The policy computes optimal action, message pair which results in a maximum expected reward. Consequently, value iteration in CIPOMDP is analogous to that in IPOMDP and POMDP. The set of optimal message-action pairs, $(m_{i,s}^*, a_i^*)$ is obtained by replacing max in Eq. 2 with argmax. We call the resulting set of optimal message-action pairs $OPT(\theta_i)$. When agent i models agent j as a strict optimizer, i predicts j would choose action-message pair in OPT set with equal probability:

$$P(m_{j,s}, a_j|\theta_j) = \frac{1}{|OPT(\theta_j)|} \tag{3}$$

and that $P(m_{j,s}, a_j|\theta_j)$ is equal to zero if $(m_{j,s}, a_j)$ is not in OPT. The possibility that agents may be less than optimal is considered in [19]

Being able to compute the probabilities of messages given the preferences and beliefs of a speaker is of crucial importance when sincerity is not guaranteed. The belief update in CIPOMDPs provides the principled way to discount content of messages that may be insincere because it is in the interest of the speaker to transmit them. We give an example of this further below.

4   Approach

4.1   Message Space

We define message space, $\mathbb{M}$, as a set of marginal probability distributions over a subset of variables in the interactive states of the agent. Since the belief space is continuous we make the computation more tractable by quantizing $\mathbb{M}$ into finite set of belief points. The message space is augmented with nil representing silence, which is analogous to no-op operation in the physical action set. Limiting message space to only nil message reduces CIPOMDP to IPOMDP. Usually, a message contains information about only the subset of possible interactive states.[2] The variables that the message doesn't mention are interpreted as being marginalized. For e.g. the message received $m_{i,r}$ can provide a mapping from physical state to belief marginalizing other variables of interactive state (belief of another agent, frame, etc.). Then $m_{i,r}(s)$ denotes belief the message ascribes to physical state $s \in S$. Further, message may only contain probabilities of subset of values that the variables mentioned in message can take. We use the principle of indifference and assume that probability is uniformly distributed among the remaining values. For the variables used in the message, let W be the set of values mentioned in the message and W' be the set of values not mentioned in the message

---

[2] For example, if the physical state space, S, is factored into variables X and Y, a message, m, might be "$P(0 \le X \le 100) = 0.7$".

$$\forall_{w'} \in W'$$

$$m(w') = \frac{1 - \sum_{w \in W} m(w)}{|W'|} \tag{4}$$

4.2   Sincerity and Deception

Let X denote a set of variables describing the interactive state of the agent. $\wp(X)$ is a set of all non-empty subsets of X. The joint belief b^t of an agent can be marginalized over the subset of variables in X. Let $b_{\overline{X}}$ represent belief marginalized over variables in $\overline{X}$. Accordingly message space $\mathbb{M}$ can be factored into the sets of messages marginalized over each of $\overline{X} \in \wp(X)$.

Sincere message can be defined as a message in message space $m \in \mathbb{M}_{\overline{X}}$ which is closest to the marginalized belief $b^t_{\overline{X}}$ consistent with the true joint belief b^t of the agent at time t. The distance is defined in terms of the L1 norm. Thus the set of sincere messages is given by

$$\mathbb{M}_{sincere} = \bigcup_{\overline{X} \in \wp(X)} \operatorname*{arg\,min}_{m \in \mathbb{M}_{\overline{X}}} \| b^t_{\overline{X}} - m \| \tag{5}$$

Insincere(deceptive) message can be defined as any message in message space except the one closest to true belief b_t of the agent at time t. Thus the set of insincere messages is given by

$$\mathbb{M}_{insincere} = \bigcup_{\overline{X} \in \wp(X)} \mathbb{M}_{\overline{X}} - \operatorname*{arg\,min}_{m \in \mathbb{M}_{\overline{X}}} \| b^t_{\overline{X}} - m \| \tag{6}$$

4.3   Communication for POMDP (Level-0 CIPOMDP)

The recursion in CIPOMDP bottoms out as a flat POMDP which does not have a model of the other agent. We use the definition of literal speaker[3] from [19]. A literal listener can incorporate the incoming message as additional observation, which we describe in the following section. These assumptions enable an agent that does not model the other agent to participate in the exchange of messages.

Augmented Observation Space and Function for POMDP. We propose POMDP (θ_0) can receive the message and include it in its belief update, by augmenting its observation space and consequently observation function. Observation space now becomes a Cartesian product of usual observation space and message space.

---

[3] Literal speaker generates a message reflecting its true belief about the physical states of the world b_t with probability $1 - \alpha$ and all other messages including 'nil' with probability $\frac{\alpha}{|\mathbb{M}|-1}$.

$$\Omega' = \Omega \times \mathbb{M} \tag{7}$$

The joint probability of observation and message received is obtained by combining the likelihood function for a physical observation with message distribution. The message distribution is represented by a triangular distribution with the idea that the likelihood of a message reflecting belief about the world state should increase monotonically as the belief.

$$P(m_{i,r}|s) = \begin{cases} \frac{1}{|S|} & if \ m_{i,r} - nil \\ (m_{i,r}(s)) & otherwise \end{cases} \tag{8}$$

Given the state of the world, observation is conditionally independent of the message received. The conditional independence holds because the broadcasted message received by the agent does not depend on the sensor which is used to get a physical observation. Then the augmented observation function can be defined as

$$\forall_{m_{i,r}} \in \mathbb{M} \ and \ \forall_o \in \Omega \ and \ \forall_s \in S$$

$$O'(s, a, o, m_{i,r}) = \frac{O(s, a, o)P(m_{i,r}|s)}{\sum_{m_{i,r}} P(m_{i,r}|s)} \tag{9}$$

4.4   IPBVI-Comm Algorithm

The point-based value iteration approach backs up the alpha-vectors optimal at a fixed set of belief points in each iteration starting from horizon 1. Each iteration consists of three steps, which we describe below, and along the way we highlight the difference with IPBVI [11]. Algorithm 1 provides the interactive point based value iteration with communication. The majority of the work happens in function PointBasedUpdate which generates new set of alpha vectors utilizing alpha vectors from previous time horizon. The belief set for each horizon consists of randomly generated belief points across all interactive states. When it comes to the 3 steps of point-based value iteration, IPBVI-Comm has the complexity of the same order as IPBVI except that the time complexity for calculation of intermediate alpha-vectors now depends on the size of the message space. Let $|B|$ represent the size of sample belief space at any level. When models of level '1' are solved, we have maximum of $|B|$ number of alpha vectors for each frame. For simplicity, let's suppose we have $|\hat{\theta}|$ frames at each level. Then the number of alpha vectors at each level is bounded by $\mathcal{O}(|B||\hat{\theta}|l^2)$ The additional complexity in IPBVI-Comm stems from the augmentation of POMDP policy with a sincere message, for which the agent has to perform an exact belief update. Even if we limit the set of initial models of other agents like IPBVI and perform planning over reachable models of the other agent, exact belief update quickly becomes intractable. At $t + 1$, $|B^t||A||\Omega'|$ new models are generated.

Algorithm 1. Point based value iteration with communication

1: **function** POINTBASEDUPDATE($\Gamma^{t-1}, IS^{t-1}, IS^t, B^t, \mathbb{M}^t$)
2:     $\Gamma^{a,m_s,*} \leftarrow \emptyset$, $\Gamma^{a,m_s,o,m_r} \leftarrow \emptyset$
3:     **for** $action \in A$, $m_s \in \mathbb{M}$ **do**
4:         $\alpha^{a,m_s} \leftarrow AlphasAM(action, m_s)$
5:         $\Gamma^{a,m_s,*} \leftarrow \Gamma^{a,m_s,*} \cup \alpha^{a,m_s}$
6:         **for** $obs \in \Omega$, $m_r \in \mathbb{M}$ **do**
7:             $\alpha^{a,o,m_s,m_r} \leftarrow AlphasAOM(a, m_s, obs, m_r, \Gamma^{t-1})$
8:             $\Gamma^{a,m_s,o,m_r} \leftarrow \Gamma^{a,m_s,o,m_r} \cup \alpha^{a,o,m_s,m_r}$
9:         **end for**
10:     **end for**
11:     $\Gamma^{all} \leftarrow \emptyset$
12:     **for** $action \in A$, $m_s \in \mathbb{M}$ **do**
13:         $\Gamma^{a,m_s} \leftarrow \emptyset$
14:         **for** $b_l \in B$ **do**
15:             $\alpha^{a,m_s,b} \leftarrow \Gamma^{a,m_s,*}(action, m_s)$
16:             **for** $obs \in \Omega, m_r \in \mathbb{M}$ **do**
17:                 $\alpha^{a,m_s,b} \leftarrow \alpha^{a,m_s,b} + \arg\max_{\Gamma^{a,m_s,o,m_r}}(\alpha^{a,m_s,o,m_r}.b_{i,l})$
18:             **end for**
19:             $\Gamma^{a,m_s} \leftarrow \Gamma^{a,m_s} \cup \alpha^{a,m_s,b}$
20:         **end for**
21:         $\Gamma^{all} \leftarrow \Gamma^{all} \cup \Gamma^{a,m_s}$
22:     **end for**
23:     $\nu^t \leftarrow \emptyset$
24:     **for** $b_l \in B$ **do**
25:         $\nu^t \leftarrow \nu^t \cup \arg\max_{\alpha^t \in \Gamma^{all}}(\alpha^t.b_l)$
26:     **end for**
27:     **return** ν^t
28: **end function**

Step 1. The first step (lines 2–10) involves calculating the intermediate set of alpha vectors $\Gamma^{a_i,m_{i,s},*}$ representing immediate reward for action a_i and message $m_{i,s}$ (Eq. 10), and $\Gamma^{a_i,o_i,m_{i,s},m_{i,r}}$ representing future reward after receiving observation o_i and message $m_{i,r}$ (Eq. 11). The step is performed for all actions, observations and messages. For horizon 1, computation of immediate reward is sufficient and will be used as initial alpha set for subsequent backups.

Different from point-based algorithm for IPOMDPs, we need to calculate $Pr(m_{ir}|\theta_{j,l-1})$ and perform belief update for the other agent j which now depends on message sent by i. Due to one-step delay in message exchange, the message sent in the current time step allows computing interactive states in next time step and backup the values from next time step. Assuming sincerity for $\theta_{j,0}$, only the message closest to belief will get probability $1 - \alpha$. All the other messages, including 'nil', will share the probability α. When a message received is other than a sincere message, level-1 CIPOMDP ignores the message, and belief update proceeds as IPOMDP. For higher-level CIPOMDPs, the probability of message received is uniformly distributed among all the messages in $OPT(\theta_j)$

set, as defined in Sect. 3.3. Algorithm to calculate the probability of message given model of another agent is provided in the appendix.

$$\forall a_i \in A_i, \forall o_i \in \Omega_i, \forall m_{i,s} \in M, \forall is \in IS$$

$$\Gamma^{a_i,m_{i,s},*} \leftarrow \alpha^{a_i,m_{i,s},*}(is) = \sum_{a_j \in A_j} R_i(s, a_i, a_j, m_{i,s}) Pr(a_j|\theta_{j,l-1}) \qquad (10)$$

$$\Gamma^{a_i,o_i,m_{i,s},m_{i,r}} \leftarrow \alpha^{a_i,o_i,m_{i,s},m_{i,r}}(is) = \gamma \sum_{is' \in IS'} \sum_{a_j \in A_j} Pr(m_{i,r}, a_j|\theta_{j,l-1}) T_i(s, a_i, a_j, s')$$

$$O_i(s', a_i, a_j, o_i) \sum_{o_j} O_j(s', a_i, a_j, o_j) \delta_D(SE_{\hat{\theta}_j}(b_{j,l-1}, a_j, o_j, m_{j,s}, m_{i,s}) - b'_{j,l-1}) \alpha'(is')$$

$$(11)$$

Here, δ_D is the Dirac delta function taking the current belief and updated belief as an argument. The updated belief is returned by state estimator function $SE_{\hat{\theta}_j}$.

Step 2. The second step (lines 11–22) involves combining intermediate alpha vectors calculated in step 1 weighted by the observation and message likelihood using a cross sum operation. Due to the point-based approach, the cross sum operation in exact value iteration is simplified. The step proceeds by selecting only those intermediate alpha vectors which are optimal at any of the given set of belief points.

$$\Gamma^{a_i,m_{i,s}} \leftarrow \Gamma^{a_i,m_{i,s},*} \underset{o_i \in \Omega_i, m_{i,r} \in M}{\bigoplus} \underset{\Gamma^{a_i,o_i,m_{i,s},m_{i,r}}}{\arg\max} (\alpha^{a_i,o_i,m_{i,s},m_{i,r}}.b_{i,l})$$

$$\forall b_{i,l} \in B_{i,l} \qquad (12)$$

Step 3. In the final step, the belief points in set $B_{i,l}$ are used again to select the alpha vectors for the final set for the current iteration. Since different action, message pairs can be optimal for the modeled agent, we need to include alpha vectors corresponding to all optimal action, message pairs in the final alpha set.

$$\nu^t \leftarrow \underset{\alpha^t \in \cup_{a_i} \Gamma^{a_i,m_i}}{\arg\max} (\alpha^t.b_{i,l})$$

$$\forall b_{i,l} \in B_{i,l} \qquad (13)$$

The recursion bottoms out as level-0 POMDP which we assume to be literal speaker. Since, POMDP policy only computes physical action, we need to augment the policy with sincere message. The algorithm for augmenting level-0 POMDP policy with sincere message is provided in appendix.

5   Experiments and Results

5.1   Multi-agent Tiger Game

In this version, two agents are facing two doors: "left" and "right". Behind one door lies a hungry tiger and behind the other is a pot of gold but the agents do not know the position of either. Thus, the set of states is $S = \{TL, TR\}$ indicating the tiger's presence behind the left, or right, door. Each agent can open either door. Agents can also independently listen for the presence of the tiger, so the actions are $A = \{OR, OL, L\}$ for opening the right door, opening the left door, and listening and is the same for both agents. The transition function T, specifies that every time either agent opens one of the doors, the state is reset to TR or TL with equal probability, regardless of the action of the other agent. However, if both agents listen, the state remains unchanged. After every action, each agent can hear the tiger's growl coming either from the left, GL, or from the right door, GR. The observation function O (identical for both agents) specifies the accuracy of observations. We assume that tiger's growls are informative, with predefined sensor accuracy, only if the agents listen. If the agent opens the doors the growls have an equal chance to come from the left or right door and are thus completely uninformative.

Table 1. Neutral Reward

$\langle a_i, a_j \rangle$	TL	TR
OR, L	10	−100
OL, L	−100	10
L, L	−1	−1
OR, OL	10	−100
OL, OL	−100	10
L, OL	−1	−1
OR, OR	10	−100
OL, OR	−100	10
L, OR	−1	−1

Table 2. Friend Reward

$\langle a_i, a_j \rangle$	TL	TR
OR, L	9.5	−100.5
OL, L	−100.5	9.5
L, L	−1.5	−1.5
OR, OL	−40	−95
OL, OL	−150	15
L, OL	−51	4
OR, OR	15	−150
OL, OR	−95	−40
L, OR	4	−51

Table 3. Enemy Reward A

$\langle a_i, a_j \rangle$	TL	TR
OR, L	10.5	−99.5
OL, L	−99.5	10.5
L, L	−0.5	−0.5
OR, OL	60	−105
OL, OL	−50	5
L, OL	49	−6
OR, OR	5	−50
OL, OR	−105	60
L, OR	−6	49

Table 4. Enemy Reward B

$\langle a_i, a_j \rangle$	TL	TR
OR, L	10	−100
OL, L	−100	10
L, L	−1	−1
OR, OL	10	−150
OL, OL	−100	−40
L, OL	−1	−51
OR, OR	−40	−100
OL, OR	−150	10
L, OR	−51	−1

Reward Functions. The reward functions are chosen to simulate cooperative and competitive scenarios. Table 1 represents the scenario when the reward of the agent is independent of the action of the other agent. Table 2 is the friend reward function where the agent gets half of the reward obtained by the other agent, in addition to its own reward. In Table 3 the agent gets half of the negative of the reward obtained by the other agent, hence represents the competitive case. In other reward function Table 4, the agent gets −50 reward if another agent opens the correct door but there is no extra reward if the other agent opens the wrong door. Table 3 incentivizes the extreme lie while Table 4 incentivizes more believable lie.

5.2   Results

Table 5 shows the total reward collected in multi-agent tiger game averaged across 10000 episodes for sensor accuracy of 0.85. The message space M is limited to distribution over physical states only and has been quantized into 5 equally spaced belief points (0.0, 1.0), (0.25, 0.75), (0.5, 0.5), (0.75, 0.25), (1.0, 0.0), and nil. The value of α is fixed to 0.01. The results show that the CIPOMDP agent outperforms the IPOMDP agent in terms of the average reward collected due to the sophistication of message exchange. The difference is more prominent when the agent is able to deceive the other agent. The behavior of the agent across multiple scenarios is discussed below.

Table 5. Reward comparison for CIPOMDP agent against IPOMDP agent in different scenarios. For Enemy, reward function in Table 3 is used.

Nesting level	Agent	Opponent	Reward					
			$h = 3$		$h = 4$		$h = 5$	
			CIPOMDP	IPOMDP	CIPOMDP	IPOMDP	CIPOMDP	IPOMDP
1	Neutral	Sincere and Gullible	3.4 ± 8.92	2.84 ± 16.02	3.9 ± 8.29	2.39 ± 7.95	3.5 ± 8.037	1.067 ± 20.275
	Enemy	Sincere and Gullible	46 ± 24.69	1.53 ± 18.07	66.48 ± 42.15	1.07 ± 8.887	86.00 ± 36.57	−1.31 ± 24.79
	Friend	Sincere and Gullible	5.08 ± 10.91	4.15 ± 18.02	6.05 ± 9.42	3.56 ± 8.86	5.71 ± 17.10	−0.81 ± 23.32
2	Neutral	Enemy	3.39 ± 8.08	2.81 ± 16.02	3.9 ± 11.40	2.39 ± 7.67	3.4942 ± 8.94	1.55 ± 17.14
	Friend	Friend	5.08 ± 10.5	4.14 ± 18.02	6.21 ± 8.56	3.67 ± 8.97	5.02 ± 10.099	3.65 ± 17.94
	Enemy	Enemy	5.44 ± 10.83	1.53 ± 18.07	8.99 ± 18.88	2.32 ± 15.72	10.78 ± 18.09	0.5 ± 19.81
	Neutral	Uncertain (Enemy or Friend)	3.43 ± 7.80	1.53 ± 18.07	4.19 ± 9.162	2.44 ± 7.87	3.45 ± 8.33	0.82 ± 13.71

5.3   Algorithm Performance

Since the point-based algorithm only backs up alpha-vectors optimal at fixed set of belief points, the performance would depend on the number of belief points chosen. Figure 2 shows the comparison of expected reward for the different number of belief points.

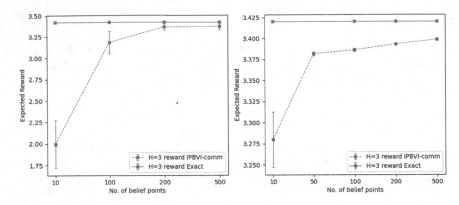

Fig. 2. The performance profile of IPBVI-Comm for level 2 (left) and level 1 (right) CIPOMDP agent, in a cooperative multiagent tiger game. The increase in expected reward is due to improvement in policy after increasing number of belief points. The figure also shows the comparison with exact value iteration

6   Discussion

6.1   Cooperative Scenario

When level 2 friend i models a friend j, agent i sends a sincere message to j reflecting its belief and further includes a message from another agent in its belief update. For e.g. after starting from uniform belief, if the agent i hears GL, it will send the sincere message $m_{i,s} = (0.75, 0.25)$, which assigns probability 0.75 to TL and 0.25 to TR.

6.2   Non-cooperative Scenarios

When a level 1 CIPOMDP agent i models a gullible agent j, it can collect a large reward by sending a deceitful message. For e.g. after starting from uniform belief and getting GL, the agent sends a message $m_{i,s} = (0,1)$ which indicates agent i is certain tiger is on the right, opposite to its own observation. When level 2 enemy i models enemy j, the sophisticated agent i can prevent itself from being deceived by j and further take advantage of the deceitful message as an extra observation. Also, since level-2 agent knows level-1 CIPOMDP models the other as a sincere agent, the former tends to deceive the latter by sending a deceitful message. When level 2 neutral agent models an enemy, it has no incentive to deceive but can prevent itself from being deceived by ignoring the message from the other agent.

6.3   Uncertainty About the Opponent

Message Non-revealing of the Agent's Type. Let's consider a scenario where the level-2 CIPOMDP agent i is uncertain about the level-1 opponent

j's type and thus assigns uniform probability over the other agent being friend, enemy or random[4]. The friend is characterized by the friend reward function (R_f) which incentivizes sincere communication while the enemy is characterized by the enemy reward function (R_e) incentivizing the deceptive behavior. Also, all other elements in the frame of the CIPOMDP agent at all levels are assumed to be the same. Level-2 CIPOMDP i uses IPBVI-Comm to solve for the anticipated behavior of modeled agents $\theta^f_{j,1}$ and $\theta^e_{j,1}$. Now let's see how the belief update proceeds for i. Note, that optimal messages from level-1 agents are not indicative of the agent type. For e.g. if the enemy received GL, it would send the message $(0.25, 0.75)$ and if the friend received GR, it would again send the message $(0.25, 0.75)$. We study the scenario when the message itself is indicative of agent type in the next section. It turns out the agent i is still able to assign a higher probability to one agent type than the other based on the observation it received. For e.g. if the observation and message received for i in two time-steps are $< GL,' nil' >$ and $< GL, (0.25, 0.75) >$, the agent is more likely to be an enemy than the friend because its observations contradict the received message. The belief update of other scenarios are provided in appendix.

Message Revealing the Agent's Type. Again we consider the scenario when there is uncertainty about the opponent type, i.e. when level 2 neutral agent i models both enemy and friend. The only difference now is that the agent modeled at level-1 $\theta_{j,1}$ has the reward function that incentivizes the extreme lie (Table 4). In this case, the higher level agent $\theta_{i,2}$ can figure out if the other agent j is friend or enemy based on the message content only. The CIPOMDP agent $\theta_{i,2}$ incorporates the message from j as a sincere message if it is closer to the belief of the modeled agent $\theta_{j,1}$ and discards the message as an insincere message if the incoming message is way off the belief of the modeled agent. For e.g. if the belief of the modeled agent is $(0.85, 0.15)$, $(0.75, 0.25)$ is considered a sincere message while $(1, 0)$ is considered insincere message. Let's suppose $\theta_{i,2}$ starts by listening at $t = 0$. After receiving GL and message nil, the belief shifts towards physical state TL but belief is equally distributed among both frames. At $t = 1$, after receiving message $(0.75, 0.25)$ and observation GL, the belief concentrates on tiger being on left and other agent being a friend. The agent is able to detect friend from enemy by calculation of sincerity term $P(m_{i,r}|\theta_j)$. When $\theta_j = (b_j, R_f)$, $P(m_{i,r}|\theta_j) = 1$ and when $\theta_j = (b_j, R_e)$, $P(m_{i,r}|\theta_j) = 0$. This happens because for level-1 CIPOMDP with enemy reward function, the optimal action would be to lie to the extreme. This would make $\theta_{i,0}$ open the door intended by the deceiver $\theta_{j,1}$, disregarding its own observation. This message reveals j as an enemy to the higher level agent i.

---

[4] Level-2 CIPOMDP might be uncertain about the strategic level of the opponent, but to simplify the illustration, we stick to level-1 models and a random model.

7   Conclusion

We started by devising a technique to incorporate the message into POMDP belief update in order to allow an agent that does not model other agents to take part in exchange of (literal) messages. We then formalized the notion of sincerity and deception in terms of belief of the agent and messages in message space. We adopted a point based solution method to CIPOMDPs to alleviate the complexities of considering communication as well as observations and physical actions. The analysis of computed policies shows the added sophistication of communication results in policies of superior quality, which is further supported by the empirical results on several experiments conducted on multi-agent tiger game. In future work, we want to explore the higher depth of nesting, and more relaxed soft maximization criterion for action selection which can give rise to richer rational communicative behavior agents can engage in. We are considering online planning method like Monte Carlo tree search for computing policy which provides scalability and with some variation, could accomodate continuous message space.

References

1. Al Amin, M.A.R., Shetty, S., Njilla, L.L., Tosh, D.K., Kamhoua, C.A.: Dynamic Cyber Deception Using Partially Observable Monte-Carlo Planning Framework, chap. 14, pp. 331–355. Wiley (2020). https://doi.org/10.1002/9781119593386.ch14. https://onlinelibrary.wiley.com/doi/abs/10.1002/9781119593386.ch14
2. Albert, S., de Ruiter, J.P.: Repair: the interface between interaction and cognition. Top. Cogn. Sci. **10**(2), 279–313 (2018). https://doi.org/10.1111/tops.12339. https://onlinelibrary.wiley.com/doi/abs/10.1111/tops.12339
3. Beautement, P., et al.: Autonomous agents and multi –agent systems (AAMAS) for the military – issues and challenges. In: Thompson, S.G., Ghanea-Hercock, R. (eds.) DAMAS 2005. LNCS (LNAI), vol. 3890, pp. 1–13. Springer, Heidelberg (2006). https://doi.org/10.1007/11683704_1
4. Breazeal, C., Takanishi, A., Kobayashi, T.: Social Robots that Interact with People. In: Siciliano, B., Khatib, O. (eds.) Springer Handbook of Robotics, pp. 1349–1369. Springer, Heidelberg (2008). https://doi.org/10.1007/978-3-540-30301-5_59
5. Bridewell, W., Isaac, A.: Recognizing deception: a model of dynamic belief attribution. In: AAAI Fall Symposium: Advances in Cognitive Systems (2011)
6. Chao, C., Thomaz, A.: Timed petri nets for fluent turn-taking over multimodal interaction resources in human-robot collaboration. Int. J. Robot. Res. **35**(11), 1330–1353 (2016). https://doi.org/10.1177/0278364915627291
7. Devin, S., Alami, R.: An implemented theory of mind to improve human-robot shared plans execution. In: 2016 11th ACM/IEEE International Conference on Human-Robot Interaction (HRI), pp. 319–326 (2016)
8. Devin, S., Clodic, A., Alami, R.: About decisions during human-robot shared plan achievement: Who should act and how? In: Kheddar, A., et al. (eds.) ICSR 2017. LNCS, vol. 10652, pp. 453–463. Springer, Cham (2017). https://doi.org/10.1007/978-3-319-70022-9_45

9. Ding, X.P., Wellman, H.M., Wang, Y., Fu, G., Lee, K.: Theory-of-mind training causes honest young children to lie. Psychol. Sci. **26**(11), 1812–1821 (2015). https://doi.org/10.1177/0956797615604628. pMID: 26431737

10. Doshi, P., Gmytrasiewicz, P.: Approximating state estimation in multiagent settings using particle filters. In: Proceeding of AAMAS 2005 (2005)

11. Doshi, P., Perez, D.: Generalized point based value iteration for interactive POMDPs. In: Proceedings of the 23rd National Conference on Artificial Intelligence, AAAI 2008, vol. 1, pp. 63–68. AAAI Press (2008)

12. Ettinger, D., Jehiel, P.: A theory of deception. Am. Econ. J.: Microecon. **2**(1), 1–20 (2010). https://doi.org/10.1257/mic.2.1.1. https://www.acaweb.org/articles?id=10.1257/mic.2.1.1

13. Evdokimov, P., Garfagnini, U.: Communication and behavior in organizations: An experiment. Quan. Econ. **10**(2), 775–801 (2019). https://doi.org/10.3982/QE809. https://onlinelibrary.wiley.com/doi/abs/10.3982/QE809

14. Foerster, J.N., Assael, Y.M., de Freitas, N., Whiteson, S.: Learning to communicate to solve riddles with deep distributed recurrent q-networks (2016)

15. Foerster, J.N., et al.: Bayesian action decoder for deep multi-agent reinforcement learning. ArXiv abs/1811.01458 (2019)

16. Gamer, M., Ambach, W.: Deception research today. Front. Psychol. **5**, 256 (2014). https://doi.org/10.3389/fpsyg.2014.00256. https://www.frontiersin.org/article/10.3389/fpsyg.2014.00256

17. George, J., Yilmaz, C.T., Parayil, A., Chakrabortty, A.: A model-free approach to distributed transmit beamforming. In: ICASSP 2020–2020 IEEE International Conference on Acoustics, Speech and Signal Processing (ICASSP), pp. 5170–5174 (2020)

18. Gmytrasiewicz, P., Doshi, P.: A framework for sequential planning in multiagent settings. J. Artif. Intell. Res. **24**, 49–79 (2005). http://jair.org/contents/v24.html

19. Gmytrasiewicz, P.J.: How to do things with words: a Bayesian approach. J. Artif. Intell. Res. **68**, 753–776 (2020). https://doi.org/10.1613/jair.1.11951

20. Gmytrasiewicz, P.J., Durfee, E.H.: Rational coordination in multi-agent environments. Auton. Agents Multiagent Syst. J. **3**(4), 319–350 (2000). https://doi.org/10.1023/A:1010028119149

21. Gneezy, U.: Deception: the role of consequences. Am. Econ. Rev. **95**, 384–394 (2005)

22. Guzman, A.L., Lewis, S.C.: Artificial intelligence and communication: a human-machine communication research agenda. New Media Soc. **22**(1), 70–86 (2020). https://doi.org/10.1177/1461444819858691

23. Isaac, A., Bridewell, W.: White lies on silver tongues: why robots need to deceive (and how), pp. 157–172 (2017). https://doi.org/10.1093/oso/9780190652951.003.0011

24. Kurakin, A., Goodfellow, I.J., Bengio, S.: Adversarial examples in the physical world. ArXiv abs/1607.02533 (2017)

25. Madani, O., Hanks, S., Condon, A.: On the undecidability of probabilistic planning and related stochastic optimization problems. Artif. Intell. **147**(1), 5–34 (2003). https://doi.org/10.1016/S0004-3702(02)00378-8. http://www.sciencedirect.com/science/article/pii/S0004370202003788. Planning with Uncertainty and Incomplete Information

26. Nair, R., Pynadath, D., Yokoo, M., Tambe, M., Marsella, S.: Communication for improving policy computation in distributed POMDPs. In: Proceedings of the Agents and Autonomous Multiagent Systems (AAMAS) (2004)

27. Nair, R., Roth, M., Yokoo, M., Tambe, M.: Taming decentralized POMDPs: towards efficient policy computation for multiagent settings. In: Proceedings of the Eighteenth International Joint Conference on Artificial Intelligence (2003)
28. Nayyar, A., Mahajan, A., Teneketzis, D.: Decentralized stochastic control with partial history sharing: a common information approach. IEEE Trans. Autom. Control **58**(7), 1644–1658 (2013)
29. Oey, L.A., Schachner, A., Vul, E.: Designing good deception: recursive theory of mind in lying and lie detection (2019). https://doi.org/10.31234/osf.io/5s4wc. https://psyarxiv.com/5s4wc
30. Olihoek, F., Spaan, M., Vlassis, N.: Dec-POMDPs with delayed communication. In: Proceedings of MSDM 2007, Honolulu, Hawai'i, USA, 15 May 2007 (2007)
31. Pineau, J., Gordon, G., Thrun, S.: Point-based value iteration: an anytime algorithm for POMDPs. In: Proceedings of the 18th International Joint Conference on Artificial Intelligence, IJCAI 2003, pp. 1025–1030. Morgan Kaufmann Publishers Inc., San Francisco (2003)
32. Ratner, N.K., Olver, R.R.: Reading a tale of deception, learning a theory of mind? Early Child. Res. Q. **13**(2), 219–239 (1998). https://doi.org/10. 1016/S0885-2006(99)80036-2. http://www.sciencedirect.com/science/article/pii/ S0885200699800362
33. Renoux, J., Mouaddib, A., Gloannec, S.L.: A decision-theoretic planning approach for multi-robot exploration and event search. In: 2015 IEEE/RSJ International Conference on Intelligent Robots and Systems (IROS), pp. 5287–5293 (2015). https://doi.org/10.1109/IROS.2015.7354123
34. Sarkadi, S., Panisson, A.R., Bordini, R.H., McBurney, P., Parsons, S., Chapman, M.: Modelling deception using theory of mind in multi-agent systems. AI Commun. **32**, 287–302 (2019)
35. Schlenker, A., et al.: Deceiving cyber adversaries: A game theoretic approach. In: Proceedings of the 17th International Conference on Autonomous Agents and MultiAgent Systems, AAMAS 2018, pp. 892–900. International Foundation for Autonomous Agents and Multiagent Systems, Richland (2018)
36. Shinde, A., Doshi, P., Setayeshfar, O.: Active deception using factored interactive POMDPs to recognize cyber attacker's intent (2020)
37. Shu, K., Sliva, A., Wang, S., Tang, J., Liu, H.: Fake news detection on social media: a data mining perspective. SIGKDD Explor. **19**, 22–36 (2017)
38. Sodian, B., Taylor, C., Harris, P.L., Perner, J.: Early deception and the child's theory of mind: False trails and genuine markers. Child Dev. **62**(3), 468–483 (1991). https://doi.org/10.1111/j.1467-8624.1991.tb01545.x. https://srcd. onlinelibrary.wiley.com/doi/abs/10.1111/j.1467-8624.1991.tb01545.x
39. Sondik, E.J.: The optimal control of partially observable Markov processes over the infinite horizon: discounted costs. Oper. Res. **26**(2), 282–304 (1978). https:// doi.org/10.1287/opre.26.2.282
40. Sukhbaatar, S., szlam, a., Fergus, R.: Learning multiagent communication with backpropagation. In: Lee, D.D., Sugiyama, M., Luxburg, U.V., Guyon, I., Garnett, R. (eds.) Advances in Neural Information Processing Systems, vol. 29, pp. 2244–2252. Curran Associates, Inc. (2016). http://papers.nips.cc/paper/6398-learning-multiagent-communication-with-backpropagation.pdf
41. Unhelkar, V.V., Li, S., Shah, J.A.: Decision-making for bidirectional communication in sequential human-robot collaborative tasks. In: Proceedings of the 2020 ACM/IEEE International Conference on Human-Robot Interaction, HRI 2020, pp. 329–341. Association for Computing Machinery, New York (2020). https://doi.org/ 10.1145/3319502.3374779

42. Wang, N., Pynadath, D.V., Hill, S.G.: Trust calibration within a human-robot team: comparing automatically generated explanations. In: The Eleventh ACM/IEEE International Conference on Human Robot Interaction, HRI 2016, pp. 109–116. IEEE Press (2016)
43. Yuan, L., Fu, Z., Shen, J., Xu, L., Shen, J., Zhu, S.C.: Emergence of pragmatics from referential game between theory of mind agents. arXiv e-prints arXiv:2001.07752 (2020)
44. Zhang, Y., Volz, R.A., Loerger, T.R., Yen, J.: A decision-theoretic approach for designing proactive communication in multi-agent teamwork. In: Proceedings of the 2004 ACM Symposium on Applied Computing, SAC 2004, pp. 64–71. Association for Computing Machinery, New York (2004). https://doi.org/10.1145/967900.967917

A Decentralized Token-Based Negotiation Approach for Multi-Agent Path Finding

Cihan Eran[1]([✉])[iD], M. Onur Keskin[1][iD], Furkan Cantürk[1][iD],
and Reyhan Aydoğan[1,2][iD]

[1] Computer Science, Özyeğin University, Istanbul, Turkey
{cihan.eran,onur.keskin,furkan.canturk}@ozu.edu.tr
[2] Interactive Intelligence, TU Delft, Delft, The Netherlands
reyhan.aydogan@ozyegin.edu.tr

Abstract. This paper introduces a negotiation approach to solve the Multi-Agent Path Finding problem. The approach aims to achieve a good trade-off between the privacy of the agents and the effectiveness of solutions. Accordingly, a token-based bilateral negotiation protocol and a compatible negotiation strategy are presented. The proposed approach is evaluated in a variety of scenarios by comparing it with state-of-the-art centralized approaches such as Conflict Based Search and its variant. The experimental results showed that the proposed approach can find conflict-free path solutions with a higher success rate, especially when the search space is large and high-density compared to centralized approaches while the gap between path cost differences is reasonably low. The proposed approach enables agents to have their autonomy; thus, it is convenient for MAPF problems involving self-interested agents.

Keywords: Multi-Agent Path Finding · Negotiation · Decentralized coordination · Self-interested agents

1 Introduction

Technological advancements in the last decades enable autonomous robots and vehicles to carry out a variety of tasks such as surveillance and transportation. To achieve their goal, they may need to navigate from one location to another. Imagine an environment in which hundreds of autonomous robots aiming to reach certain locations. Such an environment requires a coordination mechanism to avoid some potential collisions. This problem, allocating conflict-free paths to agents so as to navigate safely in an environment, is well-addressed in the field of Multi-Agent Systems and known as Multi-Agent Path Finding (MAPF) problem [26]. A vast number of studies tackle this problem; some propose a centralized solution while others focus on decentralized solutions [25].

Centralized solutions rely on full access to all relevant information regarding the agents and properties of the given environment so that a global solution can be derived. In contrast, decentralized solutions decouple the problem into local

© Springer Nature Switzerland AG 2021
A. Rosenfeld and N. Talmon (Eds.): EUMAS 2021, LNAI 12802, pp. 264–280, 2021.
https://doi.org/10.1007/978-3-030-82254-5_16

chunks and address the conflicts locally [10]. Without any time constraints, centralized approaches can find optimal solutions if there exist. However, the performance of centralized solution approaches can suffer in high density and complex environments [8,24]. Besides, full information may not always be available due to the limitation of communication, sensors, or privacy issues. On the one hand, decentralized approaches can deal with uncertainty and scalability issues and produce admissible solutions. However, they may overlook a potential optimal solution and end up with suboptimal solutions.

This work pursues a decentralized approach to the MAPF problem targeting a good trade-off between privacy and effectiveness of the solutions. As agents can resolve their conflicts for varying problems from resource allocation to planning through negotiation [3,13,15,19], we advocate to solve the aforementioned problem in terms of negotiation and accordingly propose a token-based alternating offers protocol. In the proposed approach, agents share their partial path information with only relevant agents that are close to them to some extent. If they detect any conflict on their partial path, they encounter a bilateral negotiation to allocate required locations for certain time steps. To govern this negotiation, this study introduces a variant of alternating offers protocol enriched with token exchanges. By enforcing the tokens' usage, the protocol leads agents to act collaboratively and search unexplored paths so that there is no conflict anymore. A path-aware negotiation strategy is also presented in line with the protocol. There are a few attempts to solve the MAPF problem in terms of negotiation [14,21,22]. Either they require sharing full path information with others, or they consider one-step decisions such as who will move to a certain direction at the time of conflict, or they aim to resolve the conflict in one shot (i.e., collaborate or reject). In contrast, our approach aims to reduce the complexity of the problem by resolving the conflicts in subpath plans iteratively instead of the entire path plans, thereby respecting the agents' privacy to some extent.

This paper is organized as Sect. 2 describes the problem addressed in this paper, while Sect. 3 lays out the proposed solution approach, introduces a new variant of Alternating Offers Protocol and a compatible negotiation strategy in line with that protocol. Experiment setup and results of the experiments are presented in Sect. 4. This paper's main contributions and planned future work are discussed in Sect. 6.

2   Problem Statement

Multi-Agent Pathfinding (MAPF) as defined in [26], is the problem of assigning conflict free paths to agents from their respective starting locations to their destinations. Formally, we have k agents denoted by $A = \{A_1, A_2, ..., A_k\}$ navigating in an undirected graph $G = (V, E)$ where starting and destination location for each A_i are denoted by $s_i \in V$ and $g_i \in V$ respectively. The path of each agent A_i is denoted by π_i, a sequence of vertices indexed by each time step $0 \to n$, $(s_i^0, ..., g_i^n)$. $\pi_i^t \in V$ corresponds to current location of A_i at time step t. At any time step, the agents cannot be located in the same vertex – $\pi_i^t \neq \pi_j^t$ $\forall$

$i \neq j$, and traverse the same edge. A swapping conflict occurs when $\pi_i^t = \pi_j^{t+1}$ $\wedge \pi_i^{t+1} = \pi_j^t \; \forall \; i \neq j$.

In this paper, agents are located in a $M \times M$ grid-like environment where each cell corresponds to a vertex as illustrated in Fig. 1a. Each agent has an initial path to follow in the addressed problem to reach their destination, shown by dashed lines in the grid. For the current example, we have three agents A, B, and C whose planned paths are colored in their respective colors (i.e., red, blue, and green). Here, an agent located in a cell can only move to their vertical and horizontal adjacent neighboring cells (i.e., cardinal directions). For instance, Agent A located in $(2, 2)$ can move to one of the following cells: $(1, 2)$, $(3, 2)$, $(2, 1)$, and $(2, 3)$. In the proposed framework, agents cannot wait at a certain cell unless agents reach their destinations. That is, $\pi_i^t \neq \pi_i^{t+1}$ whereas $\pi_i^t \neq g_i$. As seen in the example, there is a conflict between Agent A and B at time step t = 2 (cell $(3, 3)$). They need to resolve this conflict to achieve their goals. Final solutions will be evaluated under the objective of some of the individual costs, $\sum_{i=1}^{k} |\pi_i|$ where individual cost of each agent i corresponds to their path length denoted by $|\pi_i|$. Furthermore, when an agent reaches its destination, it stops there to act as an obstacle for other agents. This behavior makes this problem a *stay at target* MAPF problem.

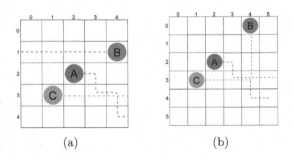

Fig. 1. Example environment & field of view representation

3   Proposed Approach

This work presents a decentralized solution in which agents autonomously negotiate with each other in order to refine their path to avoid possible collisions. The main challenge is to deal with the uncertainty about the environment due to the limited capacity of the sensors, communication, or some privacy concerns. Most real-world applications are partially observable where the agents can perceive some relevant aspects of the environment. For instance, a robot may not perceive all objects that are far from its current location. Light detection and range finding sensors can detect up to a certain distance. Similarly, wireless communication systems also have limited communication capabilities. Agents may not exchange information with each other if their distance is above a threshold value. Besides, full information is not always available due to the characteristics of the environment. For example, drivers in traffic do not know where other drivers are going. Furthermore, agents may be reluctant to share all information due to their privacy. For instance, they may not be willing to reveal their destination.

In our framework, agents are located in a grid as shown in Fig. 1b. Initially, each agent knows only their starting location, destination, and a path plan to reach their destination. Those planned paths are shown in colored dot lines in the grid for each agent. For simulating the aforementioned partially observable environment, we adopt the concept of *field of view*. The framework enables agents to access a limited portion of other agents' planned paths within a certain proximity and share their own. In other words, an agent's field of view determines the scope of its communication and perception capacity. An agent can only observe and communicate with other agents if they are within its field of view. That is described as a certain number of cells d from its location. For instance, when d is equal to 1, the boundary of the field of view is shown by a red rectangle for Agent A. In such a case, Agent A can receive/send information from/to only Agent C, which is located in the scope of Agent A's field of view and vice versa. However, in the given snapshot, Agent B cannot communicate or see other agents at that time.

In this framework, agents broadcast their sub-planned path. Agents are free to determine to what extent the path to be shared with other agents in the field of view. In our experiments, agents share their current subpath with a length of $2d$. If any conflict is detected by one of the agents, they can engage in a negotiation session. For example, when d is equal to 1, agents will share their current subpath with a length of 2 (i.e., its next two moves) with the agents located the scope of their field of view. Agent A broadcasts its current subpath as $Broadcast : [\pi_A^{t=1} = (3,2), \pi_A^{t=2} = (3,3)]$ while Agent C shared its own as $Broadcast : [\pi_C^{t=1} = (2,3), \pi_C^{t=2} = (3,3)]$. Since agents would detect a conflict in the vertex $(3,3)$ at $t = 2$, Agent A and C start negotiating on the allocation of vertices on their path since they detect a conflict in $(3,3)$.

When an agent detects a conflict with more than one agent, which negotiation to be held first is determined in *first come first serve* basis. For example, if d is 2, then Agent B and Agent C will share their subpaths with a length of 4 with Agent A. Agent A may first negotiate with Agent B if Agent B's message has been received before Agent C's one. Afterward, it can encounter a bilateral negotiation with Agent C. After carrying out any successful negotiation, agents will update their path accordingly. A number of negotiation sessions might be held until resolving current conflicts. If there are no conflicts left in the current field of view, agents move to their next location in their path. Once an agent reaches its desired destination, it will not encounter a negotiation anymore. The negotiation between agents is carried out according to the proposed token-based negotiation protocol. The details of this protocol and a specific bidding strategy particularly designed for this protocol to tackle the MAPF problem are explained in the following sections.

3.1   Token-Based Alternating Offers Protocol (TAOP)

The proposed framework requires agents to engage in negotiation to resolve conflicts in their paths. At a given time, the conflict may occur either between two agents or among multiple agents. When it happens among more than two agents, we can formulate it as multiple bilateral negotiations and consider it a multilateral negotiation. As it may be harder to find a joint agreement, especially when the number of participants is high [4], the proposed approach aims to solve the conflicts in multiple consecutive bilateral negotiations. For simplicity, agents perform their bilateral negotiations consecutively. That is, a new negotiation can start after completing the previous one.

In the proposed approach, when there is a conflict in two agents' sub-path, agents negotiate on allocating the relevant vertices for certain time steps. Following the previous example illustrated in Fig. 1b, Agent A may claim to allocate the vertices at $(3, 2)$ at time $t = 1$, $(3, 3)$ at time $t = 2$ while Agent C may aim to allocate the vertices at $(2, 3)$ at time $t = 1$, $(3, 3)$ at time $t = 2$. Depending on how the negotiation proceeds, they may concede over time and change their request on vertex allocations to come up with an agreement. If agents find an agreement, they are supposed to obey the allocation for the other party. That is, agents are free to change their own path as long as their current path allocation does not violate the agreed vertex allocation for the other party. For example, when Agent C accepts Agent A's vertex allocation for time steps $t = 1$ and $t = 2$, Agent C confirms that it will not occupy those vertices to be allocated by Agent A for the agreed time steps.

The interaction between agents needs to be governed by a negotiation protocol. In automated negotiation, agents mostly follow the Stacked Alternating Offers Protocol [5] in which they exchange offers in a turn-taking fashion until reaching a predefined deadline. This protocol does not force the agents to come up with an agreement. If both agents are selfish, they may fail the negotiation. However, finding a consensus plays a key role in the context of MAPF. Therefore, agents preferably follow a protocol leading them to reach an agreement. Accordingly, we introduce a novel token-based negotiation protocol namely *Token-based Alternating Offers Protocol* (TAOP) inspired from Monotonic Concession Protocol (MCP) [23] and Unmediated Single Text Protocol (USTP) [16]. According to MCP, agents make simultaneous offers in a way that either they can stick to their previous offer or make a concession. If both parties stick to their previous offers, the negotiation ends without any consensus. Otherwise, agents continue negotiation until reaching an agreement or failing the negotiation. This protocol leads agents to complete the negotiation without setting a predefined deadline. However, there is a high risk of ending up with a failure. In USTP, agents interchangeably are becoming a proposer or voter during the negotiation. Initially, a number of tokens are given to each agent where agents can use those tokens to override other's reject votes. One agent starts with a random offer, and the other agent votes to accept or reject it. If the other agent accepts, it is considered as the most recently accepted bid. This interaction is repeated multiple times, and the most recently accepted bid is updated over time. At the end of the negotiation, the most recently accepted bid is considered as the agreement. Here, the tokens are used to incentivize truthful voting of agents to not manipulate the system by rejecting all offers. Since this protocol is particularly designed for large-scaled negotiation problems, the generated bids are variants of an initial random offer, not directly applicable to our problem. On the other hand, the token idea can enforce the agents to concede over time in a fairway.

Basically, the proposed token-based alternating offers protocol is a variant of alternating offers protocol enriched with token exchanges. One of the agents initiates the negotiation with an offer. The receiving party can accept this offer, make a counteroffer, or end the negotiation without agreement. The main difference is that agents are not allowed to repeat their previous offers unless they pay for them. The protocol assumes that each agent owns a predefined number of tokens, $\mathcal{T}$. Those tokens are used to enable an agent to make one of its previous offers during that negotiation. Different from MCP, agents are not required to make conceding moves. The essential requirement for agents is to make unproposed offers during the negotiation or pay tokens to repeat an offer. In addition to the given offer, agents send an acknowledgement message specifying the number of tokens to be used to repeat an offer previously made by the same agent. The general flow of the proposed protocol is given below:

1. One of the agents makes an offer specifying its request to allocate some vertices for certain time steps and sends an acknowledgement message regarding the usage of its token in the current negotiation. Initially, the usage of tokens is set to zero.
2. The receiving agent can take one of the following actions:
   - ends the negotiation without any consensus.
   - accept the received offer and complete the negotiation successfully.
   - makes an offer specifying the vertices allocation for itself that has not been offered by that agent yet and sends the acknowledgement denoting the accumulated usage of its tokens.
   - can repeat one of its previous offers, increase the usage of its tokens by one, and sends the token acknowledgement message.
3. If the agent accepts or ends the negotiation, negotiation is finished. The accepting agent receives tokens amounting to the calculated token usage difference from its opponent, $min(\mathcal{T}_{opp,self} - \mathcal{T}_{self,opp}, 0)$ where $\mathcal{T}_{opp,self}$ and $\mathcal{T}_{self,opp}$ denote the total number of tokens used by the opponent and the accepting agent during the entire negotiation respectively. If the accepting agents spend more tokens than its opponent, it does not receive any tokens. Otherwise, the receiving agent can take any action mentioned in Step 2.

Considering the scenario given in Fig. 1b, an example negotiation trace between Agent A and C is illustrated in Fig. 2. Agent A initiates the negotiation with its offer P_{A1} requesting to claim the vertices $(3, 2)$ for $t = 1$ ad $(3, 3)$ for $t = 2$. Agent C does not accept this offer and makes its own offer specifying the allocation for itself, such as $(2, 3)$ and $(2, 4)$. Since Agent A insists on its previous offer, it increases its token usage by one. As seen from the example, agents send an acknowledgement message and their offer in each turn. In the fourth round, Agent C accepts Agent A's offer. It confirms that Agent C will not move to $(3,2)^{t=1}$ and $(3,3)^{t=2}$. In return, Agent A will pay 2 tokens ($T_{A,C}$-$T_{C,A}$). It is worth to note that the token exchange is performed at the end of the negotiation depending on who accepts the offer. If an agent needs to pay tokens, but it has an insufficient number of tokens, the agreement is not committed (i.e., negotiation fails).

Fig. 2. Example interaction between negotiating agents

3.2   Path-Aware Negotiation Strategy

Existing negotiation strategies focus on only which offer to make at a given time and when to accept a given offer [6]. Therefore, there is a need to design a new strategy taking token exchanges into account. Hereby, we propose a negotiation strategy determining when to repeat an offer or to generate a new offer. The proposed strategy, namely *Path-Aware* negotiation strategy, aims to utilize the information available to determine when to insist on its current path. It is worth noting that each agent generates its possible paths leading them to their destination by using A-Star Algorithm in a way that the generated paths would not conflict with the neighbor agents' current path. Afterward, they sort those paths in descending order with respect to their path cost.

Algorithm 1 describes how an agent negotiates according to Path-Aware Negotiation Strategy. At the beginning of the negotiation, the current path in the field of view ($P_{current}$) is the relevant part of the optimal path (i.e., the shortest path to its destination). It corresponds to the first offer in the negotiation. When the agent receives an offer from its opponents, it checks whether it is possible to generate a path that is of equal length or shorter than its current path to the destination (Line 1). If so, it accepts its opponent's offer (Line 2). Note that the path generation function takes the opponent's offer, $O_{opponent}$ as a constraint while generating the best possible path to the destination. If the agent's remaining tokens are greater than the length of the remaining path to the destination (Line 4), it decides to repeat its previous offer and updates its remaining tokens accordingly (Line 5). Recall that for each repetition, the agent needs to use one token. Otherwise, it concedes and sets the next possible best path from the sorted path space P_{Space}, as its current path in its field of view (Line 7). Accordingly, the agent offers its previous path in the field of view $P_{current}$ (Line 9). Note that agents have to concede if they don't have any tokens left.

Algorithm 1: Negotiation Strategy of Path-Aware Agent

Data:
$T_{remaining}$: Agent's remaining tokens count
$P_{remaining}$: Agent's remaining path to destination
$P_{current}$: Current path in FoV
P_{Space}: Sorted path space
$O_{opponent}$: Opponent offer

1   **if** $|P_{current}| \geq |generatePath(O_{opponent})|$ **then**
2   accept()
3   **else**
4   **if** $T_{remaining} > |P_{remaining}|$ **then**
5       $T_{remaining} - -$
6   **else**
7       $P_{current} \leftarrow P_{Space}.next()$
8   **end**
9   offer($P_{current}$)
10 **end**

---

4 Evaluation

We evaluated the proposed approach empirically from three different perspectives: by comparing its performance with centralized solutions, by comparing the performance of the Path-aware negotiation strategy with a baseline strategy, and by studying the effect of field of view (FoV) in the proposed approach. The following sections will explain our experimental setup and result elaborately.

4.1 Experimental Setup

To inspect the performance of our decentralized approach against centralized approaches to resolve conflicts in MAPF, we make a comparison with two well-known centralized methods, namely Conflict-Based Search (CBS) [24] and CBS with the Weighted Pairwise Dependency Graph Heuristic and Rectangle Reasoning by Multi-Valued Decision Diagrams, named WDG+R in [17]. These centralized solutions are detailed below. We used the code of WDG+R provided by its authors. We removed wait-action (no movement in a time step) from the action space of agents in all solvers to be suitable for the problem definition in Sect. 2. All experiments were carried on machines with the computing power of 16-Core 3.2 GHz Intel Xeon and 32 GB RAM. Each scenario configuration experimented with 100 different scenarios in no obstacle, 8×8, and 16×16 grid environments.

- **CBS:** Conflict-Based Search (CBS) [24] is a two-level algorithm for centralized and optimal MAPF. At the low-level search, a single path is planned by an optimal shortest-path algorithm, like A*, under given constraints. A constraint is a tuple (i, v, t) where agent a_i is prohibited from occupying vertex v at time step t. At the high-level search, a constraint tree (CT) is operated to resolve conflicts between paths. CT is a binary tree of constraint nodes. Each CT node consists of a set of constraints for each agent. When a conflict is found between two agents, two child nodes are generated. In each child node, one agent in the conflict is prohibited from using conflicted vertex or edge by adding a constraint, and a new path is searched for that agent at the low level under the new constraint set.

- **WDG+R:** It is one of the recently enhanced variants of CBS and a state-of-art optimal MAPF solver. WDG+R operates smaller CTs by using an admissible heuristic in the high-level search named the Weighted Pairwise Dependency Graph (WDG) Heuristic. WDG represents the pairwise dependencies requiring some cost increase to resolve conflicts. Value of the minimum vertex cover of WDG serves as an admissible heuristic of a lower bound to cost increase to resolve conflicts. Besides, it efficiently resolves the rectangle conflicts by a reasoning technique introduced to CBS in [18]. A rectangle conflict occurs when two locations are required to be taken by both agents simultaneously, which means a certain cost increase to resolve the conflict. These enhancements provide a large factor of speedup compared to CBS.

We generated MAPF scenarios from the MAPF benchmark datasets provided by [25]. Table 1 provides the information of experimented MAPF scenarios. We set eight different problem configurations, which are 10, 15, 20, and 25-agent scenarios in an empty 8×8 grid, and 20, 40, 60, and 80-agent scenarios in an empty 16×16 grid. For each configuration, 100 different scenarios have experimented with randomly distributed path lengths between 2 and 14 for 8×8 grid scenarios, and 4 and 24 for 16×16 grid scenarios. We determined the number of agents in the environment to such levels to observe remarkable breakdowns in success rates of CBS and WDG+R, which helps to see which MAPF problem complexity levels these centralized MAPF solution approaches become to fail at. 8×8 grid scenarios are experimented to benchmark CBS specifically and our proposed solution considering the performance evaluation of CBS done in [24]. In 16×16 grid scenarios, we aim to see when the scaling capability of centralized and decentralized solutions are discriminated by changing the number of agents with large increments.

We set the runtime of CBS and WDG+R to 30 min 8×8 for grid scenarios and 1 h for 16×16 grid scenarios in favor of obtaining optimal solutions for a

Table 1. Scenario types

Configuration name	Grid size	Number of agents	Initial path range
Config-1	8×8	10	2–14
Config-2	8×8	15	2–14
Config-3	8×8	20	2–14
Config-4	8×8	25	2–14
Config-5	16×16	20	4–24
Config-6	16×16	40	4 24
Config-7	16×16	60	4–24
Config-8	16×16	80	4–24

rigorous evaluation of experiments, although CBS benchmarked in 5 min by [24] and WDG+R benchmarked in 1 min by [17]. However, the runtime metric does not represent the success capability of our decentralized solution since it would proceed in real-time. Nevertheless, we limited the simulation runtime of the decentralized MAPF framework. In addition, decentralized solution can fail to find a solution, when inactive agents close off movement to destination (Fig. 3a), or surround others (Fig. 3).

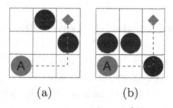

(a)   (b)

Fig. 3. Agent and destination blocked by agents reached destinations

The field of view (FoV) is set to 2 for all agents to experiment with all 8×8 and 16×16 scenarios. Setting FoV to 1 corresponds that agents can be aware of conflicts just a one-time step before, limiting the practicality of negotiation to resolve conflicts. To observe the effect of FoV in our framework's solution performance, we repeat the experiments of Config-6 and Config-7 scenarios, setting FoV to 2, 3, and 4 for all agents. We do not test the effect of field of view in 8×8 grid environment since it is not much practicable to change the range.

4.2 Experimental Results

Each metric for the results of each solution method is averaged over scenarios solved by itself throughout the evaluations in the following subsections.

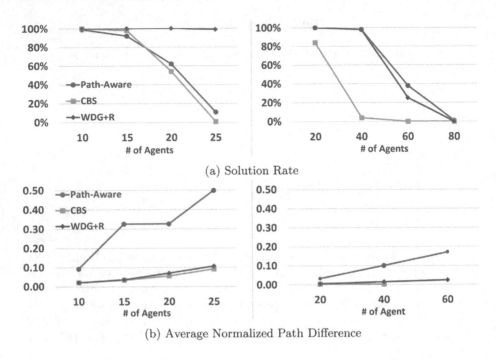

(a) Solution Rate

(b) Average Normalized Path Difference

Fig. 4. Decentralized versus centralized approach results

Decentralized Versus Centralized Approach: Solution rate (R) of the decentralized MAPF framework with Path-aware agents (PA) and the centralized solutions for 8×8 and 16×16 grids are represented in Fig. 4a where the left chart corresponds for 8×8 grid results, and the right chart corresponds for 16×16 grid results. Although the decision complexity of agents is essential to measure the framework performance, this basic agent strategy outperforms CBS in 8×8 grid scenarios and also WDG+R in 16×16 grid scenarios in terms of R. However, PA results are not desirable 8×8 grid scenarios when the solution quality is considered according to the left chart in Fig. 4b. To measure how much extra cost is produced to resolve conflicts in optimal paths, we use a metric named Average Normalized Path Difference (D_{avg}), which is equal to $(C_1\text{-}C_0)/k$ where C_0 is the cost of initial paths of all agents and C_1 is the sum of individual path costs (SIC) value attained in a solution. This metric means how much-added cost is yielded to resolve conflicts compared to C_0. D_{avg} gives the information of how much cost increase occurs in which environments for the side of the self-interested agent only consider its own cost valuation based on its initial path cost. Figure 4b shows that PA performs well in the scenarios of the high number of agents in larger maps, which indicates the scalability of the decentralized solution compared to centralized solutions. However, only one scenario of Config-8 was solved by PA because agents cannot negotiate to resolve a conflict caused due to the demonstrated situations in Fig. 3. We note

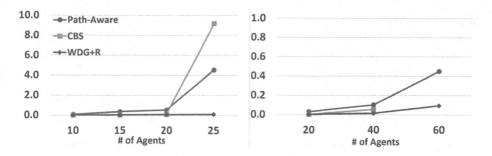

Fig. 5. Average normalized path difference/solution rate

that Config-8 scenarios are not evaluated in the following metrics since optimal solutions could not be obtained for them.

As all scenarios are not solved by WDG+R, we do not have the complete information to measure the solution quality of the decentralized solutions since optimal solutions are taken as the basis for it. It is not a health assessment to compare the cases that CBS and WDG+R can solve with the scenarios they cannot solve, but PA solves. For this reason, there is a need for a variable that shows the relationship between solution rates and normalized path differences more dynamically, which is D_{avg}/R. Figure 5 has enabled dynamic changes to be observed in a wide range with D_{avg}/R. Although CBS seems to be more successful than PA in 8×8 grid scenarios in terms of D_{avg}, Fig. 5 shows that Path-Aware agents are more successful when considering the performances in new metric solution rates. It is observed that CBS fails dramatically in scenarios involving 25 Agents. When the 8×8 and 16×16 grid scenarios are compared, it is observed that the performance of the WDG+R remained the same, while the performance of the Path Aware Agents was 10 times better. This result shows that in larger domains, decentralized and intelligent agents such as Path-Aware have less performance difference from optimal solvers and high privacy support.

Effect of Intelligence of Agents: To figure out the effect of intelligence of agents in our framework, a baseline representing a random decision behavior for the negotiation protocol is needed. Therefore, we present a basic decision mechanism adapted by an experimental agent named *Random Agent*. Random Agent accepts its opponent's offer with %50 probability. Otherwise, it repeats its previous offer with %50 probability if it has enough tokens. It generates its offer space exactly in the same way as the Path-aware strategy. The main difference is about accepting and deciding the usage of tokens. We highlight that Random Agent provides a lower bound performance for any prospective self-interested rational agent designed for the proposed decentralized MAPF framework.

Figure 6a shows the total number of token exchanges in a session for both agent types. Negotiation between Path-Aware agents results in less number of token exchanges compared to negotiations of Random agents, which shows that Path-Aware agents insist on their offers only to maintain their own cost balance,

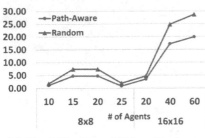
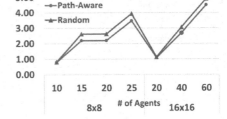

(a) Total Number of Token Exchange   (b) Number of Negotiations/Agent

Fig. 6. Path-aware agent versus random agent

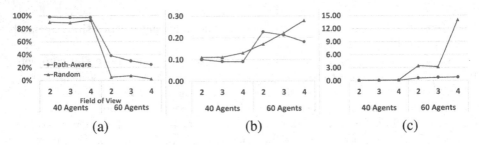

(a)   (b)   (c)

Fig. 7. (a) Solution rate with FoV, (b) Average normalized path difference with FoV, (c) Average normalized path difference/Solution rate with FoV

whereas Random agents insist or concede randomly. Negotiations between Path-Aware agents reach an agreement faster than random agents in all environments, as seen in Fig. 6b. The number of negotiations by Random agents represents a baseline for the negotiation protocol if the agent decides indifferent to counter's bids. So, it can be concluded that when agents behave more analytical, they can reach an agreement faster with our proposed negotiation protocol. Since the solution rates of the decentralized solution with Random agents (RA) and the decentralized solution with Path-Aware agents (PA) is low, we do not seek a trend for the curves in Fig. 6.

Effect of Field of View: We experiment with 40 and 60-agent scenarios in 16×16 grid with different FoV values to figure out how the perception and information broadcast range of agents relate to the solution performance of the decentralized MAPF approach. This relation branches in three aspects, R, D_{avg}, and D_{avg}/R. Figure 7 presents the related curves for PA and RA. Change in FoV of Random agent has no general trend in R in all scenarios, while the increase in FoV decreases R in all scenarios when all agents are Path-Aware. This decrease is 1% for 40-agent scenarios and 14% for 60-agent scenarios, which shows that Path-Aware agents struggle to agree in dense environments when they have a wider FoV. On the other hand, Path-Aware agents can have better paths with wider FoV according to D_{avg} trend in Chart B. Besides, the third chart in Fig. 7

shows that the solutions achieved with PA are much better in terms of D_{avg}/R compared to RA solutions. So, it can be concluded that intelligent agents can preserve their own path cost interest by negotiating with others under TAOP. This output is expected because Path-Aware agents change their bidding behavior based on current cost analysis (of remaining path length and the remaining token amount at the negotiation time). This evaluation becomes more useful if more information about the environment is used.

In large FoV cases, Random agents tend to perform worse as their decision-making process is stochastic. As the accepted offers are registered, having a large FoV thus results in more constraints for agents, which reduces path search space. Path-Aware Agents provide solutions to these problems both in acceptance and by spending their tokens correctly. On the other hand, Random Agents do not have a specific strategy other than entering into a negotiation and accepting long paths randomly in the face of these problems. This situation is reflected in the average number of negotiations per agent. When looking at the difference of the average negotiation per agent between FoV 2 and FoV 3, Random agents (2.17) are 2.59 times more than Path-Aware agents (0.83). When the same variable is examined between FoV 3 and Fov 4, Random agents (2.11) increased 5.90 times more than Path-Aware agents (0.35).

5   Related Work

We classify approaches to resolve conflicts in MAPF based on two factors: the centralization of solution mechanism and cooperation of agents. Centralized solution approaches to pathfinding of cooperative agents provide optimal plans [11]. If a trusted center with the information of all agents moving in a certain area and the ability to command all of them is not available, negotiation can be used for a conflict resolution mechanism [1,12,21,22,27]. One negotiation approach to allocating resources to multiple parties is Combinatorial Auction (CA). To resolve conflicts between self-interested agents in an environment, Amir et al. reduce MAPF problem to CA and implements iBundle, an iterative CA algorithm [20], for MAPF [1]. Self-interested agents might not provide their own utilization truthfully to the auctioneer. Considering this aspect of the auction, Amir et al. propose Vickrey-Clarke-Groves (VCG) auction for MAPF, a strategy-proof auction mechanism for manipulation attempts by the agents. In this iBundle auction, the auctioneer is exposed to a computational burden as agents submit their all-desirable bundles, which requires even impractical auction time. Addressing this limitation of iBundle, Gautier et al. introduce an auction design that allows agents to submit a limited number of bundles so that a feasible allocation is more likely to be found, and the auction terminates in fewer time [12]. They also provide a further auction solution procedure applied if a feasible allocation to submitted bundles is not found. Auctioneer finds some feasible allocations using a MAPF solver, and it evaluates them to maximize social welfare using its privileged knowledge gained in the bidding. Then it proposes the most valuable allocation to the agents. Auction ends when all agents accept one allocation;

otherwise, the auctioneer updates allocation values based on rejecting agents' bids and proposes the best new allocation.

Key challenges of addressing MAPF problem within the decentralized method can be summarized as establishing a framework for agents to use while interacting with the environment, defining an interaction protocol between agents, and designing agents that are able to reach a solution [2,7,9]. In their paper Purwin *et al.*, proposes a decentralized framework where agents allocate portions of the environment in which they move. Similarly, the framework proposed in this paper also allows agents to exchange vertex information while trying to allocate a conflict-free path. However, their negotiation protocol resolves the conflicts in one shot, whereas the protocol proposed in this paper allows agents to engage in negotiation sessions in length. Sujit *et al.* focuses on resolving a task allocation problem in their work, using a multilateral negotiation structure [27]. Agents only utilize the presented token structure to determine whose offer to accept in a deadlock situation that might happen, in which the agent with the least number of tokens is selected. Whereas in this paper, tokens are treated as a limitation in making repeated offers. The work of Pritchett *et al.* defines a simultaneous bilateral negotiation structure to resolve conflicts in air traffic control [21]. Their work defines a structure where agents negotiate over the trajectories that they will take. In each round of the negotiation session, the cost of all offers increases until an agreement is reached. While due to the nature of the environment, this forces agents to concede over time, the protocol proposed in this paper defines a hard constraint on how many times an agent can refuse an opponent's offer. Inotsume *et al.* demonstrates a negotiation-based approach to MAPF from the perspective of an operator [14]. In their setup, each agent tries to maximize their utility by completing tasks, reaching a certain destination in a shared space. An area manager interface manages this shared space, and each agent is expected to submit their desired paths to the area manager before they begin their movement. Here, the area manager is the entity that checks whether each path conflicts with already reserved paths or prohibited locations. As they utilize a path reservation system managed by a non-agent entity, this setup deviates from the proposed decentralized approach. Additionally, they propose a trading structure for their paths, which can correspond to token exchange. They value these tokens equivalent to each edge traversal, whereas our study values tokens in a completely different economy. Nevertheless, both systems focus on resolving path conflicts using negotiation mechanisms.

6   Conclusion

This paper addresses how self-interested agents can coordinate in a grid environment to reach their destination without any collision and proposes solving the conflicts on the paths by means of bilateral negotiations. Accordingly, we propose a novel negotiation protocol and a compatible path-aware negotiation strategy. The proposed approach enables agents to optimize their paths in real time without sharing their complete path information with everyone. This problem is harder to solve especially when the grid size gets larger and higher-density (i.e., large number of agents and long paths per agent). In such cases, the proposed approach has an edge over centralized approaches. The analysis of experimental evaluation showed that Path-aware negotiation approach finds reasonably good solutions in most of the cases and it performed better on aforementioned challenging scenarios than the state-of-the-art centralized solution such as CBS and WDG+R. As future work, we are planning to extend our approach by adopting multilateral negotiation instead of multiple consecutive bilateral negotiations and to compare its performance with the current approach. In the current work, agents should move constantly in line with their path. However, enabling agents to wait for any time step (i.e., no move action) may lead agents to discover new solutions while it increases the search space dramatically. We think of incorporating wait action to our framework as well as other variants of actions. Furthermore, it would be interesting to design more sophisticated negotiation agents thinking ahead when they use their tokens.

References

1. Amir, O., Sharon, G., Stern, R.: Multi-agent pathfinding as a combinatorial auction. In: Proceedings of the Twenty-Ninth AAAI Conference on Artificial Intelligence, AAAI 2015, pp. 2003–2009. AAAI Press (2015)
2. Atzmon, D., Zax, Y., Kivity, E., Avitan, L., Morag, J., Felner, A.: Generalizing multi-agent path finding for heterogeneous agents. In: SOCS (2020)
3. Aydoğan, R., et al.: Challenges and main results of the automated negotiating agents competition (ANAC) 2019. In: Bassiliades, N., Chalkiadakis, G., de Jonge, D. (eds.) EUMAS/AT -2020. LNCS (LNAI), vol. 12520, pp. 366–381. Springer, Cham (2020). https://doi.org/10.1007/978-3-030-66412-1_23
4. Aydoğan, R., Hindriks, K.V., Jonker, C.M.: Multilateral mediated negotiation protocols with feedback. In: Marsa-Maestre, I., Lopez-Carmona, M.A., Ito, T., Zhang, M., Bai, Q., Fujita, K. (eds.) Novel Insights in Agent-based Complex Automated Negotiation. SCI, vol. 535, pp. 43–59. Springer, Tokyo (2014). https://doi.org/10.1007/978-4-431-54758-7_3
5. Aydoğan, R., Festen, D., Hindriks, K.V., Jonker, C.M.: Alternating offers protocols for multilateral negotiation. In: Fujita, K., et al. (eds.) Modern Approaches to Agent-based Complex Automated Negotiation. SCI, vol. 674, pp. 153–167. Springer, Cham (2017). https://doi.org/10.1007/978-3-319-51563-2_10
6. Baarslag, T., Gerding, E.H., Aydogan, R., Schraefel, M.C.: Optimal negotiation decision functions in time-sensitive domains. In: 2015 IEEE/WIC/ACM International Joint Conferences on Web Intelligence (WI) and Intelligent Agent Technologies (IAT), vol. 2, pp. 190–197 (2015)
7. Bhattacharya, S., Likhachev, M., Kumar, V.: Multi-agent path planning with multiple tasks and distance constraints. In: 2010 IEEE International Conference on Robotics and Automation, pp. 953–959. IEEE (2010)
8. Desaraju, V.R., How, J.P.: Decentralized path planning for multi-agent teams with complex constraints. Auton. Robots **32**(4), 385–403 (2012). https://doi.org/10.1007/s10514-012-9275-2
9. Erdem, E., Kisa, D.G., Oztok, U., Schüller, P.: A general formal framework for pathfinding problems with multiple agents. In: Proceedings of the Twenty-Seventh

AAAI Conference on Artificial Intelligence, AAAI 2013, pp. 290–296. AAAI Press (2013)

10. Erdmann, M., Lozano-Perez, T.: On multiple moving objects. In: Proceedings of 1986 IEEE International Conference on Robotics and Automation, vol. 3, pp. 1419–1424 (1986)

11. Felner, A., et al.: Search-based optimal solvers for the multi-agent pathfinding problem: summary and challenges. In: SOCS (2017)

12. Gautier, A., Lacerda, B., Hawes, N., Wooldridge, M.: Negotiated path planning for non-cooperative multi-robot systems. In: IJCAI (2020)

13. De la Hoz, E., Gimenez-Guzman, J.M., Marsa-Maestre, I., Orden, D.: Automated negotiation for resource assignment in wireless surveillance sensor networks. Sensors (Basel, Switzerland) 15, 29547–29568 (2015)

14. Inotsume, H., Aggarwal, A., Higa, R., Nakadai, S.: Path negotiation for self-interested multirobot vehicles in shared space. In: Proceedings of the International Conference on Intelligent Robots and Systems, Las Vegas, NV, USA, pp. 11587–11594. IEEE (2020)

15. de Jonge, D., Bistaffa, F., Levy, J.: A heuristic algorithm for multi-agent vehicle routing with automated negotiation. In: 20th International Conference on Autonomous Agents and Multiagent Systems (AAMAS 2021) (2021)

16. Klein, M., Faratin, P., Sayama, H., Bar-Yam, Y.: Protocols for negotiating complex contracts. IEEE Intell. Syst. 18, 32–38 (2003)

17. Li, J., Felner, A., Boyarski, E., Ma, H., Koenig, S.: Improved heuristics for multi-agent path finding with conflict-based search. In: Proceedings of the Twenty-Eighth International Joint Conference on Artificial Intelligence, IJCAI-19, pp. 442–449. International Joint Conferences on Artificial Intelligence Organization (2019)

18. Li, J., Harabor, D., Stuckey, P.J., Ma, H., Koenig, S.: Symmetry-breaking constraints for grid-based multi-agent path finding. In: Proceedings of the AAAI Conference on Artificial Intelligence, vol. 33, no. 1, pp. 6087–6095 (2019)

19. Marsá-Maestre, I., Klein, M., Jonker, C., Aydogan, R.: From problems to protocols: towards a negotiation handbook. Decis. Supp. Syst. 60, 39–54 (2014)

20. Parkes, D.C.: Ibundle: an efficient ascending price bundle auction. In: Proceedings of the 1st ACM Conference on Electronic Commerce, EC 1999, New York, NY, USA, pp. 148–157. Association for Computing Machinery (1999)

21. Pritchett, A., Genton, A.: Negotiated decentralized aircraft conflict resolution. IEEE Trans. Intell. Transp. Syst. 19, 81–91 (2018)

22. Purwin, O., D'Andrea, R., Lee, J.: Theory and implementation of path planning by negotiation for decentralized agents. Robotics Auton. Syst. 56, 422–436 (2008)

23. Rosenschein, J.S., Zlotkin, G.: Rules of Encounter: Designing Conventions for Automated Negotiation among Computers. MIT Press, Cambridge (1994)

24. Sharon, G., Stern, R., Felner, A., Sturtevant, N.R.: Conflict-based search for optimal multi-agent pathfinding. Artif. Intell. 219, 40–66 (2012)

25. Stern, R.: Multi-agent path finding – an overview. In: Osipov, G.S., Panov, A.I., Yakovlev, K.S. (eds.) Artificial Intelligence. LNCS (LNAI), vol. 11866, pp. 96–115. Springer, Cham (2019). https://doi.org/10.1007/978-3-030-33274-7_6

26. Stern, R., et al.: Multi-agent pathfinding: definitions, variants, and benchmarks. CoRR, abs/1906.08291 (2019)

27. Sujit, P.B., Sinha, A., Ghose, D.: Multiple UAV task allocation using negotiation. In: AAMAS 2006: Proceedings of the Fifth International Joint Conference on Autonomous Agents and Multiagent Systems, AAMAS 2006, New York, NY, USA, pp. 471–478. Association for Computing Machinery (2006)

Author Index

Printed in the United States
by Baker & Taylor Publisher Services